SUPERVISION
A REDEFINITION

SUPERVISION

A REDEFINITION

FIFTH EDITION

Thomas J. Sergiovanni
Robert J. Starratt

McGRAW-HILL, INC.

New York   St. Louis   San Francisco   Auckland   Bogotá   Caracas
Lisbon   London   Madrid   Mexico   Milan   Montreal   New Delhi   Paris
San Juan   Singapore   Sydney   Tokyo   Toronto

This book was set in Palatino by Arcata Graphics/Kingsport.
The editors were Phillip A. Butcher and Ira C. Roberts;
the production supervisor was Leroy A. Young.
The cover was designed by Rafael Hernandez.
R. R. Donnelley & Sons Company was printer and binder.

SUPERVISION

A Redefinition

2 3 4 5 6 7 8 9 0 DOC DOC 9 0 9 8 7 6 5 4 3

ISBN 0-07-056339-X

Library of Congress Cataloging-in-Publication Data

Sergiovanni, Thomas J.
    Supervision: a redefinition/by Thomas J. Sergiovanni, Robert J.
Starratt. — 5th ed.
        p.   cm.
    Includes bibliographical references and index.
    ISBN 0-07-056339-X
    1. School supervision—United States.   2. School management and
organization—United States.   3. School personnel management—United States.
I. Starratt, Robert J.   II. Title.
LB2806.4.S47   1993
371.2´00973—dc20   92–10031

ABOUT THE AUTHORS

THOMAS J. SERGIOVANNI is presently Lillian Radford Professor of Education and Senior Fellow, Center for Educational Leadership, at Trinity University. He received his Ed.D. from the University of Rochester, in joint study in educational administration and business administration. An active teacher, writer, and editor, he brings to the text his extensive experience teaching and writing about educational and business administration. He has published numerous articles in professional journals, prepared abundant papers for professional associations, and many books.

ROBERT J. STARRATT, Professor of Educational Administration, Graduate School of Education at Fordham University, is also an accomplished author and educator. He received his Ed.D. from the University of Illinois, specializing in administration and curriculum theory. Like Dr. Sergiovanni, Dr. Starratt has published extensively, including several books, papers for professional associations, articles in major educational journals, as well as numerous presentations. He is actively involved in research involving leadership theory and the process of change.

CONTENTS

FOREWORD

FOR a brief, and to me precious, moment in time, having been invited to write its Foreword, I was privileged to be one of the very few persons privy to the contents of this important book. I spread out the final drafts of the seventeen chapters on my desk, I carried some of them with me on plane trips, I read and re-read the authors' Preface and the very-focusing final chapter, and overall I enjoyed an intellectual and spiritual feast as with these experts' help I examined once again the ever-more-important place that Supervision (capital S!) plays, or at least can and should play, in the high drama that is educational renewal.

Along the way, I stole at least fifty new ideas and references to fit later into my own writings. That this work was so up-to-the-minute regarding important and relevant writings impressed me a great deal; and that the book is really a major revision rather than a cosmetic overhaul was immediately apparent to me. At the end of my careful review I felt deliciously exhausted by the effort these writers required of me, but also as refurbished as is possible for an ancient tiller of the supervision soil to be. And while there might be a few minor interpretations or conclusions that Tom, Jerry, and I could joust about, I found myself rejoicing that in a small way my name will continue to be associated with these two scholarly giants and the way they illuminate the field.

That field is no longer for minor-leaguers. It may be appropriate to offer here some generalizations about the supervision literature of which this volume continues to be an important part. Supervision has only recently reached a point where its theoretical and research bases command respect and attention. Most of the books and articles dealing with supervision prior to the mid-1980s or thereabouts were generally regarded within the academic community as "out of the mainstream" of significant educational inquiry. Professors of Supervision have been not only numerically fewer than most other professorial groups, but also somewhat less valued or influential. In school districts, the supervisory (helping) function has usually been less respected and less well financed than administrative and evaluative functions; and in terms of budget crunch it has invariably been the presumably-expendable supervisors (carrying a variety of titles) who first suffered the ax.

Even within the Association for Supervision and Curriculum Development, the association within which supervisors supposedly have their logical "home," the curriculum people have almost always sat at the head tables, and they suffered rather than embraced their supervision colleagues. Even in the American Educational Research Association, it was not until the mid-1980s that program slots and other recognitions came in the direction of supervision people. Fortunately, the times are a-changing. Yet even recently, many of the publications and university courses with "Supervision" in their titles tend, perhaps as a sort of defense mechanism, to emphasize, or at least to devote substantial space and time to, matters that are less supervision and more curriculum and/or administration.

As we move into the mid-1990s, however, it seems that the climate has begun to change and there is a growing appreciation of the role that can and must be played by those helping, emancipating, nurturing, guiding, thought-provoking, reflective, and growth-inducing behaviors for which the imperfect label "supervision" is used.

In my Foreword to the fouth edition (1988) of this book, I dared to prophesy or at least to express my wish that in a fifth edition there would be deeper pursuit of "such important questions as moral leadership, empowering teachers, nurturance of school culture, and facilitating work groups (p. xvii.)." This prophecy was fulfilled; and in the new pages all of these dimensions, especially with reference to moral leadership, have greater clarity and vitality. It is much more difficult for me to look beyond 1992–1993 and guess what edition six might look like: for the moment, this book is not only state-of-the-art but a portent-of-the-future.

I am supposing that most of the readers/users of this volume will in effect be relative newcomers to the field, and they will have very little interest in the remarkable phylogeny of the work. I am, therefore, not stopping to trace the evolution of the volume over five editions. However, I assume that having taken note of the book's history, going back to 1971, readers will probably conclude that the work must have some enduring virtues and strengths. I can confidently confirm that conclusion.

Another group of this fifth edition's readers will be not newcomers at all, but rather, experienced students and practitioners in supervision who have already encountered some of the joys and challenges of advanced graduate study and who will recognize that Sergiovanni and Starratt are among the superstars in the field. For them, as it was for me, the prospect of re-exploring supervision's frontiers with the guidance of these two scholars is a most welcome one. A third, and necessarily much smaller, audience will be those professors and others of investigative bent who are doubtless familiar with the prior editions and who are eager to learn what confirmations and surprises may lie in wait for them. To these colleagues I can confirm that there are indeed some new insights and some deeper post-holes to be encountered along the way.

As the authors indicate in their Preface, the underlying theory (or theories) of supervision seem(s) in need of redefinition; accordingly, the very title of the book had to be changed. The features, appurtenances, and underlying theoretical structures of education are in such a dynamic state, that many new ways of looking at supervision are now needed. These authors have responded well to that need.

My advice to all who are tentatively examining this volume would be first to read the Preface so that the authors' intentions can be brought into focus. Next, one could profitably turn to the final chapter (17) so that the authors' ultimate message(s) could at least be sampled. Weeks or months later, when the other sixteen chapters have been absorbed, the final chapter will, I think, have even more profound meaning. At least it did for me.

Robert H. Anderson
President, Pedamorphosis, Inc.

PREFACE

COMPLETING a book used to have a certain finality to it. One could place it in a prominent part of one's library and get on with other projects. If an author wished to change a position taken in that book in a subsequent publication, it was an easy matter of a footnote reference. This book, however, has refused to be finished.

As each of the previous editions was completed, we felt that this was the book we should have written the first time. Despite numerous changes, however, the underlying theory had remained the same. That is not the case with this edition. Expectations and assumptions about schools have changed so significantly that schooling is now being reinvented. This reinvention includes new understandings about school structures, time frames, accountability, professionalism, teaching and learning, leadership, and sources of authority for what is done. In such a dramatically altered context, supervision itself has to be redefined. This redefinition includes not only new ways to do old things but a change in the theory itself which underlies supervisory thought and practice.

The first edition focused on "human perspectives in supervision, linking human concerns which emerged from research on organizational dynamics with human concerns as found in instructional and curriculum literature." In that first edition we asserted, "Humanizing education, with its focus on self-actualization of youngsters, can be achieved only in a humanizing organization which focuses on the self-actualization of teachers and other educational professionals." The second edition unfolded similarly, giving attention to the supervisor's human concerns in organizational leadership, educational leadership, and instructional leadership. The theme of human resource development, articulated in the second edition, was carried forward in more sophisticated and expansive treatments in the third and fourth editions. We introduced more of our own thinking in the fourth edition, adding analogies such as mindscapes, clockworks, and teaching as surfing to categories such as reflective practice. Likewise, we proposed our own theory of leadership and added a chapter on a relatively new concern, supervision as moral action.

The first edition appeared under the title, *Emerging Patterns of Supervision: Human Perspectives*. Editions two through four appeared as *Supervision: Human Perspectives*. The title for this fifth edition, *Supervision: A Redefinition*, signals a new emphasis. This redefinition includes the disconnection of supervision from hierarchical roles and a focus on community as the primary metaphor for schooling. Supervision is viewed here as a more democratic and professional process, involving multiple skills that are equally available to teachers and administrators who have the word "supervisor" in their title or job description. The new supervision embraces peer clinical supervision, mentoring, action research, collective work on teaching platforms, program evaluation, group discussions of specific translations of school mission statements, and other configurations of teachers as colleagues working together to increase their understanding of their practice. In a similar vein, staff development and supervision are now joined in such a way that they are often indistinguishable.

Earlier editions included bureaucratic authority, the personal authority of the supervisor, and technical-rational authority as equally legitimate grounds for what was done in schools. This edition places professional and moral authority as the driving force behind what teachers should do and how the process of supervision should unfold. Teachers and supervisors are not viewed primarily as independent decision makers who calculate individually the costs and benefits of their actions, but rather as members of an educating community who respond to shared norms and values. Both teachers and supervisors are seen as capable and willing to sacrifice self-interest for shared ideals; these ideals are viewed as intrinsic to the definition of teaching as a profession. Furthermore, commitments to these ideals become moral commitments; their neglect is a moral perversion of the profession. In this edition professionalism itself is redefined from something that has to do primarily with enhanced competence and expert authority to something that has to do with virtue as well. The virtuous side of this equation is understood as a powerful source of authority for what teachers do and should do. Together, professional and moral authority hold a promise of promoting self-governing and self-managing teachers who in turn make traditional conceptions of supervision obsolete.

Supervision often is defined by criteria extrinsic to the moral qualities of teaching and learning. In this edition supervision takes its moral character from its close involvement with the intrinsic moral qualities of teaching and learning. That is to say, teaching of its very nature assumes a caring for the one taught and a respect for the integrity of what is being taught and its connection to the past, present, and future life of the community. Not to care for the person being taught, or to distort the meaning of what is being taught, violates the very idea of teaching. Supervision is an activity that involves another in supporting and furthering that caring for the learner and respect for the significance of what is taught. The moral authority of the supervisor is joined with the moral authority of the teacher.

In this edition the metaphor for schooling itself is changed from organization to community as a way to express the new context for supervision. Though we continue to emphasize the skills and practical applications of such traditional supervisory processes as in-class supervision, enhancing reflection about teaching and learning, teacher evaluation, and staff development, these activities are recontextualized and substantially altered. In schools as learning communities rather than organizations, these activities are more than technical components of an efficient organization. They imply deeper, professional and moral concerns at work. In the new supervision, moreover, responsibility for these functions is no longer the exclusive domain of principals, supervisors, and others positioned within the school hierarchy. Instead, they comprise a common set of concepts and skills that are shared by everyone involved in the process of improving schooling. The supervisor's role remains important but is understood differently. She or he emerges as an advocate, developer, and linking pin in relationship to the teacher's efforts to improve the process of teaching and learning.

Finally, the new supervision is seen not as a separate function removed from the dynamics of institutional reinvention that is going on in schools, but as a necessary element of such dynamics. In earlier editions, we portrayed supervision as a relatively self-contained activity, dealing with the improvement of an individual teacher's instructional activities. Because of the importance of a super-vision of what schools are supposed to be, those exercising supervisory responsibilities are in a unique position to nurture, develop, and articulate the community's vision of what a learning community can and should be. Hence, supervision is also redefined as an essential process within the complex and continuous dynamic of reinventing schools.

McGraw-Hill and the authors would like to thank the following reviewers for their many helpful comments and suggestions: Jeanne C. Baxter, Northeastern Illinois University; William Callison, California State University; Robert Donmeyer, The Ohio State University; Richard D. Hawthorne, Kent State University; and E. John Kleinert, University of Miami.

Thomas J. Sergiovanni
Robert J. Starratt

SUPERVISION
A REDEFINITION

PART ONE

PERSPECTIVES FOR SUPERVISION

CHAPTER 1

IMAGES OF SUPERVISION

INTRODUCTION: THE NATURE OF SUPERVISION

In editions one and two published in the 1970s we characterized supervision in schools as being largely ritualistic. Supervisors continued to be hired and university courses continued to be offered in the subject. But much of what took place under the name of supervision seemed not to matter very much. A good deal of the supervisor's time was spent on administrative matters. Teacher-evaluation systems tended to be perfunctory. Overall a certain complacency characterized the role and function of supervision.

The third edition published in 1984 noted that a mild renaissance of interest in supervision and supervisory activities was in the making. At the national level the Association for Supervision and Curriculum Development had begun to place stronger emphasis on supervision. The literature in the field was expanding and improving in quality. For classroom supervision, clinical strategies and artistic strategies began to emerge and to compete successfully with more traditional checklist approaches to teacher evaluation. At least this was the case in the literature and at academic conferences if not in actual practice. Publications focusing on problems and issues in supervision increased in popularity, becoming among the most popular offered by the Association for Supervision and Curriculum Development. Supervisory topics were appearing more frequently on the programs of this organization's national conference and series of National Curriculum Study Institutes. The founding of the Conference of Professors of Instructional Supervision in 1976 was clearly evidence that scholars studying problems of supervision were increasing in numbers, interested in identifying themselves and in establishing better communication networks and developing more systematic approaches to research and development.

As the fourth edition of this book appeared in 1988 supervision was becoming the "in thing" in American schooling. What previously was a mild renaissance had turned into a revolution. Supervision began to rank high on the agendas of both state policymakers and local school administrators. Many states, for example, began to mandate increases in supervision and evaluation of teachers. These mandates ranged from required "training" in the techniques of supervision and evaluation for principals and supervisors to the provision of comprehensive and standardized state systems of supervision and evaluation. Many of these systems were based on a body of research associated with the teaching effectiveness and school effectiveness movements. This research noted that "effective schools" were characterized by principals and other supervisors who exercised strong instructional leadership. It noted further that a one best way to teach could be identified, provided for, and evaluated.

Instructional leadership became the hot topic in thousands of seminars and workshops provided for administrators and supervisors by states, professional associations, local school districts, and individual entrepreneurs. Some states even went so far as to mandate that all principals and supervisors go through state-approved and state-sponsored instructional leadership training programs as a condition of their continued employment and as part of a licensing system to certify them as teacher evaluators.

The academic side of the professional educational community experienced a similar flurry of interest in supervision. In 1985, the Association for Supervision and Curriculum Development established the scholarly journal, *The Journal of Curriculum and Supervision*. Scholarly articles on supervision and evaluation began to appear more frequently in such established journals as *Curriculum Inquiry* and *Educational Evaluation and Policy Analysis. The Journal of Personnel Evaluation in Education* was established in 1986. The prestigious American Educational Research Association established a special-interest group in instructional supervision in 1983. This marked the beginning of a concentrated and continuous appearance of sessions devoted to supervision at the annual meeting of this association.

These events place supervision at a critical point in its evolution. It is clear that supervision is emerging as a key role and function in the operation of schools. At issue, however, is the form and substance of this new emergence and interest, how its influence will be felt by teachers, and what its effects will be on teaching and learning. Will this "new supervision," for example, provide support for teachers and enhance their roles as key professional decision makers in the practice of teaching and learning? Or will this new supervision result in increased regulation and control of teachers and teaching? If the latter, what are the consequences of supervision for teacher professionalism and for teaching and learning? The increased importance attributed to supervision then and now is attractive. But whether this new emphasis will develop into promises fulfilled or promises broken will depend, we believe, on the form that supervision takes.

THEORIES OF PRACTICE

Supervisors and teachers typically do not characterize their work as being informed by theory. Instead they talk about how they rely on what works, hunches about what works, the principles that they can derive from these hunches, and the new practice insights and ideas which evolve from this very practical view of their work. What at first glance seems not to be theoretical, however, turns out to be theoretical. In fact, it is very difficult to engage in teaching or supervisory practice without being theoretical. When professionals say they are not being theoretical, it is likely that what they mean is they are not aware of the theoretical assumptions and basis of their actions and behaviors. Much of the theory which guides professional practice is implicit and in-formal.

Van Miller, one of the pioneers in administrative theory, often spoke of the practical art of using theory. He noted that it was difficult to administer and supervise in schools without using theory.[1] Practices typically do not lead to other practices without some help. When practice does lead to practice di-rectly, the relationship can be depicted as follows:

$$practices \rightarrow practice$$

This is a monkey-see-monkey-do operation. One's practices are rooted in cus-tom. When something new is proposed, teachers and supervisors ask, "Where else is it being done?" and "How does one do it?"

Very few supervisory or teaching practices evolve so simply from other practices. Instead professionals think about what they are doing and form hunches. The relationship between hunch and practice can be depicted as fol-lows:

$$practices \rightarrow hunch \rightarrow practices$$

The addition of hunch shows that one is thinking about his or her practice.

Hunches, however, do not just appear. They are shaped by insights which are derived from one's broader experience with events and activities similar to the problem under consideration as well as one's assumptions and beliefs. In-sights, assumptions, and beliefs comprise informal and implicit theories. As supervisors and teachers work, they think about their practice and develop hunches which guide subsequent practices. With experience, hunches become more established and codified into formal and informal operating procedures. Practice based on operating principles is more advanced than practice based on hunches.

The relationship among hunches, principles, and practice can be depicted as follows:

$$practices \rightarrow hunches \rightarrow principles \rightarrow practices$$

Here one uses experience to select the most appropriate hunch. This use repre-sents a degree of codification which results in the development of operating principles to guide subsequent professional practice.

Operating principles stand and fall on the basis of trial and error. Further, principles become more elegant as one's hunches become more refined. One's readings, interactions with other professionals, and practical experience in as-

---

[1] This discussion of practices, hunches, theories, and principles follows closely Van Miller, "The Practical Art of Using Theory," *The School Executive*, vol. 70, no. 1, pp. 60–63, 1958.

sessing operating principles provide the basis for the development of theories of practice. When theories of practice emerge to connect hunches and principles, professional behavior is more deliberate. Supervisors and teachers are more conscious of the theoretical basis of their practice, can articulate this basis, and can continuously revise this theory of practice as a result of their actual practice. How theory fits into this chain of events is depicted as follows:

practices → hunches → theories of practice → principles → practices

With theory, the professional can reach a new step in professional decision making and practice. Theory can provide the professional with a surer view of the situation, serve as a guide to the selection of principles, and provide a basis for evolving improved practices in light of improvements in one's theoretical outlook.

In sum, rarely does teaching or supervisory practice emerge from other practices. Instead, hunches are at play and operating principles emerge as theories of practice which provide a more rational basis for what one does. Typically hunches and operating principles are implicit and when they are explicit they are not thought about systematically. The question for most supervisors and teachers, then, is not whether they are being theoretical but what are the theories (the implicit hunches and operating principles) which help shape the way they see their professional worlds and provide the basis for professional decisions and practice.

IMAGES OF SUPERVISION

Different theories of supervision and teaching compete with each other for the attention of professionals. Present supervisory practices in schools, for example, are largely based on one or a combination of four general views. Which of the four theories best matches the hunches and operating principles which govern the way you think about teaching and supervision and are likely to provide the basis for your behavior as a supervisor?

One way in which these implicit theories can be made explicit is by evaluating the decisions that you make or the ways in which you size up supervisory situations. For example, place yourself in the role of school supervisor in Metro City. A year ago another school in Metro City was selected by the superintendent and central office staff to become a model school. This school was to incorporate a new educational system featuring explicit goals and teaching objectives across grade levels and a highly structured and tightly paced curriculum linked to the objectives. The curriculum included new textbooks and workbooks for all the major subject areas as well as carefully thought out assignments and activities designed to provide students with needed practice. Daily and weekly lesson plans were provided to make things easier for teachers and to ensure that students received the same instruction and assignments. Criterion-referenced weekly, 6-week, and semester tests were included in the package. The system provided as well for test scores to be evaluated by grade level and by each class within grade level every 6 weeks to monitor student progress. Teachers were formed into quality-control committees or quality circles to discuss the scores and in instances of low scores to come up with ways in which the system might be better implemented. The administration was particularly proud of this quality-circle concept, for it wanted teacher participation.

The administration felt that teachers needed only to become familiar with the materials and that by following directions carefully and relying on their own ingenuity in presenting instruction they would teach successfully. An incentive system was also introduced. Teachers were trained in methods of teaching that reflected the teaching effectiveness research. Then an evaluation system based on this research was used to evaluate their performance. Teachers scoring the highest received cash bonuses.

To help things along, the principal received extensive training in the new curriculum and in staff supervision and evaluation. Further, a new supervisor who had a thorough understanding of the new curriculum, the testing procedures, the daily and weekly lesson plans, the needed teaching to make things work, and the evaluation system was assigned to the school. Both principal and supervisor provided instructional leadership by monitoring teaching carefully to ensure compliance with the new system and by providing help to teachers who were having difficulty in complying.

Prior to the beginning of the school year teachers were provided with a carefully planned and implemented one-week training program, receiving one week's salary for their participation. Schools ran on a half-day schedule for the first week, thus allowing additional training and debugging. The training seemed to be successful, for by the end of September teachers developed an acceptable level of understanding and competence in using the system. The central office had high hopes for the success of this new initiative and saw it as a model for export to other schools in the district.

Before the introduction of the new educational system the teachers and principal of this school enjoyed a reputation for being a closely knit faculty with high morale. This situation began to change shortly after the new system was introduced. Teachers begin to complain. They did not like the new curriculum, feeling that frequently it did not fit what they thought was important to teach. They complained of pressure from the tests. They found themselves teaching lessons and adopting teaching strategies that they did not like. They expressed displeasure too with the overall climate in the school, describing it as increasingly impersonal with respect to students and competitive with respect to colleagues. Discontent among teachers grew as the semester continued. Things really began to sour when it became apparent that student performance did not measure up to the high expectations of the administration. The administration was puzzled as to why such a well-thought-out and carefully implemented educational system was not working in this school. Shortly after the spring break the principal became disillusioned enough to request a transfer. The supervisor was equally discouraged.

With the departure of the principal imminent, the superintendent has asked you and three other supervisors to review matters at the school in an effort to determine the source of the supervision problems and to arrive at a solution to these problems. Each has been asked to work independently to develop solutions and to bring their ideas to the meeting which is to take place shortly. Below are descriptions of how the four supervisors size up the problems at this school and the solutions that they propose. Each of the supervisors is working from an implicit theory of how the world of schooling, and perhaps even the world itself, works. Which of the four descriptions best matches your own view of the situation and your opinion as to how the situation might be remedied?

Supervisor A

You feel that the present problems in the redesigned school are obviously attributable to the people who work there. If the teachers have not yet adapted to the new curriculum and its procedures, they probably are incapable of functioning in a school committed to school improvement. It is also possible that the principal and the new supervisor are not the experts they were assumed to be and are therefore to blame for inadequate monitoring of the system and for their inability to provide the teachers with the proper help and supervision needed so that they might use the system better.

If you had had your way from the beginning, you would have staffed the school with new teachers. A systemwide search would have been conducted to find the kinds of teachers who would best fit such a system: those who would carefully follow the pattern of teaching and working which the system requires. In introducing the new system at the school, you believe that too much emphasis was placed on helping existing teachers to develop a conceptual understanding of the new procedures. This resulted in too many questions, too much confusion, doubts, and other problems. All teachers needed to know was how they fit into the system, what their jobs were, and what outcomes were expected. Clearer directions and expectations combined with close monitoring would have provided the needed controls to make the system work.

You believe that the curriculum, lesson plans, materials, tests, the teaching design, and the evaluation system introduced into the school are the best available. Although you know that it is possible for snafus to occur and that no educational system can be designed perfectly, you attribute the failure in this case to the unwillingness and inability of the teachers to do what they're supposed to do. Therefore, during the upcoming meeting you plan to make it clear that the problem is not the new educational system but the teachers who are using it. The answer is not to change the system but to train teachers better and to more closely supervise the teachers or to find teachers who are willing to use the system in the way in which it is intended.

Supervisor B

You are convinced that the source of the problems at the redesigned school is the lack of emphasis on human relations. Throughout the year the teachers and other employees have been complaining. As you suspected from the outset, the teachers were not consulted about the type of curriculum or the procedures that should be used, just as they were excluded from the decision-making process that led to the development of this model of the school of the future. You believe that teachers want to feel that they have a say in the matters which influence them. They want to be remembered and noticed, to be considered important. The formula for success is simple and straightforward. When these conditions do not exist, morale sinks. When teachers are satisfied and morale is high, on the other hand, they are more cooperative, more willing to comply, and their performance improves.

The teachers state that the new curriculum and teaching procedures were too cumbersome and rigid and thus made it impossible for them to work comfortably. As you have always said, when the school fulfills its responsibility to teachers' needs, everything else falls into place and school goals are met automatically. After all, the teachers were happy before the redesigning process and student performance was then higher than it is now. Under the new system they have to cope not only with a reduction in the amount of teamwork that previously had promoted morale and satisfaction but also with new supervisors who were hired or trained because of their technical skills instead of their human skills. During the upcoming meeting you plan to discuss top management's error in judgment.

You intend to point out that teachers must be noted and appreciated; that the evaluation system is competitive and thus disruptive to group harmony; and that providing a little attention and lots of cheerleading can go a long way toward making things work. Fix up the human relationship and teachers will gladly cooperate with the administration in implementing the new system.

Supervisor C

In your opinion the problems in the redesigned school are attributable to one source: a failure to provide teachers with opportunities to fulfill their individual needs for autonomy and their natural desire to do competent work. You form this opinion on the basis of what you have learned about teachers in general as well as those at this troubled school. The teachers in this school, like those in your own school, are mature adults who, under the right motivating conditions, will want to do their best for the school; they want to enjoy their work and are capable of supervising themselves. Indeed, their performance record and their level of job satisfaction before the redesigning process prove that to be the case. The formula for success is simple and straightforward. Give people responsibility and authority to make decisions about how they are to work, and they respond with increased motivation. Provide them with opportunities to be successful in accomplishing their goals, and their performance improves. The best strategy is to provide the overall frame and let teachers figure out how to implement it. With the right climate, teachers respond to general expectations, need broad goals, and want to be held accountable if trusted and given the discretion to make the implementing decisions that make sense to them. In this school not enough attention was given to creating that climate.

In its plans to redesign the school, top administration has overlooked these facts and has chosen to treat employees like children. A new supervisor was brought in to monitor the work of teachers and a new educational system was programmed to keep track of their comings and goings. The teachers were expected to meet new organizational goals for increased student performance while their needs for achievement, autonomy, self-direction, and a sense of fulfillment were ignored. Under the circumstances, a drop in performance was inevitable. You feel strongly that the present school attitude toward teachers is counterproductive, and you plan to make your feelings known during the upcoming meeting. The instructional system in the redesigned school cannot be salvaged in its present form. A new one needs to be developed with teachers as full shareholders and decision makers in its design and implementation.

Supervisor D

You believe that the redesigned school was doomed from the start. The changes introduced were just not realistic. They did not reflect the way schools actually work or how teachers think and behave. The curriculum and instructional system and the teaching and evaluation design that were introduced featured discrete goals, structured tasks, easily measured outcomes, sure operating procedures, clear lines of authority, and single best ways to organize, teach, and evaluate. The problem, as you see it, is that these characteristics are suitable for teaching and learning environments that are stable and predictable and for instances in which student and teacher needs and styles are uniform. But schools have multiple and competing goals, unstructured tasks, competing solutions, difficult-to-measure outcomes, unsure operating procedures, and unclear and competing lines of authority. Further, teachers and students have diverse needs and styles. You hope to explain that these are characteristics of dynamic environments. What works in the first instance doesn't work in the second.

You remember reading somewhere that schools are "managerially loose and culturally tight," and you intend to build your arguments around this idea. What counts for teachers is not so much the management system but what they believe, the values they share, and the assumptions they hold. When values are held collectively they become defining characteristics of the school's culture. Changing schools, as you see it, means changing school cultures.

You plan to recommend that the present system be abandoned. You also recommend that the faculty and administration spend the next year coming to grips with the values they share about teaching and learning, what schools are for, how best to evaluate, and how they might best work together. They should then seek to identify the norms and values that are now in place in the school as evidenced by what is now going on, and come to grips with what needs changing. This sort of reflection, you believe, will enable them to reinvent their school from top to bottom. You intend to point out that in this reinvented school less emphasis will need to be given to prescribing what needs to be done and to providing direct supervision. Values and purposes, in your view, should function as substitutes for supervision and should help teachers to become self-managing.

Each of the recommendations of the four supervisors represents a different conception or "theory" of what supervision is, of how schools work, and of what is important to teachers. Make your selection by ranking the four in a way that reflects your view of supervision. Does a clear favorite emerge? Or, do you feel more comfortable by combining some of the views? By deciding, you are revealing your own personal theory. The theories of each of the supervisors are described below.

SCIENTIFIC MANAGEMENT, HUMAN RELATIONS, AND NEOSCIENTIFIC MANAGEMENT SUPERVISION

Many of the supervisory practices found in schools today and many of the policies emerging from state governments and local school boards which influence these practices are based on one or a combination of three general theories of supervision—traditional scientific management, human relations, and neoscientific management. These theories are reflected in the images of supervision portrayed by supervisors A and B. In our view, none of the three theories of supervision is adequate to provide a model for school supervision. Reasons for their inadequacy range from scientific limitations on the one hand to lack of fit with the realities of school supervision on the other. In later sections we propose human resources and normative supervision as theoretical approaches and models of practice which are more sound from a scientific point of view and more accurate in their fit to practice.

Scientific management supervision emerges from the thinking and work of Frederick Taylor and his followers during the early 1900s. Many of the ideas that shaped this theory stem from his experience and research in America's steel industries. For example, Taylor analyzed the loading of pig iron onto railroad cars at a Bethlehem steel plant. Noting certain inefficiencies, he devised techniques for increasing the workers' productivity. His techniques were "scientific" in the sense that they were based on careful observation and task analysis. He determined, for example, that the equipment the workers were using was inadequate to the task. He substituted standardized shovels and other work equipment which were designed specifically for the tasks to be done. Once the best way of doing something was established, he instructed workers to do exactly as they were told and only as they were told. By closely adhering to his methods and by using the equipment he provided, the workers were able to increase their average loading per day from 12 to 47 tons. Taylor felt that the secret to scientific management was a compliant worker who did not think too much but instead followed directions exactly.[2] The directions, of course, were to be based on "scientifically validated" methods of doing the job. The scientific management recipe is as follows: Identify the best way; develop a work system based on this "research"; communicate expectations to workers; train workers in the system; monitor and evaluate to ensure compliance.

Scientific management represents a classic autocratic philosophy of supervision within which workers are viewed as appendages of management and as such are hired to carry out prespecified duties in accordance with the wishes of management. These ideas carry over to school supervision when teachers are viewed as implementers of highly refined curriculum and teaching systems and where close supervision is practiced to ensure that they are teaching in the way in which they are supposed to and that they are carefully following approved guidelines and teaching protocols. Control, accountability, and efficiency are emphasized in scientific management within an atmosphere of clear-cut manager-subordinate relationships. Though vestiges of this brand of supervision can still be found in schools, by and large traditional scientific management is not currently in favor. Its basic premises and precepts, however, are still thought to be attractive by many policymakers, administrators, and supervisors. The ideas have not changed, as will be discussed later, but strategies for implementing these ideas have.

Human relations supervision had its origins in the democratic administration movement which emerged during the 1930s. Elton Mayo, a social philosopher and professor at Harvard University, is often considered to be the originator of human relations supervision. He believed that the productivity of workers could be increased by meeting their social needs at work, providing them with opportunities to interact with each other, treating them decently, and involving them in the decision-making process. His classic research study at the Western Electric Hawthorne plant during the 1920s gave testimony to these ideas.[3] Ultimately human relations supervision was a successful challenger to traditional scientific management. When it was applied to schooling,

---

[2] See, for example, Frederick Taylor, *The Principles of Scientific Management*, New York: Harper & Row, 1911. Reprinted by Harper & Row in 1945; Raymond Callahan, *Education and the Cult of Efficiency*, Chicago: University of Chicago Press, 1962.

[3] See, for example, Elton Mayo, *The Human Problems of an Industrial Civilization*, New York: Macmillan, 1933; F. J. Roethlisberger and W. J. Dickson, *Management and the Worker*, Cambridge: Harvard University Press, 1949.

teachers were to be viewed as "whole persons" in their own right rather than as packages of needed energy, skills, and aptitudes to be used by administrators and supervisors. Supervisors needed to work to create a feeling of satisfaction among teachers by showing interest in them as people. It was assumed that a satisfied staff would work harder and would be easier to work with, to lead, and to control. Participation was considered to be an important supervisory method and its objective was to make teachers *feel* that they were useful and important to the school. "Personal feelings" and "comfortable relationships" were the watchwords of human relations.

Human relations supervision is still widely advocated and practiced today, though its support has diminished. Human relations promised much but delivered little. Its problems rested partly with misunderstandings as to how this approach should work and partly with faulty theoretical notions inherent in the approach itself. The movement actually resulted in widespread neglect of teachers. Participatory supervision became permissive supervision which in practice was laissez-faire supervision. Further, the focus of human relations supervision was and still is an emphasis on "winning friends" in an attempt to influence people. To many, "winning friends" was a slick tactic that made the movement seem manipulative and inauthentic, even dishonest. Though this approach developed a considerable following during the thirties, forties, and fifties, it became clear that increases in school productivity would not be achieved merely by assuring the happiness of teachers.

School reforms of the early 1980s suggested a new, renewed interest in scientific management thinking, though its shape and form in practice changed considerably from the more traditional form. This *neoscientific* management is in a large part a reaction against human relations supervision with its neglect of the teacher in the classroom and its lack of attention to accountability. Neoscientific management shares with traditional management an interest in control, accountability, and efficiency, but the means by which it achieves these ends is far more impersonal. For example, there is a renewed interest in closely monitoring what it is that teachers do, the subject matter they cover, and the teaching methods that they use. But checking daily lesson plans and visiting classes daily to *inspect* teaching often breeds resentment and results in tension between teachers and supervisors. A more impersonal way to control what it is that teachers do is to introduce standardized criterion-referenced testing and to make public the scores by class and school. Since it is accepted that what gets measured gets taught, tests serve as an impersonal method of controlling the teacher's work. Within neoscientific management the task dimension, concern for job, and concern for highly specified performance objectives, all lacking in human relations supervision, are strongly emphasized. Critics feel that this emphasis is so strong that the human dimension suffers. Neoscientific management relies heavily on externally imposed authority and as a result often lacks acceptance from teachers.

Human relations supervision and the two versions of scientific management share a lack of faith and trust in the teacher's ability and willingness to display as much interest in the welfare of the school and its programs as that presumed by administrators, supervisors, and the public. Within traditional scientific management teachers are heavily supervised in a face-to-face setting in an effort to ensure that good teaching will take place. In human relations supervision teachers are provided with conditions which enhance their morale and are involved in efforts to increase their job satisfaction so that they might be more pliable in the hands of management, thus ensuring that good teaching will take place. In neoscientific management impersonal, technical, and rational control mechanisms substitute for face-to-face close supervision. Here it is assumed that if visible standards of performance, objectives, or competencies can be identified, the work of teachers can be controlled by holding them accountable to these standards, thus ensuring better teaching.

Sometimes neoscientific management and human relations are combined into one theory of action. For example, the work of teachers may be programmed by an impersonal system of regulation and control but day-to-day supervision might emphasize pleasant and cordial relationships, building teachers up (telling them, for example, how important they are), encouraging positive attitudes, and rewarding teachers who conform.

HUMAN RESOURCES SUPERVISION

In 1967, the Association for Supervision and Curriculum Development's Commission on Supervision Theory concluded its 4-year study with a report entitled *Supervision: Perspectives and Propositions.*[4] In this report William Lucio discussed scientific management and human relations views of supervision and spoke of a third view—that of the revisionists—which sought to combine emphasis on both tasks and human concerns into a new theory. Standard-bearers of the revisionists were Douglas McGregor, Warren Bennis, Chris Argyris, and Rensis Likert.[5]

Beginning with the second edition of this book, the concepts and practices associated with this new theory have been referred to as *human resources supervision.*[6] This is the theory of supervision that supervisor C relies upon. The distinction between human resources and human relations is critical, for human resources is more than just another variety of human relations. Human resources represents a higher regard for human need, potential, and satisfaction. Argyris captured the new emphasis succinctly as follows:

[4] William Lucio (ed.), *Supervision: Perspectives and Propositions,* Washington, D.C.: Association for Supervision and Curriculum Development, 1967.

[5] Douglas McGregor, *The Human Side of Enterprise,* New York: McGraw-Hill, 1960; Warren Bennis, "Revisionist Theory of Leadership," *Harvard Business Review,* vol. 39, no. 2, pp. 26–38, 1961; Chris Argyris, *Personality and Organization,* New York: Harper & Row, 1957; and Rensis Likert, *New Patterns of Management,* New York: McGraw-Hill, 1961.

[6] This distinction was first made by Raymond Miles, "Human Relations or Human Resources?" *Harvard Business Review,* vol. 43, no. 4, pp. 148–163, 1965; and by Mason Haire, Edwin Ghiselli, and Lyman Porter, *Managerial Thinking: An International Study,* New York: Wiley, 1966.

We're interested in developing neither an overpowering manipulative organization nor organizations that will "keep people happy." Happiness, morale, and satisfaction are not going to be highly relevant guides in our discussion. Individual competence, commitment, self-responsibility, fully functioning individuals, and active, viable, vital organizations will be the kinds of criteria that we will keep foremost in our minds.[7]

Leadership within this new kind of supervision was to be neither directive nor patronizing but instead supportive:

The leader and other processes of the organization must be such as to ensure a maximum probability that in all interactions and in all relationships within the organization, each member, in light of his background, values, desires, and expectations, will view the experience as supportive and one which builds and maintains his sense of personal worth and importance.[8]

Douglas McGregor, pointing out that every managerial act rests on a theory, provided a new theory more conducive to human resources management. Theory Y, as he called it, was based on optimistic assumptions about the nature of humankind and provided a more powerful basis for motivating workers than the older Theory X.

Theory X leads naturally to an emphasis on the tactics of control—to procedures and techniques for telling people what to do, for determining whether they are doing it, and for administering rewards and punishments. Since an underlying assumption is that people must be made to do what is necessary for the success of the enterprise, attention is naturally directed to the techniques of direction and control. Theory Y, on the other hand, leads to a preoccupation with the *nature of relationships,* with the creation of an environment which will encourage commitment to organizational objectives and which will provide opportunities for the maximum exercise of initiative, ingenuity, and self-direction in achieving them.[9]

The assumptions about people associated with Theory X are as follows:

1 Average people are by nature indolent—they work as little as possible.
2 They lack ambition, dislike responsibility, prefer to be led.
3 They are inherently self-centered, indifferent to organizational needs.
4 They are by nature resistant to change.
5 They are gullible, not very bright, ready dupes of the charlatan and demagogue.[10]

One can find many instances in schools when the assumptions of Theory X do indeed seem to be true. Teachers, for example, seem to work only mini-

[7] Chris Argyris, *Integrating the Individual and the Organization,* New York: Wiley, 1964, p. 4.

[8] Rensis Likert, *New Patterns of Management,* New York: McGraw-Hill, 1961, p. 103.

[9] Douglas McGregor, *The Human Side of Enterprise,* New York: McGraw-Hill, 1960, p. 132.

[10] These assumptions are quoted from McGregor's essay, "The Human Side of Enterprise," which appears in Warren G. Bennis and Edgar H. Schein (eds.), *Leadership and Motivation: Essays of Douglas McGregor.* Cambridge, Mass.: MIT Press, 1966. The essay first appeared in *Adventure in Thought and Action,* Proceedings of the Fifth Anniversary Convocation of the School of Industrial Management, M.I.T., April 9, 1957.

mally and then only under close supervision. Few instances of teacher initiative can be found. Instead they seem to be defensive and preoccupied with maintaining the status quo. McGregor argued that when such conditions exist the problem may be less with workers and more with the expectations which their administrators and supervisors have of them. Sensing negative assumptions and expectations, teachers are likely to respond in a negative way. This is an example of the self-fulfilling prophecy. Fundamental to Theory X is a philosophy of direction and control. This philosophy is administered in a variety of forms and rests upon a theory of motivation that is inadequate for most adults, particularly professional adults.

The assumptions about people associated with Theory Y are as follows:

1 Management is responsible for organizing the elements of productive enterprise—money, materials, equipment, people—in the interest of economic (educational) ends.
2 People are *not* by nature passive or resistant to organizational needs. They have become so as a result of experience in organizations.
3 The motivation, the potential for development, the capacity for assuming responsibility, the readiness to direct behaviors toward organizational goals are all present in people; management does not put them there. It is a responsibility of management to make it possible for people to recognize and develop these human characteristics for themselves.
4 The essential task of management is to arrange organizational conditions and methods of operation so that people can achieve their own goals *best* by directing *their* own efforts toward organizational objectives.[11]

Basic to Theory Y is building identification and commitment to worthwhile objectives in the work context and building mutual trust and respect. Success in work is assumed to be dependent on whether authentic relationships and the exchange of valid information are present.

Advocates maintained that school conditions created by human resources management would result in a better life for teachers and more productive schooling. Satisfaction and achievement would be linked in a new and more expansive way. Instead of focusing on creating happy teachers as a means to gain productive cooperation, the new managerial emphasis would be on creating the conditions of successful work as a means of increasing one's satisfaction and self-esteem. As Frederick Herzberg described the new emphasis:

> To feel that one has grown depends on achievement of tasks that have meaning to the individual, and since the hygiene factors do not relate to the task, they are powerless to give such meaning to the individual. Growth is dependent on some achievements but achievement requires a task. The motivators are task factors and

---

[11] McGregor in Bennis and Schein, op. cit., p. 15.

thus are necessary for growth; they provide the psychological stimulation by which the individual can be activated toward his self-realization needs.[12]

HUMAN RELATIONS AND HUMAN RESOURCES SUPERVISION COMPARED

Neoscientific management and scientific management are really the same theory, though each has a slightly different look in practice. Human relations and human resources supervision, however, are two different theories. For example, though both are concerned with teacher satisfaction, human relations views satisfaction as a means to a smoother and more effective school. It is believed that satisfied workers are happier workers and thus easier to work with, more cooperative, and more likely to be compliant. Supervisors find it easier to get what they want from teachers when human relationships are tended to. Consider, for example, the practice of shared decision making. In human relations supervision this technique is used because it is believed it will lead to increased teacher satisfaction. This relationship is depicted as follows:

The human relations supervisor
↓

| adopts shared decision-making practices | → to | increase teacher satisfaction | → which in turn | increases school effectiveness |

The rationale behind this strategy is that teachers want to *feel* important and involved. This feeling in turn promotes in teachers a better attitude toward the school and therefore they become easier to manage and more effective in their work.

Within human resources supervision, by contrast, satisfaction is viewed as a desirable *end* toward which teachers work. Satisfaction, according to this view, results from successful accomplishment of important and meaningful work, and this accomplishment is the key component to building school success. The human resources supervisor, therefore, adopts shared decision-making practices because of their potential to increase school success. The supervisor assumes that better decisions will be made, that teacher ownership and commitment to these decisions will be increased, and that the likelihood of success at work will increase. These relationships are depicted as follows:

The human resources supervisor
↓

| adopts shared decision-making practices | → to | increase school effectiveness | → which in turn | increases teacher satisfaction |

[12] Frederick Herzberg, *Work and the Nature of Man*, New York: World Publishing Co., 1966, p. 78.

Human relations supervision is much more closely aligned with the assumptions of Theory X than with those of Theory Y, even though when experienced, they result in a softer form of control. This is evident when the two sets of assumptions are contrasted, as in Table 1-1.

Let us now revisit supervisors A, B, and C.

Scientific management and neoscientific management comprise the theory of practice which governs the thinking and practice of supervisor A. This supervisor supports a highly structured and finely tuned teaching and learning system characterized by close connections among objectives, curriculum, teaching methods, and testing. Supervisor A believes that if teachers do what they are supposed to the system will produce the results that are intended.

Human relations comprises the theory of practice to which supervisor B gives allegiance. Supervisor B is concerned with the teaching system's insensitivity to teachers' needs. Further, teachers were not consulted about the system to be implemented and thus feel left out. The answer to this supervisor is to back off and try again, this time getting teachers involved and making compromises in the proposed change which get in the way of teachers' social interaction and other needs. With the right human relations strategy, supervisor B believes, any school-improvement initiative will be successful. It is just a matter of how effectively you work with people.

Supervisor C comes closest to operating from within the human resources perspective. This supervisor believes that successful teaching and school improvement occurs when teacher motivation and commitment are high. Being in charge of one's work life and being held accountable to shared values and broad goals contribute to motivation and commitment. Authentic participation in decision making and providing responsibility are viewed as key supervisory strategies by supervisor C.

Supervisor D's analysis of the problems in Metro City represents a fairly new image of supervision. Supervisor D relies much less on direct supervision, whatever its form. No matter how enlightened such supervision might be, supervisor D reasons, it still depends largely upon some external force to make things happen. Even in the case of human resources supervision, at the base is an exchange of higher-level need fulfillment for some sort of work compliance. Instead, supervisor D seeks to build substitutes for supervision into the everyday life of the school. Substitutes enable teachers and supervisors to respond from within, to become self-managing.

It is hard to put a label on supervisor D's theory of supervision. Providing substitutes, for example, suggests that supervision as it is now being practiced should be replaced by something else. Supervisor D highlights shared values as one such substitute. Shared values can take many forms. Sometimes they are expressed as professional norms or community norms or the felt need for teachers to care about each other and to help each other. These and other substitutes for supervision will be discussed in the next and subsequent chapters of this book. Perhaps a good label for this emerging theory is *normative supervision*.

TABLE 1-1
SUPERVISORY ASSUMPTIONS

Theory X soft human relations model	Theory Y human resources model
Attitudes toward people	
1. People in our culture, teachers and students among them, share a common set of needs—to belong, to be liked, to be respected.	1. In addition to sharing common needs for belonging and respect, most people in our culture, teachers and students among them, desire to contribute effectively and creatively to the accomplishment of worthwhile objectives.
2. While teachers and students desire individual recognition, they more importantly want to *feel* useful to the school and to their own work group.	2. The majority of teachers and students are capable of exercising far more initiative, responsibility, and creativity than their present jobs or work circumstances require or allow.
3. They tend to cooperate willingly and comply with school goals if these important needs are fulfilled.	3. These capabilities represent untapped resources that are presently being wasted.
Kind and amount of participation	
1. The supervisor's basic task (or in reference to students, the teacher's basic task) is to make each worker believe that he or she is a useful and important part of the team.	1. The supervisor's basic task (or in reference to students, the teacher's basic task) is to create an environment in which subordinates can contribute their full range of talents to the accomplishment of school goals. He or she works to uncover the creative resources of subordinates.
2. The supervisor is willing to explain his or her decisions and to discuss subordinates' objections to the plans. On routine matters, he or she encourages subordinates in planning and in decision making. In reference to students, the teacher behaves similarly.	2. The supervisor allows and encourages teachers to participate in important as well as routine decisions. In fact, the more important a decision is to the school, the greater the supervisor's efforts to tap faculty resources. In reference to students, the teacher behaves similarly.
3. Within narrow limits, the faculty or individual teachers who make up the faculty should be allowed to exercise self-direction and self-control in carrying out plans. A similar relationship exists for teachers and students.	3. Supervisors work continually to expand the areas over which teachers exercise self-direction and self-control as they develop and demonstrate greater insight and ability. A similar relationship exists for teachers and students.

TABLE 1-1
SUPERVISORY ASSUMPTIONS (*Continued*)

Theory X soft human relations model	Theory Y human resources model
Expectations	
1. Sharing information with teachers and involving them in school decision making will help satisfy their basic needs for belonging and for individual recognition.	1. The overall quality of decision making and performance will improve as supervisors and teachers make use of the full range of experience, insight, and creative ability that exists in their schools.
2. Satisfying these needs will improve faculty and student morale and will reduce resistance to formal authority.	2. Teachers will exercise responsible self-direction and self-control in the accomplishment of worthwhile objectives that they understand and have helped establish.
3. High faculty and student morale and reduced resistance to formal authority may lead to improved school performance. It will at least reduce friction and make the supervisor's job easier.	3. Faculty satisfaction and student satisfaction will increase as a by-product of improved performance and the opportunity to contribute creatively to this improvement.

Source: Adapted from Raymond E. Miles, "Human Relations or Human Resources?" *Harvard Business Review,* vol. 43, no. 4, pp. 148–163, 1965, esp. exhibits I and II.

Normative supervision is based on several premises that are at odds with more traditional approaches to supervision. One premise is that while self-interest may be an important source of motivation for teachers, most are capable of and willing to sacrifice self-interest for more altruistic reasons if conditions are right. Another premise is that preference, values, emotions, and beliefs are equally powerful if not more teacher motivators than are logic, reasoning, and scientific evidence. A third premise is that teachers and others do not make decisions simply as isolated individuals. Instead, what they think, believe, and ultimately do are shaped by their memberships in groups and their connections with other people.

Each of the supervisory models sketched above provides an oversimplification, and probably none is exclusively adequate. Successful supervision is shaped by the circumstances and situations which the supervisor faces, and at different times different models may be appropriate. Still, it matters greatly which of the general theories of supervision or which combination one accepts as her or his overarching framework. One important characteristic that defines each of the images of supervision is the source of authority for supervision. Supervision inevitably deals with control. Control is in turn a response to some form of authority. The source of this authority might be external, such as regulations, or internal, such as commitment to one's principles or values and one's sense of duty or obligation. Sources of authority for supervision are the theme of the next chapter.

CHAPTER 2

SOURCES OF AUTHORITY
FOR SUPERVISION

$\mathbf{T}$HE four supervisors described in the last chapter share a common commitment to improving schools. Further, they realize that improving schools means changing existing ways of thinking about teaching and learning and changing existing teaching practices. Supervisors A and B choose slightly different paths but *follow a similar route* to achieve these goals. And this is the case as well for supervisors C and D.

Each of the pairs of supervisors represents two very different conceptions of supervision, and each of the two different conceptions leads to different consequences in the school. Let us refer to these broad conceptions as *Supervision I* and *Supervision II*. Supervision I represents the traditional kind of supervision that has been in place in schools for most of this century. Supervision II, by contrast, represents an emerging pattern that can fundamentally change not only the way supervision is understood and practiced but also our understanding of how successfully to effect change, what really counts when it comes to motivating teachers, what leadership is, how to be helpful to teachers in the classroom, the meaning of staff development, and how to help teacher evaluation become more useful.

At the end of this chapter the assumptions and principles underlying Supervision I and Supervision II are compared. This comparison lays the foundation for developing a new kind of supervisory practice. To set the stage we first examine sources of authority for supervisory practice. The issue of authority is important not only in understanding different forms of supervision but also in handling the problems of change. Each of the four supervisors in the last chapter, for example, sought to bring about change by relying on different sources of authority. "Authority" refers to the power to influence thought and behavior. The success or failure of any change strategy rests in a large measure on the match that exists between the source of authority relied upon and the situation at hand.

THE ISSUE OF CHANGE

Change does not come about easily and is very difficult to mandate from the top down or from the outside. Mandated change requires more checking and monitoring to sustain than is possible to provide. Further, for change to have meaning and effect it must change not only the way things look but also the way things work. And finally, too often efforts to change are directed only toward doing the same things better. Change that counts, by contrast, is typically that which alters basic issues of schooling such as goals, values, beliefs, working arrangements, and the distribution of power and authority. This kind of change requires more than just tinkering with the existing school culture.

Teacher evaluation provides a good example. In recent years those interested in improving teaching and learning have frequently relied upon mandating new teacher evaluation systems. Yet the record to date suggests that such mandates have not made much of a difference in improving the quality of teaching and learning. For example, teachers may conform to the mandated system only when under scrutiny. Since constant checking and monitoring is not possible, such systems soon become time-consuming and expensive. Using such monitoring, the school can supply evaluation data that suggest teachers are teaching in required ways and that point to an array of new policies and procedures that are in place in the school as further evidence. Nevertheless, the teaching and learning process continues as it did before.

In the case above, changes in teaching practice are superficial rather than real. The reason for this superficiality is that the source of authority chosen for implementing changes is too limited. Present supervisory practices emerge from a particular pattern of authority. Changing these practices means changing the authority base for supervision.

THE SOURCES OF AUTHORITY

Supervisory policies and practices can be based on one or a combination of five broad sources of authority:

Bureaucratic, in the form of legal and organizational mandates, rules, regulations, job descriptions, and expectations. When supervisory policies and practices are based on bureaucratic authority teachers are expected to respond appropriately or face the consequences.

Personal, in the form of interpersonal leadership, motivational technology, and human relations skills. When supervisory policies and practices are based on personal authority teachers are expected to respond to the supervisor's personality, to the pleasant environment provided, and to incentives for positive behavior. Personal authority is enhanced by learning how to apply insights from psychology and human and organizational behavior.

Technical-rational, in the form of evidence derived from logic and scientific research in education. When supervisory policies and practices are based on the authority of technical rationality teachers are expected to respond according to what is considered the truth.

Professional, in the form of experience, knowledge of the craft, and personal expertise. When supervisory policies and practices are based on professional authority teachers are expected to respond to common socialization, accepted tenets of practice, and internalized expertise.

Moral, in the form of obligations and duties derived from widely shared values, ideas, and ideals. When supervisory policies and practices are based on moral authority teachers are expected to respond to shared commitments and felt interdependence.[1]

Each of the five sources of authority is legitimate and should be used, but the impact on teachers and on the teaching and learning process depends on which source or combination of sources is prime. Authority underlying today's supervision is a combination of bureaucratic, psychological, and technical-rational. The supervision we propose is based primarily on professional and moral authority.

Each of the four supervisors described in Chapter 1 views authority for supervision differently. Supervisor A, for example, relies heavily on a combination of bureaucratic and technical-rational authority in implementing the instructional system in Metro City. The system itself, for example, is based on the school effectiveness and teaching effectiveness research in vogue during the seventies and eighties, and supervisor A appeals to the type of authority advocated in this research. "Research says that these are the indicators of effective teaching"; "Research says that tightly aligned curriculum and teaching to objectives and then testing for mastery produces better results"; and so on. Further, the teaching, supervisory, and testing processes to be followed are specified as rule-bound standard operating procedures. A system of monitoring is provided to check compliance, and penalties are levied for noncompliance. In the ideal, supervisor A reasons, the school should recruit teachers who are willing to go along with the desired instructional system at the outset. The reason is that bureaucratic and technical-rational sources of authority exist independent of people and of situations. It matters not what is unique about a particular classroom or what hunches the teacher has. Bureaucratic and technical-rational sources of authority are not defined by idiosyncrasy.

Supervisor B, on the other hand, recommends relying on knowledge about psychology and human behavior in developing personal authority, expressed as human relations leadership, to get the job done. The instructional system itself is not questioned, and the weight of bureaucratic authority and technical-rational authority is accepted but not emphasized. Bureaucratic and technical-rational sources of authority may motivate supervisors, but not teachers. Supervisor B might say: "Yes, research says so and so, but if you want teachers to follow the research don't preach it, just treat them right"; "Procedures have to be followed, but in seeking compliance emphasize positive rewards rather than negative penalties"; or "Remember to involve teachers because they like to be involved and are more likely to work within the system as a result."

[1] The discussion of sources of authority for supervision in this chapter is based on Thomas J. Sergiovanni, "Moral Authority and the Regeneration of Supervision," in Carl Glickman (ed.), *Supervision in Transition,* The 1992 Yearbook of the Association for Supervision and Curriculum Development, Alexandria, Va., 1992; and "The Sources of Authority for Leadership," in Thomas J. Sergiovanni, *The Moral Dimensions in Leadership,* San Francisco: Jossey-Bass, 1992, chap. 3.

Supervisor C also relies on a form of personal authority but one that is different from the personal authority used by supervisor B. Bureaucratic and technical-rational sources of authority are not ignored, but they count less. Further, they are understood differently by supervisor C than by supervisor B. For example, supervisor C believes that it is okay to have a general sense of what you want to accomplish. Then you involve teachers in fleshing out this general sense into a more specific design. Bureaucratic rules in this case take the form of broad policies that guide the decision-making process. Research, too, plays a role, but is viewed less as a script to be followed and more as a series of revelations that can inform the shared decision-making process. Supervisor C relies heavily on developing the right interpersonal climate and on meeting teachers' needs for achievement, esteem, recognition, and autonomy within some general framework.

Supervisor D views sources of bureaucratic and technical-rational authority in a fashion similar to supervisor C. Personal authority also has its place. But what matters most are shared values and beliefs that become norms governing behavior. These norms are connected to the teacher's sense of professionalism, knowledge of the craft, and membership in the school as a learning community. Norms represent a form of moral authority. Professional and moral authority are the two sources relied upon most by supervisor D.

In the sections that follow we take a closer look at each of the five sources of authority, examining the assumptions underlying each one when it is used as the prime source, the supervision strategies suggested by each, and the impact each one has on the work of teachers and on the teaching and learning process.

BUREAUCRATIC AUTHORITY

As suggested above, bureaucratic authority relies heavily on hierarchy, rules and regulations, mandates, and clearly communicated role expectations as a way to provide teachers with a script to follow. Teachers are, in turn, expected to comply with this script or face consequences. There may be a place for this source of authority even in the most progressive of enterprises. But when this source of authority is *prime*, the following assumptions are made:

Teachers are subordinates in a hierarchically arranged system.

Supervisors are trustworthy, but you can't trust subordinates very much.

The goals and interests of teachers and those of supervisors are not the same; thus, supervisors must be watchful.

Hierarchy equals expertise; thus, supervisors know more about everything than do teachers.

External accountability works best.

With these assumptions in place it then becomes important for supervisors to provide teachers with prescriptions for what, when, and how to teach, and for governing other aspects of their school lives. These are provided in the form of expectations. Supervisors then practice a policy of "expect and inspect" to ensure compliance with these prescriptions. Heavy reliance is placed on predetermined standards to which teachers must measure up. Since teachers often will not know how to do what needs to be done, it is important for supervisors to identify their needs and then to "in-service" them in some way. Directly supervising and closely monitoring the work of teachers is key in order to ensure continued compliance with prescriptions and expectations. To the extent possible, it is also a good idea to figure out how to motivate teachers and encourage them to change in ways that conform with the system.

The consequences of relying on bureaucratic authority in supervision have been carefully documented in the literature. Without proper monitoring, teachers wind up being loosely connected to bureaucratic systems, complying only when they have to.[2] When monitoring is effective in enforcing compliance, teachers respond as technicians who execute predetermined scripts and whose performance is narrowed. They become, to use the jargon, "deskilled."[3] When teachers are not able to use their talents fully and are caught in the grind of routine, they become separated from their work, viewing teaching as a job rather than a vocation, and treating students as cases rather than persons.

Readers probably will have little difficulty accepting the assertion that supervision based primarily on bureaucratic authority is not a good idea. The validity of most of the assumptions underlying this source of authority are suspect. Few, for example, believe that teachers as a group are not trustworthy and do not share the same goals and interests about schooling as do their supervisors. Even fewer would accept the idea that hierarchy equals expertise. Less contested, perhaps, would be the assumptions that teachers are subordinates in a hierarchically arranged system and that external monitoring works best. Supervision today, for example, still relies heavily on "expect and inspect," predetermined standards, in-servicing teachers, and providing direct supervision. Because these practices endure, supervisors need to spend a good deal of time trying to figure out strategies for motivating teachers and encouraging them to change. Supervision becomes a direct, intense, and often exhausting activity.

PERSONAL AUTHORITY

Personal authority is based on the supervisor's expertise in providing human relations leadership, in using motivational techniques, and in practicing other interpersonal skills. It is assumed that as a result of this leadership, teachers will want to comply with the supervisor's wishes. When human relations

[2] See, for example, Karl Weick, "Educational Organizations as Loosely Coupled Systems," *Administrative Science Quarterly*, vol. 21, no. 2, pp. 1–19, 1976; and Thomas J. Sergiovanni, "Biting the Bullet: Rescinding the Texas Teacher Appraisal System," *Teachers Education and Practice*, vol. 6, no. 2, pp. 89–93, Fall/Winter 1990–1991.

[3] See, for example, Arthur E. Wise, *Legislated Learning: The Bureaucratization of the American Classroom*, Berkeley, Ca.: University of California Press, 1979; Susan Rosenholtz, *Teachers' Workplace: The Social Organization of Schools*, New York: Longman, 1989; and Linda McNeil, *Contradictions of Control: School Structure and School Knowledge*, New York: Routledge & Kegan Paul, 1986.

skills become the prime source of authority, the following assumptions are made:

The goals and interests of teachers and supervisors are not the same. As a result each must barter with the other so that both get what they want by giving something that the other party wants.

Teachers have needs, and if these needs are met at work the work gets done as required in exchange.

Congenial relationships and harmonious interpersonal climates make teachers content, easier to work with, and more apt to cooperate.

Supervisors must be experts at reading the needs of teachers and handling people in order to barter successfully for increased compliance and performance.

These assumptions lead to a supervisory practice that relies heavily on "expect and reward" and "what gets rewarded gets done." Emphasis is also given to developing a school climate characterized by a high degree of congeniality among teachers and between teachers and supervisors. Often personal authority is used in combination with bureaucratic and technical-rational authority. When this is the case very few of the things that the supervisor wants from teachers are negotiable. The idea is to obtain compliance by trading psychological payoffs of one sort or another.

Personal authority is also important to the practice of human resources leadership. In this case, however, as suggested in Chapter 1, it takes a slightly different twist. The emphasis is less on meeting teachers' social needs and more on providing the *conditions of work* that allow people to meet needs for achievement, challenge, responsibility, autonomy, and esteem; the presumed basis for finding deep psychological fulfillment in one's job.

The typical reaction of teachers to personal authority, particularly when connected to human relations supervision, is to respond as required when rewards are available but not otherwise. Teachers become involved in their work for calculated reasons and their performance becomes increasingly narrowed. When the emphasis is on psychological fulfillment that comes from the work itself (emphasizing challenging work, for example) rather than the supervisor's skilled interpersonal behavior, teachers become more intrinsically motivated and thus less susceptible to calculated involvement and narrowing of performance. But in today's supervision this emphasis remains the exception rather than the rule.

Suggesting that using personal authority and the psychological theories that inform this authority as the basis for supervisory practice may be overdone and may have negative consequences for teachers and students is likely to raise a few eyebrows. Most supervisors, for example, tend to consider knowledge and skill about how to motivate teachers, how to apply the correct leadership style, how to boost morale, and how to engineer the right interpersonal climate as representing the heart of their work. It is for many supervisors the "core technology" of their profession.

We do not challenge the importance of psychologically based supervision and leadership. Indeed, we argued for its importance in earlier editions. We do question, however, whether it should continue to enjoy the prominence that it does. Our position is that personal, bureaucratic, and technical-rational sources of authority should do no more than provide support for a supervisory practice that relies on professional and moral authority. The reasons, we argue here and elsewhere in this book, are that psychologically based leadership and supervision cannot tap the full range and depth of human capacity and will. This source of authority cannot elicit the kind of motivated and spirited response from teachers that will allow schools to work well. We hope to build a case for this assertion in Chapter 4, where we examine what is important to teachers at work.

Another reason for our concern with the overuse of personal authority is that there are practically and morally better reasons for teachers and others to be involved in the work of the school than those related to matters of the leader's personality and interpersonal skills. Haller and Strike, for example, believe that building one's expertise around interpersonal themes raises important ethical questions. In their words,

> We find this an inadequate view of the administrative role . . . its first deficiency is that it makes administrative success depend on characteristics that tend to be both intangible and unalterable. One person's dynamic leader is another's tyrant. What one person sees as a democratic style, another will see as the generation of time wasting committee work. . . . Our basic concern with this view . . . is that it makes the administrative role one of form, not content. Being a successful administrator depends not on the adequacy of one's view, not on the educational policies that one adopts and how reasonable they are, and not on how successful one is in communicating those reasons to others. Success depends on personality and style, or on carefully chosen ways of inducing others to contribute to the organization. It is not what one wants to do and why that is important; it is who one is and how one does things that counts. We find such a view offensive. It is incompatible with the values of autonomy, reason and democracy, which we see among the central commitments of our society and educational system. Of course educational administrators must be leaders, but let them lead by reason and persuasion, not by forces of personality.[4]

Carl Glickman raises still other doubts about the desirability of basing supervisory practice on psychological authority. He believes that such leadership creates dependency among followers.[5]

The perspectives of Haller and Strike and Glickman raise a nagging set of questions. Why should teachers follow the lead of their supervisors? Is it because supervisors know how to manipulate effectively? Is it because supervisors can meet the psychological needs of teachers? Is it because supervisors are charming and fun to be with? Or, is it because supervisors have something to

[4] Emil J. Haller and Kenneth A. Strike, *An Introduction to Educational Administration Social, Legal and Ethical Perspectives*, New York: Longman, 1986, p. 326.

[5] Carl D. Glickman, "Right Question, Wrong Extrapolation: A Response to Duffey's 'Supervising for Results'," *Journal of Curriculum and Supervision*, vol. 6, no. 1, pp. 39–40, Fall 1990.

say that makes sense? Or because supervisors have thoughts that point teachers in a direction that captures their imagination? Or because supervisors speak from a set of ideas, values, and conceptions that they believe are good for teachers, for students, and for the school? These questions raise yet another question: Do supervisors want to base their practice on glitz or on substance? Answering "yes" to the former alternative not only raises moral questions but also encourages a vacuous form of leadership and supervisory practice. It can lead to what Abraham Zaleznik refers to as the "managerial mystique," the substitution of process for substance.[6]

TECHNICAL-RATIONAL AUTHORITY

Technical-rational authority relies heavily on evidence that is defined by logic and scientific research. Teachers are expected to comply with prescriptions based on this source of authority in light of what is considered to be truth.

When technical rationality becomes the primary source of authority for supervisory practice the following assumptions are made:

Supervision and teaching are applied sciences.
Scientific knowledge is superordinate to practice.
Teachers are skilled technicians.
Values, preferences, and beliefs are subjective and ephemeral; facts and objective evidence are what matters.

When technical-rational authority is established, then the supervisory strategy is to use research to identify what is best teaching practice and what is best supervisory practice. Once this is known, the work of teaching and supervision is standardized to reflect the best way. The next step is to in-service teachers in the best way. For the system to work smoothly, it is best if teachers willingly conform to what the research says ought to be done and how it ought to be done. Thus it is important to figure out how to motivate teachers and encourage them to change willingly.

When technical-rational authority is the primary source, the impact on teachers is similar to that of bureaucratic authority. Teachers are less likely to conform to what research says and more likely to act according to their beliefs. When forced to conform they are likely to respond as technicians executing predetermined steps, and their performance becomes increasingly narrowed. When technical-rational authority is used in combination with personal authority, teachers tend to conform as long as they are being rewarded.

If criticism of a supervisory practice based on personal authority raises concerns, then suggesting that primary use of technical-rational authority is dysfunctional is also likely to raise concerns. We live, after all, in a technical-rational society where that which is considered scientific is prized. Because of this

---

[6] Abraham Zaleznik, *The Managerial Mystique Restoring Leadership in Business*, New York: Harper & Row, 1989.

deference to science, the above beliefs and their related practices are likely to receive ready acceptance. "Supervision and teaching are applied sciences," has a nice ring to it. And, using research to identify one best practice seems quite reasonable. But teaching and learning are too complex to be captured so simply. In the real world of teaching none of the assumptions hold up very well and the related practices portray an unrealistic view of teaching and supervision.

There is, for example, a growing sense among researchers, teachers, and policy analysts that the context for teaching practice is too idiosyncratic, non-linear, and loosely connected for simplistic conceptions of teaching to apply.[7] Teaching cannot be standardized. Teachers, like other professionals, cannot be effective when following scripts. Instead they need to *create knowledge in use* as they practice, becoming skilled surfers who ride the wave of teaching as it uncurls.[8] This ability requires a higher level of reflection, understanding, and skill than that required by the practice of technical rationality—a theme to be further developed in Parts Three and Four.

The authority of technical rationality for supervisory practice does share some similarities with the authority of professionalism. Both, for example, rely on expertise. But the authority of technical rationality presumes that scientific knowledge is the only source of expertise. Further, this knowledge exists separate from the context of teaching. The job of the teacher is simply to apply this knowledge in practice. In other words, the teacher is *subordinate* to the knowledge base of teaching.

PROFESSIONAL AUTHORITY

Professional authority presumes that the expertise of teachers counts most. Teachers, as is the case with other professionals, are always *superordinate* to the knowledge base that supports their practice. Professionals view knowledge as something that informs but does not prescribe practice.[9] What counts as well is the ability of teachers to make judgments based on the specifics of the situations they face. They must decide what is appropriate. They must decide what is right and good. They must, in sum, create professional knowledge in use as they practice.

---

[7] See, for example, Linda Darling-Hammond, Arthur E. Wise, and S. R. Pease, "Teacher Evaluations in an Organizational Context: A Review of Literature," *Review of Educational Research*, vol. 53, no. 3, pp. 285–328, 1983; Thomas J. Sergiovanni, "The Metaphorical Use of Theories and Models in Supervision and Teaching: Building a Science," *Journal of Curriculum and Supervision*, vol. 2, no. 3, pp. 221–232, Spring 1987. and Lee S. Shulman, "A Union of Insufficiencies: Strategies for Teacher Assessment in a Period of Educational Reform," *Educational Leadership*, vol. 46, no. 3, pp. 36–41, 1988; and Michael Huberman, "The Social Context of Instruction in Schools," paper presented at American Educational Research Association Annual Meeting, Boston, April 1990.

[8] Thomas J. Sergiovanni, "Will We Ever Have a TRUE Profession?" *Educational Leadership*, vol. 44, no. 8, pp. 44–51, 1987.

[9] Thomas J. Sergiovanni, "The Metaphorical Use of Theories and Models in Supervision: Building a Science," *Journal of Curriculum and Supervision*, vol. 2, no. 3, pp. 221–232, 1987.

Professional authority is based on the informed knowledge of the craft of teaching and on the personal expertise of teachers. Teachers respond in part to this expertise and in part to internalized professional values, and accepted tenets of practice that define what it means to be a teacher.

When professional authority becomes the primary source for supervisory practice the following assumptions are made:

Situations are idiosyncratic; thus no one best way to practice exists.

"Scientific knowledge" and "professional knowledge" are different; professional knowledge is created as teachers practice.

The purpose of "scientific knowledge" is to inform, not prescribe, the practice of teachers and supervisors.

Professional authority is not external but is exercised within the teaching context and from within the teacher.

Authority in context comes from the teacher's training and experience.

Authority from within comes from the teacher's professional socialization and internalized knowledge and values.

Supervisory practice that is based primarily on professional authority seeks to promote a dialogue among teachers that makes explicit professional values and accepted tenets of practice. These are then translated into professional practice standards. With standards acknowledged, teachers are then provided with as much discretion as they want and need. When professional authority is fully developed, teachers will hold each other accountable in meeting these practice standards with accountability internalized. The job of the supervisor is to provide assistance, support, and professional development opportunities. Teachers respond to professional norms, and their performance becomes more expansive.

Though it is common to refer to teaching as a profession, not much attention has been given to the nature of professional authority. When the idea does receive attention, the emphasis is on the expertise of teachers. Building teacher expertise is a long-term proposition. In the meantime much can be done to advance another aspect of professionalism—*professional virtue*. Professional virtue speaks to the norms that define what it means to be a professional. Once established, professional norms take on moral attributes. When professional norms are combined with norms derived from shared community values, moral authority can become a prime basis for supervisory practice. These themes will be explored further in the next chapter, "The School as Community."

MORAL AUTHORITY

Moral authority is derived from the obligations and duties that teachers feel as a result of their connection to widely shared community values, ideas, and ideals. When moral authority is in place, teachers respond to shared commitments and felt interdependence by becoming self-managing.

When moral authority becomes the primary source for supervisory practice, schools can become transformed from organizations to communities. Communities are defined by their center of shared values, beliefs, and commitments. In communities, what is considered right and good is as important as what works and what is effective; teachers are motivated as much by emotion and belief as they are by self-interest; collegiality is understood as a form of professional virtue.

In communities, supervisors direct their efforts toward identifying and making explicit shared values and beliefs. These values and beliefs are then transformed into informal norms that govern behavior. With these in place it becomes possible to promote collegiality as something that is internally felt and that derives from morally driven interdependence. Supervisors can rely less on external controls and more on the ability of teachers as community members to respond to felt duties and obligations. The school community's informal norm system is used to enforce professional and community values. Norms and values, whether derived from professional authority or moral authority, become substitutes for direct supervision as teachers become increasingly self-managing. The five sources of authority for supervision with consequences for practice are summarized in Table 2-1.

Community and professional norms as expressions of moral authority play major roles in Supervision II, the recommended alternative to today's supervisory practice. They are described more fully in the next chapter. Chapters 4 and 11 ("Supervision as Moral Action," and "Providing Supervisory Leadership") extend the theme by examining how moral authority is expressed in day-to-day supervisory practice.

EXPANDING THE VALUES OF MANAGEMENT

We believe that improving schools over the long run will require expanding the sources of authority for supervision to include professional and moral authority. Expanding sources, in turn, means rethinking the very values that undergird management thought.[10] Presently the official values of management, as depicted in Table 2-2, are secular authority, science, and deductive logic in the form of faith in the bureaucratic system, the findings of empirical research, and deductive reasoning, respectively. Two other management values that have gained enough legitimacy in *practice* to now be considered semi-official are sense experience and intuition. The two remain semi-official, since their acknowledgment in the academic literature is ambivalent and often expressed in the form of criticism. Sacred authority and emotion, by contrast, are two unofficial management values. Presently they have little legitimacy in the academic literature. In schools these two are expressed as faith in the authority of professional and school norms, and in the authority of one's feelings. We believe that all management values are legitimate and should be manifested in the ways in

---

[10] See, for example, Hunter Lewis, *A Question of Values*, New York: Harper & Row, 1990.

TABLE 2-1
THE SOURCES OF AUTHORITY FOR SUPERVISORY POLICY AND PRACTICE

Source	Assumptions when use of this source is prime	Leadership/ supervisory strategy	Consequences
Bureaucratic authority Hierarchy Rules and Regulations Mandates Role expectation Teachers are expected to comply or face consequences.	Teachers are subordinates in a hierarchically arranged system. Supervisors are trustworthy, but you cannot trust subordinates very much. Goals and interests of teachers and supervisors are not the same, thus supervisors must be watchful. Hierarchy equals expertise, thus supervisors know more than do teachers. External accountability works best.	"Expect and inspect" is the overarching rule. Rely on predetermined standards to which teachers must measure up. Identify their needs and "in-service" them. Directly supervise and closely monitor the work of teachers to ensure compliance. Figure out how to motivate them and get them to change.	With proper monitoring teachers respond as technicians executing predetermined scripts. Their performance is narrowed.
Personal authority Motivation technology Interpersonal skills Human relations leadership Teachers will want to comply because of the congenial climate provided and to reap rewards offered in exchange.	The goals and interests of teachers and supervisors are not the same but can be bartered so that each gets what they want. Teachers have needs, and if those needs are met at work the work gets done as required in exchange. Congenial relationships and harmonious interpersonal climates make teachers content, easier to work with, and more apt to cooperate.	Develop a school climate characterized by congeniality among teachers and between teachers and supervisors. "Expect and reward." "What gets rewarded gets done."	Teachers respond as required when rewards are available but not otherwise. Their involvement is calculated and performance is narrowed.

TABLE 2-1
THE SOURCES OF AUTHORITY FOR SUPERVISORY POLICY AND PRACTICE (*Continued*)

Source	Assumptions when use of this source is prime	Leadership/ supervisory strategy	Consequences
	Supervisors must be expert at reading needs and handling people in order to successfully barter for increased compliance and performance.	Use personal authority in combination with bureaucratic and technical-rational authority.	
The authority of technical rationality			
Informed knowledge of craft and personal expertise.	Supervision and teaching are applied sciences.	Use research to identify one best practice.	With proper monitoring, teachers respond as technicians executing predetermined scripts. Performance is narrowed.
Evidence defined by logic and scientific research	Knowledge of research is privileged.	Standardize the work of teaching to reflect the best way.	
Teachers are required to comply in light of what is considered to be truth.	Scientific knowledge is superordinate to practice.	In-service teachers in the best way.	
	Teachers are skilled technicians.	Monitor the process to ensure compliance.	
	Values, preferences, and beliefs don't count, but facts and objective evidence do.	Figure out ways to motivate teachers and get them to change.	
Professional authority			
Informed knowledge of craft and personal expertise.	Situations are idiosyncratic, thus no one best way exists.	Promote a dialogue among teachers that makes explicit professional values and accepted tenets of practice.	Teachers respond to professional norms, thus require little monitoring. Their performance is expansive.
Teachers respond on basis of common socialization, professional values, accepted tenets of practice, and internalized expertness.	"Scientific" knowledge and "professional" knowledge are different; professional is created in use as teachers practice.	Translate above into professional practice standards.	

TABLE 2-1 (Continued)

Source	Assumptions when use of this source is prime	Leadership/ supervisory strategy	Consequences
	The purpose of "scientific" knowledge is to inform, not prescribe, practice.	Provide teachers with as much discretion as they want and need.	
	Authority cannot be external but comes from the context itself and from within the teacher.	Require teachers to hold each other accountable in meeting practice standards.	
	Authority from context comes from training and experience.	Make available assistance, support, and professional development opportunities.	
	Authority from within comes from socialization and internalized values.		
Moral authority			
Felt obligations and duties derived from widely shared community values, ideas, and ideals	Schools are professional learning communities.	Identify and make explicit the values and beliefs that define the center of the school as community.	Teachers respond to community values for moral reasons. Their performance is expansive and sustained.
Teachers respond to shared commitments and felt interdependence.	Communities are defined by their center of shared values, beliefs, and commitments.	Translate the above into informal norms that govern behavior.	
	In communities:		
	What is considered right and good is as important as what works and what is effective.	Promote collegiality as internally felt and morally driven interdependence.	
	People are motivated as much by emotion and beliefs as by self-interest.	Rely on ability of community members to respond to duties and obligations.	
	Collegiality is a professional virtue.	Rely on the community's informal norm system to enforce professional and community values.	

Source: Thomas J. Sergiovanni, "Moral Authority and the Regeneration of Supervision," in Carl Glickman (ed.), *Supervision in Transition.* 1992 ASCD Yearbook. Alexandria, Va.: Association for Supervision and Curriculum Development, 1992, pp. 203–214. © Thomas J. Sergiovanni. All rights reserved.

TABLE 2-2
SOURCES OF THE OFFICIAL, SEMI-OFFICIAL, AND UNOFFICIAL VALUES OF MANAGEMENT

Sources of the official values of management	Sources of the semi-official values of management	Sources of the unofficial values of management
1. Secular authority (I have faith in the authority of the bureaucratic system)	1. Sense experience (I have faith in my experiences)	1. Sacred authority (I have faith in the authority of community, in professional norms, school norms and ideas)
2. Science (I have faith in the findings of empirical research)	2. Intuition (I have faith in my insight)	2. Emotions (I have faith in my feelings)
3. Deductive logic (I have faith in deductive reasoning)		

Source: Thomas J. Sergiovanni, *Moral Leadership: Getting to the Heart of School Improvement,* San Francisco: Jossey-Bass, 1992, p. 13.

which supervision is practiced. Seeking this legitimacy is one of the purposes of Supervision II.

SUPERVISION II

In this section some of the basic assumptions and underlying operating principles that differentiate Supervision I from Supervision II are provided. Supervision II combines Theory Y from human resources supervision with the belief that people are morally responsive and able to sacrifice self-interests for the right reasons. Supervision I, by contrast, relies heavily on the assumptions of Theory X (scientific management) and Theory X soft (human relations), as described earlier.

In Supervision I a great deal of emphasis is given to understanding, researching, and improving supervisory behavior. As will be discussed in Part Two, Supervision II emphasizes action. Behavior is very different from action. Behavior is what we do on the surface. Action, by contrast, implies intentionality, free choice, value seeking, and altruism.

Because of this difference between behavior and action, Supervision II focuses more on interpretation. There is concern not only for the way things look but also for what things mean. The metaphors "phonetics" and "semantics" can help understand this distinction.[11] Tending to supervisory and teaching behaviors and accounting for what, when, how, and under what circumstances supervisors and teachers do, comprises a phonetic view. It does not matter so much whether the supervisor is involved in leading, coaching, man-

[11] Thomas J. Sergiovanni, *Educational Leadership,* op. cit.

aging, evaluating, administering, or teaching. If the emphasis in these activities is on "the looks and sounds" of behavior, on the form or shape that this behavior takes as opposed to what the behavior means, the view is phonetic.

Identical behaviors can have different meanings as contexts change and as different people are involved. For example, a supervisor may walk through the classrooms of several teachers on a regular basis, making it a practice to comment to teachers about what is happening and to share her or his impressions. For supervisor A, teachers may consider this behavior inspectorial or controlling and view this supervisor as one who is closely monitoring what they do. For supervisor B this same behavior is considered symbolic of the interest and support which the supervisor provides to teachers. In this case, supervisory behavior is interpreted as being caring and helpful. At one level, the phonetic, the behavior is the same for both supervisors. At another level, the semantic, the behavior results in different meanings. When concerned with different interpretations and meanings, one is tending to the semantic aspects of supervision.

Motivation in Supervision I focuses primarily on "what gets rewarded gets done." Supervision II is based on "what is rewarding gets done" and "what is believed to be right and good gets done" as well. These latter emphases, as will be discussed in Chapter 4, not only reflect more completely what is important to teachers at work but also result in less emphasis on direct control-oriented supervision. When motivated by intrinsically satisfying and meaningful action, teachers become self-managing.

In Supervision I it is assumed that supervisors and teachers make "rational" decisions on the basis of self-interest and as isolated individuals. Supervision II recognizes the importance of emotions and values in making decisions and the capacity for humans consistently to sacrifice self-interest as a result. Further, Supervision II recognizes that our connections to other people to a great extent determine what we think, what we believe, and the decisions that we make. These two themes will be explored further in Chapters 4 and 5.

Supervision I takes places in the context of hierarchically differentiated roles. "Supervision" and "designated supervisor" go together. Supervision is something that supervisors do to teachers. A teacher studies to become a supervisor, becomes licensed, and thus is allowed to practice supervision. Supervision, in other words, is a formal and institutionalized process linked to the school's organizational structure.

Supervision II views supervision as a process and function that is hierarchically independent and role-free. It may be linked to hierarchy and role, but it need not be. Supervision, in other words, is not necessarily shaped by organizational structure and is not necessarily legitimized by credentials. Instead it is a set of ideals and skills that can be translated into processes that can help teachers and help schools function more effectively. Supervision is something that not only principals and hierarchically designated supervisors do but also teachers and others. Thus, such ideas as collegial supervision, mentoring supervision, cooperative supervision, and informal supervision are important in

Supervision II. In a sense these processes are often in place in schools anyway. Teachers respect each other's craft knowledge and depend on each other for help. One of the purposes of Supervision II, therefore, is to deinstitutionalize institutional supervision and to formalize the informal supervision among teachers that now takes place in schools by legitimizing it.

MODELS OF CONTROL

Supervision is a process designed to help teachers and supervisors learn more about their practice; to be better able to use their knowledge and skills to better serve parents and schools; and to make the school a more effective learning community. For these goals to be realized a degree of control over events is necessary, and in this sense supervision is about control. But it makes a difference how control is expressed in schools. The wrong kind of control can cause problems and lead to negative consequences despite the best of intentions.

Control is understood differently in Supervisions I and II. For example, the management theorist Henry Mintzberg proposes that the work of others can be controlled by providing direct and close supervision of what people are doing; by standardizing the work that needs to be done, and then fitting people into the work system so that they are forced to follow the approved script; by standardizing outputs and then evaluating to be sure that output specifications have been met; by socializing people through the use of norms of one sort or another; and by arranging work circumstances and norms in a way that people feel a need to be interdependent.[12] When referring to socializing people, Mintzberg has in mind professional norms. The norms that come from common purposes and shared values provide still another control strategy that can be added to Mintzberg's list.[13]

In Chapter 1 supervisor A relied heavily on providing direct supervision, standardizing the work, and standardizing outputs as the preferred ways to control what teachers were doing and how. By contrast, supervisor D recommended relying on the process of socialization, building interdependencies, and purposes and shared values. Which of the two views makes the most sense? In part, the answer to this question depends upon the degree of complexity of the work to be supervised.

Professional socialization, purposes and shared values, and building natural interdepencies among teachers are unique in that they are able to provide a kind of normative power that encourages people to meet their commitments. Once in place, the three become substitutes for traditional supervision, since teachers tend to respond from within, becoming self-managing. Since these strategies do not require direct supervision or the scripting of work, they are better matched to the complex behaviors that are required for teaching and

---

[12] Henry Mintzberg, *The Structure of Organizations,* New York: Wiley, 1979.
[13] Karl Weick, "The Concept of Loose Coupling: An Assessment," *Organizational Theory Dialogue,* December 1986 and Thomas J. Peters and Robert H. Waterman, *In Search of Excellence,* New York: Harper & Row, 1982.

learning to take place successfully. Professional socialization, purposes and shared values, and building natural interdependencies are the strategies that provide the framework for control in Supervision II. The three are much more difficult to implement when schools are viewed as formal organizations. Such organizations tend to nurture control systems that rely on direct supervision, standardized work, and standardized outputs. In the next chapter we propose that one way to improve schools is to change the way they are understood from organizations to communities.

CHAPTER 3

THE SCHOOL
AS COMMUNITY

Whether Supervision I or Supervision II is favored depends in part on the metaphor that shapes our thinking about schools and our understanding of the nature of teaching and learning. In this chapter we examine two different metaphors for schools and the kinds of supervision that logically evolve from their use.

A dominant metaphor for school or school system is that of organization. Schools are organizations, and what people do within them is described as organizational behavior. Organization was the guiding metaphor for the analysis of school supervision we provided in editions one, two, and three of this book. In the fourth edition more attention was given to viewing schools as communities. And, as a result, the kind of supervision we recommended in that edition was somewhat different from previous editions. In this, the fifth edition, we propose that community become the dominant metaphor for thinking about schools. Not surprisingly, the more organization is the metaphor of choice for schools, the more appropriate will be the concepts and practices of Supervision I. And, the more community is the metaphor of choice, the more appropriate is Supervision II.

THE SCHOOL AS ORGANIZATION

The words "dominant" and "more" are used above deliberately. Both organization and community are metaphors that ring true for certain aspects of how schools function. But it makes a difference which of the two provides the overarching frame for how schools are viewed.

The phrase "to organize," for example, provides a good clue as to how the metaphor of organization forces us to think about schools and school supervision. To organize means to arrange things into some kind of a coherent whole. First there has to be a reason for organizing. Then a careful study needs to be made of each of the parts to be organized. This often involves grouping them mentally into some kind of logical order. A plan needs to be developed that enables the elements to be arranged according to the desired scheme. This is a stepwise process that proceeds linearly. As the plan is being followed one must monitor progress, making corrections as needed. And finally when the work is complete the organizational arrangements are evaluated in terms of original intentions. These principles seem to apply whether we are thinking about organizing our bureau drawers or a school. Organization as an idea is explicitly rational.

The sociologist John Meyer points out that

> A useful starting point [in understanding organization] is . . . the idea that formal organizational structures are depictions of rational or rationalized activity. This idea makes sense. Almost all observers see the distinctive feature of modern formal organization, in contrast to social units by communities, societies, associations or families, as lying in its explicitly rational character. This property justifies and legitimates it and brings it into existence and into its presently dominating role. In modern society even education, medical care, and recreational activity are organized in such structures.[1]

Obtaining and maintaining legitimacy is an important goal for schools. Being considered legitimate by external forces, for example, provides the school with increased political and financial discretion and with authority. Internal legitimacy brings with it support and compliance. In our culture, formal organizations seek to maintain legitimacy by appearing rational.

What are the dimensions of rationality an organization must display in order to be considered legitimate? It must, as Meyer points out, have clearly articulated and readily measured purposes.[2] Purposes that matter are those that are standardized, can be counted and measured. Unclear and ambiguous purposes, by contrast, send the wrong messages and therefore threaten legitimacy. What should organizations do when stuck with the latter but need the former? They should convert "fuzzy" purposes into clear ones. Schools, for example, do this by breaking down complicated learning goals into achievement test score targets. Further, since accounting for what students actually know and can do is difficult, schools often rely on counting the number of courses taken, the number of days students attend school, the number of students who graduate, and other more easily stated and measured objectives as means to achieve legitimacy.

Second, according to Meyer, organizations must develop explicit management structures and procedures that give a convincing account that the proper means-ends chains are in place to accomplish purposes. In other words, schools should have not only clear purposes, but also explicit, understandable, and rational policies, processes, operating procedures, and management systems that represent designs to achieve the stated purposes. Organizing schools and school districts into departments and grade levels, developing job descriptions, constructing curriculum plans, and putting into place explicit instructional delivery systems of various kinds are all examples of organizational

[1] John Meyer, "Organizations as Idiological Systems," in Thomas J. Sergiovanni and John E. Corbally (eds.), *Leadership and Organizational Culture*, Urbana: University of Illinois Press, 1984, p. 190.

[2] Ibid. See, for example, pp. 190–194 for a discussion of the dimensions.

structures and management processes that communicate to those inside and outside the school that the school knows what it is doing. The more difficult it is to find out what the school is actually doing and what students are actually learning, the more important are substitutes such as test scores in obtaining and maintaining legitimacy. And similarly, the more important are rational organizational structures and other management processes.

Third, according to Meyer, organizations must convince sources of legitimacy that they are in control. "The simplest depiction of control is hierarchy, and modern organizations are filled with organizational charts. . . ."[3] Developing and using rules and regulations, monitoring and supervising, providing for recordkeeping, and implementing evaluation systems are the means by which this hierarchy seeks and maintains control over teachers. Teachers, in turn, develop similar schemes in efforts to control students. Control, of course, must be linked to rational processes. And these processes must be linked to explicit goals.

For the chain of events described above to work, organizations must assume that hierarchy equals expertise. Principals and supervisors, by virtue of their rank, are presumed to know more than do teachers. Central office staff are presumed to know more than do principals, and superintendents, presumably, know the most. The evaluation policies of most school districts testify to this. Each hierarchical level is responsible for evaluating the people who are at the level immediately below. This means that those lower in the hierarchy must submit to the control of those higher. Most of the literature on the supervision and evaluation of teachers is based on these assumptions. This is the kind of supervision that logically derives from viewing schools as organizations.

Meyer points out that organizations seek legitimacy in two other ways: by standardizing "inputs, throughputs and outputs" and by outlining for themselves clear boundaries that separate them from other organizations.[4] Schools, for example, take in students who are variable in every conceivable way, instructing them with teachers who are also variable. But such variability threatens the legitimacy established through clear and measurable purposes, rational and explicit processes, and hierarchical control. Unless variability in "inputs, throughputs and outputs" is reduced, other dimensions of the organization as rational system break down and legitimacy is threatened.

Unclear boundary lines create similar problems, clouding particularly the issue of school purpose. Are schools learning organizations or social welfare organizations? In school, day care centers and parent centers, for example, cloud the issue of who are the schools' direct clients. Providing psychological and social services to students clouds academic purposes. Clouding creates ambiguity and confusion, threatening rationality and in turn legitimacy.

---

[3] Ibid., p. 192.
[4] Ibid., pp. 192–193.

THE INEVITABILITY OF BUREAUCRATIC VALUES

The discussion above suggests that using the metaphor "organization" to think about schools carries with it a heavy load of baggage. The issue of legitimacy becomes central, with rationality as the means to achieve it. The meaning of school supervision under these circumstances becomes increasingly clear. Supervision becomes a process linked to clear goals, expressed in the form of instructional and management delivery and monitoring systems, legitimized by bureaucratic authority, and designed to maintain control of what teachers do in light of stated purposes and management requirements.

The typical reaction of schools to the demands that organizations require is to rely increasingly on bureaucratic values. The school administration theorist Max Abbott listed the following as examples of bureaucratic characteristics that schools typically adopt when construed as organizations. Each one of the characteristics depends heavily on direct and close supervision of teachers and their work:

1 The school organization has clearly been influenced by the need for specialization and the division of tasks. The division of the school into elementary and secondary units; the establishment of science, mathematics, music, and other departments within a school; the introduction of guidance programs and psychological services; and, indeed, the separation of the administrative function from the teaching function all represent responses to this need.

2 The school organization has developed a clearly defined and rigid hierarchy of authority. Although the term "hierarchy" is seldom used in the lexicon of the educational administrator, the practices to which it refers are prevalent. The typical organization chart is intended specifically to clarify lines of authority and channels of communication. Even in the absence of such a chart, school employees have a clear conception of the nature of the hierarchy in their school systems. In fact, rigid adherence to hierarchical principles has been stressed to the point that failure to adhere to recognized lines of authority is viewed as the epitome of immoral organizational behavior.

3 The school organization has leaned heavily upon the use of general rules to control the behavior of members of the organization and to develop standards which would assure reasonable uniformity in the performance of tasks. Whether they have taken the form of policy manuals, rules and regulations, staff handbooks, or some other type of document, general rules have been used extensively to provide for the orderly induction of new employees into the organization and to eliminate capricious behavior on the part of all school personnel, including administrators and members of boards of education.

4 Despite frequent proclamations regarding togetherness and democracy, the school organization has made extensive application of Weber's princi-

ple of impersonality in organizational relationships. Authority has been established on the basis of rational considerations rather than on the basis of charismatic qualities or traditional imperatives; interpersonal interactions have tended to be functionally specific rather than functionally diffuse; and official relationships have been governed largely by universalistic, as contrasted with particularistic, considerations. Thus, by operating in a spirit of "formalistic impersonality," the typical school system has succeeded, in part, in separating organizational rights and obligations from the private lives of individual employees.

5 Employment in the educational organizations has been based upon technical competence and has constituted for most members a professional career. Promotions have been determined by seniority and by achievement, tenure has been provided, and fixed compensation and retirement benefits have been assured.[5]

DOES THE METAPHOR FIT?

There are several reasons why viewing schools as organizations does not serve them very well. To begin with, most of the assumptions about schools being "rational" don't hold up. No matter how hard organizationists try to impose rational systems on schools, the best they can do is create symbolic rather than real ones. Schools wind up looking rational, thus fulfilling claims for legitimacy, but are not rational in operation.

There is, for example, a vast literature that makes the case for schools being loosely structured in an organizational and management sense.[6] "Loosely structured" refers to the gap that exists between the school's formal and informal structure and the gap that exists between the behavior prescribed by the systems of rules and procedures and actual behavior. To appear rational and obtain legitimacy, for example, schools as organizations develop official curricula that are presented to teachers for their subsequent delivery to students. But the curriculum in use is typically different from that presented. Teachers tend to teach what they like, what they believe is important, and what they know the most about.

Officially, for example, teaching is construed as a linear process that begins with identifying discrete learning goals, linking these goals to appropriate curricula, teaching these curricula, and assessing learning outcomes to find out whether the original goals have been learned. But in the real world of teaching

---

[5] Max G. Abbott, "Hierarchical Impediments to Innovation in Educational Organizations," in M. G. Abbott and John Lovell (eds.), *Change Perspectives in Educational Administration*, Auburn, Ala.: Auburn University School of Education, 1965, pp. 44–45.

[6] See, for example, Chester Barnard, *The Function of the Executive*, Cambridge, Mass.: Harvard University Press, 1938; James G. March and Johann P. Olsen, *Ambiguity and Choice in Organizations*. Bergen: Universitetsforlaget, 1976; and Karl Weick, "Educational Organizations as Loosely Coupled Systems," *Administrative Science Quarterly*, vol. 21, pp. 1–19, 1976.

no sequential assumptions can be made about the relationships among discrete goals, curriculum, teaching, and outcomes. Any of the four can drive the other three. Goals often are selected as a result of materials available, just as materials often are selected as a result of goals. Teaching styles and preferences determine objectives as often as objectives determine teaching styles and preferences. Outcomes become goals as often as goals determine outcomes.

Teacher evaluation provides still another example of the looseness that exists between supervisory systems and actual teaching behavior. It is becoming increasingly clear that what happens in classrooms during the time they are being scrutinized under the official evaluation system is very different from what happens the rest of the time. For example, Texas is one of the states that uses a state-mandated system of evaluation. The system relies heavily on the Texas Teacher Appraisal System (TTAS) to observe teachers on a regular basis. Evaluators are trained by and must be certified by the state. The TTAS is comprised of 55 behaviors gleaned from the teaching effectiveness research popular during the 1970s. A high number of required behaviors displayed under observation results in a high score and a high opinion of the teacher. Teachers with high scores are rewarded and those with low scores are remediated. High-scoring teachers, for example, increase their chances of advancing on the state's career ladder and thus winning financial incentives.

The financial and career advancement stakes in Texas and in other places where such systems are used are high. Further, complying with the required evaluation system makes administrators and supervisors happy. And happy administrators and supervisors makes life easier for teachers. For these reasons, when teachers are being observed they tend to demonstrate the required behaviors. But what happens when they are not being observed? The evidence is compelling that teachers often do not comply with the system, choosing instead to teach in their own way.[7]

From a practical point of view it appears that the management and supervisory systems that are logically derived from schools construed as organizations just don't fit schools very well. Though these systems may look good on paper and sound good when talked about, they seem not to work. They are not effective without intensive monitoring. Pushing compliance, as suggested in Chapter 2, doesn't help. The results of pushing are that teaching becomes narrowed, teachers use fewer of their skills, and ultimately teachers become alienated from their work.[8]

The practices associated with the school as organization raise professional and moral questions as well. Bureaucratic values, for example, communicate a set of expectations that are at odds with professional expectations. From a bureaucratic point of view teachers are concerned with cases, functions, means, codes, roles, and behavior. From a professional point of view these dimensions

---

[7] See, for example, Thomas J. Sergiovanni, "Biting the Bullet: Rescinding the Texas Teacher Appraisal System," *Teacher Education and Practice*, vol. 6, no. 2, Fall/Winter 1990–91, pp. 89–94.

[8] See, for example, Linda McNeil, *Contradictions of Control: School Structure and School Knowledge*, Politics of Education Yearbook, 1987, pp. 199–216.

are understood as people, relationships, ends, norms, persons, and intentions. From a bureaucratic point of view teachers and teaching and learning are about uniformity; from a professional point of view they are about uniqueness. The bureaucratic emphasis is on efficiency of teaching. The professional emphasis is on achieving goals and embodying values. Finally, the values of bureaucracy provide for uniform application of rules to problems thought to be routine. The values of professionalism stress the development of idiosyncratic solutions to problems thought to be varied.

Uniformities expected in organizations can lead to actions questionable from a moral point of view. The demand for a standard curriculum, embodied in textbooks, may, for example, suppress the legitimate place of women or minorities in history courses. The stress on "public knowledge," central to standardized tests, may displace the legitimate and necessary personal appropriation and expression of knowledge. The emphasis on conformity may rob young people of even the thought of dissent and thereby destroy one of the important elements in any social democracy. In all these cases, schools seem to disenfranchise youngsters from legitimate sources of self-esteem and personal growth. In other words, youngsters are morally violated by an overemphasis on uniformity, order, predictability, and quantifiable outcomes. Teachers who are forced or socialized to support this system are likewise morally violated. Their integrity as professionals and, more important, as responsible adults is compromised.

There is, in sum, wide agreement that bureaucratic values do not serve schools very well. The problem is that schools cannot become free of bureaucratic values and practices by merely tinkering with present policies and structures. Enlightened organizationists prescribe such practices as shared decision-making and promoting job satisfaction in efforts to improve schools. But as long as the schools are defined exclusively as organizations, the same problems will remain. Things may look different, but they work the same in the end. Getting rid of bureaucratic values and practices means changing the metaphor for schools from organization to community.

THE SCHOOL AS COMMUNITY

Supervisor D's analysis of the failed restructured school described in Chapter 1 relies heavily on the belief that though schools may be loosely connected in an organizational and management sense, they are tightly connected in a normative sense. Supervisor D commented, "The changes . . . did not reflect the way schools actually work or how teachers think and behave." And later, "What counts for teachers is not so much the management system but what they believe, the values they share, the assumptions they hold." Supervisor D's recommendation? View the school as a *community*. Develop a set of shared norms and values that define what this community is and how it works. Community norms, supervisor D believes, combined with the norms and values that define teachers as professionals, provide substitutes for management controls, instructional systems, and close supervision by helping teachers to become self-managed.

Supervisor D's ideas about schools and supervision do not make sense in schools understood as organizations. By the same token the ideas of supervisors A and B do not make sense in schools understood as communities. For example, we often talk about the process of teaching and learning as if it were an instructional delivery system. This is an image generated by the metaphor organization. As you think about the idea of instructional delivery system, your thoughts tend to revolve around such themes as how to identify and carefully develop the targets, goals, steps, procedures, timetables, and schedules that will become the basis for establishing the best routes for delivering instruction; how to properly in-service deliverers and then provide them with clear instructions as to what to do and how to do it; how to develop a system of monitoring to ensure that instruction is delivered properly; how to provide additional training to correct mistakes and better align what deliverers do with what they are supposed to do; and how to put into place an evaluation scheme that measures the extent to which the system is working. But instructional delivery systems are larger than teachers. They are intended to reduce discretion and to force teachers to assume narrow roles. Since teachers don't like this narrowing, heavy reliance is placed on external motivation and monitoring. Instructional delivery systems, in other words, become supervisory-intensive.

Now imagine the issues that come to mind when schools are viewed as learning communities. In this case it is likely you will be concerned with how this community will be defined; what the relationships will be among parents, students, teachers, and administrators; what the shared values, purposes, and commitments are that bond this community; how community members will work together to embody these values; what kinds of obligations to the community members should have; and how these obligations will be enforced.[9] These concerns require a kind of supervision different from that needed for instructional delivery systems.

UNDERSTANDING SCHOOLS AS LEARNING COMMUNITIES

We believe that schools should be understood as learning communities. Communities are defined by their centers. Centers are repositories of values, sentiments, and beliefs that provide the needed cement for bonding people in a common cause. As the sociologist Edward A. Shils explains,

> The center, or the central zone, is a phenomenon of the realm of values and beliefs. It is the center of the order of symbols, of values and beliefs, which govern the society [community]. It is the center because it is ultimate and irreducible. . . . The central zone partakes of the nature of the sacred. In this sense, every society [community] has an official "religion." . . . The center is also a phenomenon of the realm of

9 Thomas J. Sergiovanni, *The Moral Dimension in Leadership*, San Francisco: Jossey-Bass, 1992.

action. It is a structure of activities, of roles and persons. . . . It is in these roles that the values and beliefs which are central are embodied and propounded.[10]

In sum, centers express what is of worth to the school and provide a set of norms that guide behavior and give meaning to school community life. The norms become compass settings and sometimes road maps. "They answer such questions as what is this school about? What is our image of learners? What makes us unique? How do we work together as colleagues? How does the school as community fit into the larger school community? How do parents fit into the picture? Why are all these questions worth asking and answering?"[11]

In schools, community norms are intermingled with the norms that define teaching as a profession. And together the two sets of norms provide the basis for what should be done and how. Teachers, for example, are not only responsive to shared values, conceptions, and ideals within the school but also bring to the school shared values, conceptions, and ideals that define them as professionals.

THE NORMS OF PROFESSIONALISM

When first thinking about professionalism, attention is drawn to issues of competence. Professionals are experts, and this expertise entitles them to be autonomous. But expertise is not enough to earn one the mantle of professionalism. Though society often refers to expert safecrackers, hairdressers, gamblers, and baseball players as being professionals, the reference is colloquial. Being a professional has to do with something else besides being competent. Society, for example, demands not only that physicians, physicists, teachers, and other professionals be skilled but also that their skills be used for good intentions. Professionals enjoy privileges because they are trusted. It takes more than competence to earn trust. One might refer to this "something else" as professional virtue.[12]

What are the dimensions of professional virtue? At least four are related to this discussion[13]:

A commitment to practice in an exemplary way
A commitment to practice toward valued social ends
A commitment not only to one's own practice but to the practice itself
A commitment to the ethic of caring

[10] Edward A. Shils, "Centre and Periphery," in Edward A. Shils (ed.), *The Logic of Personal Knowledge: Essays Presented to Michael Polanyi.* London: Routledge & Kegan Paul, 1961, p. 119.

[11] Sergiovanni, op. cit, p. 46.

[12] This discussion of professional virtue follows Sergiovanni. Ibid., pp. 52–56.

[13] The first two dimensions are from Alastair McIntyre, *After Virtue*, Notre Dame, Ind.: Notre Dame University, 1981. The third is from Albert Flores, "What Kind of Person Should a Professional Be?" in Albert Flores (ed.), *Professional Ideals*, Belmont, Calif.: Wadsworth Publishing, 1988. The fourth is from Nel Noddings, *Caring: A Feminine Approach to Ethics and Moral Education*, Berkeley, Calif.: University of California Press, 1984.

The four dimensions of professional virtue provide the roots for developing a powerful norm system that, when combined with the norm system that defines the school as community, can greatly diminish if not replace supervision as it is now practiced. For this reason establishing the virtuous side of professionalism should be a high priority for supervision.

A commitment to exemplary practice, for example, means practicing on the cutting edge of teaching, staying abreast of the latest research in practice, researching one's own practice, experimenting with new approaches, and sharing one's craft insights with others. Once established, this dimension results in teachers accepting responsibility for their own professional growth, thus greatly reducing the need for someone else to in-service them or to plan and implement staff development programs for them. The focus of professional development shifts from "training" to providing opportunities for self-renewal, for interacting with others, for learning and sharing. Much of what happens in this kind of professional development is informal and built into the everyday life of the school. Teachers accept a greater share of the responsibility for planning and carrying out both formal and informal activities and programs.

The second dimension of professional virtue, a commitment to practice toward valued social ends, represents a commitment to place oneself in service to students and parents and to agreed-upon school values and purposes. Such a commitment raises the issue of purpose to a prime position in ongoing conversations about the school and its work and in planning, doing, and evaluating teaching and learning.

When relying on purposes, an idea and value structure emerges in the school that can greatly reduce the need for hierarchically based controls or for supervisors working hard to provide deft interpersonal leadership. Teachers, for example, would do things not because they are forced to by controls or cajoled by personality but because they are persuaded by merit defined by purposes. When compliance for teachers must be required and the weight of this compliance comes from school purposes rather than rules of personality, professional and moral sources of authority are activated. These sources of authority have the capacity to transform the work of the school from something technical and secular to something sacred.

The third dimension of professional virtue, a commitment not only to one's own practice but also to the practice of teaching itself, forces teachers to broaden their outlook. On the one hand teachers become concerned with the broad issues of teaching policy and practice. On the other, teachers become concerned with the practical problems and issues of teaching and learning faced every day in their own school as seen in relationship to these issues and policies. Such a commitment requires that teaching be transformed from individual to collective practice. In collective practice, for example, it would not be acceptable for one teacher to teach competently in the company of others having difficulty, without being concerned, without offering help. It would not be acceptable to have special insights into teaching and not to share them with others. It would not be acceptable to define success in terms of what happens in one's own classroom when the school itself may be failing.

When teaching is conceived as collective practice then collegiality emerges as an expression of professional virtue. Teachers feel compelled to work together not so much because interpersonally they enjoy relief from isolation and not because administrative arrangements (teaming or cooperative teaching and learning) force them together but because of internally felt obligations. With professional virtue intact, collegiality becomes a reciprocal form of meeting obligations in a collective practice. Its source of authority becomes professional and moral.

A commitment to the ethic of caring, the fourth dimension of professional virtue, shifts the emphasis from viewing teaching as a technical activity involving the execution of validated teaching moves, more toward viewing teaching as a professional activity involving concern for the whole person. The word "person" is key. Too often technical conceptions of teaching, complete with their language systems of labels and categories, regard students as cases to be treated rather than persons to be served. The caring ethic speaks not only to how students should be regarded and to the quality of relationships but also to teaching itself. Teachers, as Nell Noddings observes, act as models of caring when they model "meticulous preparation, lively presentation, critical thinking, appreciative listening, constructive evaluation, general curiosity."[14] The ethic of caring, in sum, provides still another substitute for direct, close, formal supervision. As the ethic is internalized, teachers are motivated more from within, thus requiring less external supervision.

IMPLICATIONS FOR SUPERVISION

The theme of this chapter is that, despite the best of intentions, efforts to improve schools that do not seek first to change the metaphor for schooling are not likely to work in the long run. Working hard to introduce new supervisory systems, curriculum development projects, teacher arrangements, and staff development programs in schools understood as organizations is at best likely to result in doing the same things as before, only more efficiently. The metaphor of organization forces us to understand supervisory practice in a particular way, a way that does not fit how schools work or what counts most to teachers and others who work in schools.

One purpose of supervision is to provide the leadership needed to transform schools from organizations to communities. Supervision, in other words, should be directed to community building. In 1957 Philip Selznick wrote:

> The art of the creative leader is the art of institution [community] building, the reworking of human and technological materials to fashion an organism that embodies new and enduring values. . . . To institutionalize is to *infuse with value* beyond

[14] Nel Noddings, "Fidelity in Teaching, Teacher Education, and Research for Teaching," *Teacher Education and Research for Teaching*, vol. 56, p. 503, Nov. 4, 1986.

the technical requirements of the task at hand. The prizing of social machinery beyond its technical role is largely a reflection of the unique way it fulfills personal or
group needs. Whenever individuals become attached to an organization or a way of
doing things as persons rather than as technicians, the result is a prizing of the device for its own sake. From the standpoint of the committed person, the organization
is changed from an expendable tool into a valued source of personal satisfaction.
. . . the institutional [community] leader, then, is primarily an expert in the promotion and protection of values.[15]

With the transformation of the school from organization to community as
the purpose, the policies and practices of Supervision I must give way to those
of Supervision II. Teachers, of course, are key not only in this transformation
but also in any vision to improve schools. Little or nothing can happen without their support. In the next chapter we turn our attention to teachers, their
workplace, and what is important to them. Do we understand correctly what
matters to teachers at work? What kind of supervision can best respond to
their images of what is important?

---

[15] Philip Selznik, *Leadership in Administration*, Berkeley, Calif.: University of California Press,
1957, p. 28.

CHAPTER 4

SUPERVISION AS MORAL ACTION

Even 10 years ago, it would have seemed embarrassing for professionals and scholars in the field of supervision to talk of supervision as moral action. The literature on supervision had been and continues to be dominated by language and imagery borrowed from the mainstream social sciences of psychology and sociology. Those sciences had attempted to model themselves on the natural sciences in an effort to reproduce similarly objective findings, "value-free" facts and theories, generated by methods that were supposed to screen out subjective impressions, ideological points of views, imaginative speculation, philosophical perspectives, and all such nonempirical data.

In the last 20 years there have been challenges to this positivistic, reductionistic approach to explaining social systems. More sociologists and social psychologists have begun to include human beings in all their complexity as a central factor in their study of why social systems do or do not work.[1] In these emerging perspectives, the person is seen in a much richer light, as someone questing for meaning and purpose in daily life, as exercising moral agency and seeking self-fulfillment. Moreover, life in organizations is coming to be seen as far more complex, as involving not only rational thinking, but also emotional responses, political influence peddling, ego investment, shifting power alliances, etc.

With this recent shift in mind, in this chapter we consider supervision as moral action. Our view of morality sees moral action as taking place in a context of limits, limits of understanding, limits of maturity, limits of virtue, limits of power. In a sense morality is never a given; it is always something to be negotiated, it is always something only partially achieved. The values we seek are always, in a sense, beyond us. Our actions become moral only as we reach out for what lies beyond those limits and the definition of human possibility which those limits tend to impose. Supervision as moral action, therefore, can be understood as an effort on the part of supervisors to participate in a community of other moral agents, each of which is struggling to do "the right thing," according to some sense of values, according to some sense of what it means to be or become a human being.

---

[1] Bruce J. Jennings, "Interpretive Social Sciences and Policy Analysis," in Daniel Callahan and Bruce Jennings (eds.), *Ethics, The Social Sciences and Policy Analysis*, New York: Plenum, 1983, pp. 3–35.

THE MORAL IDEAL OF TEACHING

We will not argue for the need of supervisors to encourage the moral commitment of teachers, as though that is lacking on the part of teachers. On the contrary, the action of supervision takes place within an existing moral environment created by the professionalism of teachers. We will better understand the moral dimensions of supervision by a close look at the moral dimensions involved in the ideal of teaching, an ideal which the large majority of teachers subscribe to, and which makes up the core of their general concept of professionalism.[2]

Consider the content knowledge that is required to carry on the activity of teaching in a normal class. This knowledge is not a linear collection of concepts and facts, although textbooks tend to present knowledge that way. It is, rather, knowledge of and within a dynamic, existential field. A piece of knowledge can be abstracted from the field for purposes of analysis and discussion (for example, a discussion in a social studies class of a piece of legislation such as prohibition against alcohol), but in isolation from the dynamic field of social history, that piece of knowledge is decontextualized. A teacher has a responsibility to both the field of knowledge from which the material is selected, as well as to the youngsters who are to learn something from studying the material. The teacher is always involved with a specific context at a particular moment of time, trying to sort out a plan of action that respects and responds to the content being studied and to the multiple contextual strands of the tapestry that make up any classroom moment.[3] That construction of a unit of the curriculum by the teacher implies a moral responsibility both to present the material in nondistorted fashion, and to present it in such a way that it is useful to the students as they encounter this piece of social history.

Responsiveness to the context of students implies a sensitivity to their life connections. When a situation involves the need, for example, to clean up toxicity in a lake, the expert has to consider the sources of toxicity, the impact of various treatments on the whole ecology of the lake, the current chemical composition of the lake, the support of a food chain for various living systems, the seasonal variations in relation to rainfall and drainage, etc. When the situation involves a teacher and an individual student, it involves understanding the student's family background, his or her talent and interests, fears and aspirations, as well as the student's developmental capabilities for cognitive and affective responses. The teacher must take into account this constellation of student variables when assessing the potential of a variety of learning activities to

---

[2] Magdalene Lampert and Christopher M. Clark, "Expert Knowledge and Expert Thinking in Teaching: A Response to Floden and Klinzing," *Educational Researcher*, vol. 19, no. 5, pp. 21–23, June–July 1991.

[3] For a treatment of the moral implications of teaching see John I. Goodlad, Roger Soder, and Kenneth A. Sirotnik, *The Moral Dimensions of Teaching*, San Francisco: Jossey-Bass, 1990; M Buchmann, "Role Over Person: Morality and Authenticity in Teaching," *Teachers College Record*, vol. 87, pp. 529–544, 1986.

stimulate learning readiness within each student. That knowledge of all these variables does not exist "out there" in some uniform, objective package, as though it could be fed into 20 computers, all of which would prescribe the same learning activities. Teachers are not separated from their knowledge of the content and of the context. It is something which they generate from their own prior education and their embedded personal understanding of the subject matter, as well as their diagnostic understanding and sensitivity, which in turn are colored by their cultural and class background, their own values and beliefs, and their degree of understanding of or attending to other potential variables which might enter into their decision-making processes. The knowledge upon which professional teaching decisions are based is partly derived from the knowledge base of the profession (which is itself imperfect and inconsistent), but it is also a knowledge that is personal, intuitive, and interpersonal. By saying that a teacher's knowledge is interpersonal, we add a further complication to the teacher's ability to arrive at professional decisions. The teacher knows only what each student chooses to disclose about him- or herself. A student may reveal a problem in understanding what the teacher is trying to teach, but may not be able to say why he or she does not understand. The cause of the problem may be one of several possibilities.

When we compound the difficulties involved in decision-making knowledge when teaching one student, by considering that most teachers deal with from 20 to 120 students a day in classes of approximately 20 to 30, then we begin to understand some of the complexity of teaching and the complexity of the professional expertise required of teachers. Being responsive simultaneously to the enormous variety of interests, talents, learning blocks, emotional states, and cultural backgrounds within any given classroom of 20 to 30 youngsters requires an artistry of high complexity.

The large majority of experienced teachers manage to meet this complex challenge. And they engage in this professional activity driven not simply by knowledge—knowledge of the youngsters, knowledge of the subject matter, knowledge of pedagogy; they are also driven by a sense of responsibility. That sense of responsibility derives from an intuitive ideal of what teachers are supposed to be doing for youngsters, namely, finding the appropriate interaction which will trigger insight, understanding, skill acquisition, curiosity, motivation, and interest in learning. Just as doctors are concerned with bringing their patients to a condition of health, and lawyers are concerned with bringing their clients into an appropriate relation with the law, teachers have the ideal of bringing their youngsters to a condition of learning. That ideal places certain obligations on teachers:

1 To know their students well enough to create learning opportunities for them that do in fact bring them to a condition of learning
2 To understand their subject matter well enough so that they can bring out its internal relationships and its connections to other bodies of knowledge
3 To discover the various illustrations, analogies, metaphors, stories, expe-

riences, sensory representations, and learning activities which will enable the students to connect with the subject matter

4 To develop a large repertory of teaching strategies which can be employed in a variety of circumstances to develop conditions of learning for their students

5 To influence, by their example and counsel, a broad array of learning which extends beyond academic learning to a variety of personal and social learning including, but not limited to, social manners, acceptance of differences, self-esteem, and a sense of social responsibility for the quality of life of the community

In other words, teachers experience their work as driven by a moral ideal. That ideal activates their integrity as human beings. That ideal is imbedded in the understanding of teaching as a profession. It is what teachers are called to do; it is their vocation.

Because teaching is a moral activity, supervision partakes of its moral qualities. Supervision is supposed to support, nurture, and strengthen the moral ideals embedded in teaching. Supervision as a professional activity, therefore, is intimately tied to both the knowledge expertise of the teacher and the moral responsibility of the profession of teaching. The supervisor must understand the complexities of teaching, its multilayered and multidimensional artistic knowledge base. Beyond appreciating that complex knowledge base and being able to converse with teachers about it, the supervisor is obliged to participate with teachers in the tasks of bringing youngsters to the condition of learning. The supervisor does this by supporting the teachers' search for improved responsiveness to their students.

That support will clearly bring the supervisor's professional knowledge base into play. In subsequent chapters we will deal with various aspects of that knowledge base. Supervision as moral activity, however, involves more than the supervisor's knowledge; it involves the supervisor's ability to engage teachers at a level of moral discourse which mirrors the moral responsibility teachers model for their students. Ultimately what teachers try to accomplish with their students is not simply the acquisition of knowledge, although that is central to their task; teachers also want the experience of knowing they have opened up the youngster to an appreciation of life, an experience of themselves as connected to a world that is challenging and complex, filled with beauty and pain and joy.[4]

Underneath all the specifics of what they are teaching, teachers basically want to share a deep part of their life with youngsters, the joy and fascination which they experience in understanding and engaging the world through a

---

[4] Among other testimonies of this moral commitment to the human growth of their students, see Tracy Kidder, *Among Schoolchildren*, New York: Avon, 1989; Philip Lopate, *Being with Children*, New York: Poseiden, 1975; Jay Mathews, *Escalante*, New York: Holt, 1988; Jo Anne Pagano, *Exiles and Communities: Teaching in the Patriarchal Wilderness*, Albany, NY, State University of New York Press, 1990.

variety of perspectives. Teachers are happy enough when their students score well on exams; however, they are most fulfilled when their students delight in what they are learning. It is at this level that a supervisor engages the teacher in the moral dimension of teaching. At this level supervisors engage in one of the fundamental aspects of empowerment.

EMPOWERING AS A MORAL ACTIVITY OF SUPERVISION

Teacher empowerment is a term with many uses and various meanings, depending on whether it is employed by teacher unions, school administrators, or school reformers.[5] We use it here to indicate a moral basis for teacher autonomy and professionalism. In order to understand this usage, we need to consider what "power" means.

For many people, power has negative overtones. It is associated with coercion, force, threat, and sometimes violence. Power is often viewed as something only a few possess; "the powerful" are thought to be able to control or influence the affairs of the community. From that vantage point, empowering people implies that those who hold power over others give them some of their power. Yet the reality is that no one person has power over another unless that person is allowed to have that power. If everyone refuses to comply with those "in power," then they have no power, as the rulers in Russia and Eastern Europe recently discovered. Even the power of persuasion implies that the listeners assent to the reasonableness of the persuader's argument. The power of the judge to impose a prison sentence is based on an assumed agreement of the people to live according to the law.

Instead of thinking of power as "power over," we may think of power as something every person possesses: a power to be and a power to do. The most unique power each person possesses is the power to be herself or himself. No one else has the power to be you. Only you can exercise that power. You may fail to use that power and instead try to live up to an idea that others have of you, or to some fantasy image provided by popular culture. That power is the power to say yes and to say no to such images. The power may be heavily circumscribed by circumstances in your present context, but it is a power you never lose. You may turn it over to other people, but it always belongs to you. It is the power to be yourself, to sing your own song, dance your own dance, speak your own poetry. It is the power to be true to your best self, rather than to the self that is fearful, jealous, or spiteful.

The paradox about this power is that although it is yours, it is given you for the benefit of the community. You can exercise the power to be you only in relationship to your community. Some mistakenly think that the power to be an individual is a power against the community, a power that necessarily defies

---

[5] See Gene I. Maeroff, "A Blueprint for Empowering Teachers," *Phi Delta Kappa*, vol. 69, no. 7, pp. 472–477, March 1988; Vicki J. Karant, "Supervision in the Age of Teacher Empowerment," *Educational Leadership*, vol. 46, no. 8, pp. 27–29, May 1989.

the community.[6] Although isolation from all social contacts, real or imaginary, is impossible except, perhaps, for autistic people, some people attempt to live as though other people are not necessary for their own fulfillment or even for their own existence. That attitude leads to varieties of narcissistic isolation, which are actually self-destructive.

You can be yourself only in relation to others, to other selves whom you value as they value you. You can express yourself only in relation to the world, to another person, to a particular circumstance that at that moment is part of your definition (such as your family, your workplace, your neighborhood, your garden).[7] You express yourself by responding to persons and events in your immediate surroundings, and that expression is an expression of giving or of taking, an expression of gratitude or of greed, an expression of celebration or of complaint, an affirmation of life or a denial of life. Insofar as your expression of yourself is giving, thankful, celebratory, and affirming, you yourself receive life, grow, and are nurtured. Insofar as your expression of yourself is taking, hoarding, complaining, and denying, you hurt yourself and those around you. The person you express in negativity is an expression of self-destruction. Hence, the power to be yourself is a moral power. It is either an enormously creative power, a power to create yourself while adding to the life around you or an enormously destructive power, a power to destroy yourself (even though that takes place by minuscule choices) and smother and depress life around you. That is why some people choose not to exercise that power; they sense the moral risk involved. Better to leave the choices in the hands of others.

There are few people for whom the power to be themselves, freely and spontaneously, is unlimited. People are victims as well as beneficiaries of their socialization, habituated to guiding their actions by the cues they pick up from those around them, especially from authority figures such as parents, older relatives, teachers, and other public figures. When people have been taught not to trust their own feelings, they rarely rely on their own intuitions or wants. Maxine Greene writes about the socialization of teachers as follows.

> Classroom teachers, assigned a relatively low place in the hierarchy, share a way of seeing and of talking about it. They are used to watching schedules, curricula, and testing programs emanate from "the office." They take for granted the existence of a high place, a seat of power. . . . The reality they have constructed and take for granted allows for neither autonomy nor disagreement.[8]

---

[6] For interesting perspectives on this point, see Robert N. Bellah, Richard Madsen, William M. Sullivan, Ann Swidler, and Steven M. Tipton, *Habits of the Heart,* New York: Harper & Row, 1985; Kenneth A. Strike, "The Moral Role of Schooling in a Liberal Democratic Society," in Gerald Grant (ed.), *Review of Research in Education,* Volume 17, Washington, DC: American Education Association, 1991, pp. 413–483; Gregory Bateson and Mary Catherine Bateson, *Angels Fear: Towards an Epistemology of the Sacred.* New York: Macmillan, 1987; Edward Shils, *Tradition,* Chicago: University of Chicago Press, 1981.

[7] See John MacMurray, *Persons in Relation,* London: Faber and Faber, 1961; and David E. Hunt, *Beginning with Ourselves,* Cambridge, Mass.: Brookline Books, 1987.

[8] Maxine Greene, *Landscapes of Learning,* New York: Teachers College Press, 1979, pp. 44–45.

For a wide variety of reasons, some psychological, some cultural, some political, people are limited in their power to be themselves. Yet the most basic moral task in life is precisely to be uniquely oneself. It is a task never fully achieved. Saints get close, but even they have their devil's advocate.

TEACHING AS AUTOBIOGRAPHY

Recent studies of teachers seem to be pointing in the same direction: Each teacher brings her or his unique constellation of personality traits, interests, talents, prior educational and psychological influences, and prior professional experiences to bear on classroom practice.[9] Even in situations where teachers experience uniform staff development programs and agree to implement schoolwide changes, their classroom activity reflects elements of their personality and their unique ways of responding to perceived needs of students. Whereas previously that may have been perceived as an unavoidable deficit by those attempting to implement teacher-proof innovations, it is now being seen as an asset to be encouraged.[10] Clearly, the power to be themselves, when combined with experience and a professional teaching culture, enables teachers to enrich the learning experiences of their students through, for example, self-constructed or self-discovered learning activities, through reference to life lessons from their own experience, and through the teacher's obvious excitement and commitment associated with various units of the curriculum.[11] This is not to glorify an extreme form of individualism and isolationism on the part of teachers; clearly, teacher professionalism requires collaboration on instructional and curricular improvements. What these studies are emphasizing, on the other hand, is the need to balance collaboration with individual autonomy in the practice of everyday life in school.[12] The mix of teacher personalities, backgrounds, personal histories, talents, and interests creates a rich experience of adult community for students, an experience that profoundly educates in its own tacit manner throughout the students' years in that community.

[9] See Michael G. Fullan, "Staff Development, Innovation, and Institutional Development, in Nancy B. Wyner (ed.), *Current Perspectives on the Culture of Schools*, Cambridge, Mass.: Brookline Books, 1991, pp. 181–201; Michael Huberman, "The Social Context of Instruction in Schools," paper presented at the American Educational Research Association Annual Meeting, Boston, April 1990; David E. Hunt, "From Single Variable to Persons-in-Relation," in L. Fyans (ed.), *Achievement Motivation: Recent Trends in History and Research*, New York: Plenum, 1980, pp. 447–456.

[10] D. Jean Clandinin and F. Michael Connelly, "Rhythms in Teaching: The Narrative Study of Teachers' Personal Practical Knowledge of Classrooms," *Teaching and Teacher Education*, vol. 2, pp. 377–387, 1986; Freema Elbaz, *Teacher Thinking: A Study of Practical Knowledge*, New York: Nichols, 1983.

[11] Virginia Richardson, "Significant and Worthwhile Change in Teaching Practice," *Educational Researcher*, vol. 19, no. 7, pp. 10–18, October 1990.

[12] Andy Hargreaves, "Individualism and Individuality: Reinterpreting the Teacher Culture," paper presented at the American Educational Research Association Annual Meeting, Boston, April 1990.

SUPERVISORS AND EMPOWERMENT

While no one can give a person the power to be herself or himself, it is possible to limit or enlarge that power, especially when one is perceived to have "power over" that person. Supervisors, by creating a trusting and supportive relationship with teachers, can enlarge the relational space which teachers need to be more fully themselves. That relational space allows for a mutual process of discovering what the power to be and the power to do means in a particular school, what positive qualities are attached to the exercise of that power, and what limitations are imposed by the circumstances of the communal effort at schooling. Such a process of empowerment involves mutual respect, dialogue, and invitation; it implies recognition that each person enjoys talents, competencies, and potentials which are being exercised in responsible and creative ways for the benefit of the students. It implies that teachers legitimately and necessarily model what it means to be genuine in the way they conduct their relationships with their students and in the way they engage them in the learning material itself. In this empowering relationship, both teachers and supervisors invite one another to exercise their power to be themselves in the specific relationship of teacher and supervisor. This process requires some clearing of the air, some exploration of what the relationship is supposed to entail. This leads to considerations about the moral "underside" of supervision.

THE UNDERSIDE OF SUPERVISION

Many stories told by teachers of their experiences of "being supervised" are anything but uplifting.[13] Again and again teachers tell of being placed in win-lose situations, of experiencing powerlessness, manipulation, sexual harassment, and racial and ethnic stereotyping. At best, their encounters with supervisors lead directly to evaluative judgments based on the skimpiest of evidence. At worst they are destructive of autonomy, self-confidence, and personal integrity. In other words, supervision as practiced by many supervisors is not only nonprofessional, it is dehumanizing and unethical.

The most traditional exercise of supervision is the formal observation of a teacher in his or her classroom. Despite some semblance of clinical supervision, most encounters result in the supervisor making evaluative judgments about the appropriateness and effectiveness of various teaching behaviors. These judgments are usually recorded and placed in the teacher's file. Classroom observations which start out with preconceived formulas for what con-

---

[13] *Impact*, New York State Association for Supervision and Curriculum Development, vol. 19, no. 1, Fall 1983. The whole issue is devoted to dealing with these less than altruistic motives. Arthur Blumberg raises penetrating questions in his treatment of the "cold war" between teachers and supervisors in *Supervisors and Teachers, a Private Cold War*, Berkeley, Calif.: McCutcheon Publishing, 1974.

stitutes good practice tend not to be very helpful.[14] Moreover, the supervisor's underlying but unspoken assumptions about teaching and learning frequently defeat the supervisory experience right from the start, because they tend to be simplistic and reductionistic. Teachers' decision making, whether flawed or appropriate, is based on an awareness of an extremely complex, multilayered field of human beings in dynamic interaction over extended periods of time. Supervisors who observe that group of human beings interacting in one slice of time cannot be aware of all that is going on.[15] Hence, evaluation of teachers' performance is a very complex and imperfect art which, in practice, few have mastered.

Beyond professional issues, there are other attitudes and behaviors which undermine supervisors' activity. These have to do with the desire to dominate and control others; with insecurities which must be covered over by aggressive and controlling actions and words; with racial, sexual, and ethnic stereotypes which prevent genuine communication and mutual respect. Some older teachers are disdainful of younger supervisors; some older supervisors are disdainful of younger teachers. A black supervisor raises problems for a white teacher; white supervisors raise problems for black teachers. Women supervising men and men supervising women have to deal with agendas beyond the explicit professional agenda. When racial and cultural differences are mixed with gender differences, the possibilities for misunderstanding and harm are multiplied.

The expanding literature by women about the challenges of being a woman teacher deserves much greater attention within the field of supervision. As more and more women teachers find their voice and explore ways of being more fully themselves in their work, rather than acting according to the roles they have been socialized to assume, supervisors need to be much more sensitive to this growth process.[16] For some women, this exploration of new personal terrain is a moral challenge. Male supervisors may be unprepared for this emerging phenomenon among women teachers. Our advice would be to hurry up and begin the dialogue with women about what is afoot. This valued, growing female voice points to a need for more women supervisors.

When these negative issues dominate the supervisory experience, they subvert any possibility of open, trusting, professional communication, and can lead to manipulative words and actions on the part of the supervisor, the teacher, or both. Sometimes the supervisor and the teacher are not aware that they are being offensive to each other. Sometimes one consciously seeks to control, dominate, or intimidate the other. Often teachers go through the motions, play a superficial role, act as though everything is perfectly understand-

---

[14] Susan Stoldowsky, "Teacher Evaluation: The Limits of Looking," *Educational Researcher*, vol. 13, no. 9, November 1984, pp. 11–18.

[15] Jane Juska, "Observations," *Phi Delta Kappa*, vol. 72, no. 6, pp. 468–470, February 1991.

[16] Nell Noddings, "Feminist Critiques in the Professions," in Courtney Cazden (ed.), *Review of Research in Education*, Vol. 16, 1990, esp. pp. 406–416; Madeleine R. Grumet, "Women and Teaching: Homeless at Home," *Teacher Education Quarterly*, vol. 14, no. 2, pp. 39–46, 1987.

able, and keep feelings and honest communication at a safe distance. More often than not, supervisory encounters take place without either teachers or supervisors revealing their true feelings toward each other or toward the game they are playing. It is simply an organizational ritual that must be completed to satisfy some political or legal necessity. In the above instances, supervision is the opposite of moral action, implying hypocritical, dishonest, disloyal, vicious, or dehumanizing intentions. Sometimes supervision is immoral simply because it wastes so much time of so many people.

THE MORAL HEURISTICS OF SUPERVISORY PRACTICE

If supervision is to be moral action, it must respect the moral integrity of the supervisor and the supervised. That is to say, the exchange between the supervisor and the teacher must be trusting, open, and flexible in order to allow both persons to speak from their own sense of integrity and to encourage each person to respect the other's integrity. In other words, the exchange must begin with an honest discussion of what will be helpful for the teacher and the students. For this to happen, supervisors need to explore those conditions necessary to establish and maintain trust and honesty and open communication. This means that supervisors need to discuss the ground rules ahead of time. Hence, supervisors need to explore with teachers what procedures will be followed, what rights and responsibilities will be defined ahead of time, who controls what, whose needs are being served, the purpose of the exchange, etc. This discussion in itself is a kind of moral action, a negotiation of guidelines to be followed so that fairness and honesty can be maintained. These exploratory discussions on how to initiate and maintain a genuine exchange comprise the heuristics of moral action.

Beyond the heuristics of setting the parameters and guidelines, there is the exchange itself, an engagement of another person in all his or her complexity, fragility, and ambiguity. Embedded in the process of making contact with that other person are the moral imperatives of acceptance, honesty, respect, and care. These comprise the moral activity of empowerment, the willingness to let people be who they are, and beyond that willingness, an appreciation of what they have to contribute. These moral imperatives are not experienced as some abstract, Kantian principles, reference to which deductively leads to specific conclusions. Rather, they are intuitive, instantaneous responses to the other person in the ebb and flow of the interaction. After the fact, through reflection, both supervisor and teacher can understand the moral aspects of those responses.

PROMOTING A MORAL COMMUNITY

Besides concern for the empowerment of individual teachers, supervisors have a responsibility to nurture the moral environment of the school. In fact, both moral concerns support each other. Everyday life in the school contains within it many moral challenges, but often supervisors do not know how to name them. Often institutional practices in the school convey a sense of impersonality. Communications contained in faculty memos, announcements to the students over the intercom, administrative changes in student disciplinary policies, average class sizes, or the length of the school day can convey paternalistic, authoritarian, or adversarial attitudes. School practices—in grading and testing, in assigning students to tracked curriculum groups, in choosing textbooks and assembly speakers—can be questioned in terms of fairness, equity, respect for cultural pluralism, and other moral criteria. The imposition of uniform class schedules, the labeling of some children as gifted and others as disabled, the practice of suspending students from class and from school attendance, the absence of important topics and points of view in textbooks, the process of calculating class rank, the absence of alternatives in student assessments, the criteria for student and faculty awards—these and other institutional procedures carry moral implications, because the ends or purposes they were intended to serve are at least implicitly moral.

As with most institutions, in schools, standard operating procedures tend to rigidify and to take on a life of their own. Instead of regarding these procedures as human constructs put in place to serve a larger purpose, school personnel tend to allow means to become ends, to allow procedures to define the way things have always been and the way they are supposed to be. When institutional procedures become more important than the human beings the institution is supposed to serve, then the danger for moral mischief spreads. The institutional environment becomes inimical to human life. Values such as uniformity, predictability, efficiency, obedience, and conformity can tend to override other human values such as freedom of conscience, creativity, diversity, inventiveness, risk-taking, and individuality. Human beings should not be forced to serve institutional procedures when those procedures violate human values. Institutional procedures should serve human beings. When they do not, they should be changed.

To speak of supervisory action as necessarily moral, but at the same time restrict that activity exclusively to activity with individual teachers, is to ignore the institutional context of teaching and supervising and its potential for demoralizing, in the literal sense, the teaching-learning situation. It is also to ignore the supervisor's position within the institution. The supervisor's position often is an institutional position in a way that differs from the teacher's institutional position. The teacher's primary responsibility is to the students, to see that they learn what he or she and the school community has determined they should learn. The supervisor's responsibilities are more to the total community, to see that schoolwide goals are being achieved. Institutional arrangements impinge very directly on the teaching-learning situation, and individual teachers are not in a position to change them.

Supervisors, however, enjoy a multiplicity of institutional opportunities to initiate and sustain conversations among various groups within the school community. They can challenge the appropriateness of institutional practices which unfairly affect various segments of the community, whether they be women, ethnic groups, or students who are affected simply by the labels the institution uses to sort and serve them.[17] Supervisors function at a variety of institutional levels, and their activities intersect with a variety of offices. Because they are relatively free to structure their day, they can attend a variety of administrative and faculty meetings to bring these institutional moral concerns before the community. To ignore these issues is to allow institutional practices and policies to disempower teachers and students, to thwart the very work supervisors carry on with individual teachers.

COMMITMENT TO LARGE EDUCATIONAL VALUES

Although not the only ones responsible, supervisors are among those in the school and the school system who have to be committed to a vision of what the school can become. Most schools have mission statements which hold up high moral purposes to the learning community. Those mission statements tend to fade into thin air unless people within the community refer to them, and use them to plan and to debate school policies. Teachers and students, as well as all administrative staff, need to hear references to the higher purposes at which their collective activity is aimed. That sense of purpose is needed to encourage the school community when the daily aggravations of everyday school life wear down the patience and enthusiasm for the tasks at hand.

In schools it is customary for people to compete for scarce resources, whether they be library materials, larger classrooms, brighter students, better class schedules, etc. Moreover, group affiliations among teachers based on narrow self-interest build up and lead to group rivalry and conflict, especially when some teachers appear to have greater status and power within the school. Add to those tensions petty grievances that arise daily: a missed meeting, a favorite parking place usurped by a rival, a misconstrued remark overheard in the teachers' room—these easily lead to conflicts, hurts, loss of morale.

When people have a deep ownership of the larger goals of the school, however, attention to those goals can lead them to lay aside irritations and to work as a team. Grievances need to be cleared up, to be sure. However, there will always be someone assigned the last-period class, lunchroom duty, or a less desirable classroom. Variations in assignments during and across school years are possible, but at any given time, someone in the school will have a "nose out of joint." Appeals to the larger goals of the educational community, frequent reminders of the larger moral purposes being served by the community's collective action, will draw teachers' focus away from the small

---

[17] For a more extensive discussion of this responsibility of supervisors, see Robert J. Starratt, "Building an Ethical School: A Theory for Practice in Educational Leadership," *Educational Administration Quarterly*, vol. 27, no. 2, pp. 195–202, May 1991.

grievances and invite a pride in being part of such a community. That is clearly one of the continuing moral activities of supervisors.

THE POLITICS OF THE POSSIBLE

This treatment of supervision as moral action can be viewed as hopelessly idealistic, as out of touch with the realities of schooling. In discussing supervision as moral action, however, it was not our intention to present it as something beyond the reach of every person who serves in a supervisory capacity. Supervision can be moral action, although, it can perhaps never be untainted by traces of self-interest or manipulation. The context of schooling is a context of limited rationality, of limited altruism, of limited power, of limited efficiency—as is the context of every organization. Moral action in this context is therefore itself limited. This limitation, however, is no reason to deny its importance and its possibility.

In any given example used in the above treatment of supervision as moral action, the exercise of moral action will be limited by the circumstances of that particular experience. Some teachers may never enter into a supervisory exchange with genuine trust. In that case, the supervisor simply does what is possible. In other instances, supervisors will find that their advice to policy-makers is neither wanted nor attended to. Again, the supervisor can do only what is possible. Perhaps next year will be a more favorable time to seek a change in policy. In any given school, supervisors will find different chemistries among groups of the faculty. Those chemistries will make things either possible or impossible. Because circumstances change every year, new chemistries and hence new possibilities emerge. Because the exercise of moral action will not always be possible at any given time does not mean that it should be ruled out altogether. There will always be opportunities for some form of moral action at one level or another. The challenge and the need never go away. What is possible at any given time will always be in flux.

SUMMARY

This chapter addressed the work of supervisors as moral activity. It focused primarily on the moral implications embedded in the empowerment of teachers. The teachers' sense of the professional ideal of teaching leads to the awareness of a kind of moral imperative embedded in that ideal, an imperative to do their best to see that students learn what they are capable of. Besides working with teachers to improve their knowledge base, supervisors are called upon to nurture the empowerment of teachers so that the teachers' sense of self, their self-confidence, and their excitement about their own learning can be more easily transmitted to their students, thereby enriching the learning experiences of their students. The creation of such enabling relationships poses intrinsically moral challenges, challenges to protect the relationship from distortions and challenges to carry on the relationship with integrity and care.

Beyond their work with individual teachers, supervisors must be sensitive to the moral implications of institutional practices which destroy or limit the empowerment of teachers and students in the learning situation. In other words, supervisors have the responsibility to promote a moral environment in which the total community can better function as a community of learners and a community of moral agents.

CHAPTER 5

MOTIVATION, SATISFACTION, AND THE TEACHERS' WORKPLACE

MOST policymakers agree that improving the teachers' workplace is one important way to improve schools. But, a great deal of confusion exists about what is really important to teachers and how best to go about such improvement. As a result, and despite good intentions, regressive school policies and practices are often put into place leading to such unanticipated consequences as job dissatisfaction, lack of work motivation, and even alienation among teachers. This confusion stems in part from four common conditions within school systems:

• Labeling teachers as professionals but viewing the work of teaching as bureaucratic.

• Attributing higher standards of trust and moral responsiveness to administrators and supervisors than to teachers.

• Assuming that teachers are primarily motivated by self-interest and thus less willing to respond to work for altruistic reasons.

• Assuming that teachers make decisions about what is important and what to do as rational, objective, and isolated individuals.

The four conditions have a tendency to reinforce each other, thus creating a cycle that makes matters worse. For example, teachers are given bureaucratic work because they're not trusted with the discretion needed for professional work. That being the case, supervisors are needed to tell teachers what to do and to check up on them. Further, teachers are not deemed capable of accepting responsibility for their own professional development. Thus the need for supervisors to provide directive supervision and formal in-service programs. As a result teachers wind up being the objects of supervision. As objects, they tend to lose their sense of commitment. They either feel resentful and alienated or they become increasingly dependent upon their supervisors. This reaction then makes it necessary for them to be *motivated* by supervisors.

Given the above realities, the motivational strategies supervisors choose typically are based on the belief that the goals of teachers and those of supervisors are not the same. Teachers do not care as much about matters of schooling as do supervisors. Thus the basis for motivating teachers becomes a series of trades whereby the supervisors gives to teachers things that they want in exchange for compliance with the supervisor's requests and requirements. This, in turn, results in the further bureaucratization of the work of teaching, reinforces the supervisor's superior moral standing, places further emphasis on the use of self-interest-oriented motivational strategies, and so perpetuates this regressive cycle. Breaking this cycle requires serious rethinking about what is important to teachers.

BUREAUCRATIC AND PROFESSIONAL WORK

Rethinking the practice of referring to teachers as professionals yet considering their work as bureaucratic is a good place to begin. In today's schools it is common for teachers to be regulated and controlled by an elaborate work system which specifies what must be done and then seeks to ensure that it is done. When this is the case, the work of teachers becomes increasingly bureaucratic. But bureaucratic and professional work are different. Though both bureaucrats and professionals are part of a rationally conceived work system, bureaucrats are *subordinate* to this system. They are responsible for implementing the system according to the provided specifications, and supervision is designed to monitor this process. The emphasis is on doing things right.

Professionals, by contrast, are *superordinate* to their work system. In teaching, the work system represents a point of reference rather than a script. Teachers use the system in ways that makes sense to them as they practice. Supervision for professionals, while no less demanding, is helpful and facilitating in its orientation. In professional work the emphasis is on writing the script while practicing.

The differences between bureaucratic and professional work and the relationship of teachers to this work are illustrated in Figure 5-1. Bureaucratic work seems to fit Supervision I and professional work seems to fit Supervision II. In Supervision I the purpose is to monitor and control the approved system. In Supervision II the purpose is to empower and expand the teachers' view, enabling them to make better decisions as they create the system in use. Levels of satisfaction, commitment, and efficacy are higher when work is conceived as professional and lower when work is conceived as bureaucratic. And, as will be discussed in later sections, these conditions of Supervision II are linked to enhanced feelings of efficacy among teachers and increased student achievement.[1]

TEACHERS AS ORIGINS AND PAWNS

In successful schools teachers tend to be more committed, hardworking, loyal to their school, and satisfied with their jobs. The research on motivation to work reveals that these highly motivating conditions are present when teachers:

---

[1] Patricia T. Ashton and Rodman B. Webb, *Making a Difference: Teachers' Sense of Efficacy and Student Achievement,* New York: Longman, 1986, p. 49.

FIGURE 5-1   Supervisions I and II: The characteristics and effects of bureaucratic and professional views of teaching.

Supervision I: A bureaucratic view of teaching and supervision:
Teachers are subordinate to the system

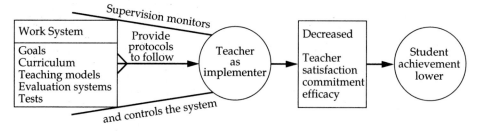

Supervision II: A professional view of teaching and supervision:
Teachers are superordinate to the system

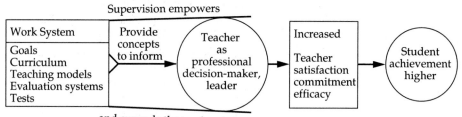

Find their work lives to be meaningful, purposeful, sensible, and significant and when they view the work itself as being worthwhile and important.

Have reasonable control over their work activities and affairs and are able to exert reasonable influence over work events and circumstances.

Experience personal responsibility for the work and are personally account-able for outcomes.[2]

When teachers experience meaningfulness, control, and personal responsibility at work, they are functioning more as "origins" than as "pawns." An origin believes that behavior is determined by his or her own choosing. A pawn, by contrast, believes that behavior is determined by external forces beyond his or her control.[3] Origins have strong feelings of personal causation. They believe that they can affect events and circumstances which exist in their envi-

---

[2] See, for example, Frederick Herzberg, Bernard Mausner, and Barbara Snyderman, *The Motivation to Work,* New York: Wiley, 1959; Thomas J. Sergiovanni, "Factors Which Affect Satisfaction and Dissatisfaction of Teachers," *The Journal of Educational Administration,* vol. 5, no. 1, pp. 66–82, 1967; J. R. Hackman and G. Oldham, "Motivation through Design of Work: Test of a Theory," *Organizational Behavior and Human Performance,* vol. 16, no. 2, pp. 250–279, 1976; and Thomas J. Peters and Robert H. Waterman, *In Search of Excellence,* New York: Harper & Row, 1982.

[3] Richard DeCharms, *Personal Causation: The Internal Affective Determinants of Behavior,* New York: Academic Press, 1968.

ronment. Pawns, by contrast, believe that forces beyond their control deter-mine what it is that they will do. Pawn feelings, according to DeCharms, pro-vide people with a strong sense of powerlessness and ineffectiveness.[4] Experts such as DeCharms believe that persons under normal conditions strive to be effective in influencing and altering events and situations that comprise their environment. They strive to be causal agents, to be origins of their own behav-ior. And when this is not the case they experience frustration, powerlessness, and often alienation.

One of the consequences of being an origin rather than a pawn is that one's sense of efficacy is enhanced. An efficacious teacher believes that she or he has the power and ability to produce a desired effect. Efficacy has to do with per-sonal effectiveness, a feeling that one can control events and produce out-comes. Recent research links sense of efficacy not only with motivation and commitment to work but with student achievement. In their study of teachers' sense of efficacy and student achievement, for example, Ashton and Webb found that efficacy was related to such teacher behaviors as being warm, ac-cepting, and responsive to students; accepting student initiatives; and giving attention to all the students' individual needs.[5] Efficacy was also related to stu-dent enthusiasm and student initiation of interaction with teachers. And fi-nally, teachers' sense of efficacy was related to student achievement. Ashton and Webb studied high school teachers of mathematics and communications. Student achievement was measured by mathematics and language basic skills tests. Their model of the relationship between teachers' sense of efficacy and student achievement is illustrated in Figure 5-2.

The factors contributing to teachers' sense of efficacy and enhanced motiva-tion and commitment are depicted in Figure 5-3. A supportive school climate, the presence of collegial values, shared decision making, and a school culture provide a sense of purpose and define for teachers a shared covenant. These characteristics (which will be discussed further in the next chapter) provide for cooperative relationships, strong social identity, a sense of personal causation, origin feelings, high responsibility for work outcomes, and a shared commit-ment to common goals.

Figures 5-2 and 5-3 provide glimpses of how the story of teacher motivation to work can end. It is a story quite different from what currently takes place in schools. To understand this story, it is important to go back to the beginning and examine some basic assumptions that can provide a basis for practicing work motivation differently.

A FRAMEWORK FOR UNDERSTANDING TEACHER MOTIVATION

Motivation is in part an expression of psychological needs and in part a func-tion of moral judgments. The motivational policies and practices of Supervi-

[4] Ibid.
[5] Ashton and Webb, op. cit.

FIGURE 5-2   The Ashton and Webb study: Relation between teachers sense of efficacy, teaching and learning behaviors, and student achievement.

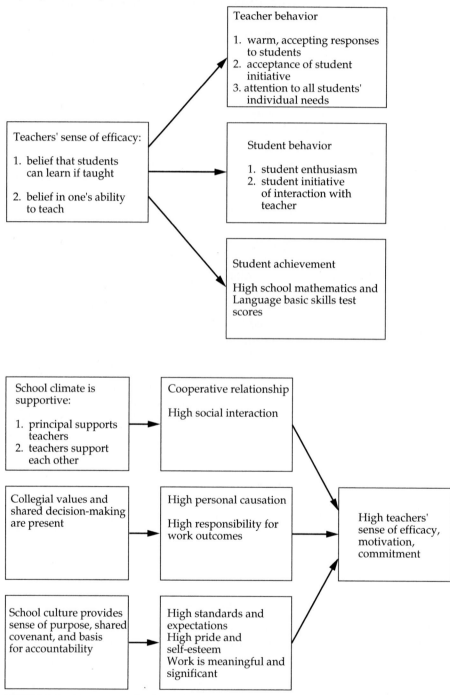

FIGURE 5-3   Factors contributing to teachers sense of efficacy, motivation, and commitment.

sion I overemphasize the former and neglect the latter. Supervision II, by contrast, seeks to join the two into an expanded theory of motivation that better reflects the full nature of human potential.

Theories of motivation can be grouped into three categories: those that emphasize the exchange of rewards or punishment for compliance; those that seek compliance by emphasizing opportunities to experience satisfaction from the work itself; and those that are based on the idea that compliance results from moral judgment. The first category relies heavily on rewards and punishments and on the promise of extrinsic gain. The second category also relies on rewards, but the rewards depend less on gains made from trades with supervisors and more on teachers finding intrinsic satisfaction in work. The third category, moral judgment, relies on the connection of teachers to professional and community norms that represent a form of moral authority. The categories can be expressed in the form of three motivational rules:

1 What gets rewarded gets done.
2 What is rewarding gets done.
3 What is good gets done.[6]

Though all three motivational rules are true, the consequences of their prime use in practice differs. The three rules are examined in the sections below.

WHAT GETS REWARDED GETS DONE

The motivational practices of Supervision I are based largely on the rule "What gets rewarded gets done." This rule works very effectively in the short term. The consequences of using the rule over time, however, are different. The famous "felt-tipped" research of Greene and Lepper is often cited as evidence that the rule can backfire when trying to motivate children.[7] In that research, preschoolers who were motivated to draw with felt-tipped markers without extrinsic rewards became less interested in this activity once such rewards were introduced. In a separate study Deci and Ryan found that not only does the motivational capacity of adults lessen with the introduction of extrinsic rewards for work, but such rewards resulted in feelings of being controlled by them.[8] These feelings had negative effects on subsequent performance and creativity.

James G. March points out that providing rewards for a performance inevitably leads to an emphasis on measuring performance. This linking of rewards and measurement typically causes problems. In his words, "A system

---

[6] The discussion of motivational rules that follows is drawn from chap. 2, "What Motivates? What Inspires?" and chap. 5, "Creating a State of Flow at Work," in Thomas J. Sergiovanni, *Moral Leadership: Getting to the Heart of School Improvement,* San Francisco: Jossey-Bass, 1992.

[7] David Greene and Mark R. Lepper, "How to Turn Work into Play," *Psychology Today,* vol. 8, no. 4, pp. 49–52, 1974.

[8] Edward L. Deci and Richard M. Ryan, *Intrinsic Motivation and Self Determination in Behavior,* New York: Plenum, 1985.

of rewards linked to precise measure is not an incentive to perform well; it is an incentive to get a good score."[9] Given March's view, teachers will work for the rewards rather than the job itself. This circumstance raises a number of important questions. What happens when extrinsic rewards are no longer available to teachers? And, what happens to other sources of motivation once extrinsic rewards are introduced?

Though "What gets rewarded gets done" may be true, it seems equally true that what does not get rewarded does not get done. The rule has a tendency to focus one's attention and narrow one's responses to work. For example, teachers who are being rewarded to teach in a certain way are not teaching in other ways. Although in some instances it might be a good idea to encourage teachers to teach in a particular way, as a general rule a policy of this sort is not a good idea. Because of the complex nature of teaching and because of the diversity that exists in student needs and teaching situations, how a teacher ought to teach at any given time cannot be validly determined beforehand. It is a decision that must be made on the spot.

In the 1970s teaching effectiveness research, for example, tended to emphasize direct instructional methods of teaching. Using this research as the basis for developing teacher evaluation systems is in effect a de facto adoption of direct instruction as a one best way to teach. The evaluation system then becomes a source of rewards and punishment for displaying the right or wrong teaching behaviors. True, direct instruction methods seem to work for lower-level learning outcomes and for students whose backgrounds and experiences are very limited. But for higher-level learning outcomes and for students who have a richer base of personal and other experience to draw upon, direct instructional methods do not work as well. Cooperative learning strategies, for example, are likely to be better choices. Rewarding the former means you do not get the latter regardless of which of the two might be appropriate.

Another problem with the motivational rule "What gets rewarded gets done" is that for it to be sustained, a busy kind of supervision is required. For example, supervisors must constantly monitor the exchange of rewards for work, must become expert at guessing which rewards are of interest to which teachers and which rewards are not, and must figure out other ways to keep this exchange going. As a result teachers become increasingly dependent upon the rewards themselves and upon their supervisors to motivate them.

The question of what happens to other sources of motivation once extrinsic rewards are introduced poses additional difficulties. Using the rule "What gets rewarded gets done" often changes a teacher's attachment to an activity from intrinsic or moral to extrinsic. For example, teachers who spend after-school hours with students in clubs or other informal activities because they enjoy it or because they think it's important often change their minds once extrinsic re-

---

[9] James G. March, "How We Talk and How We Act: Administrative Theory and Administrative Life," in Thomas J. Sergiovanni and John E. Corbally (eds.), *Leadership and Organizational Culture*, Urbana, Ill.: University of Illinois Press, 1984, pp. 27–28.

wards are introduced. Deciding to pay teachers $5 per hour for up to four hours of service a week, for example, is likely to result in very few teachers working more than four hours. And further, if the $5 rate is not increased after two or three years it is very likely that teachers will begin to give less and less during the four hours that they are required to spend after school.

What may be happening in the example above is that the teachers' attachment to their work has changed. Once involved for intrinsic and moral reasons, they now seem to be involved for calculated reasons. A fair day's work for a fair day's pay has been defined for them by the school, and a reward system has been put into place based on this definition. Teachers begin to calculate very carefully the proper equation of investments in work that matches the payoff they receive in return. Their involvement in work changes from intrinsic and moral to extrinsic reasons.

MASLOW'S THEORY AS AN EXAMPLE

One of the most popular constructs used to guide the practice of "What gets rewarded gets done" is Abraham Maslow's theory of motivation.[10] Maslow proposed that all human needs could be grouped into five categories arranged in levels of proficiency from basic to high. The most basic level is physical needs followed by security, social, esteem, and self-actualization. Basic needs, according to the theory, must be met first before a person is motivated by needs at higher levels. Lyman Porter suggested that physical needs cannot be realistically considered to have motivational potential in most work settings and thus substituted autonomy for physical as a new category.[11] The levels are often depicted in the form of a "needs hierarchy," as illustrated in Figure 5-4.

Here is how Maslow's theory is used in practicing "What gets rewarded gets done." It is assumed that teachers have needs that can be met at work. At the security level, for example, they have needs for money, benefits, tenure, and clear role expectations. At the autonomy level they have needs to influence, to become shareholders, to have authority, and so on. Supervisors, on the other hand, control the events and circumstances that allow these needs to be met. They can provide teachers with the desired need fulfillment if teachers in turn comply with required role expectations. For example, if teachers teach the right way, take on extracurricular responsibilities, volunteer for committee work, and cheerfully attend the required workshops, they can advance up the school's career ladder. Such advancement entitles them to have more control over what they do, to influence more school decisions, and to receive other benefits that help meet their needs for autonomy. If teachers don't conform to expectations, by contrast, they are likely to have less to say about what is going on in the school and are likely to be more closely watched.

---

[10] Abraham Maslow, *Motivation and Personality*, New York: Harper & Row, 1954.
[11] Lyman Porter, "Job Attitudes in Management I Perceived Deficiencies and Need Fulfillment as a Function of Job Level," *Journal of Applied Psychology*, vol. 4, pp. 386–397, December 1963.

FIGURE 5-4   The needs hierarchy.

Security	Affiliation	Self-esteem	Autonomy	Self-actualization
		Self-respect	Control	Working at top potential
	Acceptance	Respected by others as a person and as a professional	Influence	Giving all
Money	Belonging			
	Friendship		Participant	Peak satisfaction
Benefits	School membership	Competence		
				Achievement
Tenure	Formal work group	Confidence	Shareholder	
				Personal and professional success
Role consolidation	Informal work group	Recognition	Authority	

The traditional motivational rule "What gets rewarded gets done" has its place. But by itself, it is neither powerful enough nor expansive enough to provide the kind of motivational climate needed in schools. Further, overuse of the rule in motivating teachers (or, for that matter, students) can lead to many negative consequences. Some of these consequences are summed up by W. Edwards Demming, a famous quality-control expert, as follows:

> People are born with intrinsic motivation, dignity, curiosity to learn, joy in learning. The forces of destruction begin with toddlers—a prize for the best Halloween costume, grades in school, gold stars and honor to the university. On the job, people, teams, divisions are ranked—rewards for the one at the top, punishments at the bottom. MBO, quotas, incentive pay, business plans, put together separately, division by division, cause further loss, unknown and unknowable.[12]

In commenting on Demming's observations, Peter M. Senge points out that "Ironically, by focusing on performing for someone else's approval, corporations create the very conditions that predestine them to mediocre performance."[13] These comments, leveled at corporate America, seem even more appropriate when applied to schooling America.

WHAT IS REWARDING GETS DONE

"What is rewarding gets done" as a motivational rule has certain advantages over "What gets rewarded gets done." Since the basis of this rule is internal to

---

[12] Demming quoted in Peter M. Senge, "The Leader's New Work: Building a Learning Organization," *Sloan Management Review,* vol. 22, no. 1, p. 7, 1990.
[13] Ibid.

the work itself, motivation does not depend directly on what the supervisor does or on other external forces. Second, being compelled from within implies a kind of self-management that does not require direct supervision or other kind of monitoring to be sustained.

The motivational psychologist Frederick Herzberg pointed out that jobs which provide opportunities for experiencing achievement and responsibility, interesting and challenging work, and opportunity for advancement have the greatest capacity to motivate from within.[14] These are not factors that supervisors give to others in return for desired behavior but are instead factors integral to the work of teaching itself. Herzberg's research, and that of others, suggests that the following job characteristics enhance this intrinsic motivation:

> Allow for discovery, exploration, variety and challenge. Provide high involvement with the task and high identity with the task enabling work to be considered important and significant. Allow for active participation. Emphasize agreement with respect to broad purposes and values that bond people together at work. Permit outcomes within broad purposes to be determined by the worker. Encourage autonomy and self determination. Allow persons to feel like "origins" of their own behavior rather than "pawns" manipulated from the outside. Encourage feelings of competence and control and enhance feelings of efficacy.[15]

Herzberg and his colleagues Mausner and Snyderman identified two fairly independent sets of job factors that seem to be important to workers. These factors comprise the basic constructs for their motivation-hygiene theory.[16] One set of factors, called *hygienic,* affect whether people are dissatisfied with their jobs and seem to be related to poor performance. The researchers concluded that if supervisors take care of these factors to the extent that they are no longer sources of dissatisfaction, performance will improve to a level of a "fair day's work for a fair day's pay." The workers will rarely, however, be motivated to go beyond this minimum level. The word "hygiene" was used to suggest that though the factors can cause dissatisfaction if neglected, they are not sources of motivation.

The hygiene factors are related to the conditions of work but not the work itself. They include salary, interpersonal relationships with subordinates, superiors, and peers; the quality of supervision received; administrative policies; general working conditions; status; and job security. Herzberg concluded that these factors are not strong enough to motivate people for very long and certainly not without lots of effort from supervisors.

A second set of factors identified, called *motivators,* seem not to result in dissatisfaction or poor performance in work when neglected. But when the motivation factors are present the result is motivation to go beyond "a fair day's work for a fair day's pay." The motivation factors are related to the work itself

---

[14] Frederick Herzberg, *Work and Nature of Man,* New York: World Publishing Company, 1966.

[15] Thomas J. Sergiovanni, *Value-Added Leadership: How to Get Extraordinary Performance in Schools,* San Diego: Harcourt Brace Jovanovich, 1990, p. 129.

[16] Herzberg, Mausner, and Snyderman, op. cit.

and include achievement, recognition, the work itself, responsibility, and advancement. It is the work itself, Herzberg concluded, that provides the sources for intrinsic motivation, and this kind of motivation seems to make the difference.

The motivation-hygiene theory has its critics. Many feel that the findings may well be artifacts of the methods used by researchers, thus portraying an oversimplified version of reality. For example, Herzberg and his colleagues relied heavily on the critical-incident method and on in-depth interview methods. When their research is replicated using rating scales and other kinds of questionnaires the results are not so easily confirmed. But still, few dispute the overall conclusion from the motivation-hygiene theory that for most people the work itself counts as an important motivator of work commitment, persistence, and performance.

The work of Herzberg and his colleagues represents a pioneering effort to establish a tradition known as *job enrichment research.* Job enrichment research seeks to identify ways in which jobs can be restructured to allow for workers to experience for themselves greater intrinsic satisfaction. The best known is the work of Hackman and Oldham.[17] These researchers identified three psychological states believed to be critical in determining whether a person will be motivated at work.

Experienced meaningfulness. The individual must perceive his or her work as worthwhile or important by some system of values held.

Experienced responsibility. The individual must believe that he or she personally is accountable for the outcomes of efforts.

Knowledge of results. The individual must be able to determine, on some fairly regular basis, whether or not the outcomes of his or her work are satisfactory.[18]

When the three psychological states are present, according to this job enrichment theory, teachers can be expected to feel good, perform well, and continue to want to perform well in an effort to earn more of these feelings in the future. The three states become the basis for internal motivation, since teachers do not have to depend upon someone outside of themselves to motivate them or lead them.

What can supervisors do to increase the likelihood that teachers will experience meaningfulness, responsibility, and knowledge of results? The answer, according to Hackman and Oldham, is to build into teaching jobs opportunities for teachers to use more of their talents and skills; to allow teachers to engage in activities that allow them to see the whole, and to understand how their contributions fit into the overall purpose and mission (task identity); to view their work as having a significant impact on the lives of their students

---

[17] Hackman and Oldham, op. cit.

[18] J. R. Hackman, G. Oldham, R. Johnson, and K. Purdy, "A New Strategy for Job Enrichment," *California Management Review,* vol. 17, no. 4, p. 57, 1975.

(task significance); to experience discretion in scheduling work and in decid-ing classroom arrangements and teaching methods and procedures (auton-omy); and to get firsthand and from others clear information about the effects of their performance (feedback). The job enrichment model proposed by Hack-man and his colleagues is depicted in Figure 5-5.

Note that in addition to job dimensions, psychological states, and outcomes, an "implementing concepts" panel is provided. These are the suggestions the researchers offer to supervisors interested in building more of the job dimen-sions into work.

The principle of "combining tasks" suggests that fractionalized aspects of teaching should be put together in larger, more holistic, modules. Comprehen-sive curriculum development strategies, interdisciplinary approaches, and team-group teaching modes all contribute to the combining of teaching and curriculum tasks. Combining tasks increases not only skill variety but one's identification with the work as well.

Establishing "client relationships" should be easy to promote, since teachers and students already work in close contact with each other. Some patterns of organization and teaching, however, seem not to encourage close personal re-lationships between teachers and students. For example, in junior and senior high schools with 50-minute, six-period days, teachers often view students as

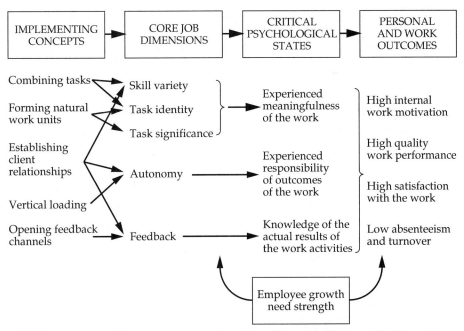

FIGURE 5-5   Job enrichment concepts and practices. *(From J. R. Hackman, G. Oldham, R. Johnson, and K. Purdy, "A New Strategy for Job Enrichment," © 1975 by The Regents of the University of California. Reprinted from California Management Review, vol. XVII, no.4, p. 64, by permission of the Regents.)*

"cases" rather than persons. This impersonality is one way teachers protect themselves from the unrelenting pace of being forced to batch-process students.

Forming "natural work units" has some interesting implications for supervision and teaching. The intent of this approach is to increase sense of ownership and continuing responsibility for identifiable aspects of the work. The self-contained elementary school classroom comes closer to this concept than does the departmentalized and quick-moving secondary teaching schedule. But even in the elementary school setting the building of teaching teams that plan and work together and whose members share a common responsibility for students is often lacking.

Vertical loading refers to the development of strategies that combine teaching and planning. Providing teachers with more control over schedules, work methods, evaluation, and even the training of less experienced teachers is an example of vertical loading. Giving teachers some budgetary control that allows them discretion in allocating available funds is another example.

"Opening feedback channels" describes what happens when supervisors motivate teachers not only by letting them know how well they are doing but also by promoting working relationships and arrangements that help teachers get feedback from each other. Teacher-evaluation strategies that are designed to provide teachers with formative feedback can be helpful. Clinical supervision, peer supervision, target setting, and other approaches with similar formats are examples. However, though providing teachers with feedback is important, it is best to create ways in which feedback occurs naturally from teachers' day-to-day activities and from working closely with colleagues.

Since virtually every decision supervisors make about school and classroom organization, curriculum development and implementation, materials selection, and teaching itself has implications for job enrichment, every decision has implications as well for either enhancing or diminishing motivation and commitment levels of teachers.

WHAT IS GOOD GETS DONE

Supervision I is based on the assumption that people are by their nature selfish. It is thought that for teachers the guiding motivational force is a desire to maximize self-interest by continually calculating the costs and benefits of options, choosing those that either make them winners or keep them from losing. Supervision I also is based on the assumption that people act rationally, seeking the most efficient means to their goals. They are capable of cold calculation and thus their emotions do not count. And finally, people make decisions as isolated individuals. Each person "keeps score" separate from others. Connections to other people and particularly the social bonds that emerge from such connections do not count very much.

Amitai Etzioni challenges the motivational assumptions of Supervision I by asking this question:

Are men and women akin to single minded, "cold" calculators, each out to 'maximize' his or her well being? Are human beings able to figure out rationally the most efficient way to realize their goals? Is society mainly a marketplace, in which self-serving individuals compete with one another—at work, in politics, and in courtship . . . enhancing the general welfare in the process? Or do we typically seek to do both what is right *and* what is pleasurable, and find ourselves frequently in conflict when moral values and happiness are incompatible?[19]

Etzioni acknowledges the importance of self-interest but suggests that people are perfectly capable of sacrificing self-interest and indeed regularly sacrifice self-interest for other interests. He provides compelling evidence that people are just as likely, if not more likely, to be motivated by what they think is right and good, by obligations they feel, and by the norms and values they consider important and just. There is, in other words, a bit of the "hungry artist" in everyone. Most supervisors agree with Etzioni when it comes to describing themselves. For example, supervisors put in demanding hours at work, often putting the job "ahead" of leisure time and family matters. Etzioni believes that the capacity to sacrifice self-interest is not limited to supervisors but is widespread. There is no reason to believe, in other words, that parents and teachers, cafeteria workers, and custodians are less likely than supervisors to respond as "hungry artists."

The belief that teachers are rational and cold calculators who are routinely capable of controlling their emotions, biases, and preferences by putting reason and logic first is also suspect. Anyone who has bought a new car understands this. Despite the best rational planning to ensure that the car chosen is both practical and within budget, in the end most people are swayed by less objective factors. Having completed the purchase, they desperately attempt to rationalize buying that "spiffy two-door with the small trunk." People strive to appear rational in an effort to cover up the fact that they are not.

Etzioni challenges as well the idea that people make decisions as isolated individuals. He provides compelling evidence that "social collectivities (such as ethnic and racial groups, peer groups at work, and neighborhood groups) are the prime decisionmaking units."[20] He acknowledges that individual decision making exists but it typically reflects collective attributes and processes, having been made within the context created by one's memberships in various groups. For teachers, membership in the profession of teaching and membership in the school as community provide the kind of collective attributes that hinder individual decision making. For example, a teacher may want to take a teaching shortcut but feels compelled to do otherwise by group norms or by having been socialized in what it means to be a teacher. Or equally likely, a teacher who wants to stay after school to help students decides otherwise as a result of pressure from other teachers who have implicitly agreed that every-

---

[19] Amitai Etzioni, *The Moral Dimension Toward a New Economics,* New York: Free Press, 1988, p. ix.

[20] Ibid., p. 4.

TABLE 5-1
MORALITY, EMOTION, AND SOCIAL BONDS IN SUPERVISIONS I AND II

Supervision I	Supervision II

Morality
  Self-interest is the driving force. People seek to maximize their gains and cut their losses. Morality is defined in terms of self-interest.
	Morality
	  People pass moral judgments over their urges and as a result often sacrifice self-interest for other causes and reasons.

Emotions
  People rationally seek the most efficient means to their goals. Emotions don't count.
	Emotions
	  People choose largely on the basis of preference and emotions.

Social bonds
  People are isolated individuals who reason and calculate individually, thus making decisions on their own. Social bonds don't count.
	Social bonds
	  People are members of groups, and the social bonds that emerge from this membership shape their individual decisions.

one should leave early. Connections are so important and the process of socialization as a result of memberships is so complete that the concept of individual decision maker appears to be more myth than reality.

Motivation in Supervision I and in Supervision II differs because of the importance the latter gives to morality, emotions, and social bonds. These differences are summarized in Table 5-1. In Supervision II, teachers regularly pass moral judgments over their urges, routinely sacrificing self-interest and pleasure for other reasons. Further, actions and decisions that teachers make are influenced by what they value and believe as well as by self-interest, and when the two are in conflict it is the former that typically takes precedence over the latter. Presently teachers represent an underutilized resource. They will remain underutilized as long as "What gets rewarded gets done" dominates the motivational scene by continuing to be the prime basis for supervisory practice. Teachers deserve more than this and schools need more than this. Changing supervision practices in a way that acknowledges the importance of "What is rewarding gets done" and "What is good gets done," we believe, are steps in the right direction. Further, this broader view of motivation is an important ingredient in developing the kinds of school climate and culture that not only enrich the lives of teachers but provide enhanced learning and development for students. These are themes of the next chapter.

CHAPTER 6

SCHOOL CLIMATE, CULTURE, AND CHANGE

THIS chapter examines school climate and school culture and their relationship to school improvement. Improving schools requires changing them. But change takes place at two levels—the way things look and the way things actually work. Changes at the first level are *structural*, resulting in altered arrangements. Changes at the second level are *normative*, resulting in altered beliefs.[1] When only first-level changes are introduced in schools it may appear that things are being done differently, but results seem not to be effected, at least not for very long.

A supervisor, for example, wants to encourage teachers to be more deliberate in their teaching and to make a better effort to teach to agreed-upon curriculum outlines. Working with a committee of teachers, she introduces a series of in-service workshops on the content of the curriculum, how to select objectives, and how to write effective lesson plans. She then establishes a policy requiring teachers to submit their lesson plans weekly for her perusal. Though she finds that the lesson plans seem to match the curriculum outlines, teachers seem to be making little progress toward improving the fit between what they teach and what they are supposed to teach. In this example the supervisor was successful in implementing change in how teachers constructed their plans, but she was not successful in changing what they were actually teaching. Normative change alters how teachers look at things, what they believe, what they want, what they know, and how they do things. Normative changes are much more likely to affect outcomes.

Though structural changes can be important, in themselves they seem not to matter much. Too often, they become "nonevents." When a junior high school changes its name to a middle school and abandons academic departments for teams that "turn teach" by subject matter specialization—this is an example of a nonevent. The introduction of supervisory and evaluation systems that elicit changes in how teachers teach when under surveillance but not otherwise is another example of a nonevent. Nonevents become events when changes are not only structural but normative as well.

Many of the practices of Supervision I often involve structural, but not normative, changes. Normative changes take into account the aspects of human nature. It is helpful to think about human nature having two sides: the psychological and the symbolic. Psychologically speaking, people have needs and

---

[1] See, for example, Michael Fullan with Suzanne Stiegelbauer, *The New Meaning of Educational Change,* 2nd ed., New York: Teachers College Press, 1991.

seek opportunities to meet these needs. Symbolically speaking, people seek to make sense of their lives by searching for meaning. The psychological side of human nature is more readily affected by *school climate* and the symbolic side is more readily affected by *school culture.* In this chapter we examine school climate first and then school culture. In each case we assess their importance in bringing about school improvement.

THE IMPORTANCE OF SCHOOL CLIMATE

School climate can help or hinder teachers as they attempt to satisfy their needs at work. One way to understand school climate is by examining your own experience with groups in schools. Recall, for example, a group that you belonged to or know about that seemed best to encourage members to learn, solve problems, and take reasonable chances. Now recall a second group that most hindered learning, problem solving, and risk taking. Briefly describe the two groups. Who were the members? What was the group trying to accomplish? How did group members work together? How did they treat one another? What were the leaders like? Using the questionnaire in Exhibit 6-1, evaluate each of the groups you recalled. Start first with the most effective learning group. *Circle* the number for each category that best describes this group. Now evaluate the less effective group, using *check marks* to indicate responses. Compare your circled and checked responses.

By describing groups that help and hinder learning and then evaluating them, you are describing and measuring dimensions of school climate. The seven item categories shown in Exhibit 6-1 are composed of several dimensions that social psychologists have found to be important in determining whether a climate is open (is supportive of learning) or closed (hinders learning). To obtain an overall climate score for the two groups you evaluated, total the score values given for each of the seven items. Reverse the scores given to item 1, conformity, for in this case a low score suggests a supportive climate. The higher the score, the more open or supportive the group is likely to be. Now, using the item categories and scores, write a few sentences that describe the helpful and hindering groups you recalled. You are now describing climate in the language of social psychologists.

Since the climate of the school is a matter of impression, it is often difficult to define with precision. Climate might be viewed as the enduring characteristics that describe the psychological character of a particular school, distinguish it from other schools, and influence the behavior of teachers and students, and as the psychological "feel" that teachers and students have for that school. Litwin and Stringer, for example, define climate as: "The perceived subjective effects of the formal system, the informal 'style' of managers, and other important environmental factors on the attitudes, beliefs, values, and motivation of people who work in a particular organization."[2]

[2]George H. Litwin and Robert A. Stringer, Jr., *Motivation and Organizational Climate,* Boston: Harvard University, Division of Research, Graduate School of Business Administration, 1968, p. 5.

EXHIBIT 6-1
ORGANIZATIONAL CLIMATE QUESTIONNAIRE

Introduction
For each of the seven organization climate dimensions described below place an (A) above the number that indicates your assessment of the organization's current position on that dimension and an (I) above the number that indicates your choice of where the organization should ideally be on this dimension.

1 Conformity The feeling that there are many externally imposed constraints in the organization; the degree to which members feel that there are many rules, procedures, policies, and practices to which they have to conform rather than being able to do their work as they see fit.

Conformity is not characteristic of this organization	1 2 3 4 5 6 7 8 9 10	Conformity is very characteristic of this organization

2 Responsibility Members of the organization are given personal responsibility to achieve their part of the organization's goals; the degree to which members feel that they can make decisions and solve problems without checking with superiors each step of the way.

No responsibility is given in the organization.	1 2 3 4 5 6 7 8 9 10	There is great emphasis on personal responsibility in the organization.

3 Standards The emphasis the organization places on quality performance and outstanding production including the degree to which the member feels the organization is setting challenging goals for itself and communicating these goal commitments to members.

Standards are very low or nonexistent in the organization.	1 2 3 4 5 6 7 8 9 10	High challenging standards are set in the organization.

4 Rewards The degree to which members feel that they are being recognized and rewarded for good work rather than being ignored, criticized, or punished when something goes wrong.

Members are ignored, punished, or criticized.	1 2 3 4 5 6 7 8 9 10	Members are recognized and rewarded positively.

5 Organization clarity The feeling among members that things are well-organized and goals are clearly defined rather than being disorderly, confused, or chaotic.

The organization is disorderly, confused, and chaotic.	1 2 3 4 5 6 7 8 9 10	The organization is well-organized with clearly defined goals.

6 Warmth and support The feeling that friendliness is a valued norm in the organization; that members trust one another and offer support to one another. The feeling that good relationships prevail in the work environment.

There is no warmth and support in the organization	1 2 3 4 5 6 7 8 9 10	Warmth and support are very characteristic of the organization.

7 Leadership The willingness of organization members to accept leadership and direction from qualified others. As needs for leadership arise, members feel free to take leadership roles and are rewarded for successful leadership. Leadership is based on expertise. The organization is not dominated by, or dependent on, one or two individuals.

Leadership is not rewarded; members are dominated or dependent and resist leadership attempts.	1 2 3 4 5 6 7 8 9 10	Members accept and reward leadership based on expertise.

Source: David A. Kolb, Erwin M. Rubin, and James M. McIntyre, *Organizational Psychology: An Experiential Approach,* 3d ed., 1979, pp. 193–194. Reprinted by permission of Prentice-Hall, Englewood Cliffs, N.J.

Climate provides a reading of how things are going in the school and a basis for predicting school consequences and outcomes. Such a barometer represents an important tool for evaluating present conditions, planning new directions, and monitoring progress toward new directions. Indeed, school climate is a key dimension of human resources supervision as described in earlier chapters.

THE HEALTHY SCHOOL

Climate can also be understood by applying the metaphor of health to the school. Matthew Miles describes the "healthy" school as one that exhibits reasonably clear and reasonably accepted goals (goal focus); communication that is relatively distortion-free vertically, horizontally, and across boundary lines (communication adequacy); equitable distribution of influence to all levels of the organization (optimal power equalization); and effective and efficient use of inputs, both human and material (resource utilization). The healthy school reflects a sense of togetherness that bonds people together (cohesiveness), a feeling of well-being among the staff (morale), self-renewing properties (innovativeness), and an active response to its environment (autonomy and adaptation). Finally, the healthy school maintains and strengthens its problem-solving capabilities (problem-solving adequacies).[3]

The 10 dimensions of health as described by Miles are listed below.[4] As you review the list, think about how you would describe the two groups you evaluated earlier according to each of the 10 dimensions.

1 *Goal focus.* In a healthy organization, the goal (or more usually goals) of the system would be reasonably clear to the system members, and reasonably well accepted by them. This clarity and acceptance, however, should be seen as a necessary but insufficient condition for organizational health. The goals must also be *achievable* with existing or available resources, and be *appropriate*—more or less congruent with the demands of the environment.

2 *Communication adequacy.* Since organizations are not simultaneous face-to-face systems like small groups, the movement of information within them becomes crucial. This dimension of organizational health implies that there is relatively distortion-free communication "vertically," "horizontally," and across the boundary of the system to and from the surrounding environment. That is, information travels reasonably well—just as the healthy person "knows himself" with a minimum level of repression, distortion, etc. In the healthy organization, there is good and prompt sensing of internal strains; there are enough data about problems of the system to ensure that a good diagnosis of system difficulties can be made. People have the information they need, and have gotten it without exerting undue efforts, such as those involved in moseying up to the superintendent's secretary, reading the local newspaper, or calling excessive numbers of special meetings.

---

[3] Matthew Miles, "Planned Change and Organizational Health: Figure and Ground," *Change Processes in the Public Schools*, Eugene, Oreg.: The University of Oregon, Center for the Advanced Study of Educational Administration, 1965.

[4] The 10 dimensions of health are abridged from Ibid., pp. 18–21.

3 *Optimal power equalization.* In a healthy organization the distribution of influence is relatively equitable. Subordinates (if there is a formal authority chart) can influence upward, and even more important—as Likert has demonstrated[5]—they perceive that their boss can do likewise with *his* boss. In such an organization, intergroup struggles for power would not be bitter, though intergroup conflict (as in every human system known) would undoubtedly be present. The basic stance of persons in such an organization, as they look up, sideways, and down, is that of collaboration rather than explicit or implicit coercion.

4 *Resource utilization.* We say of a healthy person, such as a second-grader, that he is "working up to his potential." To put this another way, the classroom system is evoking a contribution from him at an appropriate and goal-directed level of tension. At the organization level, "health" would imply that the system's inputs, particularly the personnel, are used effectively. The overall coordination is such that people are neither overloaded nor idling. There is a minimal sense of strain, generally speaking (in the sense that trying to do something with a weak or inappropriate structure puts strain on that structure). In the healthy organization, people may be working very hard indeed, but they feel that they are not working against themselves, or against the organization. The fit between people's own dispositions and the role demands of the system is good. Beyond this, people feel reasonably "self-actualized"; they not only "feel good" in their jobs, but they have a genuine sense of learning, growing, and developing as persons in the process of making their organizational contribution.

5 *Cohesiveness.* We think of a healthy person as one who has a clear sense of identity; he knows who he is, underneath all the specific goals he sets for himself. Beyond this, he *likes himself;* his stance toward life does not require self-derogation, even when there are aspects of his behavior which are unlovely or ineffective. By analogy at the organization level, system health would imply that the organization knows "who it is." Its members feel attracted to membership in the organization. They want to stay with it, be influenced by it, and exert their own influence in the collaborative style suggested above.

6 *Morale.* The implied notion is one of well-being or satisfaction. Satisfaction is not enough for health, of course; a person may report feelings of well-being and satisfaction in his life, while successfully denying deep-lying hostilities, anxieties, and conflicts. Yet it still seems useful to evoke, at the organization level, the idea of morale: a summated set of individual sentiments, centering around feelings of well-being, satisfaction, and pleasure, as opposed to feelings of discomfort, unwished-for strain, and dissatisfaction.

7 *Innovativeness.* A healthy system would tend to invent new procedures, move toward new goals, produce new kinds of products, diversify itself, and become more rather than less differentiated over time. In a sense, such a system could be said to grow, develop, and change, rather than remaining routinized and standard.

8 *Autonomy.* The healthy person acts "from his own center outward." Seen in a training or therapy group, for example, such a person appears nearly free of the need to submit dependently to authority figures, *and* from the need to rebel and destroy symbolic fathers of any kind. A healthy organization, similarly, would not re-

[5] Rensis Likert, *New Patterns of Management,* New York: McGraw-Hill, 1961, cited in Miles, op. cit.

spond passively to demands from the outside, feeling itself the tool of the environment, and it would not respond destructively or rebelliously to perceived demands either. It would tend to have a kind of independence from the environment, in the same sense that the healthy person, while he has transactions with others, does not treat their responses as *determinative* of his own behavior.

9 *Adaptation.* The notions of autonomy and innovativeness are both connected with the idea that a healthy person, group, or organization is in realistic, effective contact with the surroundings. When environmental demands and organization resources do not match, a problem-solving, restructuring approach evolves in which *both* the environment and the organization become different in some respect. More adequate, continued coping of the organization, as a result of changes in the local system, the relevant portions of the environment, or more usually both, occurs. And such a system has sufficient stability and stress tolerance to manage the difficulties which occur during the adaptation process.

10 *Problem-solving adequacy.* Finally, any healthy organism—even one as theoretically impervious to fallibility as a computer—*always* has problems, strains, difficulties, and instances of ineffective coping. The issue is not the presence or absence of problems, therefore, but the *manner* in which the person, group, or organization copes with problems. Argyris has suggested that in an effective system, problems are solved with minimal energy; they stay solved; and the problem-solving mechanisms used are not weakened, but maintained or strengthened.[6] An adequate organization, then, has well-developed structures and procedures for sensing the existence of problems, for inventing possible solutions, for deciding on the solutions, for implementing them, and for evaluating their effectiveness.

Though Miles uses the language of organizational theory in his analysis of health, the basic ideas seem to fit schools as well. The dimensions of health for any school operate in a system of dynamic interaction characterized by a high degree of interdependence. Clear goal focus, for example, depends upon the extent to which the school communicates its goals and permits inhabitants to modify and rearrange them. At another level, a high degree of health encourages school adaptiveness, while school adaptiveness contributes to, and is essential to, the health of the school.

CLIMATE AND LEARNING

An important question is, does school climate make a difference in improving learning opportunities? Susan Rosenholtz provides convincing evidence that it does. She found that the quality of work relationships that existed in a school had a great deal to do with that school's ability to improve. She defined quality as the degree of openness, trust, communications, and support that is shared by teachers. These factors encourage not only learning but job satisfaction and improved performance as well. Rosenholtz referred to schools that

---

[6] Chris Argyris, *Integrating the Individual and the Organization*, New York: Wiley, 1964, cited in Miles, op. cit.

possessed these qualities as being "learning enriched" to differentiate them from "learning impoverished" schools.[7]

Climate focuses attention on the school's interpersonal work life as it affects teachers, administrators, and supervisors. But climate affects students as well. For example, one important line of inquiry links assumptions that teachers and administrators hold for *students* to climate dimensions. This research uses the Pupil Control Ideology Scale (PCI) developed by Willower and his associates.[8] This scale measures the assumptions and attitudes of teachers and supervisors toward students on a continuum from custodial to humanistic. "Custodial schools" tend to be rigidly controlled and concerned with maintenance and order. Within custodial schools students do not participate in decision making and are expected to accept decisions without question. Further, they are viewed as being irresponsible, undisciplined, untrustworthy, and trouble-prone. As a result, strong emphasis is given to controlling students through the development and use of punitive methods. "Humanistic schools," on the other hand, resemble communities that include students as fuller members and seek their cooperation and interaction. Self-discipline is emphasized and learning is considered to be promoted and enhanced by obtaining student identity and commitment. In schools with humanistic climates teachers are more likely to cooperate with one another as they work together, to have higher morale, and to enjoy a sense of task achievement. Social interaction among teachers is also high. In custodial schools these characteristics are not found and students are likely to be more alienated. Teachers are more likely to view the school as a battlefield. Hoy and Appleberry found that in schools with more custodial climates, teachers were significantly less engaged in their work, showed less esprit, and were more aloof.[9] These are important findings that point to the link between climate and factors that directly effect the quality of teaching and knowing.

Many studies of highly successful schools confirm the importance of climate. For example, in their now famous study of 12 inner-London secondary schools, Rutter, Maughan, Mortimer, and Ouston found that important differences in climate existed between those schools which were more or less effective.[10] Effectiveness in this case was defined as higher scores on national examinations, better behavior, and better attendance. In the more effective schools

---

[7] Susan Rosenholtz, *Teachers' Workplace: The Social Organization of Schools*, New York: Longman, 1989.

[8] Donald J. Willower, Terry I. Eidell, and Wayne K. Hoy, *The School and Pupil Control Ideology*, Pennsylvania State University Studies no. 24, State College, Penn.: Pennsylvania State University, 1967.

[9] Wayne K. Hoy and James B. Appleberry, "Teacher-Principal Relationships in 'Humanistic' and 'Custodial' Elementary Schools," *Journal of Experimental Education*, vol. 39, no. 2, pp. 27–31, 1970.

[10] Michael Rutter, Barbara Maughan, Peter Mortimer, and Janet Ouston, *Fifteen Thousand Hours: Secondary Schools and Their Effects on Children*, Cambridge, Mass.: Harvard University Press, 1979.

teachers worked harder and had better attitudes toward learning, spent more time in actual teaching, relied more heavily on praising students, and were better able to involve students as active learners. Studies of highly successful schools that emphasize ethnographic techniques and the importance of culture reach similar conclusions.[11]

And finally, the work of Ashton and Web that links teachers' sense of efficacy, motivation, and commitment to teacher behavior, student behavior, and student achievement provides further evidence.[12] Their findings were summarized in Chapter 5, in Figures 5-2 and 5-3. In the accompanying discussion it was noted that students of more efficacious teachers were more enthusiastic, were more likely to initiate interactions with teachers, and scored higher on mathematics and language tests. A supportive school climate was one important contribution to teacher sense of efficacy.

SCHOOL CLIMATE AND GROUP BEHAVIOR

The concept of school climate is collective, born of the sum of teacher perceptions of the interpersonal life of the school as the faculty lives and works together. As suggested in Chapter 5, memberships in groups are important to teachers, and the norms that develop as a result influence what they believe and do. From a psychological point of view group membership provides the means for meeting many of the needs of teachers. And, from a symbolic point of view groups provide the means to enable teachers to construct their realities and to find meaning and significance. Both are important conditions that enable teachers to find satisfaction in work and to work to full potential. Etzioni suggested that teachers tend to make decisions not as isolated individuals but as members of collectivities.[13] Their teaching preferences, how they are likely to respond to school improvement initiatives, and even how cooperative they are likely to be with supervisors are all shaped by such memberships. To a great extent, changing individuals means changing groups. For this reason understanding the faculty as a work group is important. Further, helping faculties become effective work groups is an important purpose of supervision and a critical part of the school improvement process.

How can supervisors judge the extent to which faculty groups are working effectively? One indicator is the kind and nature of group outcomes. What is the group supposed to be accomplishing and to what extent is it accomplishing these aims? If outcomes are being accomplished, the group is judged to be *efficient*. But the problem with viewing effectiveness only in this way is that efficiency is only one necessary component. The other component is *growth*. An effective group is concerned not only with accomplishing its tasks but also

---

[11] See, for example, Joan Lipsitz, *Successful Schools for Young Adolescents*. New Brunswick, N.J.: Transaction Books, 1984; Sara Lightfoot, *The Good High School*, New York: Basic Books, 1983.

[12] Patricia T. Ashton and Rodman B. Webb, *Making a Difference: Teachers' Sense of Efficacy and Student Achievement*, New York: Longman, 1986.

[13] Amitai Etzioni, *The Moral Dimension Toward a New Economics*, New York: Free Press, 1988.

with improving its ability to accomplish even more difficult tasks in the future. Many studies have shown that giving primary attention to efficiency and neglecting growth may result in short-term increases in productivity, but over time the work group loses its productive edge.[14] The relationship between effective supervision and group effectiveness is becoming increasingly important as the work of supervision takes place more and more within the context of groups. Examples include peer-collegial supervision; clinical supervision; team-oriented staff-development programs; curriculum-development projects; and team, family, or group teaching.

THE SYMBOLIC SIDE OF HUMAN NATURE

Supervision II seeks to give a fuller account of what matters to teachers and of what is involved in helping them to think more carefully about their practice. A fuller account means giving attention to the symbolic side of school life as well as the psychological side.

One way to appreciate the complexity of human nature is by examining the research traditions of scholars engaged in its study. Different traditions are based on different assumptions, and different assumptions lead to different supervisory practices. Behaviorists, for example, view teachers as responders to external forces—forces in the environment and forces created for them and applied to them by their supervisors. Teachers are presumed to respond to these forces in highly predictable and determinate ways. To be helpful, supervisors provide structures and incentives that elicit the proper response. Phenomenologists, by contrast, view teachers as intentional beings who create their own reality and then direct their energies toward living this reality in some meaningful way. Teachers are presumed to derive sense and direction from interactions with others and from norm systems that they help to create. To be helpful, supervisors encourage teachers to reflect on the realities they create and to provide mirrors of their behaviors that test these realities.

Gareth Morgan and Linda Smircich identify the assumptions about human nature that emerge from six different scholarly traditions.[15] These assumptions are illustrated in Exhibit 6-2. Assumptions that view human beings as information processors, adaptive agents, and responding mechanisms tend to focus on the psychological side of human nature and suggest a practice in which school climate is considered to be of particular importance. Assumptions that view human beings as transcendental beings, creators of their own reality, and social actors tend to focus on the symbolic side of human nature and highlight the importance of school culture. Though legitimate arguments exist over which of the six views best captures the essence of human nature, few would deny that each of the views captures some aspect of human nature. Human

---

[14] See, for example, Rensis Likert, *The Human Organization*, New York: McGraw-Hill, 1967; and Rensis Likert, *New Patterns of Management*, New York: McGraw-Hill, 1961.

[15] Gareth Morgan and Linda Smircich, "The Case for Qualitative Research," Academy of Management Review, vol. 5, pp. 491–500, October 1980.

EXHIBIT 6-2
ASSUMPTIONS ABOUT HUMAN NATURE

	Humans as transcendental beings	Humans create their realities	Humans as social actors
Assumptions about human nature	Human beings are viewed as intentional beings, directing their psychic energy and experience in ways that constitute the world in a meaningful, intentional form. There are realms of being, and realms of reality, constituted through different kinds of founding acts, stemming from a form of transcendental consciousness. Human beings shape the world within the realm of their own immediate experience.	Human beings create their realities in the most fundamental ways, in an attempt to make their world intelligible to themselves and to others. They are not simply actors interpreting their situations in meaningful ways, for there are no situations other than those which individuals bring into being through their own creative activity. Individuals may work together to create a shared reality, but that reality is still a subjective construction capable of disappearing the moment its members cease to sustain it as such. Reality appears as real to individuals because of human acts of conscious or unwitting collusion.	Human beings are social actors interpreting their milieu and orienting their actions in ways that are meaningful to them. In this process they utilize language, labels, routines for impression management, and other modes of culturally specific action. In so doing they contribute to the enactment of a reality; human beings live in a world of symbolic significance, interpreting and enacting a meaningful relationship with that world. Human beings are actors with the capacity to interpret, modify, and sometimes create the scripts that they play upon life's stage.
Scholarly tradition	Phenomenology	Ethnomethodology	Social action theory
Overall perspective	Symbolic	Symbolic	Symbolic

EXHIBIT 6-2
ASSUMPTIONS ABOUT HUMAN NATURE (*Continued*)

	Humans as information processors	Humans as adaptive agents	Humans as responding mechanisms
Assumptions about human nature	Human beings are engaged in a continual process of interaction and exchange with their context—receiving, interpreting, and acting on the information received, and in so doing creating a new pattern of information that affects changes in the field as a whole. Relationships between individual and context are constantly modified as a result of this exchange; the individual is but an element of a changing whole. The crucial relationship between individual and context is reflected in the pattern of learning and mutual adjustment that has evolved. Where this is well developed, the field of relationships is harmonious; where adjustment is low, the field is unstable and subject to unpredictable and discontinuous patterns of change.	Human beings exist in an interactive relationship with their world. They influence and are influenced by their context or environment. The process of exchange that operates here is essentially a competitive one, the individual seeking to interpret and exploit the environment to satisfy important needs, and hence survive. Relationships between individuals and environment express a pattern of activity necessary for survival and well-being of the individual.	Human beings are a product of the external forces in the environment to which they are exposed. Stimuli in their environment condition them to behave and respond to events in predictable and determinate ways. A network of causal relationships links all important aspects of behavior to context. Though human perception may influence this process to some degree, people always respond to situations in a lawful (i.e., rule-governed) manner.
Scholarly tradition	Cybernetics	Open systems theory	Behaviorism Social learning theory
Overall perspective	Psychological	Psychological	Psychological

Source: Adapted from G. Morgan and L. Smircich, "The Case for Qualitative Research," *Academy of Management Review 5*, pp. 494–495, October 1980. Copyright © 1980 by the Academy of Management. Reprinted by permission.

beings are all these things, and the practices of supervision therefore should not be limited to those from the psychological perspective. Giving attention to all six views means giving attention to school culture as well as school climate.

SCHOOL CULTURE

Climate is to the psychological side of school life what culture is to the symbolic side. Teachers respond to work not only as a result of psychological needs but also as makers of meaning. Thus, studying school culture means studying how events and interactions come to be meaningful.[16] *Culture* can be defined as a set of understandings or meanings shared by a group of people. Typically these meanings are tacitly held and serve to define the group as being distinct from other groups.[17]

Communities are one kind of culture. Organizations are another kind of culture. As suggested in Chapter 3, the values and shared meanings of community cultures are more deeply held and elicit stronger feelings of loyalty and affection than is the case for organizations. Though admittedly some organizations (for example, L.L. Bean) engender in many employees and customers alike passion that stems from deeply held community values, most organizations are decidedly more instrumental and secular. Cultures of schools that are understood as communities are decidedly more sacred, having been defined by their centers of shared values. By contrast, the cultures of schools understood as organizations are more secular. Often they are contrived, having been invented and engineered by school administrators, and as a result they speak less to deeply held values of teachers, parents, and students then they do to the instrumental values of management. The noted sociologist Edward A. Shils uses the concept of "central zone" to illustrate the importance of shared values in understanding cultures:

> The central, or the central zone, is a phenomenon of the realm of values and beliefs. It is the center of the order of symbols and values and beliefs, which govern the society. . . . The central zone partakes of the nature of the sacred. In this sense every society has an official "religion." . . . The center is also a phenomenon of the realm of action. It is a structure of activities, of roles and persons, within the network of institutions. It is in these roles that the values and beliefs which are central are embodied and propounded.[18]

As repositories of values these centers are sources of identity for individuals and groups and the means by which their work lives become meaningful.

---

[16] Linda Smircich, "Is the Concept of Culture a Paradigm for Understanding Ourselves?" in Peter J. Frost et al. (eds.), *Organizational Culture*, Beverly Hills, Calif.: Sage Publications, 1985, pp. 55–72.

[17] M. R. Louis, "Organizations as Culture Bearing Milieux," in Louis Pondy et al. (eds.), *Organizational Symbolism*, Greenwich, Conn.: JAI, 1980, pp. 76–92.

[18] Edward A. Shils, "Centre and Periphery," in *The Logic of Personal Knowledge: Essays Presented to Michael Polanyi*, London: Routledge & Kegan Paul, 1961, p. 119.

Centers provide a sense of purpose to seemingly ordinary events and bring worth and dignity to human activities within the organization.

LEVELS OF CULTURE

It is useful to think about dimensions of school culture as existing at at least four levels.[19] The most tangible and observable level is represented by the *artifacts* of culture as manifested in what people say, how people behave, and how things look. Verbal artifacts include the language systems that are used, stories that are told, and examples that are used to illustrate certain important points. Behavioral artifacts are manifested in the ceremonies and rituals and other symbolic practices of the school.

The next level of school culture to be understood is the *perspectives* of people. Perspectives refer to the shared rules and norms, the commonness which exists among solutions to similar problems, how people define the situations they face, and the boundaries of acceptable and unacceptable behavior.

The third level is that of *values*. Values provide the basis for people to evaluate the situations they face, the worth of actions, activities, their priorities, and the behaviors of people with whom they work. The values are arranged in a fashion which represents the covenant that teachers share. This convenant might be in the form of an educational or management platform and statements of school philosophy. Platforms and philosophy are discussed in more detail in Chapter 8.

The fourth level is that of *assumptions*. Assumptions are more abstract than each of the other levels because they are typically implicit. Craig C. Lundberg describes assumptions as "the tacit beliefs that members hold about themselves and others, their relationships to other persons, and the nature of the organization in which they live. Assumptions are the nonconscious underpinnings of the first three levels—that is, the implicit, abstract axioms that determine the more explicit systems of meanings."[20]

IDENTIFYING THE CULTURE OF YOUR SCHOOL

The four levels of culture provide a framework for analyzing a school's history and tradition, patterns of beliefs, norms, and behaviors. For example, the questions below can help supervisors identify and describe important aspects of the culture of their schools.

---

[19] The levels are from Craig C. Lundberg, "On the Feasibility of Cultural Interventions in Organizations," in Peter J. Frost et al., *Organizational Culture,* Beverly Hills, Calif.: Sage Publications, 1985. The four levels are based on the work of Schein and Dyer as follows: W. G. Dyer, Jr., *Patterns and Assumptions: The Keys to Understanding Organizational Culture,* Office of Naval Research Technical Report TR-0 NR-7; and Edgar H. Schein, *Organizational Culture and Leadership,* San Francisco: Jossey-Bass, 1985.

[20] Lundberg, op. cit., p. 172.

The School's History. How does the school's past live in the present? What traditions are carried on? What stories are told and retold? What events in the school's history are overlooked or forgotten? Do heroes and heroines among students and teachers exist whose idiosyncrasies and exploits are remembered? In what ways are the school's traditions and historical incidents modified through reinterpretation over the years? Can you recall, for example, a historical event that has evolved from fact to myth?

Beliefs. What are the assumptions and understandings that are shared by teachers and others, though they may not be stated explicitly? These may relate to how the school is structured, how teaching takes place, the roles of teachers and students, discipline, the relationship of parents to the school. Perhaps these assumptions and understandings are written somewhere in the form of a philosophy or other statement.

Values. What are the things that your school prizes? That is, when teachers and principals talk about the school, what are the major and recurring value themes underlying what they say?

Norms and Standards. What are the oughts, shoulds, do's, and don'ts that govern the behavior of teachers, supervisors, and principals? Norms and standards can be identified by examining what behaviors get rewarded and what behaviors get punished in the school.

Patterns of Behavior. What are the accepted and recurring ways of doing things, the patterns of behavior, the habits and rituals that prevail in the school?

Corwith Hansen suggests that teachers be asked the following questions in seeking to identify the culture of their school.[21] Describe your work day both in and outside of the school. On what do you spend your time and energy? Given that most students forget what they learn, what do you hope your students will retain over time from your classes? Think of students you are typically attracted to—those that you admire, respect, or enjoy. What common characteristics do these students have? What does it take for a teacher to be successful in your school or in your department? What advice would you give new teachers? What do you remember about past faculty members and students in your school or department? If you were to draw a picture or take a photo or make a collage that represented some aspect of your school, what would it look like? How are students rewarded? How are teachers rewarded? What might a new teacher do that would immediately signal to others that he or she was not going to be successful?

"The School Culture Inventory: Identifying Guiding Beliefs" appears as Exhibit 6-3. This inventory is designed to help faculties tackle the task of identifying their culture by examining their school's belief structure. Depending on re-

---

[21] Corwith Hansen, "Department Culture in a High-Performing Secondary School," unpublished dissertation, New York: Columbia University, 1986.

EXHIBIT 6-3
SCHOOL CULTURE INVENTORY: IDENTIFYING GUIDING BELIEFS

Before a school's culture can be understood, evaluated, or changed, it needs first to be described. The list of questions which comprise this inventory can help faculties describe the culture of their school. The questions are patterned generally after those which appear in Jerry Patterson, Stuart C. Purkey, and Jackson Parker's, *Productive School Systems for a Nonrational World*. Though presented in the form of an inventory, the questions will have the most meaning when discussed by faculty. When individual and group ratings are obtained from teachers they should be supplemented by examples. To help acquaint you with the inventory items, try evaluating a school with which you are familiar using the following scale:

(*A*lways, *M*ost of the time, *P*art of the time, *N*ever)

School Purposes
To what extent does the school:
1 Communicate a set of purposes that provide a
   sense of direction and a basis for evaluating?   A   M   P   N
2 Value the importance of teachers and students
   understanding the purposes?   A   M   P   N
3 Want decisions to be made which reflect purposes?   A   M   P   N
Give examples:

Empowerment
To what extent does the school:
4 Value empowering teachers to make decisions that
   are sensible given circumstances they face?   A   M   P   N
5 Link empowerment to purpose by requiring that
   decisions reflect the school shared values?   A   M   P   N
6 Believe that teachers, supervisors, and
   administrators should have equal access to
   information and resources?   A   M   P   N
7 Believe power to be an expanding entity which
   increases when shared?   A   M   P   N
Give examples:

Decision Making
To what extent does the school:
8 Believe that decisions should be made as close to
   the point of implementation as possible?   A   M   P   N
9 Believe that value decisions should be made by
   those directly affected by them?   A   M   P   N
10 Believe that decisions should be made by those
   who are most expert, given the circumstances or
   problem being considered, regardless of
   hierarchical level?   A   M   P   N
Give examples:

Sense of Community
To what extend does the school:
11 Value a "we" spirit and feeling of ownership in the
   school?   A   M   P   N
12 Consider teachers and other employees as
   shareholders and stakeholders in the school?   A   M   P   N

13 Demonstrate commitment to helping and developing
school members?   A   M   P   N

Give examples:

Trust

To what extent does the school:

14 Believe that given the opportunity teachers will want
to do what is best for the school?   A   M   P   N

15 Have confidence in the ability of teachers to make
wise decisions?   A   M   P   N

Give examples:

Quality

To what extent does the school:

16 Value high standards and expectations for teachers
and students?   A   M   P   N

17 Believe in a "can do" attitude in teachers and
students?   A   M   P   N

18 Value an atmosphere of sharing and encouraging
within which school members "stretch and grow."   A   M   P   N

Give examples:

Recognition

To what extent does the school:

19 Value recognizing teachers and students for taking
chances in seeking new and better ideas?   A   M   P   N

20 Value recognizing the achievements and
accomplishments of teachers and students?   A   M   P   N

Give examples:

Caring

To what extent does the school:

21 Value the well-being and personal concerns of all
school members?   A   M   P   N

22 Take a personal interest in the work concerns and
career development of teachers?   A   M   P   N

Give examples:

Integrity

To what extent does the school:

23 Value honesty in words and actions?   A   M   P   N

24 Adopt a single standard of norms and expectations
for teachers, students, and other school members?   A   M   P   N

25 Value consistency?   A   M   P   N

26 Demonstrate commitment to highest personal and
ethical convictions?   A   M   P   N

EXHIBIT 6-3
SCHOOL CULTURE INVENTORY: IDENTIFYING GUIDING BELIEFS (*Continued*)

Give examples:

Diversity
To what extent does the school:

27 Value differences in individual philosophy and personality?	A M P N
28 Value differences in teaching style?	A M P N
29 Value flexibility in teaching and learning approaches in response to student differences?	A M P N
30 Link diversity in style and method to common school purposes and values?	A M P N

Give examples:

Sum of column tallys   — — — —

Scoring directions: To score the school climate inventory, multiply the sum of tallys in column A by 4; column M by 3; column P by 2; and column N by 1. Now sum the scores for each column to get a grand score. The scale below provides a *rough* indicator of the strength of your school's professional culture:

110 to 120	Strong
90 to 110	Moderately strong
60 to 90	Weak
Below 60	Very weak

Source: Adapted from Jerry Patterson, Stuart Purkey, and Jackson Parker, "Guiding Beliefs of Our School District," *Productive School Systems for a Nonrational World,* Arlington, Va.: Association for Supervision and Curriculum Development, 1986, pp. 50–51. Reprinted with permission of the Association for Supervision and Curriculum Development and Jerry Patterson, Stuart Purkey, and Jackson Parker. Copyright © 1986 by the Association for Supervision and Curriculum Development. All rights reserved.

sponses, a school can be classified generally on a continuum from having a strong to very weak culture.

From this discussion of school culture one might reasonably conclude that the concepts of culture and climate are similar. But still they are unique in many ways. Earlier we discussed the pupil control ideology (PCI) scale and its use in identifying custodial and humanistic schools. These schools differed with respect to the assumptions and beliefs that teachers made about students, discipline, and control. In many respects the PCI conception of climate is concerned with aspects of school culture suggesting that the two concepts share commonalities. Still, the climate metaphor leads one to think more about the interpersonal life in schools. Culture leads one deeper into the life of the school, into the tacit world of beliefs and norms, into the realm of meaning and significance.

PLANNING CHANGE

Acknowledging both the psychological and symbolic sides of human nature redefines the problem of how to introduce change; the problem of how to overcome the resistance of individual teachers becomes the broader problem of how to alter the culture of the school. An effective change strategy gives attention to both.

W. J. Reddin viewed individual teacher concerns as falling into three broad categories:

1 How will the proposed change affect the individual?
2 How will the proposed change affect relationships with others?
3 How will the proposed change affect the individual's work.[22]

He maintains that though these concerns are real, they are often not considered to be "legitimate" reasons for favoring or opposing a change. For this reason, teacher concerns often remain unstated. Instead the talk of resistance has to do with such issues as whether what is being proposed makes "educational sense or not."

Consider, for example, a teacher who is faced with the prospect of having to give up the safety and autonomy of teaching in a self-contained classroom for teaming with others. She may be worrying about what others will think about her teaching and about the additional time and interpersonal pressures involved in having to negotiate with others what will be taught, how it will be taught, and when. Further, she may be worrying about whether her chances of becoming an assistant principal in the school will be enhanced or diminished as a result of this new teaching arrangement. But given the formal roles played in schools, it is typically not socially acceptable to state publicly such personal concerns. Thus instead of speaking to these *real* issues, the teacher complains that students are likely to find team teaching to be impersonal, that clear lines of authority will become clouded, that discipline problems will increase, and that students will find it burdensome to adjust to several different teaching styles.

Not surprisingly, these more organizationally legitimate concerns are not real in and of themselves but are proxies for the more personal concerns of teachers. This is unfortunate, because as teachers make peace with personal concerns, the proxies have a way of disappearing. One advantage of a healthy school climate is that levels of trust and openness among colleagues are such that it becomes acceptable to raise these less legitimate reasons for being concerned about proposed changes.

You can test Reddin's ideas by applying his categories to your own personal experience. Recall, for example, an occasion when a significant change was being proposed. What was your initial reaction to this change? Think less about what you said to others about the change and more about what you ac-

---

[22] W. J. Reddin, *Managerial Effectiveness*, New York: McGraw-Hill, 1970, p. 163.

tually thought about and felt. Use Reddin's list below to identify the items that were of most concern to you:

Concern for self
How will my advancement possibilities change?
How will my salary change?
How will my future with this company change?
How will my view of myself change?
How will my formal authority change?
How will my informal influence change?
How will my view of my prior values change?
How will my ability to predict the future change?
How will my status change?

Concern for work
How will the amount of work I do change?
How will my interest in the work change?
How will the importance of my work change?
How will the challenge of the work change?
How will the work pressures change?
How will the skill demands on me change?
How will my physical surroundings change?
How will my hours of work change?

Concern for relationships
How will my relationships with my coworkers change?
How will my relationships with my superior change?
How will my relationships with my subordinates change?
How will what my family thinks of me change?[23]

A supervisor who wanted to use Reddin's theory to overcome your resistance to change would try to identify your concerns and how powerfully you held them. Then in a kind of tug of war, with the supervisor pulling at one end and you pulling at the other, the supervisor would try to change your mind about your concerns.[24] The supervisor would attempt to diminish as many of your concerns as possible by suggesting benefits of changing that outweigh them. Let's say the two most pressing concerns for you are how your informal influence with the faculty will change and the additional amount of work that will be required. The supervisor might try to convince you that teaming provides a better arena for your influence to increase. Further, the supervisor might try to counter your concern about increased work load by helping you to see the possibilities of becoming a team leader. Both of these advantages can increase your chances of ultimately becoming an assistant principal. The supervisor, in other words, seeks to overcome your resistance to change by offer-

[23] Ibid.
[24] In the parlance of social science this tug of war is called *force field theory and analysis.* See, for example, Kurt Lewin, *Field Theory in Social Science,* New York: Harper & Row, 1951.

ing attractions which increase the pull from one side of the tug of war or by re-
moving resisters that decrease the pull from the other side.

Some researchers have focused on the concerns issue in a developmental
sense, seeking to find out what are initial concerns of teachers and what concerns comes later. They reason that depending upon level of concern, teachers
are likely to focus on one set of limited issues as opposed to another. A good
change strategy, therefore, calculates carefully what the level of concern is and
gives attention to the correct corresponding issues. This work has led to the
development of the "concerns-based adoption model" of change. This model
charts the changing feelings of teachers as they learn about a proposed change,
prepare to use it, then use it, and finally make it a part of their everyday repertoire. The model proposes seven stages of concern as follows[25]:

1 Awareness	I am not concerned about it.	
2 Informational	I would like to know more about it.	
3 Personal	How will using it affect me?	
4 Management	I seem to be spending all my time getting material ready.	
5 Consequence	How is my use affecting kids?	
6 Collaboration	I am concerned about relating what I am doing to what other teachers are doing.	
7 Refocusing	I have some ideas about something that would work even better.	

The developers of the model do not assume that every teacher marches
through all the stages beginning with awareness and ending with refocusing.
Nor do they assume that the stages are mutually exclusive, with only one being tended to at a time. Instead, the stages represent the general kind of development that takes place as changes are adopted and used.

A typical pattern of progression is as follows. In the early stages teachers
are likely to have self concerns that center on learning more about the proposed innovation and how it will affect them personally. This is not unlike the
category system proposed by W. J. Reddin. Once these concerns are taken care
of teachers are then ready to focus on the management problems they are
likely to face as they begin to implement the change. Next their attention shifts
to the impact the change is likely to have on their students. Once comfortable
with answers to this question, teachers address issues of collaboration with
other teachers in an effort to implement the change and to improve its effects.
Finally, since teachers are different, they make adaptations to the innovation
in an effort to improve its fit to their own unique circumstance. In sum, the re-

---

[25] See, for example, Gene E. Hall and Susan F. Louicks, "Teacher Concerns as a Basis for Facilitating Staff Development," *Teachers College Record,* vol. 80, no. 1, 1978; and Shirley M. Hord,
William L. Rutherford, Leslie Huling-Austin, and Gene E. Hall, *Taking Charge of Change,* Alexandria, Va.: ASCD, 1977.

searchers recommend that supervisors interested in promoting change use the concerns-based model as a framework for evaluating where individuals are and for matching change strategies to these levels.

It seems clear that resistance to change occurs when one's basic needs are threatened. Though teachers have different needs, four seem fairly universal[26]:

1 *The need for clear expectations.* Most people require fairly specific information about their jobs to function effectively. People need to know what is expected of them, how they fit into the total scheme of things, what their responsibilities are, how they will be evaluated, and what their relationships with others will be. Change upsets this equilibrium of role definition and expectations.

2 *The need for future certainty.* Closely related to fit is being able to predict the future. People need to have some reliability and certainty built into their work lives. Change introduces ambiguity and uncertainty, which threatens the need for a relatively stable, balanced, and predictable work environment.

3 *The need for social interaction.* Most people value and need opportunities to interact with others. This interaction helps people to define and build up their own self-concepts and to reduce the anxiety and fear they experience in the work environment. People seek support and acceptance from others at work. Change is often viewed as threatening these important social interaction patterns.

4 *The need for control over the work environment and work events.* As suggested in Chapter 4, most people want and seek a reasonable degree of control over their work environment. People do not want to be at the mercy of the system but instead want to be origins, making decisions that affect their own work lives. When control is threatened or reduced the effect is not only less job satisfaction but also a loss of meaning in work that results in indifference and even alienation. Change efforts that ignore these four needs are likely not only to be ineffective but also to cause important morale problems.

Overcoming resistance to change by carefully calculating the appropriate level of concern of teachers involved and by helping teachers to feel safe and secure are all helpful. But resistance to change also occurs when proposed changes oppose the existing norm systems of the school. A strong change strategy seeks as well to alter the culture of the school by creating new work norms. Though tending to the psychological needs of individual teachers is important, in the end changing schools requires changing school culture. Such an ambitious goal, we will argue, requires two things: that leadership be redefined and practiced differently, and that collegiality be understood as a form

[26] Laird W. Nealiea, "Learned Behavior: The Key to Understanding and Preventing Employee Resistance to Change," *Group and Organizational Studies*, vol. 3, no. 2, pp. 211–223, 1978 as quoted in Thomas J. Sergiovanni, *The Principalship: A Reflective Practice Perspective, Second Edition*, Boston: Allyn and Bacon, 1991 p. 260.

of professional virtue. The topic of leadership is complex enough to warrant special attention, and thus it will become the theme of the next several chapters. Collegiality is discussed in the sections that follow.

COLLEGIALITY AS LINCHPIN

It is now accepted that promoting collegiality is an important way to help schools change for the better. Susan Rosenholtz's research, for example, firmly links collegiality to the amount and quality of learning that takes place among teachers.[27] In summarizing the research on collegiality and school improvement, Michael Fullan writes:

> Since interaction with others influences what one does, relationships with other teachers is a critical variable. The theory of change that we have been evolving clearly points to the importance of peer relationships in the school. Change involves learning to do something new, and interaction is the primary basis for social learning. New meanings, new behaviors, new skills, and new beliefs depend significantly on whether teachers are working as isolated individuals (Goodlad, 1984; Lortie, 1975; Sarason, 1982) or are exchanging ideas, support, and positive feelings about their work (Little, 1982; Mortimore, et al., 1988; Rosenholtz, 1989). The quality of working relationships among teachers is strongly related to implementation. Collegiality, open communication, trust, support and help, learning on the job, getting results, and job satisfaction and morale are closely interrelated.[28]

Judith Little's work is most often quoted on this issue:

> School Improvement is most surely and thoroughly achieved when:
>
> Teachers engage in frequent, continuous and increasingly concrete and precise *talk* about teaching practice (as distinct from teacher characteristics and failings, the social lives of teachers, the foibles and failures of students and their families, and the unfortunate demands of society on the school). By such talk, teachers build up a shared language adequate to the complexity of teaching, capable of distinguishing one practice and its virtue from another. . . .
>
> Teachers are frequently observed and provided with useful (if potentially frightening) critiques of their teaching. Such observation and feedback can provide shared referents for the shared language of teaching at a level of the precision and concreteness which makes the talk about teaching useful.
>
> Teachers [and administrators] plan, design, research, evaluate and prepare teaching materials together. The most astute observations remain academic ("just the-

---

[27] Susan Rosenholtz, *Teachers' Workplace: The Social Organization of Schools,* New York: Longman, 1989.

[28] Michael G. Fullan with Susan Stiegelbauer, *The New Meaning of Educational Change,* New York: Teachers College Press, 1991, p. 79. The Fullan cites are as follows: John Goodlad, *A Place Called School: Prospects for the Future,* New York: McGraw-Hill, 1984; Dan Lortie, *Schoolteacher: A Sociological Study,* Chicago: University of Chicago Press, 1975; Seymour Sarason, *The Culture of the School and the Problem of Change,* revised edition, Boston: Allyn and Bacon, 1982; Judith Warren Little, "Norms of Collegiality and Experimentation: Workplace Conditions of School Success," *American Educational Research Journal,* vol. 19, pp. 325–340, 1982; P. Mortimore, P. Sammons, L. Stoll, D. Lewis, and R. Ecob, *School Matters: The Junior Years,* Sommerset, United Kingdom: Open Books, 1988; and Susan Rosenholtz, op. cit., 1989.

ory") without the machinery to act on them. By joint work on materials, teachers [and administrators] share the considerable burden of development required by long-term improvement, confirm their emerging understanding of their approach and make rising standards for their work attainable by them and their students.

Teachers teach each other the practice of teaching.[29]

Collegiality bridges both concepts of school climate and school culture. Collegiality speaks not only to the degree of trust, openness, and good feelings that exist among a faculty, but also to the kind of norm system that bonds teachers as a collective unit. The bonding aspect of collegiality is key and is often missing in the policies and practices of Supervision I.

One problem is that too often collegiality is confused with congeniality.[30] *Congeniality* refers to the friendly human relationships that exist among teachers and is characterized by the loyalty, trust, and easy conversation that results from the development of a closely knit social group. Congeniality is often considered to be a measure of school climate. *Collegiality*, by contrast, refers to the existence of high levels of collaboration among teachers and between teachers and principal and is characterized by mutual respect, shared work values, cooperation, and specific conversations about teaching and learning. When congeniality is high a strong informal culture aligned with social norms emerges in the school. But these norms may or may not be aligned with school purposes. By contrast, when collegiality is high a strong professional culture held together by shared work norms emerges in the school. These norms are aligned with school purposes and contribute to increased commitment and improved performance. We believe that congeniality can contribute to the development of collegiality but in itself is not sufficient.

Another problem is that when collegiality *is* achieved within Supervision I it is often contrived rather than real, resulting from structural rather than normative changes. Supervisors push for collegiality by altering structures and introducing such innovations as peer coaching and team teaching without addressing the norm structure of the school. As a result, they superimpose a form of collegiality on an unaccepting culture. When this is the case collegial practices become grafted on to the existing school culture.[31] Andrew Hargreaves describes contrived collegiality as:

> Characterized by a set of formal, specific bureaucratic procedures to increase the attention being given to joint teacher planning and consultation. It can be seen in initiatives such as peer coaching, mentor teaching, joint planning in specially provided rooms, formally scheduled meetings, and clear job descriptions and training programs for those in consultive roles. These sorts of initiatives are administrative

[29] Judith Warren Little, "Norms of Collegiality and Experimentation: Workplace Conditions of School Success," *American Educational Research Journal*, vol. 19, no. 3, p. 331, Fall 1982.

[30] Roland Barth, *Improving Schools from Within,* San Francisco: Jossey-Bass, 1990.

[31] Peter B. Grimmitt, Olaf P. Rostad, and Blake Ford, "Supervision: A Transformational Perspective," in Carl Glickman (ed.), *Supervision in Transition*, 1992 Yearbook of the Association for Supervision and Curriculum Development, Alexandria, Va.: ASCD, 1992.

contrivances designed to get collegiality going in schools where little has existed before.[32]

The receiving culture is key in determining whether administratively induced collegiality is contrived or real. When it is real, collegiality results from the felt interdependence of people at work and from a sense of moral obligation to work together. From a cultural perspective, and with the right set of shared norms in place, collegiality can be considered as a form of professional virtue. When this is the case the fulfillment of certain obligations that stem from the teacher's membership in the school as community and membership in the teaching profession requires teachers to be collegial.

Collegiality as professional virtue is comprised of three dimensions: a conception of the good person who values colleagueship for its own sake; connectedness to a community that provides one with the right to be treated collegially and the obligation to treat others collegially; and interpersonal relationships characterized by mutual respect.[33] The first two dimensions are enhanced by a healthy school culture and the third by a healthy school climate.

THE SUPERVISOR IS KEY

Improving schools by helping teachers to reflect on their practice, to learn more about what they do and why, to strive for self-improvement, to share what they know with others, and to strive to improve their practice is at the heart of what supervision seeks to accomplish. This purpose often leads to a focus on how to provide staff development approaches and, in class, how to provide help that teachers welcome and find beneficial. It leads to a concern with how the talents and resources of individual teachers might be shared with others and how the evaluation process can be improved. These supervising aims and activities involve change. Change is difficult under ordinary circumstances but particularly trying unless conditions are right. The right conditions, we have argued in this chapter, are those that support both the psychological and symbolic needs of teachers; needs that are the subject matter of school climate and school culture. No matter how well-intentioned the supervisor, and no matter how hard that supervisor tries to improve the individual and collective practice of teaching in a school, little will be accomplished without first developing and nurturing the right school climate and culture. Climate and culture are affected by administrative policies; and they are affected even more by close, personal contact with the process of teaching and learning. This is the territory of supervision. For this reason, supervisors have a particularly critical role to play.

---

[32] Andrew Hargreaves, "Contrived Collegiality and the Culture of Teaching," Annual Meeting of the Canadian Society for the Study of Education, Quebec City, 1989.

[33] Thomas J. Sergiovanni, *Moral Leadership: Getting to the Heart of School Improvement,* San Francisco: Jossey-Bass, 1992.

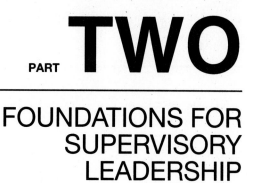

PART TWO

FOUNDATIONS FOR SUPERVISORY LEADERSHIP

SUPERVISION FOR CLASSROOM EFFECTIVENESS

BEFORE we examine clinical supervision in practice, the issue of what is good and effective teaching must be explored. Examining this issue is an important part of the supervisory process for two reasons: Insights gleaned from this process provide standards for improving teaching; and, the process itself requires the kind of deep critical reflection that helps in understanding teaching practice.

Teaching effectiveness is typically defined as bringing about desired student learning. If the objective of a particular classroom lesson or unit is to have every student spell 10 new words correctly, then the teacher who brings all the students to that happy conclusion is said to be effective. Further, the more students learn, the more effective is the teaching. Traditionally the supervisor's job has been to help teachers increase their effectiveness in bringing about increased student learnings. But effective teaching is more complex than this, and other dimensions of effectiveness must be considered. Two such dimensions are the teacher's ability to teach in a way in which learning is viewed by students as meaningful and significant, and the teacher's ability to adjust teaching strategies as warranted by changes in the teaching and learning situation.

Adding meaning and significance to the definition elevates teaching and learning from training and conditioning to educational experience. Educational experiences are characterized by the kind of intellectual and emotional involvement that results in student self-sufficiency, learning independence, and a commitment to growth not found in training and conditioning. The ability to adjust one's teaching strategy in light of changes in the teaching situation, the second dimension of teaching effectiveness we add, is a sign of reflective practice in teaching and a hallmark of professionalism.

In this chapter we review research findings on what constitutes good teaching and draw implications for supervisory practice. As with our earlier discussion on curriculum, we find that the conclusions from research on effective teaching are not all pointing in the same direction. Frequently the assumption and beliefs of the researchers lead them to focus more on certain aspects of teaching than on others. One example is the burgeoning literature of research on "effective teaching." Since many school systems provide staff-development programs based on this literature, supervisors need to be familiar with the findings of this research and need to explore ways to sensibly incorporate effectiveness strategies in their work with teachers.[1]

RESEARCH ON "EFFECTIVE TEACHING"

While the findings may sound very familiar to an experienced teacher or supervisor and appear to the ordinary citizen as good common sense, the research has been able to document that certain teacher behaviors are related to student gains on both criterion- and norm-referenced tests. Among those behaviors frequently cited by research studies are the following:

• Establish classroom rules that allow pupils to attend to personal and procedural needs without having to check with the teacher.
• Communicate expectations of high achievement.
• Start off each class by reviewing homework and by reviewing material covered in the previous few classes.
• Make the objectives of the new instructional episode clear to the students.
• Directly teach the content or skill that will be measured on the test.
• After teaching the new material, assess student comprehension through questions and practice.
• Provide for uninterrupted successful practice that is not monitored by the teacher moving around the classroom.
• Maintain direct engagement by the student on the academic task. Engaged academic time is a critical variable for student achievement.
• Assign homework to increase student familiarity with material.
• Hold review sessions weekly and monthly.

Before conclusions can be reached about the implications of these research findings for supervisory practice, they need to be seen in perspective. First of all, most of the studies that led to these findings were concentrating on the teaching of basic skills in reading and arithmetic in the earlier grades of elementary school. Whether these teaching behaviors are appropriate for higher-level learning in reading and mathematics or for learnings in other areas, such

---

[1] C. W. Fisher, N. N. Filby, R. Marliave, L. S. Cahan, M. M. Dishaw, and D. C. Berliner, "Teacher Behaviors, Academic Learning Time and Student Achievement." Final Report of Phase III-B. *Beginning Teacher Evaluation Study Technical Report Series* (Tech. Rev. V-I). San Francisco: Far West Laboratory, 1978.

Cf. *Educational Leadership*, vol. 37, no. 1, 1979, in which 12 essays on teacher effectiveness appear. One of the better collections of research reports on teacher effectiveness is Penelope P. Peterson and Herbert J. Walberg (eds.), *Research on Teaching: Concepts, Findings, and Implications*, Berkeley, Calif.: McCutchan, 1979.

Cf. Tamar Levin with Ruth Long, *Effective Instruction*, Alexandria, Va.: Association for Supervision and Curriculum Development, 1981. The annotated bibliography at the end of this book is first-rate. Three other books that contain very useful information on effective teaching are Don M. Medley, *Teacher Competence and Teacher Effectiveness: A Review of Process-Product Research*, Washington, D.C.: American Association of Colleges for Teacher Education, 1977; N. L. Gage, *The Scientific Basis of the Art of Teaching*, New York: Teachers College Press, 1978; and Doug Russell and Madeline Hunter, *Planning for Effective Instruction*, Los Angeles: University Elementary School, 1980.

as geography or art, is an open question. Indeed, as pointed out in Chapter 12, it is very likely that had effectiveness been defined differently, the same teaching-effectiveness research would have established different teaching behaviors. In this sense the indicators of teaching effectiveness are neither objective nor independent but are directly linked to how researchers define effectiveness. This point raises the question as to whether what is called "teaching effectiveness" research is properly named. A more scientific label for this research would communicate more precisely just what is involved. As a group the behaviors identified in this research describe direct or explicit teaching.[2] The research establishes that this approach to teaching is very effective in enhancing student skill acquisition and simple subject matter mastery in the basic subjects.

This research on effective teaching does not account sufficiently for other variables that may affect student achievement. Research on home influences, for example, indicates that family stability, the prior education of parents, juvenile delinquency, alcoholic or drug-addicted parents, family income, and so on can enhance or limit classroom effects.[3] While a teacher following the prescriptions of effective teaching may increase the achievement levels of most students, he or she may be unable to reach some students whose home backgrounds are so chaotic as to cripple their ability to concentrate on academic tasks. Likewise, the success of some teachers in bringing about higher achievement of their students may be enhanced by the stable family backgrounds of their students, rich in educational resources. Is it proper to rate one teacher as more effective than another whose students come from far less favorable home environments?

Research on effective schools reveals that there are schoolwide variables that can enhance or limit the impact of a given classroom teacher's efforts to move toward more effective teaching behaviors. While no one school variable of itself may account for school effectiveness, taken together a critical mass of positive school factors can support an individual teacher's effective teaching practices.[4] If all the teachers in the school have high expectations of students, a single teacher's effectiveness will be greater than if he or she is the only one in the school with high expectations. If no one else in the school assigns homework, that teacher's effectiveness will be diminished when he or she initiates the effort to assign homework.

---

[2] See, for example, Barak V. Rosenshine, "Synthesis of Research on Explicit Teaching," *Educational Leadership*, vol. 43, no. 6, pp. 60–69, 1986.

[3] See Ralph Scott and Herbert J. Walberg, "Schools Alone Are Insufficient," *Educational Leadership*, vol. 37, no. 1, pp. 24–27, 1979; James S. Coleman et al., *Equality of Educational Opportunity*, Washington, D.C.: U.S. Office of Education, National Center for Educational Statistics, 1966; and Christopher Jencks et al., *Inequality: A Reassessment of the Effects of Family and Schooling in America*, New York: Basic Books, 1972.

[4] See Gilbert R. Austin, "Exemplary Schools and the Search for Effectiveness," *Educational Leadership*, vol. 37, no. 1, pp. 10–14, 1979; and Michael Rutter, Barbara Maughan, Peter Mortimer, and Janet Ouston, *Fifteen Thousand Hours: Secondary Schools and Their Effects on Children*, Cambridge, Mass.: Harvard University Press, 1979.

SUMMARY OF RESEARCH ON TEACHING

Herbert Walberg and his associates Diane Schiller and Geneva Haertel assessed the adequacy of educational research completed during the sixties and seventies. They conducted a thorough review of research published between 1969 and 1979.[5] Of particular interest was research on teaching and instruction. They sought to demonstrate that during the decade in question the educational research community had accumulated highly useful findings addressed to policymakers and professional practitioners alike. A side benefit of this review was to demonstrate the effects of a variety of approaches to teaching and instruction. Some of the studies tabulated by Walberg and his associates are shown in Table 7-1.

The studies we select from Walberg's summary are grouped into three categories: those that support aspects of structured approaches to teaching, those that compare aspects of structured with unstructured approaches to teaching, and those that support the effects of climate on learning.

Most approaches to teaching characterized as structured are similar in their emphasis on cognitive learning, predetermined objectives, teacher direction, and carefully paced instruction. A personalized system of instruction (PSI), for example, relies on small units of written instruction, student self-pacing, mastery of subject matter at level A before proceeding to level B, and repeated testing. Mastery learning relies on diagnosis of entry-level skills and understandings, on clear objectives and specific learning procedures, on small units of learning, feedback, and flexible learning time. Direct instruction refers to methods of instruction, under tight teacher control, that focus on specific objectives. These appear to be overwhelmingly effective techniques for teaching the basic skills in reading and math and for teaching subject matter where achievement is measured by recall.

Notice in the comparisons depicted in the second category of Table 7-1 that lecturing is favored over discussion in achievement and retention of subject matter but that student-centered discussion is favored over teacher-centered discussion for building understanding of subject matter and promoting positive attitudes toward learning. It appears that the lower the level of learning (facts, simple recall), the more appropriate are direct methods of instruction.

Informal or more open teaching strategies seem superior to structured approaches in promoting creativity, self-concept enhancement, positive attitudes toward school, curiosity, self-determination, independence, and cooperation.

Teaching approaches, therefore, seem less an issue of which is the best way than of which is the best way for what purpose. Good classrooms and gifted teachers exhibit a variety of teaching approaches, mixing both formal and informal methods as circumstances require. The cautions about how the research on teaching should be interpreted are worth repeating. Teacher-effectiveness researchers and consumers of this research are naturally excited about

[5] Herbert J. Walberg, Diane Schiller, and Geneva D. Haertel. "The Quiet Revolution in Educational Research," *Phi Delta Kappan*, vol. 61, no. 3, pp. 179–183, 1979.

TABLE 7-1

SELECTED SUMMARY OF RESEARCH ON TEACHING AND LEARNING AS TABULATED BY WALBERG, SCHILLER, AND HAERTEL

I. Selected research on structured approaches to teaching		
Topics	No. of results	Percent positive
Behavioral instruction on learning	52	98.1
Personalized system of instruction (PSI) on learning	103	93.2
Mastery learning	30	96.7
Programmed instruction on learning	57	80.7
Advanced organizers on learning	32	37.5
Direct instruction on achievement	4	100.0

II. Selected research comparing more and less structured approaches		
Topics	No. of results	Percent positive
Lecture favored over discussion on		
Achievement	16	68.8
Retention	7	100.0
Attitudes	8	86.0
Student-centered discussion favored over teacher-centered on		
Achievement	7	57.1
Understanding	6	83.0
Attitude	22	100.0
Factual questions favored over conceptual on achievement	4	100.0
Open or informal education favored over traditionally structured education on		
Achievement	26	54.8
Creativity	12	100.0
Self-concept	17	88.2
Attitude toward school	25	92.0
Curiosity	6	100.0
Self-determination	7	85.7
Independence	19	94.7
Freedom from anxiety	8	37.5
Cooperation	6	100.0

III. Selected research on climate and teaching		
Topics	No. of results	Percent positive
Motivation and learning	232	97.8
Sociopsychological climate and learning		
Cohesiveness	17	85.7
Satisfaction	17	100.0
Difficulty	16	86.7
Formality	17	64.7
Goal direction	15	73.3
Democracy	14	84.6
Environment	15	85.7
Speed	14	53.8

TABLE 7-1 (*Continued*)

III. Selected research on climate and teaching		
Topics	No. of results	Percent positive
Diversity	14	30.8
Competition	9	66.7
Friction	17	0.0
Cliqueness	13	8.3
Apathy	15	14.3
Disorganization	17	6.3
Favoritism	13	10.0

Source: Herbert J. Walberg, Diane Schiller, and Geneva D. Haertel, "The Quiet Revolution in Educational Research," *Phi Delta Kappan,* vol. 61, no. 3, pp. 180–181, 1979.

the discoveries, and in their commitment to improve practice, they often make unrealistic and misleading claims as to what constitutes effective teaching. Typically, teacher-effectiveness research attempts to link certain teacher behaviors and modes of instruction (processes) to student outcomes (products). When the link is established (as in the case of direct instruction being related to higher student achievement in the basic skills), the claim is often made by researchers, and interpreted as such by practitioners, that the instructional methods investigated are generally effective. Not specifying exactly what student outcomes are of issue or what relationships between teacher behaviors and outcomes are suggested can lead to confusion and misrepresentation of the research.

Medley's comprehensive review of teacher-effectiveness research is an example of proper representation.[6] He is careful to point out that the research he reviews involves correlational studies; thus relationships observed do not prove that certain teacher behaviors *cause* particular student outcomes. These studies show only that a relationship exists. Further, the studies he reviews consist almost entirely of dependent variables defined as pupil performance on reading and mathematics achievement tests in the primary grades. Despite Medley's care in pointing out these limitations, his findings are often assumed to refer to general concepts of teacher effectiveness that apply to all students, for all outcomes, in all settings.

SOME NECESSARY CONDITIONS TO EFFECTIVE SUPERVISION AND EVALUATION

Fundamental to the process of supervision and evaluation is that the supervisor have a firm and informed knowledge of substantive aspects of educational programs and teaching. It is true that certain aspects of teaching are so obviously ascertained that even amateurs can successfully evaluate them. Picking up indicators of warmth, patterns of classroom interaction, differences be-

[6] Medley, op. cit.

tween on- and off-task behaviors, describing classroom arrangements, and detecting teacher or student boredom do not require that one be well versed in pedagogy, principles of learning, or curriculum development. But discerning the appropriateness of a teaching strategy given a particular set of objectives, commenting on the adequacy of an advance organizer, detecting whether an interest center is functioning properly, understanding how the inquiry method works, judging the adequacy of chosen curriculum materials, and commenting on the implications of a particular reinforcement pattern on student long-term motivation require a higher level of sophistication in things educational.

Teacher-effectiveness research can play an important role in increasing our understanding of supervisory issues and in helping to develop supervisory strategies. But the relationships uncovered to date are too complex and too situational to become surrogates for educated judgments. Gage's suggestions that teaching be viewed as a practical art with a scientific basis may well be worth noting:

> Scientific method can contribute relationships between variables taken two at a time and even, in the form of interactions, three or perhaps four or more at a time. Beyond say, four, the usefulness of what science can give the teacher begins to weaken, because teachers cannot apply, at least not without help and not on the run, the more complex interactions. At this point, the teacher as artist must step in and make clinical, or artistic, judgments about the best ways to teach. In short, the scientific basis for the art of teaching will consist of two-variable relationships and lower-order interactions. The higher-order interactions between four and more variables must be handled by the teacher as artist.[7]

Efforts to bring a scientific basis to teaching are important despite the fact that a one-to-one correspondence does not exist between scientific knowledge and practice. Instead, such knowledge can best serve and inform the decision-making process in supervision and enhance the art of teaching.

BELIEVING IS SEEING

An important theme in understanding supervision and evaluation is that it is difficult to separate what one considers to be effective teaching from questions of ideology. What a supervisor or a teacher, for example, considers to be evidence of good teaching is a function of both questions of meaning and truth. Further, truth is always a function of the meaning attributed to the evidence in the first place. What people believe, in other words, is what they see.[8] Many of the practices of Supervision I are based on a particular set of beliefs about teaching and learning. The practices of Supervision II are based on different beliefs. And, it is not likely that teachers and supervisors will change their su-

---

[7] Gage, op. cit., p. 20.
[8] Linda Lotto, "Believing Is Seeing," *Organizational Theory Dialogue*, vol. 3, no. 1, winter, 1983, pp. 6–26.

pervisory practices without first changing what they believe to be true about teaching and learning.

Consider, for example, the seven pairs of belief about teaching and learning listed below.[9] For each pair distribute 10 points to indicate the extent to which you believe each statement is true. For the first pair, if you believe that the *a* statement "Learning is a process of accumulating isolated bits of information and skills" and the *b* statement "Learning involves active construction of meaning and understanding" are both equally true, give each 5 points. If you believe that the *a* statement is much more true than the *b*, give the first 9 or 8 points and the second 1 or 2 points and so on.

---

1. (a) Learning is a process of accumulating isolated bits of information and skills

    (b) Learning involves active construction of meaning and understanding.

(a) _____

(b) _____ = 10

2. (a) Students are empty vessels who receive and store information that is taught.

    (b) Students' prior understandings influence what they learn during instruction.

(a) _____

(b) _____ = 10

3. (a) Learning is defined as a change in student behavior

    (b) Learning is defined as a change in a student's cognitive structure and world view.

(a) _____

(b) _____ = 10

4. (a) Teaching and learning involves interactions between teachers and students.

    (b) Teaching and learning involves active construction of meaning by students.

(a) _____

(b) _____ = 10

5. (a) Students are individual learners and motivation should be competitively based.

    (b) Learning in cooperation with others is important in motivating students and in enhancing outcomes.

(a) _____

(b) _____ = 10

6. (a) Teachers must work hard at delivering instruction to students to be successful.

    (b) Teachers must arrange for students to do the work of learning.

(a) _____

(b) _____ = 10

7. (a) Thinking and learning skills are generic across content areas and context.

    (b) Teaching and learning skills are content- and context-specific.

(a) _____

(b) _____ = 10

                                                                      70

Supervision I is based on the beliefs about teaching and learning implied by the *a* statement of each pair. Given these beliefs, Supervision I takes the form of tightly linking teachers to detailed objectives, content scripts, schedules, and

---

[9] The assumptions are summarized from James Nolan and Pam Francis, "Changing Perspectives in Curriculum and Instruction," in Carl Glickman (ed.), *Supervision in Transition*, 1992 Yearbook of the Association for Supervision and Curriculum Development. Alexandria, Va.: The Association for Supervision and Curriculum Development, pp. 44–59.

evaluation schemes and then checking to be sure that teachers are following through according to the required specifications. The act of teaching itself is thought to be expressed in the form of research-validated generic behaviors. The behaviors comprise lists that supervisors use in observing teachers to be sure that they are teaching the way in which they are supposed to.

Supervision II is based on the beliefs implied by the *b* statements. The *b* statements comprise a reality that leads to a different kind of supervisory and teaching practice. In making the case for the *b* statements, Harriet Tyson explains:

> School structures and routines should be shaped more by students' needs than by the characteristics of the disciplines, and less by teachers' and administrators' need for control and convenience. Young children learn best when they become active workers rather than passive learners. They make more progress, and are much more interested in schoolwork, when they are permitted to work together in groups to solve complex tasks, allowed to engage in class discussions and taught to argue convincingly for their approach in the midst of conflicting ideas and strategies. Even young children can do these things well with a little encouragement . . . many children, particularly those with little home support, learn best in a more familial school atmosphere.[10]

Believing that teaching is not the same as telling, Tyson concludes that

> Generic pedagogy, which has spawned generic in-service training programs and generic teacher evaluation systems, overlooks the intimate and necessary connection between a discipline and teaching methods. Powerful, subject-specific and topic-specific pedagogy, most of it in mathematics and science, is becoming available. These new techniques make the battles over relative importance of content knowledge and pedagogical knowledge seem futile. Effective teaching requires both kinds of knowledge, developed to a high degree, and applied flexibly and artistically to particular topics and students.[11]

Much of the new research on teaching leads to the conclusion that teaching is much more than script-following and supervision is much more than making sure that those scripts are being followed.[12] As teaching becomes more and more context-specific and subject-matter-dependent, supervision becomes more contextually constructed and teacher-dependent. There is no template held by supervisors to which teachers must try to fit themselves. What makes sense is not something that can be determined beforehand and arrayed as a script. Instead, what makes sense in teaching must be constructed from within

[10] Harriet Tyson, "Reforming Science Education/Restructuring the Public Schools: Roles for the Scientific Community," prepared as a background paper for the New York Academy of Sciences and the Institute for Educational Leadership Forum on Restructuring K-12 Education. New York Academy of Sciences, New York, March 1990, p. 22.

[11] Ibid., p. 24.

[12] See, for example, Lee S. Shulman, "Knowledge and Teaching: Foundations of the New Reform," *Harvard Educational Review*, vol. 57, pp. 1–22; and S. M. Wilson and A. E. Richart, "150 Different Ways of Knowing: Representations of Knowledge in Teaching," in J. Calderhead (ed.), *Exploring Teachers' Thinking*, London: Cassell, 1987.

the act of teaching itself. For example, much depends on the teacher's understanding of the subject matter she or he is teaching, and as this subject-matter understanding changes so does what makes sense. Subject-matter knowledge consists of the facts, concepts, principles, and theories underlying the structure of the discipline. "Pedagogical content knowledge" counts too.[13] This kind of knowledge refers to the teacher's ability to transform subject-matter understandings into teachable forms that make sense to students.

By totaling a and b scores you can get a rough idea of the degree to which you agree with each of the two views of teaching and learning. The newer research on teaching and the b beliefs about teaching and learning that underlie Supervision II have important implications for how supervision should be thought about and practiced. Nolan and Frances list some of these implications as follows:

   1 Teachers will be viewed as active constructors of their own knowledge about teaching and learning;
   2 Supervisors will be viewed as collaborators in creating knowledge about teaching and learning;
   3 The emphasis in data collection during supervision will change from almost total reliance on paper and pencil observation instruments [designed] to capture the events of a single period of instruction to the use of a wide variety of data sources to capture a lesson as it unfolds over several periods of instruction;
   4 There will be greater emphasis on content specific knowledge and skills in the supervisory process; and
   5 Supervision will become more group oriented rather than individually oriented.[14]

To this list we add that supervision will increasingly be viewed as a role-free process. For teachers to be active participants in knowledge and collaborators in creating new knowledge about teaching and learning, they must assume roles not only as co-supervisors with principals and other administrators but also as co-supervisors with other teachers. Indeed, the future will show that supervision involving principals and other administrators as lead people will be less important than collegial supervision involving peers. This theme is continued in Chapter 16, in which we consider options for supervision.

MATCHING TEACHING AND EVALUATION STRATEGIES

We believe that the new configurations of supervision based on more recent research and on beliefs about teaching and learning underlying Supervision II require a balanced perspective. Such a perspective embodies the following principles:

---

[13] Shulman, op. cit.
[14] Nolan and Francis, op. cit., p. 58.

1 No one teaching method is inherently better than another.

2 Supervisors and teachers need to be sensitive to the conditions under which various approaches to teaching are more and less effective.

3 Evaluation strategies need to take into account the characteristics of the teaching strategy under study in evaluating teaching.

4 Effective evaluation requires that the supervisor be well informed about such educational matters as curriculum, models of teaching, principles of learning, and classroom arrangements.

5 Asking the supervisor to develop a sense of purpose and a vision of future possibilities should not be confused with asking the supervisor to develop a narrow, rigid, dogmatic view of teaching.

6 A choice of teaching approach is *contingent* upon a number of factors found in the teaching situation such as purposes, characteristics of students, availability of materials, space, and time, and needs of teachers.

7 Adopting a variable approach to teaching does not obviate the necessity for *any* chosen approach to contain certain nurturing and human characteristics toward students.

In the sections below, we provide some guidelines in the form of questions that can help supervisors applying a balanced perspective identify evaluation issues and plan an evaluation strategy.

- What is the approach to teaching this teacher has in mind?

Assume that the teacher plans a role-playing exercise that engages students in a mock trial.

- Is this approach appropriate to the teaching purposes or outcomes sought? Is this approach appropriate to the teaching setting envisaged?

Role playing is a suitable teaching strategy for clarifying student values and addressing attitudinal issues. If the teacher envisions a lesson designed to help students learn the official names and duties of various roles common to jury trials, this method is less appropriate than direct-explicit teaching. Discussions with the teacher as to how students will be evaluated can provide clues to intended purposes. If the teacher has a matching test in mind, then probably role playing is a poor teaching choice. Perhaps the teacher is not sure of intended outcomes but feels that role playing is a good educational encounter anyway. In evaluating students the teacher might have in mind an open-ended essay as to how the student profited from the lesson. Then under these circumstances role playing might well be an excellent choice.

- Given what is known about the particular approach to teaching, how knowledgeable is the teacher about the theoretical aspects of this approach? How successful is the teacher in implementing this approach?

Evaluation strategies and methods need to take into account the purposes of the teacher and the proposed method of teaching. It would not be appropriate to criticize a teacher using direct-explicit teaching for too much teacher talk. Collecting materials used by students to assess their diversity or photographing students every 5 minutes to determine the extent to which they are engaged in a variety of learning settings does not fit this teaching method either. Certainly the supervisor can and should comment on whether direct-explicit teaching fits the purposes intended. But once teacher and supervisor agree that this method makes sense, the evaluation should do justice to the method. The same can be said for more informal or open methods of teaching. Asking all students to measure up to certain standard and predetermined criteria may well be an evaluation technique inappropriate to informal methods of teaching.

• How does this approach fit into the teacher's overall frame of reference or philosophy of teaching? How does this approach fit into the school's overall frame of reference or philosophy of teaching?

One danger in using the perspective we propose is that it can lead teachers and supervisors to conclude that anything goes. The supervisor need only ask the teacher what the intents are and evaluate accordingly. We do not accept this point of view. Schools and classrooms should operate from a set of principles and a vision of ideals. An educational platform should be developed from this broad view of the desirable and possible. This educational platform should serve as a basis for decision making and as a standard for evaluating the appropriateness of decisions about curriculum matters and broad teaching strategies. Particular teaching strategies selected by the teacher should be evaluated for goodness of fit against this standard.

• Given the array of approaches available to the teacher and acceptable to the school, does the selection of a given approach suggest a balanced repertoire of teaching strategies?

Though it is not reasonable for a school to permit teachers complete autonomy in the selection of teaching strategies, it is reasonable to expect that teachers incorporate a variety of strategies in efforts to accommodate the diverse purposes of education and the array of unique learning styles of students.

TEACHING AS DECISION MAKING

When one adopts the stance that no one teaching method is inherently better than another, the process of teaching becomes more complex than is typically portrayed in the literature or reflected in the evaluation scales of school districts and states. Teaching changes from a low-level applied technology to a high-level executive function, and teaching practice changes from faithful application of standardized teaching models (i.e., explicit teaching, informal teaching, the "lesson cycle") to the making and carrying out of decisions.

Many experts hold the view that teaching needs to be understood as a process of decision making, but differences exist as to how this decision-making process is to be understood. There is, for example, an academic view of teacher decision making as a rational and explicit process of logical steps in search of optimal solutions and in contrast, a practical view of teacher decision making as a "science of muddling through."

This latter view of decision making did not emerge from theoretical speculations about how decisions should be made but from concrete studies of how decisions are actually made in real life. In other words, the oughts and the is's of decision making are at variance with each other. This new view of decision making is based largely on the work of such theorists as Herbert A. Simon, James G. March, and Charles E. Lindblom. These scholars point out the limits of rational decision theory and provide alternative models and frames for thinking about how decision making actually occurs.

THE LIMITS OF "RATIONAL" DECISION THEORY

Rational decision making is based upon the following assumptions: Problems can be clearly defined and delineated; complete sets of alternatives can be discovered and described as a result of an extensive search; a set of consequences can be attached to each alternative; these consequences can be weighted according to some objective formula in terms of the probabilities of success in solving the problem at hand; this weighting procedure permits cardinal ordering of alternatives; and individuals can process an unlimited amount of information. James G. March and Herbert A. Simon, in their classic 1958 book *Organizations*,[15] point out numerous difficulties with this rational view. They note, for example, that the occasions when decision makers have complete and accurate knowledge of the consequences that follow various alternatives are rare, and indeed decision making typically involves high risk and a great deal of uncertainty. Thus judgments, beliefs, prior experiences, and professional and human intuition become increasingly important. They state:

> One can hardly take exception to these requirements in a normative model—a model that tells people how they are to choose. For if the rational man lacked information, he might have chosen differently "if only he had known." At best, he is "subjectively" rational, not "objectively" rational. But the notion of objective rationality assumes there is some objective reality in which the "real" alternatives, the "real" consequences, and the "real" utilities exist. If this is so, it is not even clear why the cases of choice under risk and under uncertainty are admitted as rational. If it is not so, it is not clear why only limitations upon knowledge of consequences are considered, and why limitations upon knowledge of alternatives and utilities are ignored in the model of rationality.[16]

These experts argue that except under routine or simple circumstances most decision makers seek to uncover and select satisfactory rather than optimal al-

---

[15] James G. March and Herbert A. Simon, *Organizations*, New York: Wiley, 1958.
[16] Ibid., p. 138.

ternatives, alternatives that will do the job rather than those that will do the job best. Decision makers (teachers included), in other words, do not search the haystack looking for the best needle but rather settle for the first needle that will work.

RATIONAL VIEWS OF TEACHING AS DECISION MAKING

It is presumed that teachers and supervisors should have in mind specific outcomes, and all other decisions they make about teaching should be linked to the accomplishment of these outcomes. Often complete transcripts of verbal teaching interactions are recorded and analyzed to determine the extent to which teachers and students tend to the objectives. Answers to such questions as the following are important in supervision and teaching rationally conceived: Does the transcript of teaching reveal that the teacher provides positive reinforcement when students are tending to the objectives? Do instances exist when students and teachers stray from the objectives? What can be done to get the class back on course? Are students aware of what they are supposed to do? Has the teacher instilled in students the proper mental set to learn the objectives at hand? Are lesson plans specific? Do students know beforehand what it is they are supposed to do? Are materials selected to reflect these objectives? Is this the case also with in-class and out-of-class assignments? For example, is "seat work" aligned with the objectives at hand and does the teacher monitor seat work to ensure that the students are on task?

In the real world teachers typically do not think and act in accordance with discrete goals and objectives. When they do, these goals and objectives are likely to be quite general. Instead, teachers respond to certain values and tend to certain patterns of goals and objectives that are often in competition with each other. For example, a teacher may push for "maximum" cognitive learning from students but cannot push too far for fear that students will become dissatisfied and cause trouble or perhaps even drop out. Further, the teacher is concerned with the psychological and social well-being of students and recognizes that pushing too hard in cognitive matters may incur costs in these important areas. Learning outcomes typically compete with each other. Too much drill and tedious workbook activity in teaching reading may result in students not liking reading and thus reading less in later life. Allowing students too much freedom in choosing reading material may result in omission of important works.

Though rational models assume that teaching involves a series of interconnected choices in which teachers try simultaneously to maximize several conflicting demands, in the real world typically no sequential assumptions are made about the relationships among discrete goals, curriculum, teaching, and outcomes. Indeed any of the four can drive the other three. Goals, for example, are often selected as a result of materials available as are materials selected as a result of goals. Teaching styles and preferences determine objectives as often as objectives determine teaching styles and preferences. Outcomes become goals as often as goals become outcomes.

MUDDLING THROUGH AND REFLECTIVE PRACTICE

The organizational theorist Charles E. Lindblom likens the decision-making process to "the science of muddling through."[17] To him decision making is based on successive and limited comparisons of one decision with the next as part of an intuitive process which builds out continually from current situations. It is incremental in nature and is aimed at arriving at decisions based on past experience. For example, a teacher has in mind various value patterns and goals and various favored teaching strategies but views each as being closely intertwined. That is, by habit or experience the teacher has come to learn that grouping students in a certain way makes sense and works. This teaching strategy is not arrived at by logically matching it to a set of outcomes or subject matter to be taught as if strategy and outcome were independent. Instead, having confidence in what works, the teacher searches the teaching content and various teaching outcome possibilities that fit the strategy. Since teaching means and the outcomes to achieve are not distinct, the means-end analysis of rational decision making is considered to be limited. The test of a good decision about what to teach or how to teach is a simple one. Other teachers too agree that this is the case or other teachers too operate in the same way or other teachers too arrive at the same decision place.

Similarly, Donald A. Schön, in his important book *The Reflective Practitioner: How Professionals Think and Act,* describes decision making as a process of "managing messes."[18] Instead of relying on a highly theoretical and rational process of decision making, professionals reflect on their practice in terms of their personal experience, previous successes, hopes, preferences, strengths and weaknesses, and desired outcomes. Reflection and action, according to Schön, involves "on-the-spot surfacing, criticizing, restructuring, and testing of intuitive understandings of experienced phenomena; often it takes the form of a reflective conversation with the situation."[19]

There is a certain logic and rationality to the process of muddling through. In some respects, this image is more realistic than more tidy descriptions of decision making that one finds in the traditional literature. As suggested in Chapter 13, what is assumed to be more rational can turn out to be rationalistic, and what is assumed to be less rational can turn out to be very rational. For

---

[17] Charles E. Lindblom, "The Science of Muddling Through," *Public Administration Review,* vol. 19, no. 1, pp. 79–88, 1959.

[18] Donald A. Schön, *The Reflective Practitioner: How Professionals Think and Act,* New York: Basic Books, 1983.

[19] Donald A. Schön, "Leadership as Reflection in Action," in *Leadership and Organizational Culture,* Thomas J. Sergiovanni and John E. Corbally (eds.), Urbana-Champaign: University of Illinois Press, 1984, p. 42.

example, it makes no sense for supervisors to ignore this reality and assume that decision making unfolds in a way in which it actually does not.

TYPOLOGY OF DECISION MAKING

To this point we have discussed several different decision-making situations. The situation that a teacher is likely to find her- or himself in depends in part upon the extent to which goals and learning outcomes are readily agreed to and easily identified. In those situations where low agreement exists or where outcomes are difficult to identify or need to be assessed after teaching takes place, certain approaches to decision making will be more appropriate than when there is high agreement and easy identification. The extent to which teaching means and methods are well defined and easily identified also determines the approach.

Examples of four approaches to decision making in teaching (rational, muddling through, collaborative, and garbage can) are depicted in Figure 7-1. Rational decision making is most appropriate when goals and learning outcomes are easily identified and readily agreed to and when appropriate teaching methods are well defined. In situations where it is difficult to agree on goals and learning outcomes or when they must be assessed *after* teaching takes place, but the teacher has in mind fairly well defined teaching strategies that can be readily identified, decision making is more like the science of muddling through. Collaborative decision making would be most appropriate in those instances where goals and learning outcomes are easily agreed to and are easily identified, but teaching methods are difficult to identify or are not well defined. In collaborative decision making teacher and students have in mind

FIGURE 7-1   Typology of decision-making modes in teaching

	Goals and Learning Outcomes	
	High agreement Easy to identify	Low agreement Difficult to identify
Well defined **Easy to identify** Teaching Strategies	Rational Decision Making Explicit teaching "lesson cycle" Executive plan Objectives oriented	Muddling Through Decision Making Teaching as surfing Strategic goals Contingency plans Outcome oriented
Not well defined **Difficult to identify**	Collaborative Decision Making Exploratory learning Learning contracts Group work Objectives oriented	Garbage Can Decision Making Experimental learning Discovery Playfulness Outcome oriented

what it is that needs to be accomplished and work together to decide how these outcomes will be achieved. Teaching strategies characterized by exploration, group work, and independent contracts are likely to be in evidence. And finally, where learning outcomes are either difficult to identify or agree to and where teaching means and methods remain vague or uncertain, decision making is likely to resemble the image of a garbage can. Teaching and learning activities take on the character of discovery and experimental research and are characterized by a certain playfulness. Garbage can as a metaphor for teacher decision making often makes teachers and supervisors feel uncomfortable. Yet, it can be a very productive approach. Consider, for example, the number of important medicines (or, for that matter, the array of 3M products) that have been discovered or stumbled upon because of the accidental matching of problems and solutions.

In Chapter 13 we observe that teaching for complex learning is much like surfing. Teachers ride the curl of the wave of teaching as it unfolds. This reality does not mean that supervisors are unable to assess the value of learning outcomes or to judge the adequacy of teaching decisions. It does suggest, however, that supervisors rely less on predetermined images of good teaching and more on reflection and judgment. Reflection and judgment require more collaboration than is now the case. The emphasis in supervision needs to shift from critiquing performance to understanding what is going on as agendas emerge in the process of studying teaching.

ROLES OF TEACHING

One way to understand teaching is to examine various roles teachers assume. Four such roles, described in Table 7-2, are manager, executive, mediator, and leader.

As manager the teacher executes fairly specific teaching steps according to well-defined and highly structured protocols. Rational decision making is the mode in teaching. The teacher functions as manager where teaching is conceived as a pipeline. The role of teacher as manager is to manage the flow of information through this line. Objectives are defined rather specifically for the student, motivation is extrinsic, and both the teacher and students are somewhat subordinate to the structured teaching system of which they are a part. Two different teachers assuming this role for the same purpose are likely to teach in the same way. The managerial role is most effective for teaching basic skills and simple subject-matter content.

When in the role of executive, the teacher uses the available research on teaching and principles of learning to make proper teaching decisions in light of the situation faced but within a fairly set framework for teaching. Rational decision making is the mode in teaching. There is, for example, an executive plan for teaching that is followed, and effective teaching is one which parallels this plan. Within this framework the teacher makes very important decisions about subject-matter content, grouping for and pacing of instruction, student

TABLE 7-2
ROLES OF TEACHING

Roles	Description	Characteristics	Strengths
Teacher as manager	The teacher executes explicit teaching steps according to highly structured protocols associated with direct instruction. The teacher manages student behavior accordingly.	Teaching is conceived as a pipeline. The role of the teacher is to manage the flow of information through the line. Objectives are defined for the student. Motivation is typically extrinsic. Both teacher and students are subordinate to the structured teaching protocols. Reliability in teaching, therefore, is very high.	Very effective for teaching basic skills and effective for teaching simple subject-matter content.
Teacher as executive	The teacher uses research on effective teaching and psychological principles of learning to make proper teaching decisions in light of situations faced but within a set framework which provides decision-making rules. Within this framework, for example, the teacher makes important decisions about subject-matter content, grouping for and pacing of instruction, student assignments, and other instructional features. Decisions are typically made beforehand in the form of an executive plan for teaching. Effective teaching results when this plan is followed.	Teaching is conceived as executive decision making which requires that situations be diagnosed and that established teaching principles be applied correctly. Objectives are typically defined for the student. Motivation is typically extrinsic. Students are subordinate to the system (that is, they are viewed as objects of teaching rather than partners to the teaching). Teachers are active decision makers and are in control, provided that they follow the established teaching protocols.	Very effective for teaching simple subject-matter content and effective for teaching basic skills.
Teacher as mediator	The teacher uses reciprocal and interactive teaching strategies which enable students to process new information and new learnings in light of their own personal	Teaching is conceived as a mediating process within which students, with the help of teachers, interact with information and ideas in terms of	Very effective for teaching analysis, problem-solving, and higher-order skills, complex concepts, higher levels of comprehension, and having

124

TABLE 7-2 (Continued)

Roles	Description	Characteristics	Strengths
	meanings and experiences and prior learnings. Emphasis is on helping students make sense of learning encounters by constructing new understandings and by linking new to prior learnings.	personal meanings and previous learnings. Though at times teachers decide the actual learning outcomes of teaching, a balance is sought between teacher-determined and student-determined outcomes. The intent is to move away from students as absorbers of information to students as processors, synthesizers, creators, and users of information; from students being dependent upon the learning system provided to students using the learning system provided. Motivation is frequently intrinsic.	students extend what is learned for application to new situations.
Teacher as leader	The teacher models the importance of subject matter and learning intents by the manner and enthusiasm with which teaching is provided. Modeling dimensions include time (teaching reflects a great deal of effort), feeling (the teacher cares deeply about the content, learning outcomes, and students), and focus (teaching reflects a deep understanding of the subject taught: the whys as well as the whats, the structure of knowledge; and a focus on key issues and dimensions of importance).	Teaching is conceived as a sacred activity which reflects a reverence for the importance of knowledge and of learning as ends in themselves. Through modeling students find teaching and learning to be meaningful and significant and respond with higher levels of motivation and commitment.	Very effective for communicating the importance, meaning, and significance of subject matter and learning intents; for promoting learning attitudes and values in students.

assignments, and other teaching and learning considerations. Objectives are defined for the student but motivation is typically extrinsic. Students are subordinate in the sense that they are not partners in the teaching but objects of the teaching. But teachers are active decision makers who are controlled, who are very much in control provided that they follow the established teaching protocols and the approved executive plan for teaching. This role is most suitable for teaching straightforward subject-matter content and suitable as well for teaching basic skills, though the managerial role would be much more efficient for this purpose.

The remaining two roles, mediator and leader, are associated with higher-level learning and with the development in students of attitudes and commitment to learning as something worthwhile. Decision making is more collaborative and at times resembles the garbage can or the process of muddling through. As mediator the teacher uses interaction or reciprocal teaching strategies which enable students to process new information and new learnings in light of their own personal meanings and experiences and prior learnings. The idea is not to define for the student what the nature or the value of a particular learning experience is but to have the student search for him or herself for this value.

Emphasis is on helping students make sense of learning encounters by constructing new understandings and by linking new to prior learnings. When in the mediating role the teacher helps students interact with information and ideas. Though at times teachers decide the actual learning outcomes of teaching, a balance is sought between teacher-determined and student-determined outcomes. The attempt of this kind of teaching is to move students away from being absorbers of information to being processors, synthesizers, creators, and users of information; from being dependent upon the learning system provided to using the learning system provided. Motivation is frequently intrinsic. The mediating role is very effective for teaching analysis, problem solving, and higher-order skills as well as complex concepts, higher levels of comprehension, and having students extend what is learned to new applications and new situations.

The role of teacher as leader is probably the most important of the four. The idea here is to instill in students a love for, commitment to, and appreciation of learning that carries them not only through their school years but throughout their lives. Here the teacher models the importance of subject matter and learning intents by the manner and enthusiasm with which teaching is provided. Modeling dimensions include time, feeling, and focus. That is, teaching reflects a great deal of effort, the teacher cares deeply about the content, learning outcomes, and students, and teaching reflects a deep understanding of the subject taught. The whys as well as the whats, the structure of knowledge, and key issues and dimensions of importance are emphasized. When this role is successfully implemented teaching is conceived as a sacred activity which reflects a reverence for the importance of knowledge and of learning as ends in themselves. Through modeling, students find teaching and learning to be meaningful and significant and respond with higher levels of motivation and commitment. This role is not independent of the other three but serves as a complement. That is, the qualities of leadership that are part of this role can be in evidence as the teacher assumes the role of manager, executive, or mediator. Different roles are associated with different teaching strategies and with different purposes and learning outcomes.

CHOOSING A TEACHING STRATEGY

Recognizing that in the real world of teaching there are many reasons teachers choose a particular teaching strategy (such as the availability of materials, confidence in the particular method, their own comfort zones, and previous successes) most teachers try, nonetheless, to be fairly deliberate in matching strategy to purpose and desired learning outcome. In his work on developing a "Supervision for Intelligent Teaching," Arthur L. Costa describes four general teaching strategies from which teachers might choose: directive, mediative, generative, and collaborative.[20] Directive strategies help students remember important facts, ideas, and skills. Mediative strategies help develop reasoning, concepts, and problem-solving abilities. Generative strategies help students invent new solutions, insightfulness, and the ability to communicate and extend. And finally, collaborative strategies help students to relate to each other better and to work cooperatively in groups.

The strategies and the goals and objectives for which they seem most appropriate are depicted in Table 7-3. Costa points out that when directive strategies are chosen teachers make virtually all decisions about instruction. They set the goals, decide the methods to be used and the criteria for determining whether teaching has been effective, and are responsible for motivating students. In mediative strategies the general goals are set by teachers but the methods and means are determined by students, and students assume responsibility for coming to grips with the criteria that will determine whether their learning has been successful. The source of motivation in mediative learning is more intrinsic. That is, the teacher relies on the meaningfulness and significance of the learning activity itself as the source of motivation for learning. In generative strategies goals are set by both teacher and student, though the student assumes major responsibility for determining how the goals will be met and how successful completion will be determined. In cooperative strategies goals are set by teacher and student but students as a group assume responsibility for determining how learning will take place and the criteria for success. The source of motivational learning rests with the group and tends to be normative. The Costa framework for supervision and teaching and that of others with similar views is outlined in some detail in the Association for Supervision

---

[20] Art L. Costa, *Supervision for Intelligent Teaching,* Orangevale, Calif.: Search Models Unlimited, 1982.

TABLE 7-3
CHOOSING A TEACHING STRATEGY

When the educational goals are:	And the specific behavioral objectives are to:	The appropriate strategies are:
	I. The directive	
1. Information acquisition	• Know about • Recall • Understand	1. Direct instruction Drill and practice Mastery learning
2. Remember	• Memorize	2. Mnemonics
3. Skill development	• Perform • Demonstrate	3. Rehearsal command
	II. The mediative	
1. Concept development	• Distinguish among • Formulate • Induce • Discover • Conceptualize	1. Concept attainment 2. Concept development
2. Opinion expression	• Express ideas • Consider other's opinions • Articulate • Support ideas with logical evidence	3. Open-ended discussion Circle of knowledge
3. Values awareness	• Become aware of own and other's values • Appreciate values of others when different	4. Values awareness/clarification
4. Problem solving	• Theorize • Test ideas • Validate • Develop a strategy for	5. Inquiry/discovery
	III. The generative	
1. Creativity	• Create	1. Brainstorming
2. Innovation	• Generate	
3. Fluency	• Innovate • Design	2. Creativity
4. Insightfulness	• Develop insight	3. Lateral thinking
5. Productivity	• Elaborate • Illuminate	4. Mind mapping
6. Metaphorical thinking	• Think metaphorically	5. Synectics
	IV. The collaborative	
1. Cooperation	• Cooperate • Participate in group tasks	1. Cooperative learning
2. Interdependence	• Produce insights, solutions, and products through group efforts	2. Role playing Simulations Pair problem solving
3. Socialization	• Develop social skills	3. Class meetings

Source: Arthur L. Costa, *Supervision for Intelligent Teaching: A Course Syllabus,* Orangevale, Calif.: Search Models Unlimited, 1982, pp. 134–135.

and Curriculum Development publication, *Developing Minds: A Resource Book for Teaching Thinking.*[21]

REFLECTIVE PRACTICE IN SUPERVISION AND TEACHING

A reflective practice of supervision and teaching recognizes that no one best way of teaching is inherently better than another. But still, some approaches to teaching are better than others for certain purposes. What then is the basis for choosing one teaching strategy over another? Academically speaking we have suggested that the choice of teaching strategy should reflect a number of characteristics that define the teaching situation. Different student needs and learning styles, different goals and purposes, different motives, different problems, and different desired outcomes should result in the choice of different strategies. The idea is to match strategy with situation. Though most teachers are committed to practice in this way and indeed do try to engage in this matching, other concerns also help determine choice of strategy. These include the teacher's personal preference, needs, previous successes, opinions and pressures from other teachers, likes and dislikes of the supervisor, availability of materials, time, a sense of what will fly with the students, teaching behavior indicators on an evaluation instrument, and other less lofty but nonetheless real concerns. The mix of the two reasons for choosing a particular strategy can come to light as supervisors and teachers work together as colleagues and through conferencing and other techniques within an atmosphere of trust and mutual respect.

Where does this then leave the various models of teaching that are offered to teachers? Even with the best of relationships between supervisor and teacher, how do both come to grips with what makes sense and does not make sense? Should the Hunter lesson cycle, one of the Joyce models, the direct instruction model, informal teaching, or some other model of teaching prevail? Though all the models possess a certain logic and appear scientific when described and arrayed in lists and charts in books such as this, the reality is that rarely does *any* fit exactly as described. In a sense, none of the models of teaching are true, though all can be helpful. They are frames of reference and cognitive maps that can help teachers and supervisors understand better the problems they face and help them make better decisions about how to practice.

An alternative to considering models as being "true" or "false" is to consider relative worth. A model is worthwhile if it helps one understand better the teaching events and situations under study and helps one to make informed decisions about this reality. In considering relative worth it is important to note that no matter how refined a model becomes or how precisely it is translated into practice it cannot enlarge the basic premises upon which it rests. This is the law of conservation of information that is well understood in

---

[21] Art L. Costa, *Developing Minds: A Resource Book for Teaching Thinking,* Alexandria, Va.: Association for Supervision and Curriculum Development, 1985.

the more established sciences. In discussing this law, the Nobel laureate P. B. Medawar states, "No process of logical reasoning . . . no mere act of mind . . . can enlarge the information content of the axioms and premises or observation statements from which it proceeds."[22] Taken literally and applied to all situations the dimensions of any particular model of teaching and supervision provide small premises upon which to base a science of teaching and a practice of supervision.

Models in teaching and supervision are much like windows and walls. As windows they help expand the view of things, resolve issues, provide answers, and give the surer footing one needs to function as a researcher and practicing professional. As walls these same models serve to box one in, to blind one to other views of reality, other understandings, and other alternatives.

In reflective practice supervisors are able to transcend the limitations of windows and walls. They do this by viewing research and practice models metaphorically rather than literally. That is, the models are not conceived as truth designed for application but as thought frames that inform decisions of teachers and supervisors as they practice. This reflective stance is well supported in the literature. Israel Scheffler, for example, states, "The notion that one can confidently proceed by simple deduction from theory to practical recommendations without regard to related theories, auxiliary assumptions, or possible feedback from recalcitrant cases into the theoretical assumptions themselves, is a mistaken notion."[23] On this point he quotes William James, who stated in 1892:

> You make a great, a very great mistake, if you think that psychology, being the science of the mind's laws is something from which you can deduce definite programmes and schemes and methods of instruction for immediate schoolroom use. Psychology is a science, and teaching is an art; and sciences never generate arts directly out of themselves. An intermediary inventive mind must make the application, by using its originality.[24]

Informed intuition and reflective practice are key concepts in understanding the link between knowledge and use. Neither is directly dependent upon models of teaching and supervision but neither can evolve separately from such models.

When supervisors and teachers view teaching-effectiveness, clinical, and other supervisory models reflectively, they are concerned with conceptual rather than instrumental knowledge.[25] This conceptual knowledge considered as part of a broader array of knowledge (i.e., the teacher's motives and intentions, those of the supervisor, idiosyncrasies that define the teaching and

---

[22] P. B. Medawar, *The Limits of Science*, New York: Harper & Row, 1984.
[23] Israel Scheffler, *Reason and Teaching*, New York: Bobbs-Merrill, 1973, p. 185.
[24] Ibid.
[25] Mary M. Kennedy, "How Evidence Alters Understanding and Decision," *Educational Evaluation and Policy Analysis*, vol. 6, no. 2, pp. 207–226, 1984.

learning context under study) becomes professional knowledge when decisions and actions ensue. Professional knowledge in teaching and supervision, therefore, is not the same as the knowledge of research and practice models but is created in use as teachers teach and supervisors supervise. Professional knowledge is an accumulation of the referentially based decisions that professionals make as they practice.

INDICATORS OF GOOD TEACHING

Given what is known about the complexities of teaching and best practice in supervision for classroom effectiveness, is it possible to describe the indicators of good teaching? The answer would be no if one had in mind a technical list of discrete teaching behaviors. The result would be too rationalistic and bureaucratic to be considered credible. But if one viewed teaching as being somewhat analogous to surfing and worked from a professional conception of teaching practice, then a list such as the following might be developed. Try editing the list or developing one of your own in light of your conception of good teaching and the complexities of the real world we describe. The teacher

- Behaves as a decision maker who takes charge of teaching, reflects on his or her practice, and makes defensible choices in light of intents and the requirements of the situation at hand.
- Demonstrates a keen understanding of his or her subject matter (the whys as well as the whats, the structure of the discipline, the wheat from the chaff).
- Relies on the value and interest of the subject matter and on the presentation of same as the primary means by which "classroom management" is achieved.
- Places greater emphasis on intrinsic rather than extrinsic reasons in "motivating" students. When extrinsic is necessary, can demonstrate the usual tricks of the trade in maintaining order and obtaining compliance (skillful monitoring, pacing of instruction, use of behavior modification techniques, etc.).
- Demonstrates a sense of purpose and vision which gives teaching meaning and significance.
- Is able to translate this sense of purpose and vision into operational goals and objectives.
- Uses goals and objectives "strategically" to guide planning and teaching.
- Develops "tactical" goals and objectives which are fixed and rigid for some kinds of teaching (training) but dynamic and evolving for other kinds of teaching (education).
- Aligns teaching to goals *and* goals to teaching as appropriate.
- Monitors and assesses teaching and learning activities and behaviors, making corrections as needed.
- Evaluates outcomes of teaching and learning behaviors and activities for alignment with stated goals as well as goals which emerge from teaching.

- Evaluates for outcomes and other worthwhile happy events not antici-pated prior to and during teaching.
- Knows about and uses available teaching models (direct instruction, teaching for critical thinking, informal teaching, cooperative learning, etc.) as resources (to inform intuition and professional judgment) as "tailored" deci-sions are made in response to the specific teaching and learning context.

As appropriate, students are given assignments that

- Are consistent with teaching intent.
- Provide practice in mastering subject matter.
- Extend the subject matter by requiring application, synthesis, and judg-ment.
- Are engaging, stimulating, and fun.
- Are reasonable with regard to available time and other constraints.
- Are within the capabilities of students to ensure successful completion while remaining challenging and interesting.
- Require the student to be actively engaged in learning.
- Allow students some choice within a carefully planned array of options.

In interacting with students, the teacher is

- Clear with regard to expectations.
- Sensitive to individual differences.
- Challenging to stimulate student interest and achievement.
- Supportive and respectful of the students' humanness.

Classroom climate is characterized by

- A "businesslike" environment in the sense that teachers and students know why they are in the classroom and work hard.
- A comfortable and easy feeling among students and between teacher and students.
- A free exchange of ideas.
- An exchange of helpful and supportive behaviors.
- A sense of community characterized by a common commitment to work together and a sharing of responsibility for making classroom life productive and meaningful.

CHAPTER 8

THE SUPERVISORS' EDUCATIONAL PLATFORM

THROUGHOUT this book we are emphasizing an emerging trend in supervision, what we have labeled Supervision II. This form of supervision attends to what teaching episodes mean to teachers, how students interpret the activity of the teacher, what significance a teacher places on a supervisory intervention, rather than to a prescribed formula of teacher or supervisory behaviors. We are suggesting that the professional's craft, derived from years of trial and error, is based on intuitions from the multiform signals being sent in any given situation. This kind of educator is a "reflective practitioner," one who brings many frames of reference, conceptual blueprints, normative paradigms to bear on a reality that is enormously complex and therefore contains layers of intelligibility.[1]

Besides the technical understandings which emerge from a blend of intuition and conceptual schemata, there is a floor of beliefs, opinions, values, and attitudes which provide a foundation for practice. These beliefs, opinions, values, and attitudes make up what has been called a "platform."[2] Just as a political party is supposed to base its decisions and actions on a party platform, so too educators carry on their work, make decisions, and plan instruction based on their educational platform. When a teacher is asked why a child was disciplined in a certain way, he or she frequently will respond with a generalization about how all children should be disciplined. When asked about the social usefulness of learning a certain lesson, a teacher frequently will frame his or her explanation according to a set of more general beliefs about the socialization of children.

A teacher's platform is rarely explicit. Neither is it static or one-dimensional. It is derived from life experiences, from formal education, and especially from trial-and-error experience in classrooms. Teachers are not accustomed to pause before walking into their first class of the day and recall the five or ten elements of their platform. Rather their platform is seen, if at all, in their patterns and habitual ways of interacting with students.

Whether or not a platform position is right or wrong is not the issue here. Knowing *what* the platform position is, understanding the relationship between teaching practices and platform elements, perceiving inconsistencies be-

---

[1] Donald A. Schön, *The Reflective Practitioner*, New York: Basic Books, 1983.
[2] Decker Walker, "A Naturalistic Model for Curriculum Development," *School Review*, vol. 80, no. 1, pp. 51–65. 1971.

tween platform and practice, appreciating differences between one's own platform and that of another—these are the points of emphasis in this chapter. Both teacher and supervisor need to know what their respective platforms are. They need to examine where they agree and where they differ and whether the differences are so substantial as to interfere with the growth goals of the supervisory episode. They also need to examine whether the teaching practice is sufficiently versatile to fulfill the requirements of the platform position. Finally, in the effort to encourage reflection in practice, teachers and supervisors need to take the time to articulate their platform. Most teachers tend to resist the exercise simply because they are not used to making their platform explicit. They simply act according to the feel of the situation. Yet when they do write out their platform, they experience the satisfaction of naming what they do and why they do it. Greater sense of task identity and task significance strengthens motivation, satisfaction, and commitment to one's work.[3]

What follows are several examples of at least partially developed platforms. In practice, a teacher's platform might take more of a narrative, or more of a disjointed style than the examples below. What is presented here is more a skeletal form, which tends to focus on the primary emphasis of the platform.

BASIC COMPETENCY PLATFORM

1 The purpose of schooling is to ensure a minimal competency in prescribed skills and understandings for all children. Enrichment of students' learning beyond these minimum competencies is an important but secondary aim of schooling.
2 Schools can make a great difference in the achievement of these minimum competencies; people who do not achieve them end up as unproductive citizens living on the margins of society.
3 Present and future civic and employment demands point to the absolute necessity of acquiring basic competencies. Mastery of these competencies will assist the person in other areas of personal and social growth.
4 The educator's job is to construct a highly organized environment to promote the gradual mastery of basic competencies in reading, writing, computation, and scientific processes. This implies a careful definition of learning objectives for each major unit of an intentionally sequenced series of learnings, careful assessment of entry-level skills and understandings with built-in correction of start-up deficiencies, careful monitoring of student progress with built-in remediation phases, a requirement of mastery before moving on to the next unit, and a sequential progression to broader and deeper levels of mastery of the competencies as defined by graduation requirements.
5 Almost all students, except a small percentage of more severely disabled

---

[3] J. Richard Hackman and Greg R. Oldham, "Motivation through the Design of Work: Test of a Theory," *Organizational Behavior and Human Performance*, vol. 16, p. 256, 1976.

children, are capable of mastery levels of learning in these minimum competencies, given sufficient time and appropriate instruction.

6 The most significant factor in learning is "time on task." This means that much of class time will be spent on drills and exercises that strengthen the target competency, that additional time will be afforded to those students needing it, and that daily homework will be assigned on the target competency.

7 While one approach to learning a competency may be initially stressed, alternative methodologies will be employed for students experiencing difficulty.

8 Higher-level learnings and cultural enrichment activities will tend to receive less attention, especially in the earlier grades, except for those students who have achieved mastery of the minimum competencies.

9 Classroom discipline will be controlled more by the intense concentration on the learning task than by teachers' imposition of punishments and repetition of rules.

10 All the reward systems of the school should serve to promote academic achievement as the highest priority. Rewards for other desirable behaviors or achievement should be secondary to this priority.

SCHOOLING THE SOCIAL DRAMA PLATFORM

1 Schools prepare young people for the social drama of public life. Adult life involves people in a number of social roles, roles such as worker, neighbor, citizen and voter, consumer, tourist, group member, cultural participant, etc. Schools prepare youngsters for the social drama by exposing them to the scripts, the language, the costuming, the cues, the spoken and unspoken rules, ways of framing situations, perspective-taking, etc. The challenge, of course, is somehow to be a real person while playing one's part in the social drama, to retain one's autonomy and spontaneity while keeping the social drama moving forward.

2 Youngsters need to learn large blocks of the plot of the drama, such things as the economics, the history, the ecology, and the geography of the social drama, in order to make intelligent decisions while playing their part in the drama. They are made aware that the social drama is a human construct, and as such can be changed to ensure a better outcome for the characters in the play. They are urged to take responsibility for the social drama.

3 Youngsters also need to master the language and symbols used in expressing their roles.

4 Youngsters also need to develop into authentic characters in the play; hence they need to be able to improvise on the cultural scripts they are given. Improvisation and personal appropriation of one's script will be a learning that runs throughout the curriculum.

5 Teaching involves aspects of coaching, in which teachers help individual

groups of youngsters to play out scenes in the drama. Teaching also involves directing a whole class in a variety of rehearsals of the drama. Teachers are also critics who comment on the actors' performance. And finally, teachers are themselves players in the drama, who teach by the example of their own performance.

HUMAN GROWTH PLATFORM

1 Students are unlike input factors in system designs of industrial or military organizations; for example, they are not pieces of steel that arrive at the "input station" all neatly measured and stable. Steel, wood, and stone do not grow and change during the very time when the production worker is trying to manipulate them. Students do.

2 The school makes a difference in a child's growth, but not *that* much difference. If the school were nonexistent, other influences and experiences would "educate" the child. Besides, human beings are dynamic and constantly growing. The school simply speeds up the growth process and channels it in supposedly beneficial directions, rather than leaving the student to random, trial-and-error growth.

3 Curricular-instructional programs should be designed in conformity with the growth patterns of students. The human growth needs of students should never be subordinated to objectives dictated by the needs of society and the demands of the discipline. Theoretically, these three concerns—human growth, achievement of disciplined skills and knowledge, and fulfillment of social responsibilities—should not be in conflict. In practice, however, they frequently are in conflict, and the concern for human growth usually is the one to be sacrificed.

4 The educator's primary function is to become obsolete. The job of the educator is to so influence students that the students will gradually but eventually reach the point where they do not need the teacher, where they can pursue their own learning on the basis of their acquired knowledge and skills.

5 *Active* pursuit of knowledge and understanding, an actual dialogue with reality, will produce the most significant and long-lasting types of learning. Whenever possible, therefore, the student must actively search, actively inquire, actively discover, and actively organize and integrate. The teacher's job is to guide and direct this activity toward specified goals.

DEMOCRATIC SOCIALIZATION PLATFORM

1 The primary aim of education is to enable the individual to function in society. Assuming a democratic society, the school should promote not only those qualities necessary for survival (employment, getting along with people, managing one's financial affairs, being a responsible family person, etc.) but also those qualities necessary for a healthy democratic

society (political involvement that seeks the common good, willingness to displace self-interest for a higher purpose, skills at community building and conflict resolution, an understanding of how the political process works and how to influence public policy, etc.).

2 The school should intentionally arrange itself so that learning takes place primarily in a community context. Students should be taught to collaborate on learning tasks rather than compete with one another. Team projects, peer tutoring, group rewards, and discussion of community problems should have priority even while encouraging the development of individual talents. Individual talents, however, should be prized more for what they contribute to the community than for the exclusive enrichment of the individual.

3 Learning is best nurtured in a community context. Language skills are developed by regular and varied group communication. A sense of history and culture is nurtured by a focus on the group's history and culture. Psychological needs such as self-esteem and assertiveness are best met through active involvement in the community. Acceptance of differences and the development of individuality are negotiated best when there is a sense of community. Values, laws, and social customs are best taught within the context of the community.

4 The educator stands within the learning community and yet holds a special place of authority. The educator facilitates and directs the learning tasks of the younger members of the community but allows the agenda of community dynamics to intrude on the more academic tasks when the need arises.

5 Teachers and students function best when they work in relatively small, relatively self-contained, relatively autonomous learning communities. Hence, those schools with large enrollments should be broken down into manageable learning communities that allow for closer and more continuous contact between a team of teachers and their students.

6 The curriculum should be controlled by a set of schoolwide learning outcomes for each year, but the learning community should have considerable autonomy in the ways it achieves these outcomes. The teams of teachers should be accountable for promoting required learnings but should be allowed to devise the particular learning activities that best address the students in their communities.

7 Wherever possible, the learning communities should be involved with the larger civic community through parental involvement, by using the civic community as a learning laboratory, by discussing problems in the civic community, and by promoting the value of community service.

THE CRITICAL AWARENESS PLATFORM

1 Traditionally, schools reproduce the unequal relationships found in society; schools also promote the perspectives of vested interests in the

larger society. In both the language of the curriculum as well as its content one finds stereotypes, cultural/racial/ethnic and gender bias, blind spots, and distortions. To counteract this, students should be taught a "hermeneutics of suspicion," that is, a way of questioning the official curriculum by asking: Whose interests are being served by this point of view? Who is in charge of defining the world as working in this particular way? What perspectives are left out? What are the relationships of this knowledge with social and political power?

2 Schools traditionally teach as though knowledge is "out there" waiting to be grasped by the inquiring mind. Rather, knowledge is produced by elites as a way of describing a reality which places them in a position of privilege, power, and control. True knowledge is acquired through taking action on the problems in one's life and then reflecting on the consequences.

3 Schools traditionally require students to be passive reproducers of the knowledge made available to them. Rather, they should actively create knowledge that is useful for living. Learning, moreover, should flow from dialogue, from imaginative inquiries into social possibilities, and from debate about current realities.

4 Schools traditionally stress individual achievement in competition with peers. Rather, they should stress cooperation and collective action, which encourages each student to make a contribution to the life of the community. Out of that group activity will emerge the knowledge of what is necessary for further emancipatory activity.

5 School learning should involve a struggle to define meanings in the face of cultural definitions of truth which are simply contemporary methods of containment and control; schooling should involve the questioning of the power structure within the school, which disenfranchises some students from the start.

6 Pedagogy belongs to the realm of politics. One teaches either on the side of the oppressors or on the side of the oppressed. Hence teaching will always involve going beyond the surface of the curriculum to the underlying social and political structural dynamics that support competing interpretations of the curriculum materials being presented. Specific strategies include debate, role-playing various power relationships, investigative reporting, problematizing everyday experience, inquiring into alternative possibilities.

AN ECOLOGICAL PLATFORM

1 The primary reality is neither the individual nor human society, but the entire ecosphere. Hence, the survival demands of the ecosphere and the concomitant implications for human society should comprise the primary focus of schooling.

2 Human culture can be understood analogously in ecological imagery.

Human beings live within a culture as organisms in a natural environment of food chains, cycles of life, and rhythms of seasons. Human beings understand themselves as human through the rituals, traditions, artifacts, and relationships that are elements of a living culture. Hence schools, besides teaching the primary systems and structures of the ecosphere, should teach the cultural ecology by which human survival and development is possible.

3 The individual does not stand outside of the natural or cultural environment; rather, the individual is embedded in the natural and cultural environment. Human fulfillment does not consist in escaping from this environment but in discovering harmonious ways to live with those two environments. Hence learning itself is a discovery of one's relationship to and embeddedness in the cultural and natural environment.

4 The social purposes of schooling are not so much to achieve technical control over nature or to master the culture in the service of some instrumental purpose, but to overcome those social practices and social arrangements which destroy the natural and cultural environment. This is achieved by continuously exploring those public policies and practices which sustain and respect the natural rhythms and patterns of nature and culture. Ethnocentric, nationalistic, sexist, racist, and all exploitative relationships deny the unity and integrity of the natural and human environment. When society harms the environment, it literally harms, as well, itself; similarly, when society damages the natural bonds between human beings, it damages itself. People are inextricably embedded in their cultural bonds; those bonds support humanity and feed the human spirit. People's understanding of who they are collectively is embedded in their culture.

5 Knowledge, then, is not something one individual achieves or possesses. It is rather the achievement and heritage and energy of all human beings. When one knows something, one knows it as one's culture names it. One knows something because the relationships which are grasped in knowledge contain oneself as much as one contains those relationships. Human beings always know much more than they can articulate because most knowledge is tacit and is experienced at subliminal levels of intuition. The human body knows at least as much as the human mind does; the mind has different ways of articulating that knowledge than the body does.

6 Relationships to the environment and culture are known through experience. Using a language to describe those relationships frames those relationships in ways that distort as well as clarify. Language is not a neutral tool for expression; language carries interpretations constructed and imposed by the culture. Hence, part of the task of schools is to make explicit the point of view embedded in taken-for-granted cultural understandings. Everyday language contains many class, sexist, rationalistic, economic, and ethnocentric distortions which in turn reveal distortions and

disharmonies between human beings and the natural environment, within the culture, and within human beings themselves.

7 The classroom itself represents an artificial cultural ecology which distorts how youngsters view the natural environment, how they view themselves, how they view science and rationality. Current school curricula promote values that are antithetical to both the survival of the ecosphere and the cultural unity and integrity of the human race. Hence the pedagogy employed and the curriculum and the assessment of learning must be transformed to reflect the survival demands of both the natural and the human environment.

ELEMENTS OF A PLATFORM

In stressing the importance of the teacher explicating his or her own platform, we realize that many teachers will find the exercise difficult. Their platform statements may or may not come out as clearly as the ones contained in this chapter. On the other hand, the effort to elucidate one's platform can help the teacher become more reflective about her or his practice. Such reflection can help teachers puzzle their way through instructional problems which their intuitions cannot solve. It also enables teachers to acknowledge some inconsistencies in their practice which, although not previously acknowledged consciously, may have created an occasional sense of dissatisfaction. Recognizing such inconsistencies opens up the space for changes in practice.

Furthermore, platform clarification brings greater, explicit intelligibility to what a teacher does in class everyday. It gives teachers names and words for telling their story. It enables them to talk with greater clarity among themselves, with parents, and with supervisors about what they do. The examples of platforms summarized above, provide some idea of what a platform entails. In general terms we may say that a platform contains, more or less, eight elements. All platforms need not contain all these elements; some may be expressed more in narrative form, some in a sequence of terse sentences; some may be better expressed in pictures or cartoons. Furthermore, platforms need not be cast in stone. From year to year, new elements will be added, or some stressed more than others. The important thing is to have a sense of what one's platform is, rather than to construct a prize-winning statement for the school board.

General Elements of a Platform

1 *The aims of education.* Set down, in order of priority (if possible), the three most important aims of education—not simply education in the abstract, but education for the youngsters in your school system.

2 *Major achievements of students this year.* Bring these aims down to more specific application; identify the major achievements of students by the end of the year. (For example, mastery of some academic skills up to a

certain level; the acquisition of certain basic principles that would govern behavior; more personal achievements, such as increased self-awareness or self-confidence, or trust and openness.)

3 *The social significance of the student's learning.* Some teachers emphasize vocational learning; or the utilization of learning for good citizenship; or the acquisition of a particular cultural heritage.

4 *The image of the learner.* This element tries to uncover attitudes or assumptions about how one learns. Is the learner an empty vessel into which one pours information? Some may view the learner in a uniform way—as though all learners are basically the same and will respond equally to a uniform pedagogy. Some may use "faculty" psychology to explain how students learn. Some will focus on operant conditioning; others on targeting instruction to the cognitive developmental stages of concrete operations. Still others will differentiate among various styles and dispositions for learning that point to a greater emphasis on individualization of learning.

5 *The image of the curriculum.* This element touches upon attitudes about *what* the student learns. Some say that the most important learnings are those most immediately useful in "real" life. Others say that any kind of learning is intrinsically valuable. Others qualify the latter position and consider some learnings, such as the humanities, to be intrinsically more valuable because they touch upon more central areas of our culture. Others would claim that the learning of subjects has value only insofar as it categorizes people of different abilities and interests and channels them in socially productive directions. Some might even claim that the curriculum helps youngsters to understand God better.

6 *The image of the teacher.* What basically is a teacher? Is a teacher an employee of the state, following the educational policies and practices dictated by the local, state, and federal government? Or is a teacher a professional specialist whom a community employs to exercise his or her expertise on behalf of youngsters? Or is a teacher a spokesperson for tradition, passing on the riches of the culture? Or is a teacher a political engineer, leading youngsters to develop those skills necessary to reform their society? This element tries to elicit assumptions about the role of the teacher.

7 *The preferred pedagogy.* Will the teacher dominate the learning experience? Some assume that inquiry learning is the best way to teach. Others assume that each discipline lends itself better to some forms of pedagogy than others. Some would opt for a much more permissive, student-initiated learning enterprise. While there would understandably be some reluctance to focus on *one* pedagogical approach to the exclusion of all others, nonetheless, teachers tend to settle on two or three as the more effective approaches.

8 *The preferred school climate.* This element brings various environmental considerations into play, such as the affective tone to schoolwide and

classroom discipline, feelings of student pride in the school, faculty morale, the openness of the school community to divergent lifestyles, expressive learnings, and individualistic ways of thinking and behaving. Some would describe an environment reflective of a learning community: open, caring, inquisitive, flexible, collaborative. Some would opt for order and predictability. Others would prefer a more relaxed climate, perhaps more boisterous but also more creative and spontaneous. This element is very much related to what is valued in the curriculum and to the social consequences of learning.

It becomes obvious to teachers when they test out their assumptions under each of the categories listed above that there tends to be an intrinsic logic to them. That is, there tends to be a consistency between assumptions about the nature of the learner and the preferred kind of teacher-student relationship, which in turn relates logically to teachers' beliefs about the aims of education. As educators clarify their assumptions, beliefs, and opinions under each of these eight categories, the platform they use in practice should become apparent to them. That is to say, educators usually make practical decisions about professional practice based upon convictions, assumptions, and attitudes which are not clearly or frequently articulated. Nevertheless, they do influence, some would even say dominate, actions. By bringing these convictions, assumptions, and attitudes out into the open for their own reflection, educators can evaluate internal consistency and cogency. They can also check whether they are satisfied with their platform, or whether, perhaps, they have not taken important factors into consideration. By clarifying the underlying intelligibility of their actions, educators might see a need to grow in specific areas in order to increase their effectiveness as well as to broaden their human capacities.

THE SUPERVISOR'S PLATFORM

The above analysis of key elements in a platform deals with an educational platform. This educational platform focuses on what one believes ought to happen in a process of formal education. It could belong to a teacher, a student, an administrator, or a supervisor. The supervisor can elaborate his or her own educational platform, but it becomes complete when the supervisor adds his or her beliefs about the activity of supervising. Two categories that concern supervision are the following: the purpose of supervision and the preferred process of supervision.

1 *The purpose or goal of supervision.* Some would answer from a neoscientific orientation. Others would speak from a human relations perspective. Some would tend to stress the moral activity of teacher empowerment and enriched student learning.

2 *The preferred process of supervision.* Some would express a preference for

the clinical supervision approach. Others would prefer a more eclectic process that responds to the contingencies of the situation.

Again, the point of clarifying one's convictions and unspoken assumptions about the nature of supervision is to open the door for growth, for the sharing of ideas, and for supervisory performance grounded in basic beliefs. Ideally, these last two elements of the supervisor's platform should be written down before one reads this book, and again after one has read the book. If the analysis of supervision presented between these covers has an effect, it would show up in the differences between the two platform statements.

APPROACHES TO PLATFORM CLARIFICATION

Many teachers may find the initial efforts at platform clarification very frustrating. It is not something they do often, and there can be a feeling of awkwardness. Yet everyone has an unexpressed platform. Were a sensitive observer to follow a teacher around for a day or two on the job, it would be relatively easy to guess that teacher's beliefs about how youngsters learn best, about what is important to learn, about good teaching and inferior teaching, and so on. People's actions usually reveal their assumptions and attitudes quite clearly.

Two different approaches offer supervisors and teachers a way to construct their platforms. One approach would be to work with all the teachers or a group of them in a staff-development format. The other approach would entail a supervisor and a teacher working in a one-on-one situation.

Group Approaches to Educational Platform Development

In a staff-development framework, supervisors can work with a group of teachers. Some explanation of what platforms are and how platform clarification might assist their practice should be given. Examples of platforms should then be provided. Teachers would then write out their own platform. They should be encouraged to try out a unifying image or metaphor around which all their platform elements might cluster. David Hunt, in his work with teachers, has found that metaphors help teachers bring out the theory embedded in their practice.[4] Metaphors of teaching such as guiding a journey, conducting an orchestra, pulling rabbits out of a hat, mining gold, tending a garden, captaining a ship, and directing a play contain beliefs and assumptions about learning, curriculum, social purposes of schooling, and pedagogy. Many others find the orderly process of filling out where they stand on the eight elements of the platform the most convenient beginning for the exercise. After the first draft, they may want to rearrange and amplify. Putting words onto paper may then enable them to see their guiding metaphor. Teachers can also check

---

[4] David E. Hunt, *Beginning with Ourselves*, Cambridge, Mass.: Brookline Books, 1987.

the internal consistency between elements of the platform and note points to pursue with themselves or with others during subsequent exercises. Others will prefer a less structured approach, letting their assumptions come out as they are felt and recognized, rather than having to force them into categories with which they are uncomfortable.

Some find it helpful to find a quiet place to write down their reflections. Normally, these thoughts will come out in no particular order of priority. Once teachers have written down the elements of their platform, they can with further reflection begin to group them in clusters and place them in some order of importance. Almost everyone with any experience in education, however, will feel several times during this exercise the need to qualify and add nuance to those general statements: "Which teaching strategy I'd use in a given situation depends a lot on a youngster's background. But by and large, I'd choose this approach." "While I'd place my major emphasis on mastery of basic intellectual skills, I still think it's important to spend some time teaching kids good manners." "I almost always prefer to start a lesson with a colorful advance organizer. That usually stirs up the pupils' curiosity. But there are times when I run plain, old-fashioned memory drills."

Others will find the writing exercise too tedious and will seek out a colleague with whom to discuss this whole question. The free flow of shared ideas frequently stimulates the process of clarification. In those instances, a tape recorder may help for subsequent transcription of the conversation. Others may find a combination of dialogue and writing the better way. Still others may refer to a formal statement of goals that the school or system has in print to begin the process. By studying the goals and *probing the assumptions behind them*, the teacher may discover areas of disagreement or agreement.

However teachers go about clarifying their platform initially, two other steps will prove helpful. After the first tentative statement of the platform, the teachers should compare their platform with two or three colleagues, to test out areas of agreement or disagreement. Sometimes this may lead to modification of their own platforms. It may also lead to a greater acceptance of diversity of perspectives. It certainly will help teachers to build teamwork. Knowing the biases behind one another's approach will enable teachers to work together in areas where they agree or might complement one another.

When the teachers have discussed their platforms together, they should then compare them with the school's or the system's platform. That may not exist in a written document, but, as in their own cases, it exists implicitly in the operational policies of the school or school system. They may find some genuine discrepancies between what the school's goal statements profess and what the school practices. Bringing those discrepancies to light, in itself, would be a service to the school. The purpose of examining the expressed and unexpressed (but operative) platforms of the school, however, is aimed more at a comparison between the school's platform and the teachers' platforms. If they find striking divergences between them, then the teachers and supervisors will have to seek some means of reconciling the discrepancies, modifying one or the other to make them more compatible.

The point of this exercise is not to introduce frustration and cynicism, but, on the contrary, to reduce it. If supervisors and teachers are to work toward restructuring the educational process in their schools and school systems, then this exercise may be a good place to begin. As Michael Fullan suggests, school improvement and classroom improvement necessarily overlap, and teachers must be continuously involved with both levels of improvement.[5]

The group activity with platforms can continue on to a variety of discussions. Teachers may use the discussions as a basis for considering curriculum restructuring as well as new configurations for instructional space and time arrangements. They might also use the sharing of their platforms as a launching pad for discussions about including other student learning outcomes which their present teaching is ignoring or slighting, or other ways of evaluating student learning. These follow-up discussions will depend on the particular context and frame of mind the teachers are in, or on perceived student or professional needs within the school. Discussions about platforms among groups of teachers, while worthwhile in themselves, also can lead to a variety of additional staff-development initiatives.

Individual Use of Platform Development

Supervisors can also use the group platform exercise to work with individual teachers. Discussions about the teacher's platform enable both supervisor and teacher to clarify what teaching episodes mean to the teacher. Such discussions can enable teachers and supervisors to interpret and explore possibilities within such teaching episodes and series of episodes. Making one's platform explicit also enables both supervisor and teacher to explore discrepancies between the teacher's platform in theory and the platform in use. That is to say, in particular instances, teachers may act in class in contradiction to their stated platform. Supervisors and teachers then have to discuss the apparent discrepancy and see whether such practices need to be changed to conform to their stated platform. The emphasis here is not so much on correcting faults, however, as it is on clarifying the intelligibility and intentionality of the teacher's work with youngsters. As teachers become more reflective about their work, under the influence of exercises like platform clarification, they will grow in their sense of consistency and in their responsiveness to students as well. Moreover, through discussions about the teacher's platform, supervisors will be working out of a framework of collegial conversation with the teacher based on the teacher's language and perspectives, rather than a framework of

---

[5] Michael G. Fullan, "Staff Development, Innovation, and Institutional Development," in Bruce Joyce (ed.), *Changing School Culture Through Staff Development*, Alexandria, Va.: Association for Supervision and Curriculum Development, 1990, pp. 3–25.

some generalized format for teaching. Such a basis of understanding between supervisor and teacher facilitates ongoing positive conversations, which teachers can feel comfortable with because they are dealing with their own agenda rather than a bureaucratic agenda of filling out forms containing categories constructed by someone else.

SUMMARY

In this chapter we have taken up the concept of the educational platform. When examples of educational platforms were given, it became apparent that a platform is made up of those basic assumptions, beliefs, attitudes, and values that are the underpinnings of an educator's behavior. It also became apparent that the platform tends to shape the educator's everyday practice. By encouraging teachers to clarify their platform, supervisors can stimulate a variety of teacher reflections on their practice. Some of these reflections can take place in a group setting, generating possibilities for restructuring the work of the school. Other reflections on practice in the light of the platform can take place on an individual basis. Such reflection can provide some common language and understanding between supervisor and teacher out of which can grow new insight into teaching and new possibilities for student learning.

CHAPTER 9

CURRICULUM CONCERNS
FOR SUPERVISORY
LEADERSHIP

SUPERVISION conducted in a school conceived as a community of learners brings supervisors and teachers together to reflect on questions concerning the curriculum. Sometimes curriculum is distinguished from instruction.[1] Glatthorn and others in the field would insist that since the teacher fashions the curriculum into a usable form for instruction, it cannot be separated from its embodiment in the teacher's instruction.[2] For our purposes we believe it is possible to distinguish curriculum as multiple realities, each of which is different, yet each of which bears something in common with the other. It is possible to speak of curriculum as planned, curriculum as taught, curriculum as learned, curriculum as tested, and curriculum as evaluated. In this chapter, we shall consider the supervisor and teacher reflecting on the curriculum as planned and as taught, primarily. In the next chapter, we will consider the supervisor and teacher reflecting on the curriculum as tested and as evaluated.

OBSERVING INSTRUCTIONAL ACTIVITY

Suppose you are having a busy day supervising. You visit the classes of five physics teachers. You discover that each teacher is using quite different methodologies. One teacher has divided the class into small groups that spend most of the time discussing what kind of experiments they would have to construct to study light as a particle and light as a wave. In another, the teacher is showing an animated cartoon that illustrates the different properties of light, and concludes by leaving the students in a quandary over which theory of light is correct. This teacher assigns groups of students to teams that will argue one point of view against the other. In another class, the teacher is relating Newtonian particle physics to individualistic theories of society, and contrasting that with field theory physics and more communal views of society; toward the end of class the students get into a lively discussion of the low level of student morale and the prevailing tendencies of people at the school to "do

---

[1] See the influential essay by Mauritz Johnson, "Definitions and Models in Curriculum Theory," *Educational Theory*, vol. 17, no. 2, pp. 127–140, 1967.

[2] Alan Glatthorn, *Curriculum Renewal*, Alexandria, Va.: Association for Supervision and Curriculum Development, 1987; Walter Doyle, "Classroom Knowledge as a Foundation for Teaching," *Teachers College Record*, vol. 91, no. 3, pp. 347–360. Spring 1990.

their own thing." In the fourth class you find the students in the physics laboratory performing an experiment with a ripple tank, carefully following the instructions in their lab books and recording their measurements carefully in their notebooks. There is no class discussion; the teacher merely walks around the lab, occasionally pointing out a faulty measurement notation or telling one student team to stop "goofing off." In the fifth class the students have been reading a biography of Isaac Newton and the teacher has assigned teams to prepare a model replication of Newton's laboratory. The class begins with the teacher questioning the students about the antecedent scientific knowledge to which Newton had access that might have shaped much of Newton's approach to his experiments.

You come back to your office at the end of the day with a half hour before you must leave to referee a basketball game in the league quarter finals. Tomorrow you are scheduled for individual conferences with all the teachers you have observed today. Besides the routine aspects of class management and pupil attentiveness, what will you say about the approach each teacher is using, especially as that relates to the school's curriculum? Granting the observable strengths and weaknesses of each teacher in putting on the instructional performance (self-confidence, good tone of voice, good use of questions, etc.), can you say that one approach was better than another? If you say none of the approaches is necessarily better, do you mean that they are all interchangeable, that it does not really matter which approach one uses? Or does each approach originate from a different idea of what the curriculum actually is or is supposed to be? Are these approaches mutually exclusive? Is the content learned in one approach totally different from the content learned in another? Or are there some common learnings one finds embedded in each approach? Is it fair to give one departmental exam covering material taught in such divergent ways? How would these students score on a national physics test? Does it make much difference to you if the teacher does not care much about national test scores? Before you begin to sort out these vexing questions, the bell rings and you must dash over to the gym to catch the bus for the basketball tournament.

Leaving this distraught supervisor, it is now time to return to a more dispassionate and reflective environment to put some order, sequence, and logic into this task. You might begin by asking yourself, "What were some of the questions that did *not* occur to the frantic supervisor?" It might be a good test of your own frame of reference if you were to pause at this point, close the book, and place yourself in the situation, without the press of time and the basketball game distracting you. Perhaps you could generate 10 other questions of major importance. After you write them down in the random order in which they occur to you, you might order or group them in some sequence, for example, from the more abstract to the more particular, or from those dealing with curriculum to those dealing with student achievement, to those dealing with the teacher's platform, and so on. Then ask yourself what you would do the next day in your conferences with each of these teachers.

OTHER QUESTIONS

An exercise such as the above will yield a variety of results. One salutary effect of going through the exercise and then sharing the results with others is that you quickly recognize how many potentially useful questions there are. It becomes clear that classroom observation must be preceded by at least one lengthy conference in which the teacher can indicate what his or her intentions for the class are.

Our own first attempt to complete the exercise yielded the following questions. They are by no means exhaustive. You will see subsequently that the kinds of questions you ask will emerge out of a variety of frames of reference about curriculum. But for the present, consider the following questions for purposes of illustration.

1 *Constancy of instructional methods.* Does the teacher always or usually use this method? If the teacher uses other methods, what are they? Are they related to specific curricular objectives, or are they used primarily to relieve boredom (which could also be a curriculum objective)?

2 *Instructional activity and curriculum-instructional objectives.* What is the teacher trying to do? Is the teacher trying to teach one thing or several things simultaneously? What precisely is it that she or he wants to teach? Was that clear to you? Was it clear to the students? Why did the teacher choose this precise activity as the best or, at least, as a good means to bring the students into a learning encounter with the curricular material?

3 *Effectiveness.* In your judgment, was the instruction effective? How effective was it? Was it effective for all the students or only for some?

4 *Continuity.* How does what the teacher is doing today flow out of what the students have been doing in previous classes? Is there a sequential order to the course, and if so, how does this part fit into the sequence? How much time does the teacher plan to spend on this matter of theories of light? To what level of mastery does the teacher wish to bring the students? Is the time being spent adequate for this purpose? Is that degree of mastery required to grasp the material coming later? Is there a balance between the time spent on this topic and the time spent on earlier and later topics? Who decides that? Who ought to decide that?

5 *Hidden curriculum.* Is the teacher aware of the hidden, or informal, curricula involved in this approach?

6 *Curriculum-instructional units and departmental or school objectives.* How do this class and this course fit in with the departmental or school objectives? Is there a particular focus or emphasis to the objectives that each course is supposed to reinforce? If so, was there evidence of that reinforcement in this class? Why does the department or school support, or at least tolerate, such divergent methods of teaching? Are there specific objectives that are served by these different approaches? Are these approaches the only methods encouraged in the department or school, or are there others?

7 *Curriculum-as-taught and teacher platforms.* How does this approach fit with the teacher's platform? Are there obvious discrepancies between the observable behavior and the platform? If there are, are there legitimate reasons for the discrepancies? If you knew nothing about the teacher's platform prior to the observation, could you infer what it was from the instructional activity you observed? How does the teaching method fit with your (the supervisor's) platform? Are you aware of your level of comfort or discomfort, pleasure or displeasure over the fit or lack of it? Did these feelings, perhaps unacknowledged during the classroom observation, lead either to perceptions of only weak points of the class or perceptions of only strong points? Do you need to review your observations to weed out at least some of the bias that comes from your own platform?

8 *Student readiness.* If you knew nothing of what preceded this class, what could you infer that students already knew about the topic? What could you infer about their possession of skills and understandings necessary for learning the topic of the class?

9 *Performance indicators of student learnings.* What are students expected to do with the material presented? What observable activity indicates that they got the point of the lesson?

10 *Point of view.* What perspective on the subject matter does the teacher imply (e.g., what is the view of science presented, the view of scientific activity, the view of scientific knowledge)?

11 *Connection to real life.* What is the connection of the material presented to real life as the students might experience it? Were those connections elicited? Were analogies between the material and other realities made?

By comparing your questions with these and those developed by others, you may begin to see some pattern or points of emphasis developing. But where do these questions come from, and why are they important? A little reflection will indicate that many of them come from your concepts or beliefs about the nature of learning, about what a curriculum is supposed to be, about the nature of the academic discipline, about ways to structure learning sequences, and so on. These questions are implied in an educational platform. These are the kinds of questions supervisors might ask of teachers. The ensuing conversations about these questions constitute a desirable, reflective type of post-observation conference that is appropriate in a learning community. The teacher's responses to these questions will reveal the kind of classroom knowledge which constitutes the teacher's understanding and enactment of the curriculum. The teacher's response will also reveal the quality of the teacher's reflective practice.

TEACHERS' REFLECTIVE PRACTICE

Donald Schön's work on the reflective practice of expert professionals has caused widespread interest among teacher educators and researchers into teacher practice.[3] The widespread interest in reflective practice has also spawned some misapprehensions of what Schön meant by the term.[4] Schön emphasizes that the traditional understanding of how professionals work, namely that they take theoretical knowledge learned in their own professional studies and apply that knowledge to individual cases they encounter in their practice, is erroneous. His studies show that expert practitioners generate knowledge as they engage in the particulars of a case, spontaneously forming intuitions about what is called for in a given situation. Those intuitions are formed through experience of successes and failures in their past practice. Their theoretical knowledge, such as it affects their practice, is tacit; only after the fact, when questioned by others, can they come up with explanations of their actions which are framed in intelligible theory. Even then, they may not be able to express all they know in a given situation, because so much is assumed in the activity of their practice. Their reflective practice is reflection in action; that is, it takes place *in* the action, simultaneously *with* the action. Schön did not mean reflection *on* action, which usually takes place after the fact, either alone or in discussion with a colleague. When the professional is dealing with another person or a group of people, the activity takes place in active dialogue with the client(s) being served or treated. Thus, as the professional's treatment of the client unfolds, it involves instantaneous feedback and exchange of information, so that the treatment is continually being shaped by the response of the client to the action of the professional. Thus, reflection is a kind of intense presence to the person being served, and to all the cues that are being sent in response to the initiatives of the professional. Hence, the practitioner knows what is going on in the action he or she is performing and knows the effect those actions are having on the client.

Applying this understanding of reflective practice to the supervisor-teacher relationship, you can see how the supervisor engages the teacher in the post-observation conference in reflection on the observed classroom episode, so that the supervisor can understand the *teacher's* reflective practice—the knowledge/intuitions-in-action—of that classroom episode. The supervisor is also assisting the teacher to reflect on the teacher's own reflective practice. Hence a double reflection is going on here, in which the teacher is reflecting on and explicitating his or her own tacit knowledge that was operative in the teaching activity of the observed class—in other words, the teacher reflects on the reflective practice. This exercise helps both the supervisor and the teacher to understand the tacit knowledge influencing the teacher's action in the classroom, and to see whether that tacit knowledge is reasonably accurate, adequately responsive to the students in that classroom episode, and appropriate to the curriculum outcomes being sought.

[3] Donald Schön, *The Reflective Practitioner: How Professionals Think in Action.* New York: Basic Books, 1983; *Educating the Reflective Practitioner: Toward a New Design for Teaching and Learning in the Professions,* San Francisco: Jossey-Bass, 1987.

[4] See Hugh Munby and Tom Russell, "Educating the Reflective Teacher: An Essay Review of Two Books by Donald Schön," *Curriculum Studies,* vol. 21, no. 1, pp. 71–80, 1989.

POST-OBSERVATION REFLECTION WITH THE TEACHER

You are now ready to conduct the post-observation conversation with the physics teachers whose class you have observed. What follows are possible responses to the questions generated earlier.

Post-Observation Conference #1

Supervisor: Maureen, I was intrigued by your approach to teaching that class on the wave and particle interpretations of light. Do you usually encourage the students to figure out experiments that way?

Maureen: Yes, Tom. Whenever we are starting a new unit, before we read the textbook, I explain some of the properties of the elements to be studied and try to generate at least three experiments by which we might verify the presence of these properties. So this class was following a familiar pattern for the students. You see, I want them to think like scientists, to use their imaginations as well as their logical reasoning in designing experiments. Actually, I believe some of the most creative scientific work is done in the area of designing experiments, rather than in the methodologies of measurement, which often get associated with the "real work" of science.

Supervisor: How do you respond to a student who suggests an experimental design that simply won't work?

Maureen: I encourage full discussion among the class on every design suggestion the students offer. Everyone is expected to contribute reasons why a design would work or would not work. Students are evaluated much more on their reasoning and creativity, than on whether the design would work. I want them to understand that doing science involves tons of exploratory searches, the majority of which don't work!

Supervisor: That's fascinating. Your students are getting an experience closer to the real life experiences of scientists than they would by simply memorizing the information provided in the textbook. What do you expect them to do with the design ideas they generate?

Maureen: For extra credit, students actually design their experiment and then demonstrate how it works to the class. This gives students a real pride in their accomplishment. We have been able to send six or more students to the regional science fair for the past four years, mainly, I believe, because this approach generates the imagination required to come up with the kind of science projects the fair supports. Another thing: I try to emphasize to my students that this work on designing experiments will help them in all kinds of careers, not simply in careers as scientists, because it has all kinds of problem-solving applications to other contexts.

Supervisor: Are your labs, then, made up of student demonstrations?

Maureen: Not entirely. We usually do the experiments referred to in the textbooks. On this one, we'll get to the ripple tank that Joe Schwartz is currently working on with his kids by the middle of next week.

As you can see, this conversation between Tom and Maureen has yielded significant information about the teacher's platform, about continuity with earlier and later classes in the course, student readiness for the learning, expected outcomes of the class, etc.

We will break away from this conference to look at the conference with the third teacher, the one comparing the wave and particle theory of light to theories of society.

Post-Observation Conference #3

Supervisor: Frank, I was fascinated by the far-ranging discussion in your class. Is this a regular feature of your classes?

Frank: Not exactly a regular feature, Tom. Usually at the end of a unit in the course I will spend a class like the one you saw today. I usually stick fairly close to the textbook sequence, and supplement the textbook with occasional readings of the cultural history behind some of the advances in physics. What you were seeing today is something I feel strongly about as a science teacher, namely that all the knowledge we have of the physical universe has a larger message for us as human beings. It's like a metaphor of something human. When we deal with energy, fusion, fission, relativity—concepts like that, I spend time exploring the possible human significance those realities might have for us. It's not something manufactured, simply to relieve boredom, or to conjure up an image for them to hang their scientific understanding on. Human beings are part of nature. Nature is in us. When we understand how the natural universe works, we understand ourselves better, not simply as natural beings, but as human beings, because I think that physical realities are qualitatively transformed in human experience. I know that this may sound kind of far out, but I find that after the first few discussions, kids see the point. It somehow changes the whole way they study science. I've tried sharing my approaches with other teachers in the department, but they don't seem to want to get involved.

Supervisor: Go on, Frank. Tell me how this gets worked into the classroom discussion I witnessed.

Frank: Well, it's like this. If you think that physical reality is made up of discrete things—atoms, molecules, rocks, chairs, human beings—then the problem is to understand how they can affect one another. Newton's understanding of the atom, as the smallest piece of matter, was as a discrete thing, so to speak, whose motion and speed was affected by other atoms. It would be possible to isolate each atom as discrete. I believe his view of the physical universe was consistent with the social theories of subsequent social philosophers, namely, that society is made of discrete, independent individuals, whose relationship to each other is entirely instrumental. So society, from that perspective, is nothing more than a collection of self-sufficient individuals who interact out of self-interest. But notice what happens when a different view of the physical universe becomes the metaphor for a view of society. In quantum physics, all particles make up a field of energy in which every particle is some-how connected to every other particle, and no one particle can act indepen-dently of the field. When that view of physical reality becomes a metaphor for human society, then the individual human being is connected to everyone else in that society, not by rational choice, but by nature.

Supervisor: This is pretty heavy stuff. You think the kids can grasp it?

Frank: Some of them struggle with it, but I encourage those who grasp the idea first to explain it in their own words, and then the other kids start to catch on. Some understand what I'm driving at, but think that it is too poetic or fan-ciful. Their earlier education in science has led them to totally disassociate sci-entific knowledge from knowledge about human affairs.

Supervisor: What do you expect them to do with this kind of learning, Frank? In other words, if you succeed in this effort, how would this new un-derstanding change them?

Frank: I would hope that they would see how much they depend on other people, and on the natural environment for their very existence, and that they would understand their responsibilities to honor their connections with other people. For example, I am extending this discussion to examine how the stu-dent government here in the school works. I think that kids here are struggling with the ambivalence of wanting to belong, to be accepted, and on the other hand of believing in extreme individualism, letting everyone do their own thing. I think that the way the student government works around here reflects the view of society as a collection of independent individuals. If they saw themselves differently, as a community of people who naturally belonged to one another, would they want a different student government?

Supervisor: I can see that these are pretty powerful ideas. From field theory to a new student government! Tell me, do you think that spending time on these discussions distracts from their covering the required syllabus in physics? Other teachers complain that they never have enough time to finish their course.

Frank: As a matter of fact, I think that the discussions help them to under-stand the physical concepts better. Unfortunately, none of the standard tests of knowledge of physics seem to be interested in these applications of concepts from physics. I find that the interest these discussions generate, even though they take up precious time, add to the motivation of the students to tackle the next chapters in the text.

This is quite a different platform from Maureen's. Nevertheless, Frank's dis-cussion of his approach seems to flow from a profound understanding of the connections between scientific knowledge and human understanding. Note how both Frank and Maureen's sense of the curriculum flows out of their per-sonal convictions and values.[5]

---

[5] For a clear example of this in the literature, see George H. Wood, "Teachers as Curriculum Workers," in James T. Searles and J. Dan Marshall (eds.), *Teaching and Thinking About Curriculum*, New York: Teachers College Press, 1990, pp. 97–109.

Yet another set of reflections emerges when the supervisor engages the fifth teacher in a post-observation conference.

Post-Observation Conference #5

Supervisor: I learned a lot about the relatively primitive laboratory methods of the seventeenth century yesterday. It is interesting, Marvin, how you can get across to the kids many of the early principles of scientific laboratory experimentation.

Marvin: Yeah. I think the textbook explanation of physics hides the difficulties people like Newton had to face in their work. Seeing it in its historical context helps them understand the genius of someone like Newton, as well as how much the effort of science requires the slow, painstaking work of many, many scientists who build on one another's work. Taking the time to look closely at the historical development also helps kids understand that prevailing world views and even language limits the ability of scientists to even frame the right questions. One of the amazing things the study of Newton's writings shows us is that he was aware of some of the wave-like properties of light. It was his followers who concentrated on his corpuscular explanations, creating the impression that Newton saw only that explanation. By studying the history, we can correct the inaccurate statement of our own textbook.

Supervisor: So you use this historical approach throughout your course?

Marvin: I would like to, but it is too time-consuming. Tomorrow, for example, we're going to do Newton's experiment with the convex lens and how it creates circles of various colors. The problem is that the textbook skips that experiment and the work of Huygens and goes right to Young's experiment. So after we do Newton's experiment, and Huygen's experiment of refraction of light in water, and then set up Young's experiment, I will have spent a week and a half on what the textbook expects to be covered in two classes. On the other hand, when we get to the ripple tank experiment, my kids will have a much deeper grasp of the physical properties of light than they would have had by racing through the text. So I speed up in some other places of the textbook in order to finish up with the other teachers.

Supervisor: Do your kids end up knowing as much as the kids in the other physics courses?

Marvin: Yes and no. The way I look at it, there are an almost infinite number of things to learn in physics. No matter who teaches the first course in physics, he has to choose. I try to achieve two things. One is that students have a sense of how science really got done, through years of trial and error, painstakingly building on the work of others, always with partial results. Second, that they know a good sample of physical concepts and theories reasonably well. We add to these two basic learnings a more superficial exposure to other concepts and theories, which is usually enough for them to score well on standard, multiple-choice tests of physics. You can only do so much in one course.

In each of the three post-observation conferences, you can see how the classes that were observed were part of a larger continuum of courses as designed in the plans of the three teachers. Although different, each class fit into a larger rationale of each teacher. As educators they were each convinced that they were providing valuable learnings for their students. The question facing the supervisors is, "How do I respond to these teachers?" First it may be helpful to return to the initial set of responses jotted down earlier. In the light of these post-observation conversations, would you now change your approach? If so, why? How does your sense of what supervisors are supposed to do lead you to respond?

One difficulty with this exercise is that you do not have a complete transcript of each class. You do not know how teachers performed in specific teaching strategies, such as reviewing prior information, creating a readiness set, asking leading questions, wait time after each question, use of media to illustrate the main points, positive and negative reinforcement of student responses, and the like. With more detail, you might be able to explore other possibilities with each teacher. For the moment, however, put aside considerations on technique and stay with the curriculum questions. What are the curriculum questions raised by these supervisory episodes?

One question that arises concerns the quality of student learnings. Are the students in all these different physics classes learning the essentials of physics? How would they score on a standard test of physics? Would the scores of students in one class be higher than the scores in the other four classes? Would that mean that one teacher's arrangement of the curriculum is superior? Would a pretest and a posttest be required of each class in order to determine which class learned the most?

Yet, each teacher was teaching more than concepts and theories of physics contained in the textbook. What about the learnings in each course which were legitimately related to learning physics but were not tested by the standard test? Is not the physics test itself a reflection of what a curriculum in physics should be? But who makes up the test, and does that person have the agreement of the teachers in question that it is a legitimate test for their students? Does the school not have general goals such as the promotion of democratic values, community concern, application of knowledge to problems of living, etc.? Are not all teachers expected to teach for growth in these areas as well as in academic subjects? Of the five teachers, whose students would probably have attended to those goals more successfully? Should a department seek to have all students learn the same thing? Does a preset list of learnings assume that all teachers will create the same curriculum to produce those learnings? Shouldn't teachers in that department get together more often to discuss their differences and arrive at some common learning outcomes? Even if they were to agree on common learning outcomes, given their different approaches, would the learnings, in fact, be common? What does a "common learning" mean—a memorized definition of a theory, or choosing the same item on a multiple-choice test? Or does it mean that the students in all five classes could discuss their learnings in physics intelligently, such that their differences in understandings would not defeat their ability to agree on the meaning of basic concepts in physics?

A DEEPER ANALYSIS

Other curriculum questions emerge out of a deeper analysis of what is going on in these physics courses. What is being communicated about the way scientific knowledge is achieved? Is the scientist pictured as a person who stands apart from the object of scientific study, dispassionate, objective, in control of the material under study? Is the curriculum communicating an accurate picture of how scientific knowledge is achieved, a picture of what scientific knowledge consists of, or rather a philosophical or ideological interpretation of scientific knowledge? Furthermore, is scientific knowledge presented as the purest form of knowledge, the most exact form of knowledge, such that all other forms of knowledge (such as the knowledge of the painter or musician or theologian or parent or friend) are seen as less exact, flawed, subjective, mixed with emotions? Does the curriculum ever include discussions of the public policy implications of scientific knowledge and application (for example, discussion of the pros and cons of nuclear energy plants; the pros and cons of the evidence of cancer-causing electromagnetic waves around public utility electricity generators)? Are questions posed concerning public policy decisions when the scientific evidence is contradictory or inconclusive (for example, what are the effects of radiation due to atmospheric changes caused by fluorocarbons)? Is the authority of the scientist presented as absolute, or at least more validly grounded than that of the "person on the street"? Is there an implied assumption that the ordinary citizen ought to leave more complicated technological, economic, and political decisions in the hands of experts who have access to and really understand scientific knowledge?

Is the natural universe of physical objects and forces presented as simply "out there," waiting, as it were, for human minds and scientific technologies to bump into them and discover their essential material properties, and to use this knowledge to control them and put them to productive use? Or is scientific knowledge presented as a human construct, influenced as much by the instrumentation and metaphors which human beings use to study the object as by what is out there? In the science curriculum, how often are the students encouraged to maintain a sense of reverence and stewardship for the natural universe they are studying?

Underneath the surface of the curriculum being taught, there is a substratum of ideas, assumptions, and beliefs that also makes up the curriculum. Often this substratum is not at all attended to by either the teacher or the supervisor. It might be named the "tacit curriculum"; it is very much present in the teaching and learning of the classroom, but neither student nor teacher is explicitly attending to it. It is like subliminal advertising.

The answers to these questions are not easy to come by. Upon reflection, it becomes apparent that the superficial appearance of a uniform curriculum intentionally planned and agreed to by teachers and administrators does not hold up to scrutiny. Using the example of a physics curriculum presents the matter rather simply. An analysis of social studies, or literature, or art classes would likely reveal much greater diversity and variability in the way a curriculum actually is taught and learned.[6] Recent publications which stress the importance of teaching cognitive and metacognitive processes across the curriculum reveal a wide variety of instructional approaches, cued by both contextual factors of students' age and previous educational opportunities as well as by personal frames of reference and metaphors used to model the curriculum content.[7]

ADDITIONAL CURRICULUM CONCERNS

New voices have been raised in the curriculum field to challenge traditional views on curriculum. Afro-American, Hispanic, Native American, and other scholars have recently challenged the exclusion of relevant material about their culture and communities from the school curriculum. The school curriculum, they argue, is unbalanced in favor of a Eurocentric, or white, male, middle-class perspective. These scholars would encourage a greater diversity of historical and cultural material which would provide students of various cultures with a sense of the contribution of their communities in human affairs, and would promote a greater understanding of and respect for the cultures and histories of various groups in society. More and more states are requiring courses in multicultural education for teacher certification, as well as revising textbooks to be more sensitive to multicultural concerns. These are steps in the right direction, but it is obvious that the multicultural curriculum agenda will continue to evolve, and more than likely involve local and national controversy. Feminists also have raised their voices about a curriculum that excludes a representative number of women role models and ignores women's perspec-

---

[6] See C. Evertson, "Differences in Instructional Activities in Higher- and Lower-Achieving Junior High English and Math Classes," *Elementary School Journal*, vol. 82, no. 4, 1982, pp. 329–350; William H. Clune, "Three Views of Curriculum Policy in the School Context: The School as Policy Mediator, Policy Critic, and Policy Constructor," in Milbrey W. McLaughlin, Joan E. Talbert, and Nina Bascia (eds.), *The Context of Teaching in Secondary Schools: Teachers' Realities*, New York: Teachers College Press, 1990, pp. 256–270; A. Gamoran, "The Stratification of High School Learning Opportunities," *Sociology of Education*, vol. 60, pp. 135–155, July 1987.

[7] See Beau Fly Jones, Annemarie Sullivan Palinscar, Donna Sederburg Ogle, and Eileen Glunn Carr (eds.), *Strategic Teaching and Learning: Cognitive Instruction in the Content Areas*, Alexandria, Va., Association for Supervision and Curriculum Development, 1987; Robert J. Marzano, Ronald S. Brandt, Carolyn Sue Hughes, Beau Fly Jones, Barbara Z. Presseisen, Stuart C. Rankin, and Charles Suhor (eds.), *Dimensions of Thinking: A Framework for Curriculum and Instruction*, Alexandria, Va., Association for Supervision and Curriculum Development, 1988; Lauren B. Resnick and Leopold E. Klopfer (eds.), *Toward the Thinking Curriculum: Current Cognitive Research*, Alexandria, Va., Association for Supervision and Curriculum Development, 1989.

tives on a number of issues.[8] While some textbook revision is under way to make learning materials more inclusive of women, developments of this agenda appear to be going slowly. Nonetheless, supervisors and teachers need to be more sensitive to sexist patterns in the curriculum which omit relevant historical information or present predominantly male perspectives. As many feminists have pointed out, sexism involves not only exclusionary language in the curriculum, but also the absence of awareness of women's ways of knowing.[9] As the research and analysis by women continues to develop and reach wider audiences, some lively conversations will ensue among teachers, supervisors, and curriculum developers.

Still other voices are raised in criticism of a curriculum that is excessively technocratic,[10] as reproducing the ideologies and structures of oppression found in society at large, as excessively vocational or instrumental in orientation.[11] These critics argue that the curriculum tacitly reflects ideological definitions of the way the world works. Hence the curriculum communicates values and attitudes toward authority, property, material acquisition, social conformity, work and leisure, and the like, which support the economic and political status quo.[12] Citing recent national school reform reports, these critics indicate the domination of school reform efforts by economic interests in an effort to maintain national economic hegemony/competitiveness. Hence school learning is seen as instrumental in, as oriented toward, securing employment and achieving technical literacy for the workplace. They cite the lack of concern for developing citizen participation skills and understandings, or environmental literacy.[13]

---

[8] For a small sample of such authors see Jane Roland Martin, "Sophie and Emile: A Case Study of Sex Bias in the History of Educational Thought," *Harvard Educational Review*, vol. 51, no. 3, pp. 357–372, August 1981; Jane Roland Martin, *Reclaiming a Conversation: The Ideal of the Educated Woman*, New Haven: Yale University Press, 1985; Madeleine R. Grumet "Women and Teaching: Homeless at Home," in William F. Pinar (ed.), *Contemporary Curriculum Discourses*, Scottsdale, Ariz.: Gorsuch Scarisbrisk, pp. 531–539; Madeleine Grumet, "Conception, Contradiction, and the Curriculum," *Journal of Curriculum Theorizing*, vol. 3, no. 1, pp. 21–44, Winter 1981; Lillian Robinson, "Treason Our Text: Feminist Challenges to the Literary Canon," in Elaine Showalter (ed.), *Feminist Criticism: Essays on Women, Literature & Theory*, New York: Pantheon, 1985; Jo Anne Pagano, *Exiles and Communities: Teaching in the Patriarchal Wilderness*, Albany: State University of New York Press, 1990.

[9] Jo Anne Pagano, op. cit.; Carol Gilligan, "In a Different Voice: Women's Conception of Self and Morality," *Harvard Educational Review*, vol. 47, pp. 481–517, 1977.

[10] See Robert V. Bullough, Jr., Stanley L. Goldstein, and Ladd Holt, *Human Interests in the Curriculum*, New York: Teachers College Press, 1984.

[11] See William Bigelow, "Inside the Classroom: Social Vision and Critical Pedagogy," in Steven Tozer, Thomas H. Anderson, and Bonnie B. Armbruster (eds.), *Foundational Studies in Teacher Education: A Reexamination*, New York: Teachers College Press, pp. 139–150; Michael W. Apple, "The Culture and Commerce of the Textbook," *Journal of Curriculum Studies*, pp. 191–202, July–September 1979; Henry A. Giroux, "Critical Pedagogy, Cultural Politics, and the Discourse of Experience," *Journal of Education*, vol. 167, no. 2, pp. 22–41, 1985.

[12] See Robert Dreeben's book, *On What Is Learned in School*, Reading Mass.: Addison-Wesley, 1968 as evidence by a "mainstream" scholar which supports the critics' contention.

[13] See the work of The Institute for Democracy in Education, associated with the School of Education at Ohio University, for examples of curriculum efforts to counteract this void in contemporary school reform efforts.

When their voices are added to those of the environmentalists, one can begin to get a sense of how much is missing from current school curricula.[14] Noel Gough suggests that a postmodern epistemology of knowing points to an older tradition going back to Aristotle of "phronesis"—knowing as practical judgment, a kind of knowing linked to the exercise of politics, which, in Aristotle's view, is the community seeking to come up with practical judgments about how to live its life as a community. Gough points to a new paradigm of education in which the curriculum would present the study of the natural environment as an interconnected whole.[15] This new paradigm of education would invite the community of men and women of all races and cultures to consider and seek practical judgments about how to survive and live their lives in some kind of harmony with each other and with their environment.[16]

This places knowledge—school knowledge—at the service of human and environmental needs first, and only in the light of these needs at the service of commercial needs. Hence, supervisors who would carry those concerns into classrooms would ask very different questions at the outset of their conversations with teachers.

Seen from this perspective, curriculum takes on a sense of drama. The script of this drama is concerned with human survival and the survival of the ecosphere. Schooling is seen as a drama in which the future of a society gets played out in anticipation. The curriculum can be seen as the script for this drama, but it is a script that is only imperfectly written. Teachers and students will have to improvise, experiment, and complete the script.[17] The teacher adopts a variety of postures toward instruction within this drama: at one time serving as director in rehearsing several versions of the script; at another time serving as critic of the students' performance of a script; at yet another time coaching students as they work through a problem presented by the script. From within this metaphor of schooling as a drama, teachers have to enter in as players in their own right, for they also have a stake in the outcome of this curriculum.

The above perspectives on curriculum, while calling for modifications or transformations of what most would consider the traditional understanding of curriculum, nevertheless continue to reveal that the teacher is the one who shapes the curriculum, according to very basic beliefs about the purposes of schooling, the nature of knowledge, and the varieties of learnings which make that knowledge useful or functional for the student. This theme is underscored in recent studies of teachers as shapers of curriculum based on their own per-

---

[14] See C. A. Bowers and David J. Flinders, *Responsive Teaching*, New York: Teachers College Press, 1990.

[15] Noel Gough, "From Epistemology to Ecopolitics: Renewing a Paradigm for Curriculum," *Journal of Curriculum Studies*, vol. 21, no. 3, pp. 225–241, 1989.

[16] For an approach to curriculum as embedded in a social environment, see the interesting essays contained in Joe L. Kincheloe and William F. Pinar (eds.) *Curriculum as Social Psychoanalysis: The Significance of Place*, Albany: State University of New York Press, 1991.

[17] See Robert J. Starratt, *The Drama of Schooling/The Schooling of Drama*, London: Falmer Press, 1990.

sonal history.[18] These studies indicate that teachers' personal histories shape how they think and feel about what they are teaching. Their own education, the teachers who influenced them, their way of seeing the world through the frames and experiences of their intellectual journey, their fears, disappointments, and hopes—all feed into what and how they teach. The studies point out that it is important for teachers to reflect on how their biographies influence their teaching in order to better understand themselves as teachers. This approach to understanding teachers' choices and actions relative to the curriculum they organize and teach allows supervisors to connect with a reservoir of material in the teachers' experience which enable them to converse and make meaning out of classroom events.

What the above considerations point to is an agenda for supervision that goes beyond a narrow concern with specific teaching techniques or technologies to a larger educational conversation with teachers. Such conversations, we contend, provide a much greater opportunity for teachers to consider what they are doing and to explore new possibilities for both teaching and learning.

GENERAL PRINCIPLES OF CURRICULUM AND INSTRUCTION

While the above considerations point to a curriculum agenda that remains to be worked out in practice, the supervisor and teacher, no matter where they stand on these various issues, need to reflect on some constants in the planning and teaching of curriculum. These constants are derived from both research and the experience of practice.[19] We propose them as a series of normative principles that teachers and supervisors will need to attend to in the course of their work together. As inexperienced teachers gain greater autonomy and control over the practice of teaching, and become reflective practitioners, they will tend to exhibit these principles intuitively.

1 Students must be given the opportunity to practice the kind of behavior implied by the curriculum objective. In the case of simple memorization of terminology, students should be called on often to repeat that termi-

[18] See David E. Hunt, *Beginning with Ourselves,* Cambridge, Mass.: Brookline Books, 1987; Peter Woods, "Teacher, Self and Curriculum" in Ivor F. Goodson and Stephen J. Ball (eds.), *Defining the Curriculum: History and Ethnographies,* London: Falmer Press, 1984, pp. 239–261; William Pinar, "Whole, Bright, Deep with Understanding: Issues in Qualitative Research and Autobiographical Method," *Journal of Curriculum Studies,* vol. 13, pp. 173–188, July–September, 1981; F. Michael Connelly and D. Jean Clandinin, *Teachers as Curriculum Planners: Narratives of Experience,* New York: Teachers College Press, 1988.

[19] These principles can be found under a variety of labels in the research literature: Tommy M. Tomlinson and Herbert J. Walberg (eds.), *Academic Work and Educational Excellence,* Berkeley, Calif.: McCutchan, 1986; Louis Rubin, "Instructional Strategies," in Herbert J. Walberg (ed.), *Improving Educational Standards and Productivity,* Berkeley, Calif.: McCutchan, 1982; U.S. Department of Education, *What Works,* Washington, D.C.: 1986; J. R. Mergendoller (guest ed.), "Schoolwork and academic tasks" (special issue), *Elementary School Journal,* vol. 88, no. 3, 1988; Susan Stoldolsky, *The Subject Matters: Classroom Activity in Math and Social Studies,* Chicago: University of Chicago Press, 1988; Jere Brophy and Janet Alleman, "Activities as Instructional Tools: A framework for Analysis and Evaluation," *Educational Researcher,* vol. 20, no. 4, pp. 9–23, May 1991.

nology precisely and accurately. In the case of the learning objective of application, students must be given the opportunity to make several applications and to return from time to time to other applications to reinforce the learning desired. We stress the activity of the students; unless they are actively involved in learning, they will not learn except in superficial ways.

2 The learning experience must give students the opportunity to deal with the content implied by the objective. If the objective is to develop the skill of scientific reasoning, then the learning experience must place students in a genuinely scientific setting where they encounter scientific data that can be analyzed by means of appropriate scientific instruments. Insofar as that learning experience lacks specifically scientific content, then the experience becomes diluted and fails to attain the depth of the learning desired.

3 Students must obtain satisfaction from carrying out the behavior implied by the objective. This principle insists on some sense of successful closure in the learning episode. One of the major problems in nonindividualized instructional settings is that one-third of the class seldom catches up with the rest of the class; they only partially complete their assignments. Their grades usually reflect the penalties imposed and lead to further loss of sense of worth and interest in the learning tasks.

4 The desired learnings or level of performance must be within the range of possibility for the students involved. This principle calls for an awareness on the part of both teachers and supervisors of the developmental stages and levels of cognitive, moral, and psychosocial growth. For example, some teachers expect fourth and fifth graders to engage in democratic group decision making. They will punish the miscreant who destroys the phony harmony of a simulated town meeting by laughing at the "goody-goody" who is simply trying to imitate the teacher. This is not to say that teachers should not introduce simple concepts of democracy. This principle holds for appropriate expectations of pupils' performance—appropriate to their level of development.

5 There are many particular experiences that can be used to attain the same objectives. Frequently teachers settle on only one or two examples or one or two ways to look at the problem or concept. This principle encourages more concern for diversity of student learning styles, or cultural or ethnic backgrounds. It also encourages the teacher and supervisor constantly to be enlarging their repertoire of teaching aids and resources, their "bag of tricks," in order to provide the student with a new approach to a learning task when another approach has failed to bring about the desired results.

6 The same learning activity will usually bring about several outcomes. Not infrequently a student's response to a question will take the teacher completely by surprise. Instead of rejecting the answer, the teacher should ask the student to clarify how he or she came up with that response. Frequently students come to quite legitimate learnings or insights that the

teacher had not foreseen as flowing from the assignment. This principle also alludes to the hidden, or informal, curriculum. Sometimes the teacher unwittingly communicates a value, an attitude, or a reward system that is contrary to or confuses the objectives of the instructional activity.

7 Student learnings will be strengthened, deepened, and broadened if a skill, a concept, relationships, principles, etc., are encountered and used repeatedly in several disciplines or discrete frameworks of learning. This principle points to the importance of teachers knowing what other teachers are doing in their classes. In that way a teacher can draw many comparisons, contrasts, and examples from the student's own experience. Consistent repetition in the use of learning and expressive skills will lead not only to their habitual use but also to their refinement and broader application. Repetition leads to quality and excellence.

SUMMARY

In this chapter we have touched upon a variety of curriculum concerns that supervisors might bring to their conversations with teachers. By adopting a reflective posture with teachers, supervisors facilitate a conversation in which both can explore the multidimensional realities of curriculum as planned, as taught, and as learned. We presented a variety of questions which might be explored by the supervisor and teacher, although those questions are by no means exhaustive. In some instances those questions might be surfaced among a group of teachers, as well as in individual conversations. In a school conceived as a learning community, where teaching is viewed as both a professional and a moral enterprise, everyone can approach these conversations with an openness to learning from one another and with a desire to reach for the professional and moral ideals which motivate them. As perspectives on curriculum unfolded within the chapter, it became evident that there is ample material for long, enduring conversations about practice. In the next chapter we will show how these conversations carry over into program evaluation, and into conversations about the curriculum as experienced and as learned by students.

CHAPTER 10

SUPERVISION AND PROGRAM EVALUATION

E VALUATION is a growing concern in education. From the federal and state governments down to local taxpayer groups, one finds an increasing demand for evaluation. Much of this stress on evaluation arises from a desire to find out what is wrong with the schools; why test scores are declining; why schools seem ineffective in controlling violence and vandalism, teenage pregnancies, and drug abuse. Some stress evaluation as a way of holding schools account-able to taxpayers and funding agencies for the money they spend. Others, such as university researchers, are seeking to increase information about effec-tive programs or teaching strategies.

The supervisory process, whether exercised by a superintendent, a district supervisor, a principal, or a department chairperson, inescapably involves program evaluation. In order to establish precisely what that means, however, one must make several distinctions. First, one should distinguish between evaluation that is exercised as part of a supervisory process and evaluation ex-ercised by other agents or professionals. Second, one should distinguish be-tween the object of evaluation, such as the evaluation of a school system, the evaluation of an individual school taken as a single social entity, the evalua-tion of an instructional program, the evaluation of a process, and so on. Third, one should distinguish between the various audiences for which an evaluation is intended. Fourth, one should distinguish between various types of evalua-tion procedures and the assumptions behind the procedures employed in an evaluation. Fifth, one should distinguish between the purposes of evaluation. Basically, these distinctions involve the who, what, for whom, how, and why of evaluation. Once these distinctions have been clarified, it is possible to focus on the more important and essential tasks of program evaluation with which the supervisory process is involved.

THE QUESTION OF WHO EVALUATES

Evaluation is carried on by a number of professional agents in the educational universe. At the federal level, where special programs are funded, personnel within the agencies or, more commonly, outside evaluation experts are called upon to evaluate the impact of these programs on the target populations. Head Start, for example, has been evaluated several times in order to deter-mine whether that program was accomplishing its objectives. Evaluation ex-perts from universities, state departments of education, or consulting agencies frequently are called in to use their technical expertise to evaluate special or new programs. State and regional accrediting agencies employ teachers and administrators who visit schools for cyclical reevaluations in order for the schools to retain their accreditation. Research and development centers employ evaluators to assess the impact of new or experimental programs. Foundations usually require a thorough evaluation of programs they fund, by either outside or inside evaluators. Department chairpersons evaluate new teachers. Teachers evaluate students. Supervisors evaluate teachers and programs. Therefore, when discussing evaluation in education, who is doing the evaluation makes a considerable difference to the discussion.

THE QUESTION OF WHAT IS BEING EVALUATED

Many things or many people can be the object of an evaluation. For example: The evaluation of a national program such as Head Start involves broad evaluation technologies and standardized testing of both product and process; a national evaluation of library expenditures involves the appraisal of different data; a local evaluation of a consumer education program involves the measure of outcomes different from those in a state evaluation of fair hiring procedures for school personnel. A systemwide evaluation of a reading program would differ from teacher X giving a quiz to her third-grade pupils. A supervisor's evaluation of a department's testing procedures would differ from a supervisor's evaluation of a beginning teacher. To evaluate students' reading skills involves a search for specific behaviors; to evaluate students' practices of democratic citizenship behaviors would involve a search for quite different kinds of data.

THE QUESTION OF THE AUDIENCE FOR THE EVALUATION

An evaluation report can be prepared for different audiences. The evaluation of an experimental program, when prepared for a research community, might be unintelligible to a citizens' oversight committee. A self-study report prepared by a schoolwide, faculty-parent committee would differ from a student's report card. A faculty report on new textbooks prepared for the school board would differ from a psychologist's evaluation of the match between students' stages of cognitive development and a new textbook prepared for a publishing house. Recent research on the politics of evaluation reporting indicates that not only what is evaluated but the way conclusions are drawn from the evaluation depends greatly on the audience for whom the evaluation is prepared.[1] For the supervisor, it makes a difference whether an evaluation of a

---

[1] See Ernest R. House (ed.), *School Evaluation: The Politics and Process*, Berkeley, Calif.: McCutchan, 1973; W. James Popham, "The Evaluators Curse," in Ronald S. Brandt (ed.), *Applied Strategies for Curriculum Evaluation*, Washington, D.C.: Association for Supervision Curriculum Development, 1981; and Deborah G. Bonnet, "Five Phases of Purposeful Inquiry," ibid.; Robert E. Stake, "The Countenance of Educational Evaluation," *Teachers College Record*, vol. 68, pp. 523–540, April 1967.

class is prepared for the superintendent or for the teacher who is seeking instructive information in order to test a new teaching strategy. Sometimes the audience for whom the evaluation is targeted, as well as the evaluators themselves, can seriously disrupt the very activity on which the evaluation is supposed to report.

THE QUESTION OF HOW TO EVALUATE:
PROCEDURES AND TECHNOLOGY

Currently there is a debate over the use of "hard" or "soft" evaluation procedures and technologies.[2] The earlier and more widespread practice of evaluation appears to have employed the hard procedures and technologies, namely, the quantification of what is being evaluated. Such an approach, based upon an analogy with research in the natural sciences, is seen as more "scientific" or more "objective." By quantifying data through testing or through numerical checklists, evaluators have attempted to provide a basis for comparing their data with data reported by others, using the same or similar scientific procedures, and for measuring "input" and "output."

There has been a reaction against this emphasis on quantification, a reaction that has been growing steadily over the past 10 years. Using analogies with methodologies employed in anthropology, aesthetics, literary criticism, and political analysis, the proponents of the "soft" approaches to evaluation argue that they can capture more of the human variables through "naturalistic" or ethnographic or case-study methodologies. Their argument also refers to the scale of evaluation. They claim that the individual school site or an individual classroom ought to be the locus of evaluation rather than a national, statewide, or even systemwide sample. They maintain that the study of large populations tends to diminish the unique features of smaller segments and settings. Evaluation studies that are more attentive to individual schools and individual classrooms do in fact point up significant differences between schools and between classrooms in the same school.[3]

---

[2] For a good summary of this debate see E. G. Guba and Y. S. Lincoln, *Effective Evaluation*, San Francisco: Jossey-Bass, 1981. The essays in Brandt (ed.), op. cit., aptly illustrate various approaches to program evaluation. Robert Stake argues even more strenuously for the constructivist basis of program evaluation in his "Retrospective on the Countenance of Educational Evaluation," in Milbrey W. McLaughlin and D. C. Phillips (eds.), *Evaluation and Education At Quarter Century*, Ninetieth Yearbook of the National Society for the Study of Education, Part II, Chicago: University of Chicago Press, 1991, pp. 67–88.

[3] See Michael Rutter, Barbara Maughan, Peter Mortimer, and Janet Ouston, *Fifteen Thousand Hours: Secondary Schools and Their Effects on Children*, Cambridge, Mass.: Harvard University Press, 1979; George Madaus, Peter W. Airasian, and Thomas Kellaghan, *School Effectiveness*, New York: McGraw-Hill, 1980. From a different perspective, notice the equity questions raised by between-classroom differences in Joseph Murphy and Phillip Hallinger, "Equity as Access to Learning: Curricular and Instructional Treatment Differences," *Journal of Curriculum Studies*, vol. 21, no. 3, pp. 129–148, 1989. For within class equity issues based on gender, see Myra Sadker, David Sadker, and Susan Klein, "The Issue of Gender in Elementary and Secondary Education," in Gerald Grant (ed.), *Review of Research in Education*, vol. 17, Washington D.C., The American Educational Research Association, pp. 269– 334, 1991.

While supervisory personnel do make some use of quantitative data for evaluation, it appears that much of their involvement in evaluative activity occurs within the "responsive" or "naturalistic" mode and within the smaller scale of the individual school.[4] As the scale of supervisory activity enlarges, the evaluative procedures will probably move toward the more impersonal and quantitative mode. For example, a program director at the state department of education who supervises the state-mandated program for educating sight-impaired children would probably require quantifiable information for annual reports on this program. This does not rule out using additional modes of evaluation, especially where improvements at particular sites are being sought.

THE QUESTION OF WHY: PURPOSES OF EVALUATION

Finally, the purpose for which evaluation is undertaken will shape the form and process of evaluation. If the purpose of an evaluation is to provide information about the more effective of two or three approaches to the teaching of reading, then it is supposed to lead to the choosing of one over the other(s) for future implementation or continuation. If the purpose of an evaluation is to seek improvements in an existing reading program, then it is supposed to lead to improvements in that program. An evaluation of teaching effectiveness in a department starts out with the objectives of that department and seeks to verify whether the students achieve those objectives. An evaluation of the stated objectives of a department will compare those objectives with the objectives of similar departments in other schools, or with objectives laid down by state or professional associations involved with that academic area in order to judge whether they meet accepted standards and criteria. Some evaluations may involve comparison of two or more schools in order to see which schools produce the highest student scores on national achievement tests or do best according to some other standardized criteria.

PROGRAM EVALUATION AND THE SUPERVISORY PROCESS

The supervisory process can be exercised on any level, from the supervision of a federal or state program to a districtwide program. It can involve the total educational program of a single school or, within a school, a departmental curriculum, or an individual course. Figure 10-1 highlights some of the many levels at which program evaluation takes place. At whatever level supervision is involved with program evaluation, we believe that it is exercised best when the supervisor monitors and participates in the evaluative efforts of those implementing the program. This is to say that the supervisory process ought to

[4] See Yvonna S. Lincoln and Egon Guba, *Naturalistic Inquiry,* Beverly Hills, Calif.: Sage, 1985; and Robert E. Stake, "Program Evaluation, Particularly Responsive Evaluation," in *New Trends in Evaluation,* Report #35, Gothenburg, Sweden: Institute of Education, University of Gothenburg, pp. 1–20, 1974.

LEVEL	EXAMPLE	TYPE OF EVALUATION	PURPOSE
Federal	Head Start	Statistical norm-referenced test	To report to Congress and federal officials
State	Vocational education	Statistical survey	To report to state legislature and state officials
Independent research and development center	Experimental reading programs	Highly sophisticated psychometrics; use of experimental and control groups	To isolate and measure program effects
Regional accrediting agency	Cyclical self-evaluation and assessment by visiting team	Self-report, observation by visitors, naturalistic evaluation	To judge whether school meeting minimum standards
Local school system	K–12 Modern language program	Norm-referenced and criterion-referenced testing	To judge effectiveness of their program compared to other school systems using different approaches
Single school	Volunteer community service program	Supervisor reports, agency reports, teacher reports, student reports	To assess impact on improved citizenship attitudes
Single course	Geography	Criterion-referenced tests, student in-class responses, supervisor's observation, student interviews, etc.	To improve overall course design, sequence, pacing, use of audio visuals, etc.

FIGURE 10–1   Evaluation of programs according to scale.

be separated from evaluation of the program by an evaluation expert. It is not to say that supervisors do not evaluate. Their evaluation, however, is not performed as outsiders but as insiders, working with those who are delivering the instruction or the program.

We believe that the principles that guide the supervisory process when its focus is program evaluation are best illustrated at the level of a specific program in a single school, working with teachers who are implementing the program through instructional activity. As distinguished from other kinds of evaluation activity, the supervisor's evaluation activity is exercised with and for teachers, for the purpose of program and instructional improvement, and for enhanced student learnings; it is exercised more by soft technology than by hard technology. The who, for whom, how, and why distinctions were made above in order to clarify more precisely how supervision can involve program evaluation and to distinguish supervision from the more formal aspects of program evaluation by nonsupervisory personnel. Figures 10-1 and 10-2 map out those distinctions.

Furthermore, the point of view adopted in this chapter is that supervisory evaluation of program effectiveness is exercised with teachers as they seek practical ways to improve the program as taught. That is, program evaluation activity is not extrinsic to instruction but is intrinsically involved with instructional improvement. There is a dynamic relationship between evaluating student learnings, evaluating teachers' activities in stimulating student learnings, and evaluating the effectiveness of the curriculum that teachers use. Hence our primary focus in this chapter will be the supervisor's monitoring and assisting in teachers' evaluation of their own activities for improved student learnings (program as experienced), for improved instructional activity (program as taught), and for improved program design (program as planned). Much of the teacher's evaluation and alteration of the program will depend very much on how the teacher evaluates student learnings. The supervisor, by assisting the teacher to ask the right questions when evaluating the program as learned, will also help the teacher explore ways to improve the program as taught. This is part of the supervisory process of nurturing the growth of the reflective practitioner in teachers.

THE ACTIVITY OF EVALUATION

Program and pupil evaluation formerly were thought of primarily as something that happened at the end of the term or the end of the year. At the conclusion of the course, students were evaluated on their progress in attaining the goals of the program by means of a test, a "final exam" in some form or other. When the course was over, the teacher might have spent some time looking back over the curriculum and specific instructional strategies to see whether or not some units clearly were inappropriate or unsuccessful. In the case of a new course design, the teacher and supervisor might have compared student achievement with the earlier course. They also might have asked teachers in whose classes their students subsequently enrolled whether there was any noticeable difference in student achievement after the new course.

Michael Scriven, in writing about curriculum revision, calls this type of evaluation *summative evaluation*.[5] It "sums up" the impact of the curriculum on learning, or it makes a general assessment of the student's cumulative learning of the whole curriculum. Scriven distinguishes summative evaluation from *formative evaluation* by positing formative evaluation as an ongoing process within the curriculum-instructional activity sequence. Through formative evaluation of the instructional program the teacher, learner, and curriculum designer can receive rapid feedback on the effectiveness of short-term seg-

---

[5] Michael Scriven, "The Methodology of Evaluation," in Robert E. Stake (ed.), AERA, *Monograph Series on Curriculum Evaluation*, no. 1, pp. 39–83, 1967.

WHO	ADMINISTRATORS	SUPERVISORS	EVALUATION EXPERTS
Does what	Decide whether to initiate, continue, or terminate programs, based on information received by evaluators Decide whether to alter program, or commit more resources to program, based on information received by supervisors and program implementors	Work on program improvement with implementors (teachers) of the program Examine effectiveness of small segments of the program implementation Help program implementors assess multiple effects of program on recipients (students) Explore alternative forms of implementing the program Help program implementors and recipients review the overall impact of the program	Gather data on a program Assess program effectiveness Compare this program with alternatives Report result to various sectors of the public Interpret results to various sectors of the public
How	Review reports	Conduct responsive evaluation Engage in participative observation Work with mediating variables Look for unintended effects Clarify objectives Pose alternative approaches	Clarify goals, means, and products Measure, test, observe, chart, compare Clarify relationships between program design, implementation activities, and results on tests and other hard and soft measures
Why	Are responsible and accountable to public Seek maximum effectiveness for enhanced student learning	Seek best fit between program design, learning resource materials, teacher activities, and student learning Improve program effectiveness, teacher effectiveness, and student learning	Measure what the program accomplishes Establish relationship between program and results Provide basis for making enlightened decisions about the program

FIGURE 10–2   Role of administrators, supervisors, and evaluation experts in program evaluation.

ments of the program, rather than having to wait until the conclusion of the program for the more summative type of evaluation. Since formative evaluation occurs virtually simultaneously with instructional and learning activities, it can have a formative influence on those activities. For example, the teacher may realize that his use of a particular advance organizer or a demonstration simply is not getting the students' attention or, by questions from the students, that the material is well over their heads. This kind of instant feedback probably will lead the teacher to discard that approach on the spot and to try a new tack. As another example, a student may discover that he or she has not yet mastered the rules for capital letters. The teacher and the student can then set up some exercises to ensure a more adequate grasp of those rules.

FORMATIVE EVALUATION

For the moment, we will concentrate on the activity of formative evaluation, for the supervision of evaluation activity seems to be more focused on that form. A brief overview of formative evaluation of the curriculum points to particular activities of students, other activities of the teacher, and the formative use of assessment for both learning and teaching. Depending on the situation, supervisors may or may not participate in evaluation activities, but they certainly will be expected to monitor in some fashion the effectiveness of these evaluation activities.

Student Evaluative Activity: Evaluation of the Curriculum as Learned

Consider an ordinary class setting, say, a self-contained high school honors poetry class with one teacher and 24 students. The class has just concluded a comparison of two poems. Previous classes have dealt with aspects of poetry, such as mood, figures of speech, rhythm, unity, image, and symbol. They have read a variety of poems and have done some analysis using these critical concepts. The objective of today's class is to have students use these critical concepts to compare two poems and to argue why one poem is "better" than the other. This objective fits into the larger goal of the course, which is for students to learn to discriminate between superior and inferior literary expression.

Toward the end of the class the teacher feels satisfied that most if not all of the students have demonstrated a good grasp of the analytical concepts and have applied them well in arguing for the superiority of one poem over the other. In an attempt to further reinforce the learning and to test out her impressions that the class has achieved the instructional objectives, she says, "Now let's all pause a minute and reflect on what it is we learned today. What new thing struck us? What have we understood with greater clarity? How does what we've done today fit with what went on before? Of what practical use was this whole experience, anyway?"

The following answers come back:

- "I learned that it makes a difference when you read a poem out loud. I could *hear* how superior that first poem was to the other one."
- "I learned that you can still like an inferior poem—I mean, yeah, the first poem is a better poem, by all the measures we apply to it, but I like the second poem because it expresses a feeling about being alone that I've had many times. Just because a poem is a mediocre poem doesn't mean it's no good at all."
- "I learned that I had to read both poems at least four times before they made any sense to me. It seems that with poetry, kinda like music, you gotta acquire a kind of familiarity with it before it really says anything to you."
- "I learned that all this art stuff isn't entirely a matter of feeling, you know, all from inside someone's fantasy. There's something to it, some kind of intelligence. And you can talk about poetry intelligently, instead of simply leaving it to subjective feelings of like or dislike."
- "I learned that I have no poetic imagination. I never thought those kinds of thoughts. And I'm wondering how one gets to be a poet—are you born that way, or can you develop it?"
- "I'm really having a hard time understanding what makes a poem "unified." It's a word that seems to me to mean perfect, or perfection. Like a perfect circle or something. So if a poem has unity, then it must mean that every word, every line is in a perfect place. But who could ever decide that? Maybe I need to see examples of *really* unified poems and some that are a little off-center and maybe I'll catch on."
- "I learned that it feels good to discover that a lot of people agree with my conclusions. Before the class started, I wasn't sure whether my picking the first poem as better was the right answer, you know. But when other people gave the same reasons as I had, I really felt good, because I figured—yeah, for the first time—that I'm understanding all the stuff we've been doing on poetry."

The teacher then continued the class by picking up on one student's question about what makes a poem unified. Other students were asked to come up with responses to the question, and a disjointed class discussion ensued about poetic unity. The teacher cited another student's comment that poetry is like music, and asked how one would know that a song was unified. That led to further examples, and the class moved into a distinction between narrative unity and a unity of impression, which then led to the deeper question of whether the poem itself was unified, or whether it created a sense of unity in the reader. The teacher then asked the class whether they experienced their life as a unity each day. This led to several humorous responses, and then the teacher challenged them to write a poem about an experience that conveyed to them a sense of completeness.

The example illustrates a range of student learnings that reflect not only the achievement of the teacher's objectives but also the many idiosyncratic, ancillary learnings that always occur. The example points to the importance of taking time to let students reflect on what they have learned. Obviously, the students in that honors poetry class had relatively high levels of motivation and of verbal and abstractive abilities. Students in third or fourth grade will come up with simpler responses, to be sure. But getting them into the habit early of evaluating what they are learning will pay enormous dividends as it develops into ongoing reflective habits of mind and a genuine satisfaction over knowing that they are making progress.

Students' evaluation of their appropriation of the curriculum can lead to both cognitive and affective results. By reflecting on their grasp of the learning task, they can clarify what they know. Frequently, simple recall of the class material or unit will reinforce a student's grasp of the material. When this reflection is done in a nonthreatening environment, students can also clarify and admit what they have not yet grasped or understood. They can trace back the instructional sequence until they get to the point where the teacher or the textbook lost them. This clarification of what one does not know will often lead to a desire to learn that material.

On the affective level, students also can be encouraged to review what they have learned, not so much for intellectual understanding but simply for enjoyment. The youngster who felt the need to read the poems many times was discovering how poems are meant to be enjoyed. This kind of enjoyment is not limited to those subjects within the humanities. A sensitive biology teacher or a physical education teacher can lead students into a kind of repetitive appreciation of what they have learned. Sometimes that leads to genuine wonderment.

On either a reflective or an affective level, student evaluation of this learning can lead to ownership. Recognizing what they have learned, what it means, how it is related to what they have learned before, how they can use it, what a sense of excitement or enjoyment comes with that mastery of a skill or discovery of a surprising piece of information—all of this leads students to appropriate that learning as theirs. Once appropriated, the learning tends to be effective, which is to say that the student owns it and can use it in many ways in the immediate future. Unfortunately, many teachers fail to take the time to encourage this sense of ownership. What they miss by not encouraging student self-evaluation is the genuine satisfaction of knowing how much their students have actually absorbed and the fascination of observing the individual subtleties in learning that manifest themselves through such feedback. Moreover, much of the formative evaluation the teacher engages in does not pick up the obvious clues that students put forth in their self-evaluation. A supervisor who helps a teacher to initiate student self-evaluation may have provided a stimulus for instructional and program improvement more effective than several semesters of in-service lectures on the topic.

In the example of the honors poetry class, the teacher used a spontaneous assessment of the students' learning to carry the lesson forward, to get them to probe for deeper understandings of the material. She was also able to use the assessment to relate the material to their own personal experience, and then to use that for writing their own poetry. In this example, one can see how easily formative evaluation can flow into curriculum elaboration; evaluation becomes part of the program as taught.

The Teacher's Formative Evaluation Activity: Evaluation of the Curriculum as Taught

By means of student self-evaluation, brief quizzes, and questions that are asked during instructional activity, by checking ongoing projects and homework assignments, and through informal out-of-class conversations, teachers can gauge the effectiveness of the curriculum unit as well as of their teaching strategies. It will take a multiplicity of feedback mechanisms rather than the single mechanism of an occasional test to provide the formative information.[6] Sometimes a test itself is the real problem because it has been poorly constructed.[7]

The teacher's formative evaluation activity has more than one focus. The teacher must try to evaluate how well the student is encountering and mastering the learning task. There may be several reasons the student is having difficulty: For example, emotionally upsetting conditions may exist at home; a fight in the school yard that morning could have made concentration on schoolwork impossible; the pace of the class may be too fast; the examples used to illustrate a point may have been too obscure; the student may have been distracted briefly at the beginning of the class and missed one of the initial steps in an explanation.

If most or all of the class is showing disinterest or confusion, then the teacher has to evaluate what is lacking in his or her teaching. Or is the learning unit design in the textbook confusing or flat? Sometimes the only way to identify the cause is to ask the students. From time to time, however, the teacher is not all that aware of the deficiency in the textbook or in his or her teaching. Sometimes the problem does not surface for a week or two, when a test shows a consistent gap in the sequence of learning.

Some teachers are perpetually unaware of how they smother student initiatives to learn. Giving low grades is the way these teachers punish what they perceive as the recalcitrance and general laziness of youth. Here, the formative evaluation of the teacher is almost totally ineffective because the source of the problem is ignored. It is a case of blaming the victim.

Supervisors can help teachers address the difficult task of formative evaluation primarily by communicating a respect for the teacher's ability to refashion

---

[6] There has been a significant groundswell urging variety and multiplicity in assessment mechanisms. See the theme issue of *Educational Leadership*, vol. 46, no. 7, April 1989, devoted to this topic. For a recent review of the research behind this effort, see Dennie Wolf, Janet Bixby, John Glenn III, and Howard Gardner, "To Use Their Minds Well: Investigating New Forms of Student Assessment," in Gerald Grant (ed.), *Review of Research in Education*, op. cit. pp. 31–74.

[7] See Richard J. Stiggins, "Revitalizing Classroom Assessment: The Highest Instructional Priority," *Phi Delta Kappan*, vol. 69, no. 5, pp. 363–368, January 1988, for a commentary of teachers' faulty construction of classroom assessments.

his or her curriculum-instructional plan more effectively. Some inexperienced teachers think that a textbook is too sacred to be altered one iota. On the contrary, the teacher is in the best position to know what will work with his or her students and should deviate from the textbook when that is called for. The supervisor can work alongside the teacher, exploring alternative strategies, testing out an idea on one or two students before trying it with the whole class, and looking for gaps and blind spots and filling them in so that students can move easily from one thing to another. Once the teacher gains self-confidence, he or she will be much more likely to carry on such self-corrective activities independently.

When substantial program revision is called for, the supervisor can enlist the assistance of someone more skilled in curriculum design to work with several teachers. However, the teacher ought to be the central person in his kind of formative evaluation, not the supervisor. Frequently the most important activity of the supervisor is to convince the teacher that he or she can, should, and must do an evaluation. Familiarity with a variety of evaluation techniques will equip the supervisor with a repertory of approaches, some of which may be useful to get the teacher started.

A formative use of testing can be a key source of feedback that will provide insight into any problems that teachers and students might have. More often than not, quizzes and tests are not carefully reviewed. The grades are entered into the mark book, and the papers are handed back to the students, who look at the grade and toss it in the basket. A careful review of tests and quizzes, however, can be turned into a very effective learning experience. First, there is usually a high level of student interest because of the grade involved. By reviewing the quiz or the test, students have a chance to see where they made their mistakes, thereby clearing up what could be a lingering problem if not corrected. It also provides the teacher with some clues to why some students failed to achieve the objective of the instruction. Such information often leads to more appropriate remedial exercises. In the exchange of information, the teacher can accomplish other goals, such as reinforcing the main point of the instruction, reviewing previous learnings leading up to the material under study, clarifying the level of exactitude or logic or basic English required in the course, pointing out the necessity to ask questions in class when points are unclear, and so on.

Students who scored well have an opportunity to review the essentials of the previous class or learning unit. Students whose performance was poor because of one key deficiency have the opportunity to see the principle or concept or formula or rule as such, that is, as a generalization that applies to many particulars; through review, these students can gain the general insight that may have been lost in the details of day-to-day instruction.

Such review also allows students to debate the precise meaning of a word or phrase in a question. Sometimes a student has a legitimate complaint when the wording of a question can be construed in different ways and therefore can elicit more than one valid response. The teacher's review of the test can help clear up such problems before some disgruntled youngster goes home to enlist the support of his or her parents, who in turn become disgruntled and demand an appointment with the principal.

Again, supervisors can help teachers get far more instructional mileage out of their assessments. Rather than being extraneous to instruction, this kind of formative evaluation can become one of the regular tools of instruction. Only in this way can assessment be restored to its proper place as an aid to instruction rather than being a specter dominating both instruction and student motivation.

Learning Activities in Program Evaluation

Curriculum units often provide opportunities for students to take a concept introduced by the teacher and apply it to classroom exercises and activities. For example, a teacher might introduce a mathematical operation, provide a model problem to explain how the operation applies, and then give students two or three word problems to work through in order to grasp the operation. A geography teacher might introduce the subject of primitive forms of irrigation and then assign teams of students to design an irrigation system that would work in a simulated semi-arid, mountainous setting. Many laboratory activities in science classes are of this nature, requiring students to apply principles and concepts explained earlier by the teacher to a hands-on experiment.

Recent work by Jere Brophy and Janet Alleman provides a framework for evaluating activities as instructional tools.[8] They indicate that learning activities are not always appropriate to the program goals, are sometimes poorly designed, or are not sufficiently supported with clear instructions on how to proceed. Brophy and Alleman provide a helpful series of principles by which a teacher and a supervisor can evaluate the learning activities embedded in the program. Some of their principles may be summarized as follows.

I. **Primary principles**
   A. The activity must be clearly and developmentally related to an important program goal, such that the completion of the activity leads to the achievement of the program goal clearly and unambiguously.
   B. The activity must be sufficiently difficult to stretch the student in the intended area of learning, but not so difficult as to frustrate the student. This may require some initial structuring and scaffolding of the activity differentially provided for different students.
   C. The activity must be feasible within the constraints of space, time, equipment, type of students.
   D. The benefits derived from the activity must justify its anticipated

---

[8] Jere Brophy and Janet Alleman, "Activities as Instructional Tools: A Framework for Analysis and Evaluation," *Educational Researcher*, vol. 20, no. 4, pp. 9–23; also Vito Perrone (ed.), *Expanding Student Assessment*, Arlington, Va.: Association for Supervision and Curriculum Development, 1991.

costs in time and effort. These benefits can relate to specific program goals, cross-disciplinary goals, or schoolwide goals.

II. **Secondary principles** (desirable, but not absolutely necessary)
  A. Activities that simultaneously accomplish many goals are preferred.
  B. Learnings that connect subject fields make certain activities desirable.
  C. Activities that develop the understanding of central ideas and their applications are preferred over isolated skill or concept-focused activities.
  D. Activities that require whole-task completion are preferred over activities that deal with partial or limited learnings.
  E. Activities which involve students in higher-order thinking (interpretation, debate, generation of alternatives, sustained argument, etc.) are preferred.
  F. Activities which enable students of various degrees of ability to participate are preferred over those that cannot.

III. **Implementation principles** (how teachers structure activities)
  A. Each activity should have a clear introduction, then some scaffolding so that students understand what they are expected to do and can begin the activity intelligently.
  B. Each activity should involve students working independently from the teacher, although the teacher monitors and intervenes when necessary.
  C. Each activity should conclude with assessment, feedback, reflection, and debriefing, so that both student and teacher have a sense of whether the learning goals were reached.

As with the list of general principles for curriculum and instruction enumerated in the last chapter, these principles should provide some evaluative guidelines in most settings. In pre-observation conversations, supervisors might review with the teacher the activities associated with the unit the supervisor will be observing. As the teacher explains the expected outcomes from the activities, the supervisor can get a sense of whether the principles enumerated above are tacitly being honored. During class observation, the teacher and supervisor can monitor how students are performing, and thus observe where additional structuring or scaffolding might be needed, and where more direct teaching might be needed before introducing the activity.

The Supervisor's Role in Formative Evaluation

As should be evident from the above, the role of the supervisor is that of monitoring the type and effectiveness of the formative evaluating activity that goes on in the classroom. By keeping in mind that this type of evaluation is intended to improve the learning of the student, as well as the instructional effectiveness of the teacher and the curriculum program, the supervisor can help the teacher and student stay on target in their evaluation efforts. Furthermore, the supervisor should maintain enough distance from the evaluation process to identify any values introduced by a particular teacher's type and style of evaluation procedure. Evaluation is a process of assigning value and significance to actions, things, answers, or questions. Behind any evaluation activity is a host of assumptions that have value content. These assumptions usually go untested or unquestioned.

Some assumptions behind some forms of evaluation include the following:

- Knowing or understanding something means giving this particular response to that question.
- This curriculum design or this text contains the most legitimate, or the only legitimate, approach to this area of knowledge (for example, modern Latin American history seen from a North American perspective), and therefore a test of the student's knowledge of this approach indicates that he or she knows something true or objective or valid about that area of knowledge.
- Using the language of public discourse in evaluation is the best means of measuring what the student has learned (rather than using poetry or music or graphics to measure it).
- Teachers and other school officials have the authority and competency to decide the criteria for evaluating and ranking students.
- Learning primarily involves learning what others have discovered (and seldom the way they discovered it), and so evaluation monitors learning on that level.
- There is always a causal connection between learning and instruction (rather than learning and the *students'* search, inquiry, practice, trial and error, or logical deduction), and hence evaluation of learning implies an evaluation of instruction.
- The proper place for most learning is a classroom, and so evaluation never compares classroom learning (with all its constraints) with learnings in other settings.

One could go on and on, describing assumptions behind assumptions. The point of listing these is to encourage supervisors occasionally to create distance from the evaluation activity so that both they and the teacher can perceive the value assumptions that are embedded in their evaluation procedures. If nothing else, such distancing can be a healthy antidote to dogmatism; at best it will encourage flexibility and more holistic approaches to evaluation and to program development.

SUMMATIVE EVALUATION

Summative evaluation of a program involves more than asking students to answer summative-type questions on final exams. Besides assessing the program's impact on student learning, summative evaluation of the program must involve a look at the overall design of the program, its scope and sequence, the way the parts are connected and structured, the illustrative and heuristic materials used as major instructional components, the logical and psychological sequence of topics, and the relationship of the program design to the essential concepts and processes of the academic discipline the program was intended to model. Normally, curriculum specialists are involved with teachers in a formal summative evaluation of the program. Supervisors, on the other hand, can assist teachers in a less formal, summative evaluation of the program.

As discussed in the previous chapter, there are many questions both teacher and supervisor may discuss about the curriculum as planned and as taught. Some of the larger questions about the program as experienced may reveal serious deficiencies in the program taken as a whole, for example, an exclusively Eurocentric perspective in a world history course. A supervisor does not need to be a specialist in social studies curriculum to perceive such a deficiency. Other questions involved in this general summative evaluation of the program should include the following:

- *Equity.* Does the program favor the brightest students? Are there opportunities for peer coaching, for collaborative learning, for both remediation and enrichment? Are there two standards for assignments and grading?
- *Affective learning.* Does the program allow for expressive and appreciative learnings, or is it focused entirely on conceptual clarity and disciplined logic?
- *Multicultural perspectives.* Does the program honor multicultural perspectives and multicultural realities?
- *Gender sensitivity.* Is the program sensitive to both male and female perspectives and ways of knowing?
- *Social relevance.* Are significant implications for social policy and societal practice drawn out or ignored?
- *Connectedness.* Are built-in bridges to other subject areas and to life outside of school consistently highlighted within the program?
- *Schoolwide goals.* Does the program intentionally and explicitly attend to schoolwide goals?

Holding up the outline of the program to these questions sometimes suggests areas for significant modification. If some of these questions prompt a debate about "politically correct" curriculum, then perhaps such a debate might enable the faculty and administration to air some issues that have gone unexamined for some time.

The primary emphasis in the supervisor's work with teachers in summative program evaluation should be on student response to the program. These responses can take two forms. The first is an assessment of student learning at the end of the program, typically in the form of a final exam. The second form of student assessment is an examination of how the students perceived the program. Did they understand the major goals of the program? Did they perceive the program as organized and implemented to enable them to achieve those goals? If they were teaching the course, would they have developed and managed it differently? Teachers rarely employ this form of student assessment. However, they stand to learn much from student evaluations of the program. Teachers might not agree with every student comment, but they would at least have a sense of how students perceived the program.[9]

Authentic Assessment

More and more schools are attempting to redesign their final exams into authentic tests.[10] An authentic test is one which involves students in doing the very things the course is aiming to teach. For example, an authentic test in a course in public speaking would require students to deliver an oration publicly. In a science course, an authentic test would require students to solve a scientific problem using the tools of science in an appropriate scientific setting. "An authentic test enables us to watch a learner pose, tackle, and solve slightly ambiguous problems. It allows us to watch a student marshal evidence, arrange arguments, and take purposeful action to address the problems."[11]

To ensure that the assessment is accurate, several performance-based tests should be conducted using a variety of performances (in one test, constructing charts and graphs; in another, predicting future trends based on sound evidence). Thus, the teacher is able to perceive a pattern and gain an understanding of each student's success or failure. Hence, the summative evaluation is not seen as a one-shot activity, but rather as the last in a series of opportunities to discover what students have learned. This idea is consistent with the principles described in the previous chapter and in the work of Brophy and Alleman suggesting that teaching, activities, and now assessment should be concerned with the content of the curriculum.

When dealing with summative evaluation of students, supervisors can help teachers realize the significant instructional activity and learning that can take place immediately before and during summative evaluation. For example, teachers can encourage students to engage in a summative-type self-evaluation, aiming for the students' review of what significant ideas *they* think they have learned in the course. Even in a structured class review of the course prior to a final exam, students can expand on much of what they have learned. Frequently the review provides the opportunity for a whole new synthesis of learnings. What we said in our discussion of formative evaluation about re-

---

[9] See Vincent Rogers, "Assessing the Curriculum Experienced by Children," *Phi Delta Kappan*, vol. 70, no. 9, pp. 714–717, 1989, for a variety of suggestions on how to design such student evaluations, either for formative or summative use.

[10] See Grant Wiggins, "A True Test: Toward More Authentic and Equitable Assessment," *Phi Delta Kappan*, vol. 70, no. 9, pp. 703–713, 1989; Ron Berger, "Building a School Culture of High Standards: A Teacher's Perspective," in Vito Perrone (ed.), *Expanding Student Assessment*, Alexandria Va.: Association for Supervision and Curriculum Development, 1991, pp. 32–39; George Hein, "Active Assessment for Active Science," in Vito Perrone, op. cit., pp. 106–131; Dennie Wolf, Janet Bixby, John Glenn III, and Howard Gardner, "To Use Their Minds Well: Investigating New Forms of Student Assessment," in Gerald Grant (ed.), *Review of Research in Education*, op. cit., pp. 31–74.

[11] Grant Wiggins, op. cit., p. 705.

viewing test results also applies here: It is the teacher's last chance to get the point across before students move on.

The supervisor's role as facilitator of reflective practice in a learning community becomes evident in this kind of collegial work with teachers. Collaborative program evaluation points out, perhaps, a more substantive work agenda for supervisors than the more limited work of observing a class or two for the purposes of writing a report for the teacher's personnel file. It places the supervisor squarely with the teacher in seeking school renewal through classroom and program improvement.

SUMMARY

This chapter has focused on the supervisor's role in program evaluation. In order to clarify what that role is and to distinguish it from that of the evaluation expert, we presented an overview of program evaluation, of its different levels and technologies and audiences and purposes. We presented the thesis that a supervisor's role in program evaluation is primarily to work alongside teachers as they engage in the ongoing task of reflective practice, of evaluating the impact of the program on students.

We established the distinctions between formative and summative evaluation. We pointed out that students can engage in the self-evaluation process in both formative and summative evaluation. This is a central activity that reveals to the teacher how the student is personally appropriating the program as taught. We also pointed out that in the teacher's use of both formative and summative assessments, valuable learning can take place. Evaluation can be and ought to be viewed as intrinsic to both teaching and learning, and as an indispensable tool for program improvement.

CHAPTER 11

PROVIDING SUPERVISORY LEADERSHIP

THE preceding chapters in Part Two have progressively moved the supervisory process into the heart of the educational enterprise: teaching, teacher beliefs and goals, curriculum, and student learning. The supervisory process is seen not so much as the performance of bureaucratic functions such as rating teacher and student performance according to prescribed behaviors, but as facilitating both teacher and student progress in the learning tasks at hand. We have moved into the essential meaning of Supervision II. However, the more we explored what Supervision II might mean, the more it became apparent that the process of supervision could not be tied to any one role or position. It could be exercised by a principal, a district supervisor, a lead teacher, a teaching colleague, and indeed, by a student. What is essential to the process is reflection on the significance of what is happening.

As a process, supervision involves a "standing over," a "standing above," in order to achieve a larger or deeper view of the educational moment, to gain a vision of the whole as it is reflected and embodied in its parts. In short, supervision is not so much a view of a teacher by a super-ior viewer; it is a super-vision, a view of what education might mean at this moment, within this context, for these particular people. Perhaps more accurately, the process of supervision is the attempt by a segment of the community of learners to *gain* this super-vision of the educational moment within their reflective practice, so that their in-sight into the possibilities of that moment can lead to the transformation of that moment into something immensely more satisfying and productive for them.

What becomes more apparent in the exploration of the significance of Supervision II is that the process requires an open, flexible, inquiring attitude. The process is not directed at judging behaviors according to a fixed, seemingly objective set of standards. Rather, the process leads to the construction of understanding and practical judgment, which leads to tentative, experimental choices which the participants see as responsive to the particulars of the context in which they find themselves. The participants, in their reflective practice, decide whether those choices are appropriate and productive for them. This is not to say that those pragmatic choices, guided by reflective practice, will be the perfect choices. On the contrary, teaching and learning are carried forward in the reflective give and take concerning, in this particular situation, what works and what does not work, what makes sense and what does not make sense, what facilitates student performance and what does not. Neither the teacher, the students, nor the supervisor knows ahead of time what will result until they engage the material in a specific way.[1] They are constantly constructing the teaching-learning moment. Super-vision, performed by whomever, is the attempt to see that teaching-learning moment in all its multidimensionality and all its possibility.

THE SUPERVISOR AS A PROFESSIONAL

Although it is possible and desirable for students to participate in this process of supervision, the responsibility for the more formal exercise of supervision is a professional responsibility of members of the educational staff—teachers, administrators, and professional support staff. In order to exercise this professional responsibility, those engaged in the supervisory process need to have some sense (by no means ever complete) of the substance of the super-vision. In other words, they have to have some vision of an ideal educational moment or an ideal educational tapestry woven of many threads. As discussed earlier, one's educational platform is usually the unspoken foundation of such a vision, namely, a sense of how children learn, a sense of what is most valuable to learn, a sense of the social significance of what is learned, a sense of ways to orchestrate learning, a sense of the importance of community and self-governance and social character in learning and for learning. Many teachers possess this vision tacitly, but the vision becomes narrowed by the daily routine of fragmented learning tasks. Through collaborative, reflective conversations in a supervisory process, teachers can regain that super-vision for themselves and for their students.

As professional educators, those who engage in supervision need to have a large sense of the purposes of schooling. They have to bring to the supervisory process a sense of how *this* educational moment of *this* teacher and *these* students might embody the larger purposes of this school, given its neighborhood context, the socioeconomic realities of the community, the cultural make-up of its families, and the human potential and social capital such a community represents. Such an educational awareness does not come with state certification. It requires a sustained effort to be present to the cultural and social realities of the students, an attempt to understand empathetically what their world feels like and means to them. It also requires an understanding of the learning task from the inside, as it were, not simply as a proposition on a page in a textbook or course outline. Supervisors must imagine a variety of ways of entering into and working at the learning task. They must be willing to learn by trial and error what teaching strategies work in a particular instance. When one approach does not work, then both supervisor and teacher should say openly, "This isn't working. Let's try another way of looking at this."

[1] Michael Huberman, "The Social Context of Instruction in Schools," paper presented at the Annual Meeting of the American Educational Research Association, Boston, April 1990.

Gaining super-vision through the reflective practice of teaching is not a de-ductive, logical, linear type of reasoning, moving from a clearly spelled out vi-sion to a three- or four-step process that ends up choosing a specific learning activity. Rather, it is highly specific involvement with the task at hand that is illuminated by an intuition of how it is working, and by further intuitions flowing from the exchanges with the students that enable the teacher to see that this is an instance of the larger purpose or value which the school is pro-moting. The super-vision flows out of the insides of the task, rather than from a temporary pause to rise to a philosophical level of reasoning. The experi-enced teacher knows the super-vision tacitly in the particularity of the task, as Michael Polanyi would say.[2]

Such intuitions, however, come only with time, experience, and reflection. Having a sense of these complex realities is not easily gained. It requires intel-ligent inquiry, reflective assessment, and deep familiarity with the material be-ing taught. It also requires a critical assessment of the institutional barriers to teaching and learning, given all the contextual variables just mentioned. In other words, the work of supervision is intellectual work. Not exclusively in-tellectual work, but certainly work that must be enlightened by an effort to un-derstand, to develop intelligible frameworks for interpreting what happens between teachers and students and for proposing how it might happen more felicitiously. It should not be characterized as work that relies on checklists of supposedly correct teacher behaviors, or on assumptions of superior knowl-edge granted by administrative position, or on a romanticized personal experi-ence as a teacher. In other words, the practice of Supervision II places chal-lenging demands on those who exercise it.

The practice of Supervision I tends to promote incremental changes within the status quo. Hence, relatively uniform formulas define "good teaching." A relatively superficial notion of what constitutes academic knowledge suffices as a measure of effectiveness. A complacency with institutional arrangements of classroom schedules, physical arrangements of the learning space, proce-dures for grading and promotion, and so forth, assumes that teaching and learning must take place within these boundaries. A view of knowledge as something that exists independently somewhere—in the textbook, in the li-brary, in the teacher's head—and is to be communicated to the students, all of whom will receive it as some uniform package suitable for testing, informs the way Supervision I judges and rates the work teachers do.

The practice of Supervision II challenges all these assumptions. But these assumptions cannot be challenged unless one is prepared to argue intelligently for their displacement. Hence, when we say that Supervision II requires a larger professional commitment, we mean that it requires a commitment to a studied understanding of teaching and learning, a new view of the variety of settings and stimuli which can nurture learning, a new awareness of the com-plexity of student assessment, a revised concept of professional authority as a

---

[2] Michael Polanyi, *The Tacit Dimension*, Garden City, N.Y.: Doubleday Anchor, 1967.

necessary complement to hierarchical, legal authority, and an imaginative sense of the possibilities for flexible redesign of the process of schooling itself.

Supervision II requires of those who implement it to shift from the traditional roles defined by Supervision I to those of facilitator, policy innovator, resource finder, inventor, collegial experimenter, intellectual, critic, coach, institutional builder, community healer, visionary. Supervision II views the process of supervision as involving not simply observation of a teacher's class and discussion of what transpired; it starts with the belief that the whole school needs renewal, a commitment to bring the super-vision into reality in this school, a sense that work with individual teachers and groups of teachers is one aspect of a large, communal effort of transforming the school into a learning community. In other words, Supervision II assumes the exercise of leadership.[3]

EMERGING PERSPECTIVES ON LEADERSHIP

It is useful to turn to recent developments in the study of leadership for help in articulating our understanding of supervisory leadership. These theories of leadership may provide useful frameworks and imagery to interpret and describe our sense of the challenges supervisory leadership implies.

Among current scholars of leadership, Peter Vaill, James MacGregor Burns, Warren Bennis and Bert Nanus, John Gardner, and Bernard Bass provide helpful frameworks and imagery for thinking about leadership.[4]

Peter Vaill refers to an earlier scholar of leadership, Philip Selznick, and his descriptions of two essential functions of the leader as the "definition of institutional mission and role" and the "institutional embodiment of purpose."[5] Vaill coins the word "purposing" to describe one of the essential activities of the leader of a high-performing system. By purposing, he means "that continuous stream of actions by an organization's formal leadership which have the effect of inducing clarity, consensus, and commitment regarding the organization's basic purposes."[6]

The leader feels strongly about the mission of the organization and hence constantly speaks about it. The leader is very clearly focused on those basic purposes and hence knows how to translate those basic purposes into priori-

[3] For a clear exposition of the role of supervisors and administrators in school renewal, see Joseph Murphy, *The Landscape of Leadership Preparation: Patterns and Possibilities*, Berkeley, Calif.: Corwin/Sage (in press).

[4] See the following works: Peter Vaill, "The Purposing of High Performing Systems," *Organizational Dynamics*, pp. 23–39, Autumn 1982; Peter Vaill, *Managing as a Performing Art*, San Francisco, Calif.: Jossey-Bass, 1989; James MacGregor Burns, *Leadership*, New York: Harper Torchbooks, 1978; Warren Bennis and Bert Nanus, *Leaders*, New York: Harper & Row, 1985; John Gardner, *On Leadership*, New York: The Free Press, 1990; Bernard Bass, *Leadership and Performance Beyond Expectations*, New York: The Free Press, 1985.

[5] See Philip Selznick, *Leadership in Administration*, New York: Harper & Row, 1957.

[6] See Peter Vaill, "The Purposing of High Performance Systems," in Thomas J. Sergiovanni and John E. Corbally (eds.), *Leadership and Organizational Culture*, Urbana, Ill.: University of Illinois Press, 1984, p. 89.

ties and into those key elements of the organization that support those basic purposes. Through the leader's dedication to achievement of those purposes no matter the cost, he or she comes to embody the values to which the institution is committed.

In his Pulitzer prize–winning book, *Leadership,* James McGregor Burns calls attention to a distinction between transactional and transformational leadership. Transactional leadership frequently involves a quid pro quo between the leader and a follower, an exchange of a favor for a vote, a granted request here for a future request there. These transactions are governed by instrumental values or modal values such as fairness, honesty, loyalty, integrity. In transactional leadership the leader sees to it that procedures by which people enter into agreements are clear and aboveboard, and take into account the rights and needs of others. It is the leadership of the administrator who sees to the day-to-day management of the system, listening to the complaints and concerns of various participants, arbitrating disputes fairly, holding people accountable to their job targets, providing necessary resources for the achievement of subunit goals, etc. Transactional leadership deals with people seeking their own individual, independent objectives. It involves a bargaining over the individual interests of people going their own separate ways.

Transformational leadership, on the other hand, involves an exchange among people seeking common aims, uniting them to go beyond their separate interests in the pursuit of higher goals. Transformational leadership is concerned with end values such as freedom, community, equity, justice, brotherhood. It is that leadership which calls people's attention to the basic purpose of the organization, to the relationship between the organization and society. Transformational leadership changes people's attitudes, values, and beliefs from being self-centered to being higher and more altruistic.

John Gardner, long known for his thoughtful involvement with public affairs and himself a leader of several organizations, recently has added to his distinguished works a graceful book on leadership. He, too, reaches beyond the narrow empirical categories of earlier theories to elaborate on leadership characteristics culled from his reading of history and from his own experience. He posits six characteristics that distinguish leaders from typical administrators.

1 Leaders think longer-term; they look beyond immediate problems.
2 Leaders look beyond the agency or unit they are leading and grasp its relationship to larger realities of the organization, as well as to the external environment.
3 Leaders reach and influence people beyond their own jurisdiction.
4 Leaders emphasize vision, values, and motivation; they intuitively grasp the nonrational and unconscious elements in the leader-constituent interaction.
5 Leaders have political skills to cope with conflicting requirements of multiple constituencies.

6 Leaders never accept the status quo; they always think in terms of renewal.

Warren Bennis and Burt Nanus have brought the term "vision" onto center stage in their discussion of leadership. Around that term they have built a theory of leadership and a program for leadership training. They interviewed 90 people whom their colleagues identified as exceptional leaders, and out of those interviews they culled four major themes. These leaders:

1 Focused their own attention and the attention of others on a vision.
2 Communicated through symbol, rhetoric, and action the meanings embedded in their vision.
3 Positioned themselves strategically within the field of competition to maximize their own organization's strengths to embody and communicate the vision.
4 Embodied in their own person the quest for the vision through their competence and persistence.

Bernard Bass, well known for his encyclopedic survey of the literature on leadership,[7] has taken Burns's distinction between transformational and transactional leadership and developed it by means of many empirical studies using a survey instrument he and his colleagues have developed. Bass has characterized transformational leaders as charismatic, inspirational, intellectually stimulating, and considerate of individuals. "Charisma" refers to the inspiration and excitement followers derive from their association with a leader, and "intellectually stimulating" refers to the leader's ability to get followers to rethink ideas and to look at problems from different perspectives. Bass has advanced the field of leadership studies by providing empirical credibility to terms such as "charisma," and "transformational" leadership, terms previously held suspect by the more empirically fixated segments of the research community.

Bass and others have resurrected the concept of charismatic leadership from its relative neglect after Max Weber first began to use the notion to describe certain kinds of leadership. S. N. Eisenstadt has attempted, perhaps, the most ambitious treatment of that concept in his commentary on Max Weber.[8] Charisma is seen as grounded in a profound grasp of core meanings central or essential to human life (somewhat like Burns's "end values," which shape the inspiration of the transformational leader). The charismatic leader and followers eventually institutionalize those meanings in an organizational or institutional framework. The organization then carries on the visionary work of the founders. The history of most social institutions can be charted from the charismatic founding through the periodic returns to or reinterpretation of the founders' vision.

---

[7] Bernard M. Bass, *Bass and Stogdill's Handbook of Leadership,* New York: The Free Press, 1990.
[8] See S. N. Eisenstadt, *Max Weber: Charisma and Institution Building,* Chicago: University of Chicago Press, 1968.

IMPLICATIONS FOR SUPERVISORY LEADERSHIP

Vision, symbolic meanings, purpose, charisma, transformation, mission—
these relatively new terms (or old terms revisited) in the literature on leadership allow for a more comprehensive framework within which to view supervisory leadership. This framework enables us to highlight the connections
between various elements of Supervision II. We view supervisory leadership
as consisting of five basic elements.

1 It is grounded in essential meanings about human persons, society,
   knowledge, growth, learning, and schooling.
2 It is energized by a vision of what education might and should be.
3 It involves the articulation of that vision and the invitation to others to a
   communal articulation of a vision of schooling that all can embrace.
4 It seeks to embody the vision in institutional structures, frameworks, and
   policies.
5 It celebrates the vision and seeks its continuous renewal.

With this as a basic framework for thinking about supervisory leadership, it
becomes clear how Supervision II flows into practice. Supervision II begins
with new understandings of the meaning of learning, of knowledge, of teaching. Behind those meanings (elements of the supervisor's platform) lie beliefs
about the potential of human beings, their sacred value, the moral quality of
human striving, the mutual nourishing of the individual by the community
and the community by the talent and gifts of individuals, the necessity as well
as the difficulty of self-governance.Those meanings fuel a vision of schooling,
of the social, intellectual, cultural, economic, and political purposes of schooling. That vision is made up of a sense of the social construction of knowledge,
of the moral implications of the social construction of knowledge, of the importance of placing knowledge at the service of the human community—not
only for generating wealth, but also for creating cultural expressions of the human spirit, for exercising stewardship toward the natural environment, and
for re-creating a more humane social environment. The moral demands placed
on the "intellectual capital" which teachers and students create help to shape
the learning activities in which both teachers and students participate. That vision encompasses a community of learners whose sense of community flows
out of their awareness of their mutual reliance on one another to anticipate the
world of tomorrow, to explore the possibilities and promises of that tomorrow, so that the community can survive and flourish. However the vision is
expressed, it will communicate the degree to which the present institution of
schooling falls short of its potential. It will image new ways of learning, new
environments for teaching, new ways of collaborating.

Supervision II requires leadership that invites other members of the community to talk about their vision of schooling. It invites that conversation, not
in some secluded mountain resort, but in the very reflective practice of teachers in their classrooms. It invites super-vision, so that the potentialities of the

educating moment might be discovered between professionals. Through those shared visions, a new energy can begin to generate in teachers' various explorations of restructured institutional arrangements to enhance rather than constrain authentic learning. Such conversations need not initially generate grand or total visions. Rather, they can start with the context of *this* class, with smaller visions that will stretch the immediate institutional constraints on learning. As teachers and supervisors test the limits of specific institutional boundaries, new images of what might be possible can begin to emerge. More "What if we did such and such . . . ?" type of questions need to be asked, and as it becomes more customary to ask them, a consenses can begin to emerge.

The leadership of Supervision II has to be involved in the institutional redesign of education. Conversations involving super-vision have to move toward some form of embodiment of that vision in the institution. Where the image of the school as a learning community is the centerpiece of that vision, it is natural to encourage that community to study the way it conducts its business. The sense of being moral agents, of being professionals who can control the context of their work—at least to a greater extent than is now the case—needs to be supported continually in Supervision II. Out of that sense of moral agency and professional responsibility can rise the necessary motivation to tackle the difficult task of institutional renewal.

There are numerous examples of communities of educators who have chosen to take their destiny in their hands, whether as members of national networks such as the League of Essential Schools, or as individual schools. They have shown that it is possible to redesign the learning environment; reallocate the organizational supports (such as time schedules, semester calendars, and media resources); simplify, deepen, and enrich the curriculum; and revise graduation requirements. Such transformations begin with the sharing of visions, progress to the shaping of a communal vision, and continues with the hard work of translating that communal vision into the realities of a redesigned school.[9]

In those schools that have created a culture of community and a commitment to authentic learning, leaders create opportunities to celebrate the vision they espouse. These celebrations can take the form of weekly displays of students' work throughout the school, teacher- and parent-of-the-month awards, school assemblies, or special days with ceremonies to accentuate some identifying feature of the community (a musical celebration of the cultural diversity of the school community, a costume parade to kick off a special reading week, a food fair or art fair that encourages cross-cultural appreciation, etc.).

In all these activities, the school celebrates and identifies itself. It says, "This is who we are, what we stand for, what we are proud of, what we believe in."

[9] See Joan Lipsitz, *Successful Schools for Young Adolescents,* New Brunswick, N.J.: Transaction Books, 1985; Lynn Olson, "Children Flourish Here: 8 Teachers and a Theory Changed a School World," *Education Week,* January 27, 1988. For examples of transformed schools, see Thomas J. Sergiovanni, *Value Added Leadership,* San Diego, Calif.: Harcourt Brace Jovanovich, 1990.

These activities also embody dreams and aspirations of a community not yet realized either at the school or in the civic community. They are ritual ways of deepening the culture of community at the school. They also provide a kind of cultural capital that enables the community to weather the inevitable conflicts, the disappointments, the failures that wear the fabric of community thin. Finally, those celebrations of the identity of the community fuel the efforts to continue renewal of the institution. The vision of what is possible will never be realized perfectly, or even very well. Renewal is the only antidote to the disease of institutional complacency and stagnation. Yesterday's experiment becomes tomorrow's dogma; yesterday's creation becomes tomorrow's routine; yesterday's invention becomes tomorrow's definition of eternity. Without reminders through ritual and celebration of what is held dear, of what is worth sacrificing for, it is easy to allow the details of everyday life to define reality, to place a horizon on a dream, to replace the super-vision. Hence supervisors need to promote those rituals and celebrations that keep the dream alive, that facilitate conversations about new possibilities.

Having identified five crucial elements to supervisory leadership, we need to explore what they mean in greater detail. First we need to clear up a potential misunderstanding. Sometimes leadership is presented in such favorable language and management is presented as such a prosaic activity that the two might be seen as in conflict with one another or as polarized. On the contrary, schools need supervisors who fulfill both leadership and management roles. Sometimes leadership and management talent reside in the same person; at other times those talents are found in different people. Leadership alone will not get the job done; there must be someone to administer schedules, complete reports, manage budgets and resources.

The differences between the two sets of talents can be starkly differentiated as though polarized at two extremes of management activity, as represented in Figure 11-1. In practice, one can see how the two sets of talents can be brought together in a more realistic and productive harmony, as in Figure 11-2.

Leadership in supervision will always be exercized in the zone between demands and constraints.[10] There are expectations or demands, which, if not fulfilled, can lead to loss of one's job. For example, in some systems, supervisors are required to file their reports in teachers' personnel files. Failure to do so, or refusal to do so, may cause one to be fired. Constraints also hinder the leadership of supervisors. Teacher union contracts may prohibit certain collaborative efforts between supervisors and teachers. Within the demands and constraints, there are many possibilities for leadership. There are many things supervisors can do that are neither required nor prohibited. Hence, although the opportunities for leadership are not limitless, there are many ways supervisory leaders can initiate alternatives to routine practice. One way of exercising leadership

---

[10] See Thomas J. Sergiovanni, *Value Added Leadership*, San Diego, Calif.: Harcourt Brace Jovanovich, 1990, chap. 4, for a discussion of the discretion leaders enjoy. This same topic is taken up from a structuration theory perspective in Robert J. Starratt, *The Drama of Leadership*, London: Falmer Press, 1992, chap. 2.

LEADER	MANAGER
Is concerned with growth	Is concerned with maintainance
Is a director	Is a stage manager
Writes the script	Follows the script
Reflects moral authority	Reflects legal and bureaucratic authority
Challenges people	Keeps people happy
Has vision	Keeps lists, schedules, and budgets
Exercises power of shared purpose	Exercises power of sanctions and rewards
Defines what is real as what is possible	Defines what is real as what is
Motivates	Controls
Inspires	Fixes
Illuminates	Coordinates

FIGURE 11-1 Polarized distinctions between leadership and management.

LEADER	LEADER-MANAGER TEAM	MANAGER
Is concerned with growth	Is concerned with institutional growth	Is concerned with maintainance
Is a director	Engages reflective practice management	Is a stage manager
Writes the script	Communicates meanings of script	Follows script
Challenges poeple	Channels challenges into morally fulfilling and productive programs	Keeps people happy
Has vision	Institutionalizes vision	Keeps lists, schedules, and budgets
Exercises power of shared purpose	Enables power of professional and moral community	Exercises power of sanctions and rewards
Defines what is real as what is possible	Defines reality as what is possible for now, for our circumstances; tomorrow may be different	Defines what is real as what is
Motivates	Facilitates reflective practice	Organizes
Inspires	Encourages	Fixes
Illuminates	Cheerleads; celebrates	Coordinates

FIGURE 11-2 Collaboration of leadership and managerial talent.

discretion, of course, is to study the *meaning* behind the demands and the constraints in search of justifiable reasons for *interpreting* the demands and constraints as consistent with a desired course of action. Supervisory leadership can be and must be exercised, not in some fantasy, ideal world, but in specific schools with all their limitations.

One way of exploring possibilities for supervisory leadership within institutional structures is to imagine the school as being comprised of layers resembling an onion, as shown in Figure 11-3.

The surface layer represents the operational level of the school. This is the level of school life experienced on walking into a school building, seeing children on their way to class; hearing bells ring; seeing teachers in classrooms drawing diagrams on the blackboard, monitoring seat work, explaining a concept to a class; and seeing a principal standing in the corridor with a scowl or a smile on his or her face.

Underneath that layer is the organizational level of the school. This layer is made up of all those organizing structures of the school such as the weekly schedule of classes, the assignment of students and teachers to classrooms, the allocation of resources to various segments of the school, the various departments or groupings in the school, the yearly calendar, the bus schedules, and so on. Without this layer, the operations of the school would descend into chaotic anarchy.

The next layer is made up of the programs of the school. This includes the various components of the academic program as well as extracurricular pro-

FIGURE 11-3   Dimensions of school life.

grams, the guidance program, the discipline program, parent-teacher programs, and so on. School programs channel the everyday activities of the operational level toward anticipated outcomes.

Under the program layer is the policy layer. This layer comprises the policies by which the school is run: grading policies, promotion policies, suspension policies, policies covering the teachers' conditions of work as covered in the contract, pupil personnel policies, and so on. These are the general rules that govern the day-to-day decisions made by everyone in the school community.

Beneath that layer is the goals and purposes level. This level includes the general goals of the school, the mission statement (if there is one), sometimes even a philosophy of education statement. These basic statements communicate what the school community is striving to do or become or achieve.

Near the center or core is the level of beliefs and assumptions. This is the school's tacit educational platform. We say "tacit" because most of the beliefs and assumptions rarely are explicit. People assume that children come to school to learn; people believe that parents have the best intentions for their children; people assume that teachers want children to learn something in the classroom; people assume that society is rational; people believe that the state has the best interests of the children at heart in enforcing mandatory school attendance laws, and so on. The list of beliefs and assumptions is potentially infinite, for it pertains to the most basic matters in life.

At the core, sometimes flowing into the layer of beliefs and assumptions, are the myths and meanings by which people make sense out of their lives, by which they define value, by which human striving is judged, by which individuals place themselves in a definable order of things. This core is almost beyond articulation. Philosophers and anthropologists and artists might rummage around in that core of myth and meaning, but most people live their lives in quiet confidence that life holds together and that circumstances of their lives have some kind of ultimate meaning. Nevertheless, it is in that core of myth, meaning, and belief that leaders find the foundation for their vision of what the school can and ought to become. The core includes myths of heroism, human destiny, the sacred nature of all life. It includes myths about humanity's relationship with nature, about the values underlying the nation's identity, about those virtues considered to be the essence of humanity. The core also includes myths about the nature of society, about the source of order in the universe, about the large meanings found in human history. Those myths, often embodied in story, in poem, in highly symbolic literature, shape people's convictions, beliefs, and attitudes toward most things. These universal myths enable people to reach consensus on their beliefs and assumptions.

As illustrated in Figure 11-4, schools exist in which those deep meanings are seldom referred to, in which the core might just as well be empty, because these schools focus totally on surface tasks. In contrast, Figure 11-5 illustrates a

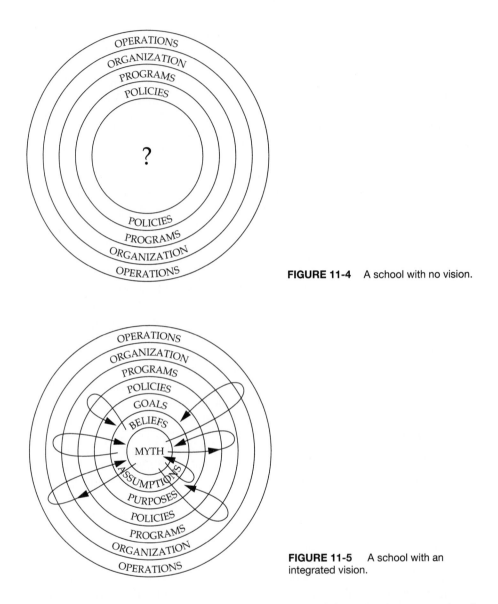

FIGURE 11-4   A school with no vision.

FIGURE 11-5   A school with an integrated vision.

school in which the myths and beliefs at the core of the school are articulated in a communal vision and penetrate every layer of school life. Every program and policy refers to a core of meanings that unify and provide identity to the community.

LEADERSHIP AND INSTITUTIONAL RENEWAL

In our framework for supervisory leadership we spoke of the leader's vision of the school, and how that is made up of meanings about fundamental values in life. It becomes apparent that those meanings are grounded in universal myths about communal destiny, national identity, humanity's relationship to nature, and so on. The vision normally employs metaphors and imagery: "Our classrooms are like gardens"; "In our class we compose a symphony of joyful music"; "Being at this school is like going on a journey"; "We voyage into the unknown on the fragile barque of science"; "Sycamore School is like a family." The vision is not a developed blueprint; rather it is like a symbolic compass, pointing toward an ideal.[11] A vision statement, a gathering together of the school's communal vision, may consist of three or four paragraphs, but it should not turn into a full-blown philosophy statement or a long-range plan. Much of its power comes from capturing three, maybe four central meanings that are open to multiple applications and representations within the school. The vision statement should create a value framework that enables daily, routine activities to take on a special meaning and significance, making the school a *special* place, instilling feelings of ownership, identity, participation, and moral fulfillment. Peter Block offers an interesting tip about vision statements: If your vision statement sounds like Motherhood and Apple Pie and is somewhat embarrassing, you are on the right track![12]

In our framework for supervisory leadership, we identified one of the basic elements of leadership as embedding the vision in institutional structures and processes. An examination of the layers of school life can show how this effort is worked out in practice. At the operational level of everyday classroom activities, supervisors can reflect with teachers on how the vision is expressed thematically in student learning activities and in the way people treat each other in the classroom. As supervisors and teachers reflect on institutional constraints that impede the fuller realization of this vision in classroom learning activities, they may find that the organizational layer of the school does not at all reflect the vision that is supposed to guide the school. For example, a school day divided into eight or nine periods is too distracting to sustain any quality learning; students are carrying too many subjects—as many as seven—to sustain quality learning; classrooms are definitely not user-friendly spaces. From a more realistic perspective, supervisors and teachers may discover their vision by recognizing the mechanistic countervision that drives the daily schedule. That is to say, they may realize what they have been looking for by encountering its opposite.

Going further, the supervisor may discover contradictions to the vision in the way the curriculum program is packaged or, on a deeper level, in policies that govern major decisions at the school, for example, how grades and class rank are determined, or how standardized tests are used to place children in various academic tracks. The schoolwide goal of bringing children up to grade level in standardized reading and math tests may be a legitimate goal for the

[11] See Thomas J. Sergiovanni, op. cit., chap. 5.
[12] See Peter Block, *The Empowered Manager: Positive Political Skills at Work,* San Francisco, Calif.: Jossey Bass, 1987.

school, but an exclusive insistence on that goal may smother other equally legitimate goals of the school. Furthermore, such a focus on standardized tests may distort the very process of teaching authentic reading and math, as research tends to show.[13]

The vision statement does not have an impact on student learning unless it is institutionalized in the various layers of school life. By enlarging the view of reflective practice from the individual teacher to include the community of learners, a sense of how school renewal can take place begins to form. One of the reasons schools remain dysfunctional is that the community fails to confront the organizational structures and dynamics that create the dysfunction. The concept that school life is manifest in layers provides a heuristic tool for identifying sources of contradiction in the vision, and a framework for building a school whose vision is integrated into the total fabric of the school as an institution.

It is becoming apparent why leaders and managers need each other. While leaders tend to focus on the vision, managers often are the ones who know how to make things work. As summarized in Figure 11-6, supervisors who wear a managerial hat tend to focus more on the operational aspect of the school, and supervisors as leaders feel more comfortable with the vision aspect of the school. They work together best when embedding the vision in policies,

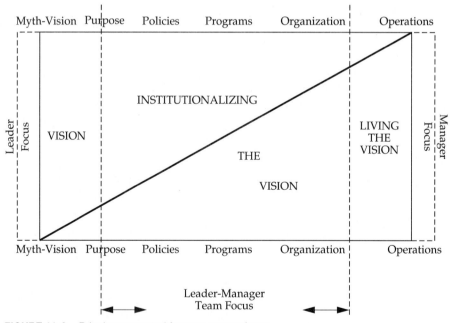

FIGURE 11-6   Bringing separated focus to a team focus.

[13] Michael Kirst, "Interview on Assessment with Lorrie Shepard," *Educational Researcher*, vol. 20, no. 2, pp. 21–23, 27, March 1991.

ROOTS OF THE VISION	ARTICULATION OF THE VISION	INSTITUTIONALIZATION OF THE VISION	OPERATIONALIZATION OF THE VISION
Meaning associated with: Human destiny The nature of the individual The nature of human society View of the past and of the future Frequently embedded in imagery, metaphor, myth, and story	Beliefs about: – the human mind and how one knows – how children develop as full human beings – how children should be socialized – varieties of learning – moral values – political values – religious values – what kind of future the young will face	Formal Organization Policies Programs Procedures – Graduation requirements – Curriculum – Course selection and assignment – Grading criteria – Discipline – Student activities – Staffing – Budget Informal Organization Community spirit Style of communications Tone of relationships Informal group Informal curriculum	Woodrow Wilson School A school that opens its doors and looks like: People coming and going to – classes – activities – interactions making up a fabric of experience – meanings – patterns – rituals – symbolic action – celebration
	Formal Statement of the Mission of the School Cultural purposes Political purposes Academic purposes Moral purposes Economic purposes Social purposes Religious purposes Processes of Communicating the Vision – Thematic purposing – Rituals – Celebrations – Championing – Heroes – Rewards		
MYTH	ASSUMPTIONS, BELIEFS	GOALS, OBJECTIVES	POLICIES, PROGRAMS, STRUCTURES
			OPERATIONS

FIGURE 11-7 The communal institutionalization of vision.

197

programs, and organizational structures. Managers are relatively comfortable manipulating the variables in these areas, but they need leaders to talk through the implications of the vision at a level of specificity so that institutional forms of the vision can be fashioned.

Finally, the ways in which the vision can be integrated with the various levels of the school organization are illustrated in Figure 11-7. There the elements of the framework of supervisory leadership build on one another, resulting in the renewal of the school in its day-to-day life. While this view of supervisory leadership may seem rather ambitious, it is clearly the framework called for by Supervision II. The supervisor's work with the individual teacher does not make a whit of difference in the effort toward school renewal unless it is actively linked to the school *community's* effort to renew itself. Supervisors can make a substantial contribution to this effort. When we reflect on the relative isolation of the field of supervision from the national conversation over school reform, it seems due to supervision being conceived as narrowly focused on bureaucratic management functions. Yet, when reflecting on the leadership possibilities of supervision, it appears that participation in this ambitious agenda of reform may provide supervision its only real justification.

SUMMARY

The succeeding chapters will return to the details of practice. Part Two has raised important questions about the educational leadership of supervisors. That leadership is to be exercised in reflective practice with individual teachers and with the community of teachers in the context of school renewal. In the chapters to come, the lofty language of vision, transformation, and myth will be replaced by the language of practice, as it is found in classrooms. The moral here should not be missed. It is imperative for supervisors to have a vision, to push for a super-vision of what is possible in various learning situations. The work, however, should be carried forward in everyday language, in teachers' language, rather than the language of theory and the language of the research university. The work may appear more humble when described in the language of practice, but it remains filled with sacred significance. Hence the reader is asked not to forget what underlies the practice of supervision as it is explored in the following chapters, for though educators may become immersed in practice, they are energized by the vision of the possibilities for transforming schools—it is to that end that Supervision II labors.

PART THREE

THE PRACTICE OF CLASSROOM SUPERVISION

CHAPTER 12

A FRAMEWORK FOR
CLASSROOM SUPERVISION

TO many supervisors teacher evaluation means the rating, grading, and classifying of teachers using some locally standardized instrument as a yardstick. Generally the instrument lists traits of teachers assumed to be important, such as "The teacher has a pleasant voice," and certain tasks of teaching considered to be critical, such as "The teacher plans well." The evaluator usually writes in comments as, increasingly, does the teacher.

This evaluation instrument is filled out after a classroom observation of the teacher, often lasting from a half hour to one hour. The observation visit is usually preceded by a conference, which varies from a brief encounter to a session where lesson plans, objectives, and teaching strategies are discussed. Sometimes a post-observation conference follows, wherein comments and ratings are discussed and negotiated. Usually, the teacher-evaluation procedure is concluded when both parties sign the instrument. The instrument is then forwarded to the district archives. This teacher-evaluation procedure may occur once or twice a year for the tenured teacher and two to four times a year for novices. Many teachers report having been observed in the classroom only a handful of times, and reports of almost never being observed after achieving tenure are common.

In an effort to correct this problem some states have passed laws that require a much more intensive evaluation, often using state-provided standardized instruments. The instruments are comprised of teaching behaviors claimed to be linked to the "teaching effectiveness" research and thus are considered to be "scientific" and "objective." As we shall point out, the systems turn out to be neither scientific nor objective and the teaching-effectiveness research upon which they claim to be based is often misrepresented.

By and large neither teachers nor administrators and supervisors are satisfied with present procedures. More damaging, many supervisors privately view the procedures as lacking in credibility. What are the likely effects of participating in a system characterized by such doubts? The system takes on a certain artificial or mechanical quality, a routine functioning that becomes an end in itself.

Some schools practice classroom supervision by remote control. This scientific-management view assumes that if the focus is on educational program administration and supervision through development of a materials-intensive curriculum, usually linked to a detailed curriculum syllabus or detailed predetermined objectives, then teachers can be supervised from a distance. Teaching behavior becomes more predictable and reliable as teaching objectives and materials become more detailed, structured, and standardized. Thus, what teachers do is controlled by controlling the objectives they pursue, the materials they use, the curriculum they follow, the assignments and tests they give, and the schedules they follow.

Seeking to control classroom practices by remote control raises nagging questions. How can supervisors be sure that teachers are indeed performing prescribed duties up to standard? What evaluation technologies can be used to answer this question? The problem is that technologies of classroom observation and evaluation are too often shrouded in scientism not found even in the more legitimate sciences. Yet most teachers and supervisors privately believe that *teaching is far more an artistic enterprise than a scientific one.*

In the next several chapters we propose artistic and reflective approaches to supervision and evaluation that are more consistent with how teachers think and what they do and with the complexities involved in the work of teaching and learning. This chapter begins the discussion with theoretical aspects of supervision, paying close attention to the differences between theories associated with Supervision I and Supervision II. Chapter 13 examines clinical supervision in practice, Chapter 14 examines the controversial problem of teacher evaluation, Chapter 15 examines the link between supervision and staff development, and Chapter 16 argues for the provision of options in supervision and evaluation.

Basic to the discussion in all the chapters in Part Three is the view that supervision must be less connected to roles. It must become a process and sometimes a set of skills available to teachers and principals alike. Indeed the future we advocate is a supervision based less and less on bureaucratic authority and more and more on professional and moral authority—a supervision firmly in the hands of both teachers and principals.

THE FOCUS OF CLINICAL SUPERVISION

In the interest of focusing attention on classroom supervision, some experts distinguish between classroom supervision and out-of-class supervision, with the former being clinical and the latter general. Morris Cogan, for example, cites two purposes of clinical supervision in his popular book entitled *Clinical Supervision:* "The first is to develop and explicate a system of in-class supervision that, in competent hands, will prove powerful enough to give supervisors a reasonable hope of accomplishing significant improvements in the teacher's classroom instruction. The second purpose is to help correct the neglect of in-class or clinical supervision and to establish it as a necessary complement to out-of-class ('general') supervision."[1]

In a similar vein Robert Goldhammer refers to clinical supervision as follows:

[1] Morris L. Cogan, *Clinical Supervision,* Boston: Houghton Mifflin, 1973, p. xi.

First of all, I mean to convey an image of face-to-face relationships between supervisors and teachers. History provides the principal reason for this emphasis, namely, that in many situations presently and during various periods in its development, supervision has been conducted as supervision from a distance, as, for example, supervision of curriculum development or of instructional policies framed by committees of teachers. "Clinical" supervision is meant to imply supervision up close.[2]

General and clinical supervision are, of course, interdependent. Meaningful classroom interventions are built upon healthy organizational climates, facilitated by credible leadership and premised on a reasoned educational program. Though general supervision is an important and necessary component of effective supervision, without clinical supervision it is not sufficient.

Clinical supervision refers to face-to-face contact with teachers with the intent of improving instruction and increasing professional growth. In many respects, a one-to-one correspondence exists between improving classroom instruction and increasing professional growth, and for this reason staff development and clinical supervision are inseparable concepts and activities. How does evaluation fit into this picture? Evaluation is a natural part of one's professional life and occurs continuously. Every decision that teachers, administrators, and supervisors make is preceded by evaluation (often implicit) of some sort. Evaluation is valuing, and valuing is judging. These are natural events in the lives of educational professionals and, of course, are critical aspects of clinical supervision and staff development.

But evaluation can have a number of focuses, some of which are more compatible with events, purposes, and characteristics of supervision than others. Evaluation experts, for example, make an important distinction between *formative* evaluation and *summative* evaluation.[3] Teacher-evaluation procedures typically found in school can be classified as summative. Evaluation that emphasizes ongoing growth and development would be considered formative. Consider the following distinctions:

1 Summative evaluation of teachers has a certain finality to it—it is terminal in the sense that it occurs at the conclusion of an educational activity. In evaluating a teacher's performance, summative evaluation suggests a statement of worth. A judgment is made about the quality of one's teaching.

2 Summative evaluation is a legitimate and important activity which if done carefully can play a constructive role in a school's total evaluation strategy.

3 Formative evaluation of teachers is intended to increase the effectiveness of ongoing educational programs and activity. Evaluation information

[2] Robert Goldhammer, *Clinical Supervision: Special Methods for the Supervision of Teachers*, New York: Holt, 1969, p. 54.

[3] Michael Scriven, "The Methodology of Evaluation," in Robert Stake (ed.), *AERA Monograph on Curriculum Evaluation*, no. 1, Chicago: Rand McNally, 1965. See also Benjamin Bloom, Thomas Hastings, and G. F. Madaus, *Handbook on Formative and Summative Evaluation of Student Learning*, New York: McGraw-Hill, 1971.

is collected and used to understand, correct, and improve ongoing activity.

4 With respect to teaching, formative evaluation is concerned less with judging and rating the teacher than with providing information which helps improve teacher performance.

5 In the strictest sense formative and summative evaluation cannot be separated, for each contains aspects of the other, but it is useful nevertheless to speak of a formative focus and a summative focus to evaluation.[4]

The focus of clinical supervision should be on formative evaluation. The supervisor is first and foremost interested in improving teaching and increasing teachers' personal development. Does this emphasis conflict with demands that teachers be held accountable for their actions? We think not. A formative evaluation emphasis is entirely consistent with holding teachers accountable in a professional, not bureaucratic, sense. Professional accountability is growth-oriented and implies a commitment to consistent improvement. Bureaucratic accountability is not growth-oriented at all but merely seeks to ensure that teachers measure up to some predetermined standard.

From time to time supervisors will indeed be engaged in a more summatively focused evaluation. Though the supervisor's major commitment is to formative evaluation, occasional problems occur and incompetent teachers or teachers whose philosophy and orientation differ markedly from that of the school will be discovered. As a result, withholding tenure or dismissal of a tenured teacher may well be considered. Personnel actions of this sort are so intertwined with existing local administrative policies and state statutory restrictions and requirements that a totally different mind-set is needed. Such a procedure is best placed in the hands of a line administrative officer of the district. In the case of a principal who assumes both supervisory and administrative roles, the teacher should be informed of the focus and the tone of the evaluation procedure that is to follow. The school attorney would most likely be consulted regarding due process if administrative guidelines on this question are wanting. In Toledo and other school districts the teachers' union is involved in the process, working cooperatively with "management" to ensure due process on the one hand and *warranted* dismissal on the other. Many state education agencies and state school board associations publish pamphlets and other guidelines on this controversial and increasingly legalistic problem. These issues are discussed further in Chapter 14.

Practically speaking, improving classroom instruction must start with the teacher. Sustained changes in teacher behavior and sustained improvements in classroom functioning occur when teachers are committed to these changes. That being the case, supervisors are forced to depend upon the cooperation of teachers. Indeed, supervisors rarely change teachers but help them to change, a condition more suited to formative evaluation.

[4] Thomas J. Sergiovanni, *Handbook for Effective Department Leadership Concepts and Practices in Today's Secondary Schools,* Boston: Allyn and Bacon, 1977, p. 372.

GETTING THE THEORY RIGHT

If the theory is wrong, the practice is wrong. Many teachers and supervisors claim they do not practice according to theory, but in response to the realities they face and the experiences they accumulate. Nonetheless, their practice *is* theory-based, though the theories may be implicit. Whether supervisors and teachers rely on theories that emerge from scholarly speculation and research or rely on subjective theories based on their intuition and experience (or some combination of both) the effect is the same: *theory-based practice.* Thus the caution "If the theory is wrong, the practice is wrong" is a serious one. To understand and improve current practice, an examination of the adequacy of underlying theories is necessary.[5]

Many educators dream of building a body of knowledge, a method of inquiry, and patterns of practice that will provide the basis for a true profession of teaching and clinically oriented supervision comparable with that of architecture and medicine or perhaps the performing arts professions. We believe that it is possible for supervision and teaching to become established and recognized fields of inquiry and professional practice. The question is: Are educators going about this process the right way? Presently, theorizing and model building is patterned too closely after the physical sciences. Unfortunately, this patterning is simplistic. The problems addressed, the theorizing, how research is conducted, the conclusions drawn, and the building of practice models based on this inquiry are not sufficiently complex or comprehensive to be considered scientific by the established scientific community. Nor do they meet the standards of scientific and professional rigor that characterize the established professions. Persistence in spite of these obstacles leads to the development of *rationalistic* theories and practices.

According to Terry Winograd and Fernando Flores, "The rationalistic tradition is distinguished by its narrow focus on certain aspects of rationality which . . . often leads to attitudes and activities that are not rational in a broader perspective."[6] Further, as the philosopher Charles Taylor suggests, rationalistic theories and models are typically implausible given the realities of practice and tend to lead to bad science by being either wordy elaborations of the obvious or by dealing with trivial questions.[7] Stated in our context, rationalistic

---

[5] For a more in-depth analysis of the point of view provided in the chapter see Thomas J. Sergiovanni, "Expanding Conceptions of Inquiry and Practice in Supervision and Evaluation," *Educational Evaluation and Policy Analysis,* vol. 6, no. 3, pp. 355–365, 1984; "Landscapes, Mindscapes and Reflective Practice in Supervision," *Journal of Curriculum and Supervision,* vol. 1, no. 1, pp. 5–17, 1985; "Understanding Reflective Practice," *Journal of Curriculum and Supervision,* vol. 6, no. 4, pp. 355–365, 1986; "The Metaphorical Use of Theories and Models in Supervision: Building a Science," *Journal of Curriculum and Supervision,* vol. 2, no. 3, pp. 221–232, 1987; "We Need a TRUE Profession!" *Educational Leadership,* vol. 44, no. 8, 1987; and "Science and Scientism in Supervision and Teaching," *Journal of Curriculum and Supervision,* vol. 4, no. 2, pp. 93–102, 1989.

[6] Terry Winograd and Fernando Flores, *Understanding Computers and Cognition,* Norwood, N.J.: Ablex Publishing Corp., 1986, p. 8.

[7] Charles Taylor, *Philosophy and the Human Sciences Philosophical Papers,* vol. 2, London: Cambridge University Press, 1985.

theories and models do not fit the real world of teaching and supervision. When such models are used anyway, teaching typically suffers, and teachers and supervisors experience frustration, combined with a loss of confidence in what sound theory and research can provide.

Building generic models of teaching and supervisory practice based on the "teaching effectiveness" research is an example of rationalistic rather than rational thinking. This research reveals that the explicit or direct teaching model is an effective way to teach basic reading and computational skills and simple subject-matter mastery to elementary school children. Assuming that this method represents "effective teaching" and thus prescribing this teaching as a means by which all learning should take place is hardly a rational approach to model building and to teaching practice. Yet consultants, workshop specialists, contributors to widely circulated professional publications, and others have been quite successful in convincing many policymakers and professionals that explicit teaching is indeed the same as effective teaching. One popular example at this writing is the adoption by school districts and in some cases by entire states of teacher-evaluation checklists and other instruments composed of items primarily or exclusively based on this research. This results in uniform use of an instrument that might be appropriate for a limited range of teaching and learning outcomes but is invalid for other teaching and learning outcomes.

HOW SCIENTISTS AND PROFESSIONALS THINK

In the professions and sciences advances have been made in understanding the nature of knowledge that are not sufficiently reflected in mainstream supervisory thought. There is, for example, remarkable agreement that human thinking influences scientific reality. The psychologist Joseph McGrath states, "We can never know anything independently of the ways we found it out; empirical knowledge is always contingent on the methods, populations, situations and underlying assumptions involved in the process by which knowledge was acquired."[8] Throughout the social sciences there is wide acceptance of the notion that scientific decisions are human choices and thus what counts as scientific evidence is often little more than an artifact of these choices. Different choices result in different scientific evidence. Gestalt psychologists are fond of demonstrating how human decisions help to create reality. One well-known example they use is the picture of a vase made of two profiles. Is it a vase or two profiles? One can see either, but one cannot see both at the same time. One must decide which reality one is going to see, and it is one's decision that creates reality.

The link between human decisions and existing reality is true as well in the physical sciences. The examples most often cited are drawn from the strange

---

[8] Joseph E. McGrath, Joanne Martin, and Richard Kulka, *Judgment Calls in Research*, Beverly Hills, Calif.: Sage, 1982, p. 105.

behavior of light and matter in quantum mechanics. For example, the principle of complementarity provides that in some cases complementary concepts whose meanings exclude each other are, nonetheless, different representations of the same thing. With respect to light, particle representations and wave representations are complementary properties of electrons. Whether an electron appears as a particle or as a wave (the nature of scientific reality for that electron) depends upon how it is measured. One method of measurement provides a particle representation and the other a wave representation. Thus the representation of an electron cannot be determined separate from a human decision as to how it will be measured. That decision, in a very large sense, *creates* the nature of scientific reality.[9]

David Gooding provides a compelling case for linking scientific observation and experiment in all fields with human actions and decisions.[10] He believes that scientists are involved as much in making meaning as they are in discovering truth. Truth seeking gets the attention in part because the making of meaning is hidden by the accepted scientific protocols for conducting and writing up experimental research. According to the protocols, theory testing in physics, chemistry, psychology, and many other areas is expected to be represented by and written up as a logically structured narrative as follows:

1 Derive research hypothesis from theory.
2 Derive *observable* hypothesis from research hypothesis.
3 Design controlled environment in which the research set up (methods, procedures, etc.) yields the observable hypothesis.
4 Conduct the experiment.
5 Observe results.
6 Compare observed results with observable hypothesis.
7 If observed results equal observed hypothesis then assume research hypothesis is implied and that the theory itself is implied.

If observed results do not equal observed hypothesis then assume that research hypothesis is not implied. Research hypothesis not implied assumes that either the theory is not implied or that the experimental set up was either not correct or not realized.[11]

Logically structured narratives, however, do not describe what really happens in research. Throughout, the process of research is subjective and judgmental, as decision after decision and interpretation after interpretation are made. Decision A instead of decision B or interpretation 1 instead of interpretation 2 changes the experiment, realizes different evidence, and leads to different conclusions about what is and is not accepted as truth. For example, in

---

[9] For a popular discussion of this theme see Heinz R. Pagels, *The Cosmic Code: Quantum Physics as the Language of Nature,* New York: Simon and Schuster, 1982. For further applications to supervision see Sergiovanni, op. cit., "Expanding Conceptions of Inquiry and Practice in Supervision and Evaluation."

[10] David Gooding, *Experiment and the Making of Meaning Human Agency in Scientific Observation and Experiment,* Boston: Kluwer, 1990.

[11] See, for example, ibid., p. 136.

the above case it makes a difference which theory the researcher chooses as the overarching framework. Once the theory is chosen it makes a difference which research hypotheses are selected for study. A critical subjective step in any research is the transformation of research hypothesis to observable hypothesis. For example, in researching the effects of teacher warmth on student learning, when "warmth" is operationally defined as frequency of smiling, the results may be quite different from those derived from other operational definitions. Further, a research design decision to assess warmth by tracking teacher behaviors instead of student behaviors (having kindergartners check a smiling face, for example) may produce different results.

Gooding points out that the research experiment involves the creation of meaning because at every step, from formation of the initial idea by an individual researcher to final acceptance by the academy, scientific knowledge involves human reconstruction.[12] The textbook writer, for example, provides knowledge expositions of scientific exemplars that represents a synthesis of articles and other scholarly treatises. These papers are in turn summaries and extensions of research papers and monographs that detail experiments that followed the logically structured narrative form described above. The original experiments reported in the narrative were very likely shaped by numerous conversations the researcher had with colleagues and by the writing and circulation of drafts and proposals. The researcher's meaning, at this stage, is influenced by the shared meanings with colleagues. At the root of it all are the original insights and ideas about the problem to be studied as recorded in the researcher's private notes. This progression from notebook to textbook is one of constant reconstruction of knowledge. As ideas are written and rewritten and as interpretations are made, meanings change accordingly. In the final stages of reconstruction accepted meaning in practice is often shaped by textbook writers, workshop providers, and other individuals who may not know the researcher or the research firsthand.

Returning to the "teaching-effectiveness" research example, the indicators of effectiveness commonly cited are an artifact of how the researchers decided to define effectiveness. Had they defined effectiveness differently, different indicators would have been discovered. The indicators, therefore, are not independent or objective but a function of human decisions. Imagine what the consequences of redefining effectiveness would be in schools and indeed states that use evaluation instruments based on the original teaching-effectiveness research? Since the instrument behaviors would no longer be "valid," teachers thought to be "winners" might well be "losers" and vice versa. Winning and losing in teacher evaluation is never objective but always an artifact of the evaluation system used.

THE MISMATCH WITH PRACTICE

Rationalistic models of teaching and supervision are not only unscientific but also are mismatched with the realities of practice. Rationalistic models empha-

---

[12] Ibid., pp. 6–7.

size uniform answers to problems, value-free teaching strategies, separation of teaching and evaluation process from context, objectivity, and a uniform-technical language system. Patterns of supervision and teaching practice found in the real world, however, are characterized by a great deal of uncertainty, instability, complexity, and variety. Further, value conflicts and uniqueness are accepted aspects of educational settings. Since the real world of teaching is characterized by unique events, uniform answers to problems are not likely to be very helpful. Since teachers, supervisors, and students bring to the classroom beliefs, assumptions, values, opinions, and preferences, objective and value-free supervisory strategies are not likely to address issues of importance. Since reality in practice does not exist separate from individuals involved in the processes of teaching and supervision, knowing cannot be separated from what is known. Since evaluation reality in teaching is linked to the observer and to decisions she or he makes about methods of evaluation, it is not independent or objective but an artifact of this situation. Since supervisory reality is context-bound and situationally determined, the practical language of actual classroom life and actual teaching events is more meaningful than the theoretical language or generic language that may be inherent in rating scales and other measurement devices associated with the rationalistic view.

What changes are needed in the ways in which educators think about, inquire, and practice if teaching and supervision are to become less rationalistic and more rational? First, mindscapes of how schools work and how life in classrooms unfolds need to change. Mindscapes help people construct their reality. Different realities lead to different supervisory and teaching practices. Teaching, for example, often thought of as a tightly connected process that resembles the throwing of teaching pitches into a learning outcome zone. There is always the danger that some pitches will miss the zone and thus be declared balls. Therefore, supervision, within this mindscape, focuses on increasing the likelihood of teaching strikes being thrown. The emphasis is on programming and monitoring the practice of teaching to ensure that the process unfolds in a reliable and predictable manner. The problem with this mindscape is that it does not reflect the realities of practice, provides a limited and unsophisticated view of the nature of teaching and learning, and provides a regressive view of the role of the teacher.

PATTERNED RATIONALITY

When teaching is conceived as pitching, detailed goals and objectives are considered critical. But teachers typically do not think and act in accord with discrete goals and objectives as much as they do in value patterns. Reading teachers are as concerned with the students' ability to synthesize and extend as they are with the mastery of reading fundamentals. They recognize that both goals need to be pursued in a manner that makes the experience of reading a joyful activity. But the three goals are often in competition. Too much emphasis on one can negatively affect each of the other two. The issue for the teacher is how to achieve a balance between and among competing values; the rationality that is appropriate is not linear or bureaucratic but pursues a pattern of outcomes. Some experts refer to this rationality as *patterned rationality.*[13] Since teachers are concerned with outcomes that produce a sensible pattern, it is difficult to ask them to think specifically in terms of this outcome or that or even several outcomes discretely.

The surfing metaphor is much more descriptive of how teachers think and act. Teachers ride the wave of the teaching pattern as it uncurls. In riding the wave they use various models of teaching and learning not rationalistically to prescribe practice but rationally to inform intuition and enhance professional judgment. A rational science of supervision and teaching places more emphasis on developing strategies that reflect a higher concern for values than goals, for patterns than discrete outcomes, and for learning how to ride the pattern of the wave of teaching.

Craft knowledge reveals that when teachers do think about goals and objectives they're just as likely to think about discovering them in the act of teaching as they are in setting them beforehand. Teachers adopt a more strategic than tactical view of goals and objectives. When "surfing," they gear their practice toward broad and often changing goals and rely heavily on assessing what was worthwhile after learning encounters have been concluded. Teachers are not likely to declare that something worthwhile did not count simply because they did not anticipate it beforehand. This reality is not sufficiently accounted for in rationalistic models of teaching and supervision.

CONFUSING EVALUATION AND MEASUREMENT

Rationalistic thinking is encouraged by the confusion that exists between measurement and evaluation. For example, much of what passes as evaluation isn't evaluation at all but measurement. Suppose you are interested in buying blinds for a window in your home. You would first need to know the size of the window. The window is 22 inches wide by 60 inches long. This set of figures is now your standard. You find some extra blinds in the attic. Using a ruler, you carefully measure the blinds and learn that none "measures up" to your standard. Though you had a role to play in this process it was really the ruler that counted. Someone else using the same ruler would very likely have reached the same conclusion.

Though measurements need to be accurate and some skill is involved in the process, the standard against which measurements are weighed and the measuring device are more important than the person doing the measuring. Ideally, measurement should be "personproof" in the sense that each person measuring should reach the same conclusion. Interrater reliability is highly valued. Thus in measurement-oriented evaluation systems the role of the evaluator is *diminished*. Principals and supervisors are *less important* than the instruments

[13] Jean Hills, "The Preparation of Educational Leaders: What's Needed and What's Next?" UCEA Occasional Paper 8303, Columbus, Ohio: University Council for Educational Administration, 1982.

and procedures they use. Further, when a measurement-oriented evaluation system is imported to a school or state, principals, supervisors, teachers, and the public forfeit the right to decide for themselves what is good teaching—what is the kind of teaching that makes sense to them given their goals, aspirations, the characteristics of their community, and so forth. Measurement-oriented evaluation systems, therefore, not only frequently result in rationalistic practices; they can threaten one of the fundamental values undergirding schooling in America—the right to choose.

Evaluation, by contrast, is a distinctly human process that involves discernment and making informed judgments. Evaluation is never value-free or context-free. In our example above, having decided on the size of blinds needed, all subsequent decisions are a matter of preference, taste, and purpose. What effect do you want to create in the room you are decorating? Do you prefer wooden or metal blinds, a soft or bold look, warm or cool colors? How will the available options fit into the broader decorating scheme of the room? In matters of evaluation "interrater reliability" is not highly valued. Instead the evaluator's judgment given desired effects is what counts. Evaluation is a distinctly human rather than mechanical process.

IMPROVING THE ACCURACY OF EVALUATION

Accuracy and precision are the standard criteria used by the more established disciplines and professions to judge the adequacy of knowledge claims and the applicability of these claims to practice. Accuracy refers to the relevance and importance of problems pursued and resulting findings. Precision refers to the cogency and rigor with which problems are pursued. In the established disciplines and professions accuracy is never sacrificed on behalf of relevance. Medical researchers and physicists, for example, do not pursue trivial questions at the expense of important ones simply because they lend themselves to greater scientific rigor and study. The Nobel laureate P. B. Medawar states, "It has been shrewdly observed that an experiment not worth doing is not worth doing well."[14] Emphasizing precision over accuracy follows the reasoning of the person who lost his keys in the middle of the block but looked for them at the street corner because the light was better.

Rationalistic decisions are made every time educators opt for teaching and supervisory models because they are clearly stated and easy to learn and use, and because the dimensions they address are readily observable and measurable with little regard for whether they address what really is important in teaching. A rational approach accepts the fact that it is far better to find an approximate answer to the right question no matter how vague than an exact answer to the wrong question which can always be made precise.[15] Much of the

[14] P. B. Medawar, *The Limits of Science,* New York: Harper & Row, 1984, p. 79.
[15] John Tukey as cited in R. Rose, "Disciplined Research and Undisciplined Problems," Carol Weiss (ed.). *Using Social Research in Public Policy Making,* Washington, D.C.: Heath, 1977, p. 23.

appeal of rationalistic models of teaching and supervision is in their precision, regardless of whether they are accurate or not. They look scientific, they are easy to use, and too often that's all that seems to matter.

"Validity" and "reliability" are the official psychometric terms for accuracy and precision. Rationalistic thinking and practice is widespread with respect to validity and reliability. Such well-known evaluation experts as Michael Scriven and Ernest House, for example, point out that validity is frequently sacrificed for reliability, and often reliability substitutes for validity, creating an evaluation error of the first magnitude.[16]

THE PHONETICS AND SEMANTICS OF TEACHING

Teaching and supervision can be examined at two levels—the level of observed behavior and the level of meaning and understanding. The level of observed behavior represents the phonetics of teaching and the level of meaning and understanding the semantics. Phonetic teaching is easily observed and lends itself to "scientific" measuring with a great deal of reliability. In contrast, the semantic side of teaching, because it refers to the deep structure and meanings that people attribute to and derive from teaching behaviors and events, is not so easily understood.

Take, for example, the common prescriptions for teaching: communicate expectations, monitor to ensure that students comply, solicit frequent responses, provide corrective feedback, and reteach as necessary. Carefully assessing teaching behaviors to ensure that these prescriptions are in evidence leaves unanswered the questions of what this approach to teaching means to students, how this teaching is to be understood by teachers and supervisors, whether the steps fit teaching purposes, and what useful personal meanings different students might derive from the same teaching. Consider how the color yellow is understood differently against fields of white and black. At one level yellow is yellow but at another level yellow against a white field is quite different from yellow against a black field. Considering yellow to be "yellow" regardless of the field emphasizes too much the phonetic aspect of this word rather than the semantic. Consider as well the meaning of winks exchanged by a grandparent or child. How can one tell the wink of affection from that of conspiracy or of deception? A wink is a wink. But then again, a wink is not a wink. Phonetically, one can find a dictionary definition of the word *wink*, but semantically winks have different meanings.

Teaching too needs to be understood in light of the circumstances at hand. The common prescriptions for teaching described above may represent good teaching when it is important to direct students toward a common performance goal requiring low-level and noncontroversial skill acquisition. But for

---

[16] Michael Scriven, "Objectivity and Subjectivity in Educational Research," *Philosophical Redirection of Educational Research,* National Society for the Study of Education, 1972; and Ernest R. House, *The Logic of Evaluative Argument,* Los Angeles, Calif.: Center for the Study of Evaluation, University of California, 1977.

more complex learning purposes where students are required to discern and judge, synthesize and extend, create and problem-solve, the same teaching prescriptions are neither meaningful nor effective. From a rational perspective, as teaching intents and circumstances change, teaching steps and behaviors take on different meanings and must be understood and valued differently.

MODES OF INQUIRY

A theory of practice should improve things, bring about higher standards, and cause individuals to strive for a better life. It should, in other words, have purposive and practical qualities and should account for the particularistic and phenomenologic qualities of human activity. Such a theory should provide a variety of modes for inquiring, analyzing, and understanding teaching and supervision.

Noreen Garman suggests that modes of inquiry should be viewed as alternate ways of knowing, with no one mode designed to rival others. Instead, modes give attention to and highlight different issues of interest in supervision and evaluation. She proposes five modes, as follows:

Discovery has as a goal the inductive search for a well-articulated phenomenon and appropriate questions inherent in the classroom scenario. Both qualitative and quantitative data are appropriate here. The analysis often begins by identifying the teacher's stated intent of the lesson and the signs of consistency or inconsistency as a result of subsequent actions. . . .

Verification is a deductive mode that provides for a degree of objectivity (which suggests that others using the same method with the same data can arrive at similar conclusions). When the salient features of the lesson have been discovered, it is imperative that the supervisor verify, usually with quantitative methodology, the extent to which the discovery was justified. Objectivity is also regarded as a general frame of mind that helps the supervisor assume a detached and neutral posture. Hypothesis testing is a feature of this verification mode.

Explanation is both inductive and deductive. Its purpose is to explain the verified phenomena through inference derived from the content analysis of stable data. The supervisor and teacher bring their subjective "best estimates" of what is happening from their own reality base. Concept formation is a vital part of the process since this becomes the means for the two to share their construed realities from both worlds. Understanding through language is the basis for explanation.

Interpretation is the search for meaning in the events under study. The interpretive mode often provides a way to get to what really matters, to derive mature interpretations from that which has been verified and explained. Through appropriate methodology one has the sanction to go beyond the literal, encouraged to look for deeper meanings than the inferences derived through explanation. The supervisor understands internally by intuitively referring to his/her experience and externally by searching for symbolic acts which reveal insights about the myths and predispositions of those involved. Through the interpretive mode the supervisor and teacher are able to seek deeper significance beneath the surface content that may appear trivial.

Evaluation is a normative mode which addresses values and judgments about the events under consideration. Evaluative methods are used to determine the effectiveness of a particular action or the worthiness of the meaning. They help the teacher answer such questions as "How well have I performed?" or "Am I doing what I should be doing?" By valuing, the supervisor and teacher come to know the internal and external criteria for setting priorities and making judgments in the evaluation mode.[17]

ISSUES OF COMPREHENSIVENESS

A good supervisory and evaluation system is one that is sufficiently comprehensive to serve a variety of purposes. As suggested earlier, the typical system now in place in most schools is measurement-oriented, seeking to establish the extent to which each teacher measures up to some preexisting standard. This standard is presumed to represent some minimum level of basic competence in teaching and is presumed to provide a yardstick for comparing one teacher or group of teachers to others who are being held to the same standard.

This *standards-referenced teacher evaluation* may have an important role to play in school district evaluation systems, but it is always a limited one.[18] For legal and other reasons school districts use standards-referenced teacher evaluation to establish for the record that teachers have met minimum requirements. But once teachers have proved themselves by passing this test, it no longer makes sense to continue to require them to pass the test again and again, year after year. Repeated use of standards-referenced teacher evaluation for the same people not only is a poor use of supervisory time, but also focuses the evaluation on minimums rather than on discovery, experimentation, and growth. Further, continued use makes evaluation ritualistic rather than something that teachers consider meaningful and useful.

Standards-referenced teacher evaluation is typically conducted using an instrument that records the presence or absence of teaching behaviors and teaching characteristics. The instrument is designed to track whether teachers are following accepted basic protocols. Reliability is very important to the success of standards-referenced teacher evaluation. Each evaluation should be duplicated exactly by another evaluator. To achieve this reliability, architects of standards-referenced teacher evaluation systems work hard to rule out judgments of goodness. Recording the presence or absence of behaviors, characteristics, or protocols, for example, requires little judgment. It is a measurement task rather than an evaluation one. Ideally, standards-referenced teacher evaluation should be "supervisor-proof."

In a comprehensive supervisory and evaluation system the emphasis

[17] Noreen Garman, "A Clinical Approach to Supervision," in T. J. Sergiovanni (ed.), *Supervision of Teaching*, 1982 Yearbook, Association for Supervision and Curriculum Development, Alexandria, Va., 1982, pp. 50–51.

[18] The discussion of standards-referenced, criterion-referenced, and personally referenced teacher evaluation approaches parallels Elliot Eisner's discussion of norm-, criterion-, and personally referenced student evaluation. See Elliot W. Eisner, *The Enlightened Eye: Qualitative Inquiry and the Enhancement of Educational Practice*, New York: Macmillan, 1991, pp. 101–103.

should be on two other types of evaluation: *criterion-referenced teacher evaluation* and *personally referenced teacher evaluation.*[19] Criterion-referenced teacher evaluation seeks to establish the extent to which a teacher's practice embodies certain goals and purposes and values considered important to the school. Assuming that the following questions reflect a particular school's shared purposes and values, such an evaluation might ask: Does the teacher provide a classroom climate that encourages openness and inquiry? Do teachers accept students without question as individuals? Do teachers teach for understanding? Are students enrolled as "workers" and teachers as facilitators or managers of the teaching and learning environment? Do students have responsibility for setting learning goals and deciding on learning strategies? Is cooperation emphasized over competition? Is diversity respected? Different values lead to different norms, and different norms lead to different questions for guiding the evaluation.

Criterion-referenced evaluation is in many respects a form of inquiry that is constructed around the issues deemed important by teacher and supervisor. For this reason evaluation extends throughout the teacher's career. As time goes on the nature of the questions that guide the evaluation should evolve from "Does the teacher's practice reflect a given value?" to "Are there better ways to do it?" and "What is the worth of the value in the first place?" Criterion-referenced teacher evaluation does not lend itself to instruments very well. Other forms of supervision such as clinical supervision, peer supervision, action research, and portfolio development are better options. These approaches to supervision will be discussed in later chapters.

Personally referenced teacher evaluation emphasizes the teacher's personal goals and comparisons between past and present performance given these goals. No external standards or norms are used to fix baselines for making such comparisons. Instead the purpose of personally referenced teacher evaluation is to help teachers understand and critically appraise their practice in light of their preferences, purposes, and beliefs.

ISSUES OF CREDIBILITY

Credibility is an important issue in teacher evaluation, particularly if the evaluator goes beyond description to interpretation, identification of themes, and appraisal of worth. In using case study methods to develop portraits of classrooms that lend themselves to evaluation, Eisner identifies three standards of credibility: structural collaboration, consensual validation, and referential adequacy.[20] The three sources of credibility apply as well to the evaluation of teaching.

---

[19] See, for example, ibid., p. 102, for a discussion of these concepts as applied to student evaluation.

[20] Ibid., pp. 110–114. See also Elliot W. Eisner, *The Educational Imagination,* 2d edition, New York: Macmillan, 1985.

The collaboration standard asks if multiple sources of information are used in providing descriptions, forming judgments, and reaching conclusions about a particular teacher's teaching. Is classroom observation backed up with other sources of information? Such sources might include interviews with teachers, examples of student work, photo essays, data descriptions of teacher-student interaction patterns, movement flow charts, case studies of students, an analysis of books read by students, student performance exhibits, a folio of tests, homework assignments and other assignments given by the teacher, and so on. In supplying multiple sources of information about his or her teaching, the teacher must become a partner in the process. The teacher, after all, is in the best position to decide what sources of evidence are most appropriate to the particular form of evaluation.

The consensus standard seeks agreement among competent others that sources of evaluation information make sense, that descriptions are sound, that interpretations are compelling, and that the conclusions drawn are plausible. The key partners to any agreement are, again, the teacher whose work is the focus of the evaluation and the person or persons (principal, other teachers, teams of teachers) assuming the supervisory role. Failing agreement at this level, third-party agreement may be necessary if conclusions need to be reached to resolve certain personnel matters such as retention or tenure. The consensus standard should not be confused with interrater reliability as understood in standards-referenced evaluation. The consensus standard seeks more holistic agreement about the adequacy of the evaluation process itself and about what it means for the teacher in question. For less contentious evaluation, all that is needed is a serious study of the evidence and the rendering of an opinion backed up by a simple statement of a paragraph or two. The art, drama, or film critic might serve as a helpful metaphor: The critic rates the subject and then provides a vivid assessment of that subject to validate that rating.

When teacher and supervisor disagree and the consequences for employment or reputation or both are significant, the consensus standard may require two or more independent evaluations complete with detailed writeups in the form of case studies. The studies are then compared. Each critic's opinion is considered, and the reasoning provided is assessed. The specifics of the case studies, the evidence gathered, the interpretations made, and other details need not overlap. In fact, they can be quite different. But for consensus to be judged to exist the evidence needs to lead to the same conclusion. If consensus is not reached, a further step may be necessary. Different critics may be focusing on different aspects of the teacher studied, and may bring different perspectives that lead to different conclusions. For this reason, evaluators or critics need to be brought together in conversation to discuss this possibility. If differences cannot be reconciled by negotiation, the evaluation may have to be invalidated and the process repeated with different evaluators.

The standard of referential adequacy can be met by examining the nature of the evaluation writeup itself. In assessing referential adequacy, Elliot Eisner asks if the description of events is rich enough and detailed enough so that others are able to see things and understand things that would be missed without the benefit of the writeup. According to Eisner, an evaluation writeup "is referentially adequate to the extent to which a reader is able to locate in its subject matter the qualities the critic addresses and the meanings he or she ascribed to them."[21] The evaluation, in other words, speaks for itself.

THE BASIC QUESTIONS

In the remaining sections we wish to emphasize the interpretive aspects of supervision, the search for meaning. This emphasis recognizes that searching for meaning is an exercise of little value without having established as well what is and what ought to be in the evaluation of teaching. We conclude by suggesting some modes of inquiry that need to be developed if a rational theory of practice in supervision and evaluation of teaching is to emerge.

Three major avenues of inquiry are suggested as being important in a theory of supervisory practice. Interpretation is an art that is enhanced by multiple perspectives on reality, and meanings are sufficiently idiosyncratic to require that avenues of inquiry be pursued in partnership by teachers and supervisors. The avenues of inquiry are suggested by three questions.

1 *What is going on in this classroom?* How does this work? Can it be explained and predicted? What laws and rules govern behavior in this context? How can classroom events be described accurately and vividly?

   "Thin" descriptions of reality are important in presenting an overall map of classroom events. Such a map gives a general orientation of the classroom's breadth and scope, much like a road map provides for a particular region. "Thick" descriptions of reality are important in identifying and recording aspects of the hidden curriculum, estimates of quality, and indicators of cultural imperatives that provide a more vivid portrayal of classroom life. The maps in a travel atlas, for example, present a general descriptive orientation of a particular region; the accompanying text and photographs describe the mind and pulse of this region. Each is useful to the traveler.

2 *What ought to be going on in this classroom?* What cultural imperatives should determine action? What values should be expressed? What qualities of life should be in evidence? What standards should be pursued? What visions of excellence should prevail?

   "Ought" dimensions of classroom life can be obtained and verified from empirically established standards (i.e., teacher-effectiveness research) on the one hand and from cultural preferences, values, and beliefs (i.e., conservative or humanistic ideology) on the other. Admittedly, the two sources are more easily separated in word than in action. Symbolic

[21] Ibid., p. 114.

interactionists, for example, would suggest that values are products of interaction among people and are qualities of mind that arise through such interaction on the one hand and through symbolic meanings on the other.

Establishing that a particular level of student achievement can be obtained if teachers follow closely a given set of teaching procedures suggests a standard of fact. Such relationships ought to be rigorously pursued and empirically established as *teaching facts*. However, deciding that the particular level of student achievement that might be obtained is valuable and that the trade-offs of what is lost to students and others by obtaining this gain in achievement or by adopting this method of teaching are acceptable does not necessarily follow from teaching facts. Making decisions among alternatives is the establishment of *teaching values*. Strong teaching facts scientifically determined are important prerequisites for establishing teaching values but are not substitutes for these values. The establishment of both teaching facts and teaching values is important in the development of the theory of supervisory practice.

3 *What do events and activities that constitute the "is" and "ought" dimension of classroom life mean to teachers, students, supervisors, and significant others?* What is the cultural content of the classroom? What implicit educational platforms exist? What values are suggested by actual behavior and events? What are the meanings implicit in discrepancies between the espoused and in-use theories?

The discovery of meaning and the creation of meaning await the further development of the art of interpretation in the supervision and evaluation of teaching. The work of Eisner is an important step in this direction.[22]

It may be helpful in illustrating the importance of teaching facts and teaching meanings in evaluation to distinguish between *picturing* and *disclosure*.[23] Picturing models of evaluation try to be as much like the teaching activity and classroom life under study as possible. In contrast disclosure models contain key characteristics of the teaching activity and classroom life under study but move beyond picturing per se to the interpretation of meaning by raising issues and testing propositions about the phenomenon. Picturing and disclosing models will be discussed further in Chapter 13. In examining the disclosure side of the ledger, emphasis is given to going beyond the data in the strictest sense to telling a story represented by the data. The data are enriched in disclosure as a means of communicating more vividly and fully. But disclosure is not invention, and the story developed is based on the social facts present in teaching. Meaningful disclosure requires accurate picturing.

[22] Ibid.
[23] Ian Ramsey, *Models and Mystery*, London: Oxford University Press, 1964.

A TURNAROUND IS POSSIBLE

What will it take for supervision and teaching to evolve into disciplined fields of inquiry and practice? We think a better understanding of rationality is needed. Present attempts at rationality seem not to hold up when evaluated against the standards of rationality that characterize the physical sciences, the social sciences, or the established professions. All these fields recognize, accept, and work with multiple and often conflicting goals and purposes that resemble value patterns; a mode of inquiry and practice more like surfing than simplistic linear thinking; subjective reality linked to human perceptions and decision; accuracy in pursuing problems regardless of difficulty in method; evaluation as discernment and judgment; and the semantic level of knowledge development and use.

What responsibilities should researchers, synthesizers, model builders, and practicing professionals each have in ensuring rationality? Researchers have a responsibility to become much more school-based and practice-focused as they seek to create new knowledge. They bring to their inquiry a commitment quite different from the commitment professionals bring to their practice. Though not neglecting relevancy to practice, the researchers' rightful obligation is to the process of inquiry itself and to the development of independent research findings. The synthesizers of knowledge have a responsibility to be much more realistic, open, and modest as they work to bring order and interrelatedness to existing research findings, concepts, and theoretical generalizations. The articles and books they write need to present a more accurate and modest picture of the available knowledge base. In the discussion of theory in Chapter 1 we pointed out that the greatest threat to rationality comes from the "intermediaries" who translate knowledge synthesis into models of practice and communicate these models to professionals through workshops, consultation, and the writing of textbooks and articles. At this point in the knowledge chain theoretical and research knowledge has already undergone two independent interpretations (synthesis and model building). Rationality requires that models of practice not be viewed as truths to be applied but as useful frames of reference that can enhance the vision of professionals at work and inform their intuition and judgment as they practice.

In the final analysis the guardians of rationality are teachers and supervisors. They have a right to expect more than rationalistic prescriptions from the knowledge developers and model builders and an obligation to demand more. Will supervision and teaching evolve into disciplined fields of inquiry and practice? That depends on the extent to which teachers and supervisors exert their rights and fulfill their obligations.

We began this discussion with the assertion that "If the theory is wrong, the practice is wrong"; we conclude with the same thought. Theory exists in the mind and guides practice, whether people admit it or not. This being the case, practices cannot be discussed fairly or rationally without first coming to grips with governing theories. You now know what our theories are and hopefully have begun a critical appraisal of yours.

CHAPTER 13

CLINICAL SUPERVISION AND TEACHER EVALUATION

THE form supervision takes depends in part on the purposes envisioned. For example, when meeting minimum standards is the purpose, supervision emphasizes quality control. In this case the supervisor is responsible for monitoring teaching and learning by visiting classrooms, touring the school, and talking with teachers about their work. As teachers become more competent and more committed to the professional ideal, supervision becomes less necessary to maintain quality control. Indeed, one measure of an effective supervisory practice is that quality control becomes increasingly less important as time goes by. When professional development is the purpose of supervision, supervisors commit themselves to helping teachers grow and develop in their understanding of teaching and classroom life, in improving basic teaching skills, and in expanding their knowledge and use of teaching repertoires. Another important purpose of supervision, one often overlooked, is building and nurturing motivation and commitment to teaching, to the school's overall purposes, and to the school's defining educational platform. A good supervisory system reflects these multiple purposes.

No supervisory system based on a single purpose can succeed over time. A system that focuses only on quality control, for example, invites difficulties with teachers and lacks needed expansive qualities. A supervisory system concerned only with providing support and help to teachers is not sufficiently comprehensive to ensure that minimum standards are being met.

Different teacher-evaluation purposes require different teacher-evaluation standards and criteria. When the purpose is quality control to ensure that teachers measure up, standards, criteria, expectations, and procedures take one form. When the purpose is professional improvement to help increase teachers' understanding and enhance teaching practice, standards, criteria, expectations, and procedures take a different form. In evaluation for quality control the process is formal and documented; criteria are explicit and standards are uniform for all teachers; criteria are legally defensible as being central to basic teaching competence; the emphasis is on teachers meeting requirements of minimum acceptability; and responsibility for evaluation is in the hands of administrators and other designated officials. When the purpose of teacher evaluation is professional improvement, the process is informal; criteria are tailored to the needs and capabilities of individual teachers; criteria are considered to be appropriate and useful to teachers before they are included in the evaluation; the emphasis is on helping teachers reach agreed-upon professional development goals; and teachers assume major responsibility for the process by engaging in self-evaluation and collegial evaluation, and by obtaining evaluation information from students.

The outcome of evaluation for quality control is the protection of students and the public from incompetent teaching. Unquestionably this is an important outcome and a highly significant responsibility for principals and other supervisors. The outcome of evaluation for professional improvement is quite different. Rather than ensuring minimum acceptability in teaching, professional improvement guarantees quality teaching and schooling for the students and the public.

The 80/20 quality rule spells out quite clearly what the balance of emphasis should be as schools, school districts, and states engage in teacher evaluation. *When more than 20 percent of supervisory time and money is expended in evaluation for quality control or less than 80 percent of supervisory time and money is spent in professional improvement, quality schooling suffers.* The 80/20 quality rule provides a framework for those responsible for evaluation of teachers to evaluate whether their efforts are indeed directed toward quality schooling. In making this assessment, less attention should be given to the rhetoric (what those responsible for teacher evaluation say their purposes are) and more to the standards and procedures that are used. The standards and procedures associated with each of the two purposes of evaluation are outlined in Table 13-1. For example, if the standards to the left of the table are emphasized, quality control is the purpose of the evaluation regardless of what is said about the purposes.

SCIENTIFIC AND ARTISTIC ASSUMPTIONS

The thorny issue of teacher evaluation for quality control and other personnel decisions is considered in the next chapter. Here we focus on supervision for professional improvement. More specifically we examine clinical supervision as one particularly powerful model. Peer supervision, target setting, action research, mentoring, and other models are discussed in Chapter 16, "Providing Options for Supervision." Supervisory purposes and models as instruments of practice are never theory-free. Instead, they are shaped both in planning and in practice by the basic assumptions and values and beliefs held about what good teaching is, the nature of expertise, and how both should be evaluated and understood.

At present the dominant view of teacher evaluation is characterized by a commitment to such technical-rational values as predetermination and the scientific method. As pointed out in Chapter 12, predetermination is evidenced by establishing specific objectives and competency levels to be exhibited and by otherwise specifying the rules of the game, or the blueprint for evaluation, before the evaluation takes place. The scientific method is characterized for example, by an emphasis on empirical design characteristics in the evaluation process and on a primary concern for precision in measurement. Though "sci-

TABLE 13-1
DIFFERENT PURPOSES, DIFFERENT STANDARDS FOR EVALUATION

Purposes	
Quality control (ensuring that teachers meet acceptable levels of performance)	Professional improvement (increasing understanding of teaching and enhancing practice)

Standards	
The process is formal and documented.	The process is informal.
Criteria are explicit, standard, and uniform for all teachers.	Criteria are tailored to needs and capabilities of individual teachers.
Criteria are legally defensible as being central to basic teaching competence.	Criteria are considered appropriate and useful to teachers.
Emphasis is on meeting minimum requirements of acceptability.	Emphasis is on helping teachers reach agreed-upon professional development goals.
Evaluation by administrators and other designated officials counts the most.	Self-evaluation, collegial evaluation, and evaluation information for students count the most.

Outcome	
Protects students and the public from incompetent teaching.	Guarantees quality teaching and schooling for students and the public.

The 80/20 Quality Rule: When more than 20 percent of supervisory time and money is expended in evaluation for quality control *or* less than 80 percent of supervisory time and money is expended in professional improvement, quality schooling suffers.

entific" supervision is offered as being rational, it turns out instead to be rationalistic.

In recent years a number of prominent evaluation experts have developed and tested artistic alternatives to this technical-rational approach that rely less on the scientific method and more on the intuitions, aspirations, and capabilities of those involved at both ends of the evaluation.[1] Theirs is an approach that sees value in discovering as opposed to determining, and in describing as opposed to measuring. Though the primary focus of this pioneering work is

[1] See, for example, Robert E. Stake, *Program Evaluation, Particularly Responsive Evaluation*, paper 5 in Occasional Paper Series, Kalamazoo: Western Michigan University, Evaluation Center, November 1975; Robert E. Stake (ed.), *Evaluating the Arts in Education: A Responsive Approach*, Columbus, Ohio: Merrill, 1975; Elliot W. Eisner, "Emerging Models for Educational Evaluation," *School Review*, vol. 80, no. 4, 1972; Decker Walker, "A Naturalistic Model for Curriculum Development," *School Review*, vol. 80, no. 1, 1971; Michael Scriven, "Goal-Free Evaluation," in Ernest House (ed.), *School Evaluation: The Politics and Process*, Berkeley, Calif.: McCutchan, 1973; George Willis, "Curriculum Criticism and Literary Criticism," *Journal of Curriculum Studies*, vol. 7, no. 1, 1975; and John S. Mann, "Curriculum Criticism," *Teachers College Record*, vol. 71, no. 1, 1969.

on program evaluation, its underlying assumption, characteristics, and design features apply to teacher evaluation as well.[2]

In Table 13-2 key assumptions and practices associated with technical-rational approaches to teacher evaluation are contrasted with those associated with artistic approaches. Though it would be a mistake to choose one of those views exclusively, the nature of reality in teaching practice suggests that the emphasis should be on the artistic assumptions.

In the sections that follow, several strategies for supervision and evaluation are described that build upon scientific but are more characteristic of artistic assumptions and are more consistent with the nature of teaching and learning practices. Well-known traditional methods have a place in teacher evaluation, but they should play a minor role compared with the alternatives proposed.

CLINICAL SUPERVISION

Clinical supervision is a powerful model for professional development for two reasons: It works, and it provides a conceptual framework that can be transferred to other models of supervision and evaluation also directed to professional development. The basic conceptual underpinnings and theoretical understandings behind clinical supervision, in other words, apply as well to peer supervision, mentoring, and target setting. Clinical supervision, nonetheless, refers to a specific cycle or pattern of working with teachers that was pioneered by Morris Cogan, Robert Goldhammer, and others and is perhaps best known through Cogan's book *Clinical Supervision*.[3]

Emerging from the real world of professional practice, this technique evolved from a series of problems faced by supervisors as they worked with teachers and would-be teachers. The essential ingredients of clinical supervision include the establishment of a healthy general supervisory climate, a mutual support system called "colleagueship," and a cycle of supervision comprising conferences, observation of teachers at work, and pattern analysis.

Clinical supervision is based on a number of assumptions that differ from those of traditional rating and evaluating and prescribes a pattern of action that departs substantially from present practice. In clinical supervision it is assumed that the school curriculum is, in reality, what teachers do day by day, that changes in curriculum and in teaching formats require changes in how

---

[2] See, for example, Elliot Eisner, "The Perceptive Eye: Toward the Reformation of Educational Evaluation," Washington, D.C.: AREA, Division B, Curriculum and Objectives, 1975, invited address; Morris Cogan, *Clinical Supervision*, Boston: Houghton Mifflin, 1973; James Raths, "Teaching without Specific Objectives," *Educational Leadership*, vol. 18, no. 7, 1971; and T. J. Sergiovanni, "Expanding Conceptions of Inquiry and Practice in Supervision and Evaluation," *Educational Evaluation and Policy Analysis*, vol. 6, no. 3, pp. 355–365, 1984.

[3] Clinical supervision evolved from a series of techniques developed as a result of the pioneering work of Morris Cogan and Robert Goldhammer in the Harvard MAT program of the late fifties and early sixties. Robert H. Anderson was an enthusiastic supporter of this effort and subsequently further developed the clinical supervision model. Originally conceived as a component of preservice teacher education, the technique has since been developed for in-service use. Morris Cogan, *Clinical Supervision*, New York: Houghton Mifflin, 1973.

TABLE 13-2
CONTRASTING TEACHER EVALUATION ASSUMPTIONS

Scientific	Artistic
1. Evaluation can be viewed as a process designed to determine the worth of something—a teacher, teaching episode, or performance.	1. But evaluation is also valuing something. Before one can begin to value something fully, one needs to understand it. Therefore, evaluation is seeking to understand something. What is going on in this classroom and why? What does it mean?
2. The emphasis is often on observing words and behavior and not on intuition and understanding. Indeed, intuition can be considered as something to be controlled because of its impressionistic rather than scientific nature, and understanding is often a luxury that may distract the evaluation process from its true course.	2. But words and behavior are only proxies for understandings and meanings and therefore much is missed by focusing only on the proxies. The evaluation is designed to inform the supervisor's intuition, not to replace it.
3. At times it is appropriate for the evaluator to follow a blueprint and evaluate the teacher according to the specifications called for in the blueprint.	3. But at times the evaluator should develop a representation of events that have taken place—a portrait of the teaching episode. Thus "specifications" not previously determined are included in the evaluation.
4. The blueprint characteristics of the evaluation specify what is of worth and define meanings and understandings. This is an exclusive process.	4. The portrait characteristics of the evaluation assume that multiple and sometimes contradicting understandings and meanings exist. The evaluator's job is to identify and describe them. Portraits of teaching episodes often reveal a hidden curriculum more potent than that intended and the achievement of unanticipated outcomes that may have more value than those intended by the teacher or specified in the lesson planned. This is an inclusive process.
5. Sometimes what is important to the evaluator are the stated intents of the teacher and the predetermined objectives held for the student.	5. Sometimes what is important to the evaluator are the implicit assumptions and guiding platform statements that teachers bring to the classroom, the manner in which these assumptions and platform statements are articulated as classroom activities and practices, and the implications and effects of these activities and practices.
6. When using scientific approaches, the evaluator is primarily concerned with methodology. He or she asks, How can I be sure that I can describe and measure without error the extent to which predetermined objectives are being met by the teacher and that this teacher exhibits predetermined competency levels in teaching?	6. When using artistic approaches, the evaluator is primarily concerned with discovering, describing, and measuring important things that occur. He or she is willing to choose methods suited to important things even though they may be weak or considered by others as subjective or impressionistic.

TABLE 13-2   (Continued)
CONTRASTING TEACHER EVALUATION ASSUMPTIONS

Scientific	Artistic
7. The evaluator relies heavily on rating scales and other teacher-evaluation instruments. These help him or her to be objective, to treat all teachers the same, and to ensure that the focus of the evaluation is on important events.	7. The evaluator believes that rating scales and other teacher-evaluation instruments often prevent him or her from fully understanding classroom events and prevent the evaluator and teacher from becoming personally involved in the evaluation process. The evaluator prefers to use data from the situation at hand to help define the parameters of the evaluation and to help understand crucial evaluation issues. He or she prefers to use videotape, teacher and student interviews, artifact collections, and evaluation portfolios and considers these as better methods of representation than instruments and rating scales.
8. The evaluation is primarily concerned with estimating the worth of a particular teaching performance and by inference the teacher. The teacher assumes a subordinate role in the process. The evaluator is the expert. Evaluation is something done to teachers by evaluators.	8. The evaluator is primarily interested in increasing understanding and stimulating thought and in extending the experiences of the teacher being evaluated. The teacher assumes a key role in the process. The evaluator and teacher share the expert role and evaluation is something done together.
9. Even when it makes sense to use more scientific approaches to evaluation, artistic aspects cannot be ignored.	9. Even when it makes sense to use more artistic approaches to evaluation, scientific aspects cannot be ignored.

Source: Thomas J. Sergiovanni, "Reforming Teacher Evaluation: Naturalistic Alternatives," *Educational Leadership,* vol. 34, no. 8, 1977.

teachers think about and understand their teaching and how they behave in classrooms; that supervision is a process for which both supervisors and teachers are responsible; that the focus of supervision is on teacher strengths; that given the right conditions teachers are willing and able to improve; that teachers have large reservoirs of talent, often unused; and that teachers derive satisfaction from challenging work.

Clinical supervision is a partnership in inquiry whereby the person assuming the role of supervisor functions more as an individual with experience and insight (or, in the case of equals, with a better vantage point in analyzing another colleague's teaching) than as an expert who determines what is right and wrong. The issue of authority is very important in the process. The clinical supervisor derives her or his authority from being able to collect and provide information desired by the teacher and from being able to help the teacher to use this information in the most effective way. This authority is functional, as compared with formal authority derived from one's hierarchical position. Functional authority is associated with higher levels of teacher satisfaction and performance.

Following these assumptions, clinical supervision is an in-class support system designed to provide assistance directly to the teacher. In practice, clinical supervision requires a more intense relationship between supervisor and teacher than that found in traditional evaluation, first in the establishment of colleagueship and then in the articulation of colleagueship through the cycle of supervision. The heart of clinical supervision is an intense, continuous, mature relationship between supervisors and teachers with the intent being the improvement of professional practice.

The purpose of clinical supervision is to help teachers to modify existing patterns of teaching in ways that make sense to them. Evaluation is, therefore, responsive to the needs and desires of the teacher. It is the teacher who decides the course of a clinical and supervisory cycle, the issues to be discussed, and for what purpose. Obviously, those who serve as clinical supervisors will bring to this interaction a considerable amount of influence; but, ideally, this influence should stem from their being in a position to provide the help and clarification needed by teachers. The supervisor's job, therefore, is to help the teacher select goals to be improved and teaching issues to be illuminated, and to understand better her or his practice. This emphasis on understanding provides the avenue by which more technical assistance can be given to the teacher; thus, clinical supervision involves, as well, the systematic analysis of classroom events.

During the last decade, interest in the development of clinical supervision has been substantial. Representative of this progress is the appearance of the second and third editions of Robert Goldhammer's classic book *Clinical Supervision: Special Methods for the Supervision of Teachers*, first published in 1969. The second and third editions were revised by Robert H. Anderson and Robert J. Krajewski.[4] The original version was pioneering, and the revised edition sets a new standard for the state of the art in clinical supervision. The 1986 appearance of *Learning about Teaching through Clinical Supervision*, edited by John Smyth and published by Croom Helm of London, attests to widespread international interest in clinical supervision. *Promoting Reflective Teaching Supervision in Practice*, by Norwegians Gunnar Handal and Per Lauvas,[5] is yet another example of the many international publications on the topic. The good news, as reflected in these books and in developments of other scholars interested in clinical supervision,[6] is a decided shift from emphasis on the steps of clinical supervision themselves to its concepts, assumptions, and basic framework. In-

---

[4] Robert Goldhammer, Robert H. Anderson, and Robert J. Krajewski, *Clinical Supervision: Special Methods for the Supervision of Teachers*, 2d ed., New York: Holt, 1980. The third edition is in press at this writing.

[5] Gunnar Handal and Per Lauvas, *Promoting Reflective Teaching Supervision in Practice*, Milton Keynes: The Society for Research into Higher Education and Open University Press, 1987.

[6] See, for example, Noreen Garman, "A Clinical Approach to Supervision," in Thomas J. Sergiovanni (ed.), *Supervision of Teaching*, 1982 Yearbook, Association for Supervision and Curriculum Development, Arlington, Va.: 1982, pp. 35–52.

creasingly, clinical supervision is viewed as an overall pattern of working with teachers that operationally should take a number of forms and follow a number of paths. Consistency is needed, of course, at the strategy level where assumptions and the overall framework come into play. But diversity is needed in developing operational tactics if clinical supervision is to accommodate itself to the array of needs of supervisors and teachers and to the particular characteristics of teaching situations. Clinical supervision is, therefore, basically a design for working with teachers within which a number of technologies, perspectives, and approaches can be used.

Some excellent "hands-on" books and articles are available that provide specific operational techniques for use within the clinical supervision framework. One we especially recommend is Keith A. Acheson and Meredith Damien Gall's *Techniques in the Clinical Supervision of Teaching.*[7] Many highly developed observational systems are also available for use in collecting information within the clinical supervision framework. The Galloway, Flanders, Blumberg, Kounin, and Morine systems are some examples. Respectively, they provide techniques and instruments for accurately recording nonverbal behavior in classroom interactions, student-teacher verbal interaction in classrooms, interaction of supervisors and teachers in conference, teacher-classroom management techniques, and a system for observing behaviors teachers find most important. As useful as these hands-on materials may be, as a *group* of techniques available to clinical supervision, they are still underdeveloped. Too much emphasis is given to objective and systematic collection of *readily observable* data. They tend to emphasize "low-inference" tactics rather than "high-inference." High-inference tactics require that judgments be made and data be interpreted to assess unique meanings given actual persons in situations involved in teaching. Low-inference tactics, by contrast, more precisely define behaviors to be observed and the data-collection strategies to be used. All in all, not enough attention is given to artistic perspectives in clinical supervision, a topic to be pursued later in this chapter. This bias toward the scientific and neglect of the artistic may well reflect the present state of the field, with better balance between the two forthcoming as clinical supervision continues to mature.

THE CYCLE OF CLINICAL SUPERVISION

In a few pages we are not able to provide all the techniques and know-how associated with clinical supervision. Competency will come with practice as supervisors team together in learning the skills of clinical supervision. The intent here is to describe the cycle of supervision, to provide some basic principles and concepts underlying clinical supervisory practice, and to suggest some

[7] Keith A. Acheson and Meredith Damien Gall, *Techniques in the Clinical Supervision of Teaching*, 3d ed., New York: Longmans, 1992.

techniques and tools which supervisors might find useful as they begin to develop competencies as clinical supervisors.

Cogan identifies eight phases in the cycle of supervision.[8]

1 *Phase 1 requires establishing the teacher-supervisor relationship.* This first phase is of particular importance, for upon its success rests the whole concept of clinical supervision. Teachers are suspicious of evaluation in general, and the intense sort of supervision prescribed by Cogan can be even more alarming. Further, the success of clinical supervision requires that teachers share with supervisors responsibility for all steps and activities. The supervisor has two tasks in Phase 1: building a relationship based on mutual trust and support, and inducting the teacher into the role of co-supervisor. Cogan believes that both tasks should be well advanced before the supervisor enters the teacher's classroom to observe teaching. Phase 1 establishes the colleagueship relationships deemed critically important by Cogan.

2 *Phase 2 requires intensive planning of lessons and units with the teacher.* In Phase 2 teacher and supervisor plan, together, a lesson, a series of lessons, or a unit. Planning includes estimates of objectives or outcomes, subject-matter concepts, teaching strategies, materials to be used, learning contexts, anticipated problems, and provisions for feedback and evaluation.

3 *Phase 3 requires planning of the classroom observation strategy by teacher and supervisor.* Together teacher and supervisor plan and discuss the kind and amount of information to be gathered during the observation period and the methods to be used to gather this information.

4 *Phase 4 requires the supervisor to observe in-class instruction.* Cogan emphasizes that only after careful establishment of the supervisory relationship and the subsequent planning of both the lesson or unit and the observation strategy does the observation take place.

5 *Phase 5 requires careful analysis of the teaching-learning process.* As co-supervisors, teachers, and supervisors analyze the events of the class. They may work separately at first or together from the beginning. Outcomes of the analysis are identification of patterns of teacher behavior that exist over time and critical incidents that occurred that seemed to affect classroom activity, and extensive descriptions of teacher behavior and evidence of that behavior. It is believed that teachers have established persistent patterns of teaching that are evidenced and can be identified as a pattern after several carefully documented observations and analysis.

6 *Phase 6 requires planning the conference strategy.* Supervisors prepare for the conference by setting tentative objectives and planning tentative processes, but in a manner that does not program the course of the con-

---

[8] Cogan, op. cit.

ference too much. They plan also the physical settings and arrange for materials, tapes, or other aids. Preferably, the conference should be unhurried and on school time. Cogan notes that it may well be necessary to arrange for coverage of a teacher's classroom responsibilities from time to time.

7 *Phase 7 is the conference.* The conference is an opportunity and setting for teacher and supervisor to exchange information about what was intended in a given lesson or unit and what actually happened. The success of the conference depends upon the extent to which the process of clinical supervision is viewed as formative, focused evaluation intended to help in understanding and improving professional practice.

8 *Phase 8 requires the resumption of planning.* A common outcome of the first seven phases of clinical supervision is agreement on the kinds of changes sought in the teacher's classroom behavior. As this agreement materializes, the eighth phase begins. Teacher and supervisor begin planning the next lesson or unit and the new targets, approaches, and techniques to be attempted.

As one reviews the cycle of clinical supervision, it appears as though the cycle describes that which many supervisors have been doing all along. But a quick review of the assumptions basic to clinical supervision, particularly the concept of co-supervisor, suggests that the resemblance may be superficial. The supervisor works at two levels with teachers during the cycle: helping them to understand and improve their professional practice and helping them to learn more about the skills of classroom analysis needed in supervision. Further, while traditional classroom observation tends to be sporadic and requires little time investment, clinical supervision asks that supervisors give 2 to 3 hours a week to each teacher. Supervisors can better manage their time by involving only part of the faculty at a time—perhaps one-third for 3 months in rotation. As teachers themselves become competent in clinical supervision and assume increased responsibility for all phases, they should participate in clinical supervision as a form of collegial supervision. No hard-and-fast rules exist that exclude teachers from assuming roles as clinical supervisors. Collegial supervision and clinical supervision are quite compatible.

EDUCATIONAL PLATFORM

In Chapter 12 we pointed out how tempting it often is to view teaching as a rational set of activities, directed to clearly stated and understood objectives. Indeed, one is often led to believe that classroom activity is a logical process of determining objectives, stating them in acceptable form, developing learning experiences, and evaluating the outcomes of these experiences in relation to predetermined objectives. This view assumes that the teaching arena is objective and that teachers come to this arena with a clean slate, free of biases, willing and able to make rational choices.

In reality, however, most supervisors know that teaching is not nearly as objective and explicit as one might think. Indeed, teachers, supervisors, and others bring to the classroom a variety of agendas, some public, many hidden, and probably most unknown, each of which influences the decisions they make. The agendas tend to fall into three major categories: what one believes is possible, what one believes is true, and what one believes is desirable. Together the three are the essential ingredients of one's *educational platform*.[9] A platform implies something that supports one's action and by which one justifies or validates one's own actions. An approximate analogy would be that of a political platform. This platform states the basic values, critical policy statements, and key positions of an individual or group. Once known, the political platform can be used to predict responses that a politician or political party is likely to make to questions on various campaign issues. The concept of education platform, particularly as it affects curriculum and educational program matters, is discussed at length in Chapter 8. Here our attention is focused on platform as it relates to clinical supervision.

Assumptions, Theories, and Beliefs

The components of one's educational platform are the assumptions, theories, and beliefs one has formed concerning key aspects of effective teaching, such as the purpose of schooling, perceptions of students, what knowledge is of most worth, and the value of certain teaching techniques and pedagogical principles. For purposes of illustration, consider each component below, recognizing that operationally they are inseparable.

Assumptions that teachers hold help answer the question "What is possible?" Assumptions are composed of one's beliefs, the concepts one takes for granted, and the ideas one accepts without question about schools, classrooms, students, teaching, learning, and knowledge. Assumptions help the teacher to define what classrooms are actually like and what is possible to accomplish within them. Assumptions are important to the decisions that teachers make, because they set the boundaries for what information will or will not be considered and for other possibilities and actions at the onset of instruction.

Theories help answer the question. "What is true?" Theories are beliefs about relationships between and among assumptions one considers to be true. Theories form the basis for developing teaching strategies and patterns of classroom organizations.

Beliefs about what is desirable in classrooms are derived from assumptions and theories that one holds regarding knowledge, learning, classrooms, and students. What is desirable is expressed in the form of intents, aims, objectives, or purposes.

Consider, for example, a teacher whose educational platform includes the

[9] Decker Walker, "A Naturalistic Model for Curriculum Development," *The School Review*, vol. 80, no. 1, pp. 51–65, 1971.

assumptions that "Little or no knowledge exists that is essential for everyone to learn" and that "Youngsters can be trusted to make important decisions." The two assumptions might well lead to the theory that "Students who are allowed to influence classroom decisions will make wise choices and will become more committed learners." That being the case, a corresponding aim for that teacher might be "to involve students in shared decision making," or perhaps "to have students interact with subject matter in a manner that emphasizes its concepts and structure rather than just its information."

Contrast this with a teacher whose educational platform includes the assumption that "The only justifiable evidence of good teaching is student acquisition of subject matter as specified by the teacher" and the assumption that "Motivation of students should reflect the realities of the world outside the school, where good behavior and performance are publicly rewarded and poor behavior and performance are publicly punished." The two assumptions might well lead to the theory that "Students need to be motivated, on the one hand, and disciplined, on the other, to get the behavior and performance that leads to acquiring the most subject matter in the least amount of time." In this case a corresponding aim might be "to provide rewards and privileges to students who behave and perform to the teacher's expectations and punishment to those who do not."

Educational platforms are powerful determinants of the nature and quality of life in classrooms. For example, imagine the fate of students in the classrooms of people who consider themselves teachers of French or biology and not of students, as compared with teachers who view instruction in a more holistic and integrated way. Consider next the fate of the supervisor who wants the first type of teacher to be more sensitive to individual differences of students and to emphasize the joy of learning French or biology as well as mastery of subject matter, but does not take into account the teacher's educational platform. Unless the supervisor is a master at behavior modification and the teacher witless enough to respond passively to stimuli from the supervisor, change in teaching behavior will require some altering of educational platforms.

Known and Unknown Platform Dimensions

In the world of the classroom the components of educational platforms are generally not well known. That is, teachers tend to be unaware of their assumptions, theories, or objectives. Sometimes they adopt components of a platform that seem right, that have the ring of fashionable rhetoric, or that coincide with the expectation of important others, such as teachers whom they admire, or of groups with which they wish to affiliate. Though teachers may overtly adopt aspects of educational platforms in this manner, covertly, or unknowingly, they are often likely to hang onto contradictory assumptions, beliefs, and theories. Publicly they may say (or espouse) one thing and assume that their classroom behavior is governed by this statement, but privately, or even unknowingly, they may believe something else that actually governs their classroom behavior. Indeed, teachers are not aware that often their classroom decisions and behavior contradict their espoused platform.

THEORIES GOVERNING TEACHER BEHAVIOR

It has been suggested that the classroom is an artificial setting where form and function are influenced largely by the stated and implied assumptions, theories, and aims of individual teachers. Together these beliefs form an educational platform that supports teachers' actions and by which they justify or validate their actions. As has been suggested, many aspects of a teacher's platform are unknown or perhaps known but covert. When covert dimensions differ from espoused, the former are likely to constitute the *operational* platform for a given individual.

The clinical supervisor needs to be concerned with two theories that the teacher brings to the classroom—an *espoused theory* and a *theory in use*. As Chris Argyris and David Schön suggest:

> When someone is asked how he would behave under certain circumstances, the answer he usually gives is his espoused theory of action for that situation. This is the theory of action to which he gives allegiance, and which, upon request, he communicates to others. However, the theory that actually governs his action is his theory in use. This theory may or may not be compatible with his espoused theory; furthermore, the individual may or may not be aware of the incompatibility of the two theories.[10]

When one's espoused theory matches one's theory in use, they are considered congruent. Congruence exists, for example, for the teacher who believes that self-image development in youngsters is desirable in its own right and is related to student achievement and whose teaching behavior and artifacts of that behavior confirm this espoused theory. Lack of congruence between a person's espoused theory and the theory in use, *when known*, proposes a dilemma to that individual. A second teacher, for example, shares the same espoused theory regarding self-concept, but his or her pattern of questioning, use of negative feedback, use of the bell curve, and insistence on standard requirements may reveal a theory in use incongruent with the espoused theory. The social studies teacher who believes in and teaches a course in American democracy in a "totalitarian" manner represents another example of incongruency between espoused theory and theory in use.

THE JOHARI WINDOW

A useful way of understanding how known and unknown platform dimensions of teachers fit into clinical supervision is by examining the *Johari Window*

---

[10] Chris Argyris and David A. Schön, *Theory in Practice: Increasing Professional Effectiveness*, San Francisco: Jossey-Bass, 1974, p. 7.

	What the supervisor knows about the teacher	What the supervisor does not know about the teacher
What the teacher knows about himself	Public or open self 1	Hidden or secret self 2
What the teacher does not know about himself	Blind self 3	Undiscovered or subconscious self 4

FIGURE 13-1   Johari Window and educational platform. *(From Thomas J. Sergiovanni,* Handbook for Department Leadership Concepts and Practices in Today's Secondary Schools, *Boston: Allyn and Bacon, 1977.)*

as it relates to espoused theories and theories in use.[11] This relationship is illustrated in Figure 13-1.

The Johari Window in this case depicts the relationship between two parties, teacher and clinical supervisor. The relationship revolves around aspects of the teacher's educational platform known to self and others, known to self but not others, not known to self but known to others, and not known to self or others. Four cells are depicted in the Johari Window, each representing a different combination of what the teacher knows or does not know about his or her teaching as contrasted with what the supervisor knows and does not know about that teacher's teaching.

In the first cell, *the public or open self,* the teacher's knowledge of his or her teaching behavior and other aspects of his or her professional practices, corresponds with the supervisor's knowledge. This is the area in which communication occurs most effectively and in which the need for the teacher to be defensive, to assume threat, is minimal. The clinical supervisor works to broaden, or enlarge, this cell with the teacher.

In the second cell, *the hidden or secret self,* the teacher knows about aspects of his or her teaching behavior and professional practice that the supervisor does

[11] Joseph Luft, *Of Human Interaction,* New York: National Press Books, 1969. The Johari Window was developed by Joseph Luft and Harry Ingham and gets its name from the first names of its authors.

not know. Often the teacher conceals these aspects from the supervisor for fear that the supervisor might use this knowledge to punish, hurt, or exploit the teacher. The second cell suggests how important a supervisory climate characterized by trust and credibility is to the success of clinical supervision. In clinical supervision the teacher is encouraged to reduce the size of this cell.

In the third cell, *the blind self,* the supervisor knows about aspects of the teacher's behavior and professional practice of which the teacher is unaware. This cell, though large initially, is reduced considerably as clinical supervision for a given teacher develops and matures. This is the cell most often neglected by traditional teacher-evaluation methods. Indeed, clinical supervision is superior to most other supervising strategies in helping teachers understand dimensions of teaching found in the "blind self."

In the fourth cell, *the undiscovered self,* one finds aspects of teacher behavior and professional practice not known to either teacher or supervisor. The size of this cell is reduced as clinical supervision progresses. Teachers and supervisors discover and understand more and more about their beliefs, capabilities, strengths and weaknesses, and potential.

HELPING TEACHERS CHANGE

Creating a condition for change greatly facilitates the change itself. For example, if individual teachers are unaware of inconsistencies between their espoused theories and their theories in use, they are not likely to search for alternatives to their present teaching patterns. One way in which search behavior can be evoked is by identifying dilemmas. Dilemmas become apparent when teachers learn that their theories in use are not consistent with their espoused theory.

Dilemmas promote an unsettled feeling in a person. Their espoused educational platforms mean a great deal, and what they stand for and believe is linked to their concept of self and sense of well-being. Dilemmas that emerge from inconsistencies between these images and actual behavior are upsetting and need to be resolved. Indeed they are likely to lead to a search for changes either in one's espoused theory or in one's theory in use.[12]

Readiness for change is a critical point in the process of clinical supervision. It is at this point that an appropriate support system needs to be provided. Part of this support system will be psychological and will be geared toward accepting and encouraging the teacher. But part must also be technical and will be geared toward making available teaching and professional practice alternatives to the teacher.

Argyris and Schön point out that congruence is not a virtue in itself. Indeed a "bad" espoused theory matched to a theory in use may be far less desirable,

---

[12] Leon Festinger, *Theory of Cognitive Dissonance,* Evanston, Ill.: Row, Peterson, 1975; and Milton Rokeach, "A Theory of Organizational Change within Value-Attitude Systems," *Journal of Social Sciences,* vol. 24, no. 21, 1968.

from the supervisor's point of view, than a "good" espoused theory insufficiently matched.[13]

SOME EVIDENCE

To this point in our discussion of developing a theory of clinical supervision we have suggested that:

A teacher's classroom behavior and the artifacts of that behavior are a function of assumptions, theories, and intents the teacher brings to the classroom. Together these compose the teacher's educational platform.

Educational platforms exist at two levels: what teachers say they assume, believe, and intend (their espoused theory), and the assumptions, beliefs, and intents inferred from their behavior and artifacts of their behavior (their theory in use).

Espoused theories are generally known to the teacher.

Theories in use are generally not known to the teacher and must be constructed from observation of teacher behavior and artifacts of that behavior.

Lack of congruence between a teacher's espoused theory and the teacher's theory in use proposes a dilemma to the teacher.

Faced with a dilemma, a teacher becomes uncomfortable, and search behavior is evoked.

Dilemmas are resolved by teachers modifying their theory in use to match their espoused theory. It is possible that espoused theory will be modified to match theory in use, but because of the link between espoused theory and self-esteem, and self-esteem with the esteem received from others, the more common pattern will be the former.

Though a number of studies suggest that indeed teachers are likely to respond as suggested,[14] a number of caveats are in order. For example, in reviewing the literature on consistency theory, William McGuire notes that search behavior is only one of several possible reactions to dissonance. Additional examples of dissonance reduction, he notes, are *avoidance*, whereby one represses the matter by putting the inconsistency out of mind; *bolstering*, whereby the inconsistency is submerged into a larger body of consistencies so as to seem relatively less important; *differentiation*, whereby one sees the situation causing dissonance to be different in a particular case ("I wasn't actually putting down the youngster but just giving her a taste of her own medicine");

---

[13] Argyris and Schön, op. cit.

[14] Using Flanders's interaction-analysis techniques as a means of collecting information and as a basis for producing verbal feedback. Tuckman, McCall, and Hyman conclude that "behavior and self-perception of experienced, in-service teachers *can* be changed by involving a discrepancy between a teacher's observed behavior and his own self-perception of his behavior, and then making him aware of this discrepancy via verbal feedback." See Bruce W. Tuckman, Kendrick M. McCall, and Ronald T. Hyman, "The Modification of Teacher Behavior: Effects of Dissonance and Feedback," *American Educational Research Journal*, vol. 6, no. 4, pp. 607–619, 1969.

substitution, whereby one changes the object about which he or she has an opinion rather than the opinion itself ("It is true that I said all school administrators are petty bureaucrats, and they are, but he is a statesman, not a bureaucrat"); and *devaluation,* whereby one downgrades the importance of the inconsistency in question, thus making it more tolerable.[15] The extent to which a teacher faces up to inconsistencies between espoused platform dimensions and those actually in use may well depend, as suggested earlier, upon the quality of climate and setting the supervisor provides—colleagueship, in Morris Cogan's language.[16]

In an extensive review of the literature, Frances Fuller and Brad Manning conclude that self-confrontation and discrepancy analysis, though achieving uneven results, is by and large a powerful supervisory technique. In addition they note that "if the person is not too stressed, or closed, or anxious, or distracted, the self-confrontation experience 'takes,' i.e., the person notices some discrepancy. This is either a difference between what he thought he was doing and what he was actually doing (an incongruence discrepancy), or a difference between what he was doing and what he wanted to do (a deficiency discrepancy)."[17] This again highlights the importance of the climate that accompanies the process of clinical supervision. But as Fuller and Manning point out, a supportive climate is a necessary but not sufficient requirement for success: "Change is said not only to require the presence of facilitative conditions such as acceptance and empathy, but also 'confrontation.' . . . The teacher will not benefit from seeing her video tape alone since there is no confrontation. . . . Feedback that is not accompanied by some focus has been found to change behavior little, if at all."[18]

Alan Simon developed and field-tested a supervisory strategy that incorporates many of the features of clinical supervision described above.[19] Using videotaping techniques, Simon, as the supervisor, interviewed teachers, asking them to specify aspects of their espoused educational platform as it applies to education in general and to a particular lesson. He then videotaped the teachers actually teaching the lessons described. The videotape was then reviewed

---

[15] William J. McGuire, "The Current Status of Cognitive Consistency Theories," in Shel Feldman (ed.), *Cognitive Consistency, Motivational Antecedents, and Behavioral Consequents,* New York: Academic, 1966, pp. 10–14.

[16] Cogan, op. cit., p. 67.

[17] Frances F. Fuller and Brad A. Manning, "Self-Confrontation Reviewed: A Conceptualization for Video Playback in Teacher Education," *Review of Educational Research,* vol. 43, p. 487, 1973.

[18] Ibid., p. 493.

[19] Alan Simon, "Videotapes Illustrating Concepts of the Argyris and Schön Model in Instructional Supervisory Situations," doctoral dissertation, Urbana: University of Illinois, Educational Administration and Supervision, 1976. See also Alan Simon, "Analyzing Educational Platforms: A Supervisory Strategy," *Educational Leadership,* vol. 34, no. 8, pp. 580–585, 1977. For a further extension of this work and its application to high school teachers see Michael Hoffman, "Comparing Espoused Platforms and Platforms-in-Use in Clinical Supervision," doctoral dissertation. Urbana: University of Illinois, Educational Administration and Supervision," 1977; and Michael Hoffman and Thomas J. Sergiovanni, "Clinical Supervision: Theory in Practice," *Illinois School Research and Development,* vol. 14, no. 1, pp. 5–12, 1977.

by the supervisor, sometimes with the help of outside experts not familiar with the teachers' espoused platform, and from this analysis a theory in use, as perceived by the supervisor, was constructed. This theory in use was also recorded on videotape. Together, the supervisor and teacher viewed the videotape now containing the teacher-espoused theory, an example of the teacher at work, and the supervisor's perception of the teacher's theory in use. The teacher was then interviewed to determine whether the videotaped espoused platform actually represented his or her thoughts before the lesson, whether the videotaped lesson represented his or her teaching, and whether the supervisor's videotaped rendering of the theory in use was fair and accurate. Overall the teachers verified the accuracy and fairness of the videotapes. Interviewing continued, to determine attitudes toward the process and to obtain perceptions of the effectiveness of the process from the teachers. Judges, listening to the audiotaped interviews, concluded that overall the teachers had positive attitudes toward the process and found it helpful. Further, by grouping teacher responses into defensive and open categories, judges concluded that indeed dilemmas had surfaced and that search behavior had been evoked.

Many forms of clinical supervision resemble artistic approaches. Such forms are artistic when they rely on developing a complete representation of a teaching episode and when they use this representation as a basis for making inferences and building understanding of events. Videotaping is the most common method of representation associated with clinical supervision. Clinical supervision uses the data at hand (actually generated from the environment and activities being evaluated) rather than data that fit a preconceived rating form or a set of instrument specifications, and it places the teacher in a key role as generator, interpreter, and analyst of events described.

Sometimes clinical supervisors take too seriously the need to "scientifically" and "objectively" document events. Sometimes they focus too intensely on the stepwise or work-flow aspects of clinical supervision. Sometimes they rely too heavily on predetermined objectives or on specifying detailed blueprints and plans that subsequently determine the direction of the evaluation. But clinical supervision can be geared to discovering and understanding rather than determining, and in that sense it has artistic potential. Additional artistic strategies that can be used either separate from clinical supervision or as a part of clinical supervision are described in the sections that follow. These techniques are powerful means for providing rich descriptions of classroom activity from which theories in use might be inferred.

CONNOISSEURSHIP AND CRITICISM

It is difficult to discuss artistic alternatives to present teacher-evaluation practices without reference to the work of Elliot Eisner.[20] Eisner is concerned with

---

[20] Elliot Eisner, "Applying Educational Connoisseurship and Criticism to Education Settings," Stanford, Calif.: Stanford University, Department of Education, undated, mimeo; see also his

developing in supervisor and teacher the qualities and skills of appreciation, inference, disclosure, and description. He refers to these qualities as the cultivation of educational connoisseurship and criticism. It is through the art of connoisseurship that one is able to appreciate and internalize meanings in classrooms and through the skill of criticism that one is able to share or disclose this meaning to others. Eisner uses references to wine connoisseurship and art criticism as illustrations of these concepts. The art of appreciation is the tool of the connoisseur and the art of disclosure the tool of the critic. James Cross uses the example of sports commentators and writers to illustrate the combined application of connoisseurship and criticism.

> Most of us are familiar with some of the techniques employed by commentators in describing and remarking on well-executed plays or potentially victorious strategies. Plays executed with finesse are often seen in stop action, instant replay, slow motion or are recounted in stirring detail on sports pages. One of the major contributions of these commentators is their great knowledge of sports, familiarizing them with possibilities so they know whether a flanker reverse, off tackle run, screen pass or drawplay was used or has potential for gaining yardage in a given situation, or when the bump and run, blitz, or single coverage was used or likely to prevent gain. Knowledge about educational potentials is also necessary. The potentially worthwhile tactics of teaching or those in use—the bump and runs or flanker reverses of schooling—need to be described and conveyed.[21]

The commentator's ability to render play-by-play action in a fashion that permits an audience to see and feel the game as he or she does depends upon a feel of intimacy with the phenomena under study not permitted by mere attention to game statistics and other objective information and upon a quality of disclosure more vivid than a box score. And in education, the evaluator's ability to describe classroom life in a fashion that permits other educators to see and feel this environment as he or she does depends upon a similar intimacy with classroom phenomena (educational connoisseurship) and a rendering of this intimacy (educational criticism) well beyond that provided by a brief observation or two accompanied by a series of ratings or a teacher-evaluation checklist. Eisner maintains that educational connoisseurship is to some degree practiced daily by teachers and supervisors:

"Emerging Models for Educational Evaluation," op. cit.; and "The Perceptive Eye: Toward the Reformation of Educational Evaluation," op. cit. Eisner notes that, unfortunately, to many the word "connoisseurship" has snobbish or elitist connotations, and criticism implies a *hacking* or negativistic attitude. In his words, "Connoisseurship, as I use the term, relates to any form of expertise in any area of human endeavor and is as germane to the problem involved in purse snatching as it is to the appreciation of fine needle point." And "criticism is conceived of as a generic process aimed at revealing the characteristics and qualities that constitute any human product. Its major aim is to enable individuals to recognize qualities and characteristics of a work or event which might have gone unnoticed and therefore unappreciated." Quoted from "The Perceptive Eye: Toward the Performance of Educational Evaluation," footnote 2.

[21] James Cross, "Applying Editorial Connoisseurship and Criticism to Supervisory Practices," doctoral dissertation, 1977, Urbana: University of Illinois, Educational Administration and Supervision.

The teacher's ability, for example, to judge when children have had enough of art, math, reading or "free time" is a judgment made not by applying a theory of motivation or attention, but by recognizing the wide range of qualities that the children themselves display to those who have learned to see. Walk down any school corridor and peek through the window; an educational connoisseur can quickly discern important things about life in that classroom. Of course judgments, especially those made through windows from hallways, can be faulty. Yet the point remains. If one knows how to see what one looks at, a great deal of information . . . can be secured. The teacher who cannot distinguish between the noise of children working and just plain noise has not yet developed a basic level of educational connoisseurship.[22]

Eisner believes that the existing level of connoisseurship found in teachers and supervisors can and should be refined, that perceptions can be enhanced and sharpened, and that understanding can be increased. He further points out that

. . . connoisseurship when developed to a high degree provides a level of consciousness that makes intellectual clarity possible. Many teachers are confronted daily with prescriptions and demands from individuals outside the teaching profession that are intended to improve the quality of education within the schools. Many of these demands the teachers feel in their gut to be misguided or wrong-headed; the demands somehow fly in the face of what they feel to be possible in a classroom or in the best interests of children.[23]

In this context he notes: "Many teachers, if you ask them, are unable to state why they feel uneasy. They have a difficult time articulating what the flaws are in the often glib prescriptions that issue from state capitols and from major universities. Yet, the uneasiness is not always, but often justified." And further: "Many teachers have developed sufficient connoisseurship to feel that something is awry but have insufficient connoisseurship to provide a more adequate conceptualization of just what it is."[24]

When applied to supervision, educational connoisseurship is a necessary but insufficient art. Classroom understanding needs to be described and communicated, and this aspect of the process, the art of disclosure, is what Eisner refers to as educational criticism. There is much to learn about cultivating the art of connoisseurship and the skills of disclosure. Much will depend upon the ability of educators to regain confidence in themselves, in their ability to analyze and judge, in their willingness to rely on intuition and perception—all today often considered dubious skills, ones to be discounted in the face of objective and scientific demands for accountability.

MORE THAN DESCRIBING

Unique to artistic approaches to supervision and evaluation is the emphasis on identifying meanings in teaching activity and classroom life rather than *only*

[22] Eisner, "The Perceptive Eye," p. 9.
[23] Ibid., pp. 10–11.
[24] Ibid., p. 11.

TABLE 13-3
COMPARING PICTURING AND DISCLOSURE MODELS OF TEACHER EVALUATION

Picturing	Disclosure
1. Intent	
To describe the teaching phenomenon under study as exactly as possible. To develop a replica, photo image, or a carbon copy of reality. Agendas and issues are those embedded in the data.	To interpret the teaching phenomenon under study. To illuminate issues, disclose meetings, and raise hypotheses or propositions. Agendas and issues are those that emerge from the data.
2. Analogies	
Legal transcript, videotape, photo-replica, interaction-analysis, electronic portrait, music or dance score, play script, historical chronology.	Impressionistic painting, collage, book review, interpretive photo, music, dance or play performance, story.
3. Key Questions	
What exactly happened in this class? How can I describe events objectively?	What issues emerge from the study of this class? How can I represent or illuminate these issues in a meaningful way?
4. Validity Check	
Are events described accurately?	When actual events are observed, do they reasonably lead to the inferences and interpretations?

describing teaching and classroom events. For example, many advocates of clinical supervision recommend that the supervisor develop an accurate and objective record of teaching. Often videotapes of teaching, exact transcripts of teacher-student talk, or tally sheets of some sort that record data of interest to the teacher and the supervisor are recommended. Typically, the supervisor is expected to avoid interpretation, leaving the extraction of the meaning behind events to the teacher or, when a particularly good relationship exists between teacher and supervisor, to both parties during the conference phase of a clinical supervision cycle.

When using more artistic approaches to clinical supervision, supervisors try to go beyond description to the interpretation of teaching events. Following Ian Ramsey,[25] John Mann distinguishes between *picturing* and *disclosure* models.[26] Picturing models of evaluation try to be much like the teaching activity and classroom life under study. Disclosure models, on the other hand, contain key characteristics of the teaching activity in classroom life under study but move beyond to interpreting meaning, raising issues, and testing propositions about this phenomenon. Some of these distinctions are suggested in Table

[25] Ian Ramsey, *Models and Mystery,* London: Oxford University Press, 1964.
[26] John S. Mann, "Curriculum Criticism," *The Teachers College Record,* vol. 71, no. 1, pp. 27–40, 1967.

13-3. As you examine the disclosure side of the ledger in Table 13-3 notice the emphasis given to going beyond the data in the strictest sense, to telling a story represented by the data. For example, consider the following excerpt from the "disclosure" of a classroom by Robert Donmoyer:

> All these forces combined to produce a profound effect upon the teacher and to profoundly influence her behavior in the classroom. She becomes, as she herself has said, an accountant. Most of her day is spent checking and recording what students have and haven't done. Math, spelling, and language assignments must be checked, and if there are mistakes (and there usually are) they must be rechecked and, sometimes, rechecked again. Then checked assignments must be checked off on each student's math, spelling, or language contract. When each contract is completed, each contract must be checked out. After this is done, the student must take home the work included on this contract and bring back a note signed by his parents indicating they saw the work. This note, of course, must be checked in.
>
> This checking and rechecking and checking out and checking in is all performed with mechanized precision. The teacher's face remains immobile except for an occasional upward turn at the corners of her mouth, the eyes never smile.
>
> The teacher exhibits great economy of movement and gesture. It's almost as if Ms. Hill were a marionette whose strings are too tight, hence her gestures must be tight and close to her body.[27]

Notice that Donmoyer does not provide a detailed description of the number of times the teacher checks this or that, but offers instead the word "accountant" not only to suggest the actual checking of student work but to communicate a meaning that transcends the particular issues of checking and rechecking and to comment on an important dimension of the climate and quality of life in this particular classroom.

The concepts of picturing and disclosure might be viewed as range parameters within which a supervisor can work. At times picturing events as accurately as possible might make sense, and at other times moving toward the disclosure end of the range might be more appropriate. One can catalog approaches to supervision and evaluation used by a particular school or a particular supervisor on such a range scale as a way of identifying the array of possibilities that exist in the school. It should be noted, however, that the more a supervisory and evaluation strategy approaches the disclosure end of this range, the more important is the quality of the relationship between teacher and supervisor to the success in this approach. Disclosure strategies of supervision and evaluation require a particularly strong climate of trust and understanding among those involved in the process of supervision and evaluation. The relatively safer picturing end of this continuum may be appropriate initially, and as the supervisory relationship matures, movement could then progress toward the disclosure end.

---

[27] Robert Donmoyer, "School and Society Revisited: An Educational Criticism of Ms. Hall's Fourth-Grade Classroom," as quoted in Eisner, *The Educated Imagination*, op. cit., p. 231.

SUMMARY OF CONCEPTS BASIC TO ARTISTIC EVALUATION

In summarizing concepts basic to artistic approaches to supervision and evaluation Elliot Eisner identifies the characteristics he considers important:

1 Artistic approaches to supervision require attention to the muted or expressive character of events, not simply to their incidence or literal meaning.

2 Artistic approaches to supervision require high levels of educational connoisseurship, the ability to see what is significant yet subtle.

3 Artistic approaches to supervision appreciate the unique contributions of the teacher to the educational development of the young, as well as those contributions a teacher may have in common with others.

4 Artistic approaches to supervision demand that attention be paid to the process of classroom life and that this process be observed over extended periods of time so that the significance of events can be placed in a temporal context.

5 Artistic approaches to supervision require that rapport be established between supervisor and those supervised so that a dialogue and a sense of trust can be established between the two.

6 Artistic approaches to supervision require an ability to use language in a way that exploits its potential to make public the expressive character of what has been seen.

7 Artistic approaches to supervision require the ability to interpret the meaning of the events occurring to those who experience them and to be able to appreciate their educational import.

8 Artistic approaches to supervision accept the fact that the individual supervisor with his or her strengths, sensitivities, and experience is the major "instrument" through which the educational situation is perceived and its meaning construed.[28]

CRITICISMS OF ARTISTIC APPROACHES

Artistic approaches to supervision and evaluation are often criticized for lacking precision and for being subjective. These criticisms are undeniable, but the alternative, to limit analysis of teaching and supervisory practice to only what is precise and objective, is neither scientific nor helpful and thus is unacceptable. As we suggest in Chapter 12, a helpful and effective system of supervision must give prime attention to data that make sense to teachers. "Brute" data become sensible when interpreted and as meanings are established. But can such a subjective system of supervision be fair? How can the validity of the system be verified? The key to solving these problems rests in the person who assumes responsibility for establishing meanings. Some protections are offered, for example, if proposed meanings are offered as hypotheses and if accepted meanings are arrived at cooperatively by teacher and supervisor.

The precision issue remains important. Some argue that only data that can be accurately and precisely observed and recorded should be part of the eval-

---

[28] Elliot W. Eisner, "An Artistic Approach to Supervision," in Thomas J. Sergiovanni (ed.), *Supervision of Teaching*, 1982 Yearbook, Alexandria, Va.: Association for Supervision and Curriculum Development, 1982, p. 66.

uation process. Unfortunately, evaluation issues that can meet this rigorous, albeit artificial, standard are often less important than those that cannot. Limiting the evaluation to issues that lend themselves to precision can lead to a serious measurement error, often referred to as an "error of the third type." In this type of error, statistical confidence limits are correctly set and precise measurements standards are applied but the *wrong problem* is addressed. As suggested in Chapter 12, this misplaced cogency might best be summed by John Tukey's admonition: "Far better an approximate answer to the right question, which is often vague, than an exact answer to the wrong question, which can always be made precise."[29] A more helpful approach in sorting out the extent to which artistic approaches to clinical supervision are useful and the circumstances under which they are useful is to understand their limitations as well as their strengths.

THE EVALUATION PORTFOLIO

Videotaping is a common technique associated with clinical supervision and with the arts of educational connoisseurship and criticism. Indeed, videotaping can provide a useful and readily accessible representation of teaching episodes and classroom activities. But because of the selective nature of lens and screen, this technique can also frame perception and evoke slanted meanings. Further, what the screen shows always represents a choice among possibilities and therefore provides an incomplete picture. And finally, some aspects of classroom life do not lend themselves very well to lens and screen and could be neglected.[30]

Artifacts analysis and/or portfolio development, when used in conjunction with videotaping, can help provide a more complete representation of classroom life and therefore can increase meaning.[31] These approaches, however, can stand apart from videotaping and indeed can stand apart from each other.

Imagine a classroom or school deserted suddenly 20 years ago by its teacher and students and immediately being sealed. Everything there remains exactly as it was at the moment of desertion—desks, chairs, interest centers, work materials, test files, homework assignments, reading center sign-up lists, star reward charts and other "motivational devices," bulletin boards, workbooks, student notebooks, grade books, plan books, library displays, teacher workroom arrangements, student lounge-area arrangements, and so on.

Twenty years later you arrive on the scene as an amateur anthropologist intent on learning about the culture, way of life, and meaning of this class (its goals, values, beliefs, activities, norms, etc.). As you dig through the class-

[29] Quoted by R. Rose, "Disciplined Research and Undisciplined Problems," in C. Carol H. Weiss (ed.), *Using Social Research and Public Policy Making,* Lexington, Mass.: Heath, 1977, p. 23.

[30] This discussion follows Sergiovanni, "Reforming Teacher Evaluation," op. cit.

[31] See Patricia Scheyer and Robert Stake, "A Program's Self-Evaluation Portfolio," Urbana: University of Illinois at Urbana-Champaign, Center for Instructional Research and Curriculum Evaluation, undated mimeo, for a discussion and application of this concept for program evaluation.

room, what artifacts might you collect and how might you use them to help you learn about life in this school? Suppose, for example, you were interested in discovering what was important to teachers, how teachers viewed their roles in contrast to that of students, what youngsters seemed to be learning and/or enjoying, and how time was spent. In each case what might you collect? What inferences might you make, for example, if you were to find most of the work of students to be in the form of short-answer responses in workbooks or on ditto sheets, no student work displayed in the class, all student desks containing identical materials, and a teacher test file with most questions geared to the knowledge level of the taxonomy of educational objectives?

Portfolio development represents a teacher-evaluation strategy similar to that of artifacts analysis but with some important differences. The intent of portfolio development is to establish a file or collection of artifacts, records, photo essays, cassettes, and other materials designed to represent some aspect of the classroom program and teaching activities. Though the materials in the portfolio should be loosely collected and therefore suitable for rearrangement from time to time to reflect different aspects of the class, the portfolio should be designed with a sense of purpose. The teacher or teaching team being evaluated is responsible for assembling the portfolio and should do it in a fashion that highlights their perception of key issues and important concerns they wish to represent.

Like the artist who prepares a portfolio of his or her work to reflect a point of view, the teacher prepares a similar representation of his or her work. Together supervisor and teacher use the collected artifacts to identify key issues, to identify the dimensions of the teacher's educational platform, as evidence that targets have been met, and to identify serendipitous but worthwhile outcomes. A portfolio collection could be used, for example, to examine such issues as:

Are classroom activities compatible with the teacher's espoused educational platform and/or that of the school?

Do supervisor and teacher have compatible goals?

Are youngsters engaging in activities that require advanced cognitive thinking or is the emphasis on lower-level learning?

Do youngsters have an opportunity to influence classroom decisions?

Is the classroom program challenging all the students regardless of academic potential or are some youngsters taught too little and others too much?

Are the youngsters assuming passive or active roles in the classroom?

Is the teacher working hard? That is, is there evidence of planning, care in preparation of materials, and reflective and conscientious feedback on students' work, or are shortcuts evident?

Does the teacher understand the subject matter?

What is the nature and character of the hidden curriculum in this class?

Though portfolio development and artifacts analysis share common features, the most notable of which is the collection of artifacts, portfolio development is the responsibility of the teacher. The teacher decides what will be represented by the portfolio and the items to be included in its collection. Together the teacher and supervisor use this representation to identify issues for discussion and analysis.

A CAVEAT ON THE USE OF PORTFOLIOS

The evaluation portfolio is a good idea. But, as is the case with many other good ideas, when portfolio use is uniformly mandated or linked to a bureaucratic and measurement-oriented system of evaluation it becomes both ritualistic and burdensome. Items are collected and filed not because of reasons that make sense to teachers and supervisors but because of the characteristics of the evaluation system. In a worst-case scenario, supervisors wind up using portfolio items as a way to play "gotcha" with teachers, and teachers develop padded portfolios to cover all the bases or to logjam the evaluation system.

The best protection against misuse of the portfolio is to take to heart the basic meanings and intentions behind clinical supervision. Basic to understanding supervision is the view that teaching practices are governed by the interplay of two theories: an espoused theory, which represents the teacher's public educational platform, and a theory in use, which represents the teacher's actual educational platform or platform in use. Often this actual platform is tacitly held. Clinical supervision seeks to infer the teacher's actual platform by examining what is going on in the classroom and assessing its meaning. This is done through observation in the classroom, analysis of videotapes, collection of artifacts and portfolios, and other techniques. When a supervisor confronts a teacher with the fact that the teacher's theory in use is not consistent with his or her espoused theory, dilemmas can be identified. Once these dilemmas are discovered, the teacher can attempt to resolve them. This process of resolution acts as a stimulus to change.

The portfolio is an artistic metaphor entirely compatible with conceptions of supervision and evaluation as forms of connoisseurship and criticism. Taken together, these ideas place clinical supervision in the realm of discovery, reflection, self-understanding, and professional improvement. As described in this chapter both clinical supervision and its conceptual underpinnings, when applied to other models of supervision aimed at professional development, should be at the center of supervisory practice.

CHAPTER 14

SUPERVISION AND SUMMATIVE EVALUATIONS

Every community is made up of individual personalities. Those individuals have their own talents, hang-ups, dreams, idiosyncrasies—all of which both enrich the community as well as place a collective strain on it. There is a need to keep alive the sense of community identity, a sense of what distinguishes that community from other communities, a sense of something special that holds people together. Sometimes that sense of identity derives from the central purpose that the community was founded to serve; other communities are bound together by their ethnic, religious, racial, or cultural traditions; other communities are made up of people who choose a certain lifestyle or recreational interest. In most communities there are certain requirements for initial membership and other requirements for maintaining membership. Sometimes these requirements are formalized through admission procedures and initiation rites, and through periodic ritual restatements of commitment to the community (renewal of marriage vows, celebrations of anniversaries, annual awards ceremonies, the publication of annual reports, tenure review, annual corporate retreats, and so on). Sometimes membership comes from simply remaining in the community long enough to be accepted. Most communities, however, need rituals by which they can assert their identity, maintain their identity, and protect their identity.

A school as a community of learners brings together youngsters, families, and other adults. Though belonging to a variety of other communities, these people form a community with a mission to perpetuate and renew the life of the larger civic community by exploring ways to carry the culture and the polity forward in the next generation. One of the mechanisms or rituals by which this community reasserts its identity as a learning community is through periodic evaluation. Through evaluations the community agrees to assess what progress they are making in their mission as a community. For students, these evaluations take the form of tests, oral and written quizzes, final exams, projects, competitions, etc. For teachers, they take a variety of forms. Formal teacher evaluations have traditionally been sources of tension, alienation, and conflict. Some of that is inescapable, and perhaps even healthy (when it involves arguments about what constitutes an authentic expression of the mission of the school community). Much of the discomfort concerning evaluation can be eliminated, however, if it is treated as a community exercise in self-governance, as a way for the school community to maintain and strengthen its identity as an entity committed to learning, rather than as a mechanism of control exercised over segments of the community. One significant way to make the evaluation process a community exercise is to require that all members be evaluated, including supervisors, administrators, and evaluators.

In the previous chapters we have been emphasizing supervision as a process for promoting teacher growth and enhanced student learning. Within the distinction between formative and summative evaluation, we have been emphasizing formative evaluation, that is, that kind of interaction with teachers that develops information, points of view, questions, and inquiries into alternatives, all of which teachers can use as part of an ongoing reflection on and within practice.

In this chapter we turn to summative evaluation. This kind of evaluation involves coming to a conclusion or making a judgment about the quality of the teacher's performance. This kind of evaluation rates the teacher's performance as meeting, exceeding, or falling below some standard of teaching competence or some level of acceptable teaching performance. Often summative evaluations are tied to a formal personnel decision, such as a decision whether to grant a teacher tenure, whether to promote a teacher to a higher position or rank, or whether to renew a tenured teacher's contract. A summative evaluation may be used to rate a tenured teacher according to a scale, which may or may not affect the teacher's salary or "rif number." Formative evaluations *assume* membership in the learning community; summative evaluations invite a more structured reflection on the demands and meanings of membership in a learning community with a specific mission. Summative evaluation employs clear standards of membership; the basic identity of the community is identified in and safeguarded through summative evaluation. Formative evaluations are ways to enliven and enrich that identity, although both forms of evaluations can serve that purpose.

Supervisors are excluded from some summative evaluations that are considered the responsibility of administrators. Sometimes administrators are also supervisors, as in the case of principals or assistant principals. In that instance they have to decide whether a particular involvement in summative evaluation requires them to wear an administrative hat or a supervisory hat. Sometimes personnel who are not administrators but who engage in supervision of teachers for formative purposes are asked to participate in a summative evaluation of a teacher.

Whether a supervisor acts in an administrative capacity or is functioning in a purely supervisory capacity, there should be very clear, formally described distinctions between supervision for formative evaluation, supervision for summative evaluation, and supervision for administrative evaluation and decision. The process of supervision for promoting teacher growth and enhanced student learning should be clearly distinguished from the process of supervision for personnel decisions; where possible, separate personnel should perform them. Where that is not possible, teachers should know beforehand what the differences among the various processes are, and which one is being used at that time. Leaving such distinctions fuzzy and indefinite engenders widespread lack of trust among teachers and undermines the formative potential of formative supervision. When the supervisory process is carried on as though the various types of evaluation are one and the same, then the supervisory episode is perceived as threatening and adversarial.

CLARIFYING THE DISTINCTION

Teachers and administrators in the school should know the difference between formative and summative supervision. Summative evaluations differ according to purpose. Each format should have a structured series of steps, with mutual responsibilities clearly spelled out. Depending on the kind of personnel decisions to be made, the structure of the evaluation may vary. The following hypothetical examples from Sunlight School may communicate how different summative evaluations might be structured.

I. Summative evaluation for nontenured teachers at Sunlight School.
  A. Six months prior to the tenure decision, the nontenured teacher will be provided an oral and written evaluation of his or her teaching performance. This evaluation will be structured according to the evaluative criteria presented to the beginning teacher within the first month of his or her teaching duties.
  B. Prior to the summative evaluation report, the beginning teacher's classes will have been visited at least six times a semester. Each visit will be followed by an extensive discussion of the teacher's performance. Suggested improvements will be noted. At least two people will have participated in those class visits in order to ensure at least two voices in the gathering of observational data.
  C. At least three people, one of whom will be the principal or someone else designated by the superintendent, will discuss the class observation data and follow-up discussions, and the three will prepare the summative evaluation report and attach their names to it.
  D. The criteria for evaluating beginning teachers will have been decided by the tenured teaching faculty.
  E. If the evaluation is unfavorable, the teacher will have one month to show why the evaluation is incorrect, or why he or she should be granted tenure despite the evaluation.
  F. During the months following an unfavorable evaluation, the beginning teacher will participate in a series of discussions with administrators and teachers chosen for this task to determine whether to stay in teaching as a career, consider what steps may be required to do so, or consider looking into some other career.
II. Summative evaluation of a tenured teacher recommended for termination of contract at Sunlight School
  A. Termination of a tenured teacher's contract shall be justified for the following reasons only: legal or moral turpitude; clear and repeated

violations of school policies; repeated demonstration of incompe-
tence as a teacher, after repeated warnings about the need to improve performance; clear and repeated neglect of duties as a professional member of the staff. All these are considered indications that
the teacher has opted out of membership in the school community
and, as such, require the community to verify whether such options
are indeed being exercised. If they are, then membership should
cease. In the case of evidence of a serious crime, the teacher will be
suspended until a legal disposition of the matter is reached.

B. The teacher must be notified by the appropriate administrator of a
serious deficiency in his or her performance and of the need to correct that deficiency as soon as it is perceived, or if the teacher has
been rated as probationary on the periodic evaluation.

C. If the teacher believes the complaint is incorrect or unjustified, both
the teacher and the administrator may ask others to verify the presence of the deficiency.

D. If the complaint is not verified, then the teacher is not required to
take any action. If the complaint is verified, the teacher must take
steps to correct the deficiency within a specified time frame. The
teacher is listed, in this case, as "on probation," and an account of
the matter is entered into that teacher's personnel file.

E. If, after the specified time, it appears that the teacher has not corrected the deficiency, at least two other professionals on the staff
must verify that the deficiency has not been corrected.

F. If the deficiency is verified, then the teacher may be notified that his
or her contract will not be renewed. Notification of nonrenewal
must be made before February 1 of the present contract year. If the
case warrants, however, the contract may be terminated immediately.[1]

Notice the difference between the two evaluation procedures. In comparison with nontenured teachers, tenured teachers have more opportunities to
turn the situation around; there are more opportunities to engage colleagues
in making additional evaluations to prevent unfair treatment. Notice the difference between these procedures and the following procedures, which might
be employed in what is considered a more normal evaluation experience.

III. Periodic evaluation of tenured teachers at Sunlight School
    A. Every 3 (or 5) years each tenured teacher will undergo an in-depth
evaluation. This evaluation is an opportunity for the teacher to
demonstrate how he or she has maintained or grown in commit-

---

[1] For a more detailed treatment of approaches to dealing with incompetent teachers, see Edwin
M. Bridges, *The Incompetent Teacher*, London: Falmer Press, 1986; Jim Sweeney and Dick Manatt,
"A Team Approach to Supervising the Marginal Teacher, *Educational Leadership*, vol. 41, no. 7, pp.
25–27, April 1984.

ment to the mission of this community of learners. It is an opportunity for the community, acting through persons delegated for that purpose, to assess the contribution each teacher is making to the life of the school.

B. Upon receiving tenure, each teacher is required to present a 3-year growth plan. This plan will include all or some of the following: efforts to improve in areas noted as needing improvement in the prior evaluation; efforts to develop one's knowledge base through university courses, staff-development opportunities in the district and in the region, or other avenues of study; efforts to expand one's repertory of teaching strategies, and to improve diagnostic abilities to assist students with difficulties; efforts to network with other teachers in the school, in the system, or in the region for professional development purposes; cultural enrichment; and so on. Every teacher will maintain a portfolio that contains evidence of systematic progress on their growth plan.

C. At the beginning of the year in which the in-depth evaluation is to take place, an administrator or senior teacher will be assigned to work with the teacher involved. That person (the evaluator) will review with the teacher what progress has been made on the growth plan and together they will prepare a report to be included with the in-depth report for review by the principal. That person will also prepare a plan with the teacher, outlining how the in-depth evaluation will take place during that year.

D. At the opening meeting the teacher will choose one of the five in-depth evaluation formats chosen by the faculty and spelled out in the faculty contract, or, with approval of the principal, some other format that appears suited to the teacher's particular needs and that satisfies the general purposes for these in-depth evaluations.

E. At the opening meeting the teacher will review with the evaluator the format of the final report of the in-depth evaluation, especially the criteria for arriving at each of the four general ratings (superior, satisfactory, less than satisfactory, and probationary). Those ratings have consequences for the type of growth plan to be submitted at the end of the year. Those receiving superior ratings will undergo the next in-depth evaluation in 5 years and are free to devise their growth plans in ways that serve both the needs of the school and the needs of their own professional growth. Those receiving satisfactory ratings will undergo the next in-depth evaluation in 3 years and may devise a growth plan in ways that serve the needs of the school and their own professional growth. Those receiving a less than satisfactory rating must submit a growth plan that is targeted at improving in those areas that caused the unsatisfactory rating and will undergo their next in-depth evaluation in 3 years. Those who are rated as probationary will be required to undergo the procedures called for by that evaluation process beginning with the next semester.

F. During the initial meeting the evaluator will arrange to hold five lengthy sessions with the teacher during the in-depth evaluation year. They will be followed by a concluding meeting for a review of the evaluation report prior to its submission to the principal. The format for those five sessions will be shaped by the evaluation format chosen by the teacher.

G. If, in the course of those sessions, disagreements arise over what the evaluator perceives to be a problem, each is free to request other members of the faculty to enter the discussion, and even to observe classes. If serious disagreements ensue from the outset, the principal and a faculty member chosen by the teacher may be called in to arbitrate the dispute.

H. The final report submitted to the principal will contain the following items:

1. An assessment of the results of the growth plan for the previous period. There should be some evidence of how involvement in that plan has influenced the teacher's classes.

2. An assessment of the teacher's present performance according to the evaluation format employed during the year. That assessment should contain, but not be limited to, the following: some assessment of the teacher's understanding of the material being taught in class (Is the teacher reflecting current understandings and trends in the field? Is that understanding of the material related to the schoolwide goals?); an assessment of the teacher's responsiveness to the students in the class(es) (Can the teacher talk about the strengths and weakness of each student in the class and how instruction is, at least occasionally, individualized to respond to individual students? Are performance assessments of students fair, challenging, and true tests of the knowledge being taught?); an assessment of the teacher's strengths and how they relate to student learning; an assessment of areas that both evaluator and teacher agree need further work, and how improvements in these areas will strengthen student learning.

3. The evaluator's overall rating of the teacher, listing the reasons for the rating.

4. Additional comments by teacher or evaluator.

5. The teacher's growth plan for the period before the next in-depth evaluation.

I. The evaluation report will be submitted no later than May 1 to the principal, who will review these reports with each teacher during the month of May.

TYPE	Administrative Evaluation	Supervisory Summative Evaluation	Supervisory Formative Evaluation
PURPOSE	– Tenure decisions – Probation Decisions – Dismissal Decisions	– Periodic, in-depth reflection – Membership renewal – Reappropriation of mission – Assessment of Growth	Ongoing reflective growth
PROCESS	Legally correct Highly structured Highly directive Either-or criteria Either-or judgments	Structured alternatives Collegial Checks & balances Multifaceted	Multiform: • Pursuit of growth targets • Staff development workshops • Clinical supervision • Peer coaching • School renewal projects • Networking with regional groups
PRODUCT	Decisions / \\ Negative Positive ↓ ↓ Dismissal Retention	Summative Evaluation / \\ Negative Positive ↓ ↓ Administrative New growth evaluation plan + Formative evalvation	• Reflective practice • Invention • Integration of classroom activities with schoolwide goals • New materials, strategies • New courses

FIGURE 14-1   Types of evaluation.

This example illustrates how, in some of the more enlightened schools, periodic summative evaluation is carried on. The system is different from that used for the untenured teacher, and from that for tenured teachers on probation. The tenured teacher participates much more in a professional evaluation process; there are more options; the evaluator and teacher can shape the evaluation to the circumstances of the teacher; there are checks and balances built into the process to protect the teacher.

Supervisors can work in either the formative or the summative process without losing trust with the faculty, as long as the evaluation systems are kept carefully distinct. Figure 14-1 provides an overview of these distinctions. Participation in the summative evaluation system will probably cost the supervisor some trust, at least initially, in establishing a formative supervisory relationship with a teacher. During the 3 or 5-year interim period between summative evaluations, teachers will remember the rating that the supervisor gave, but even more important, they will remember that the supervisor has the *power* to give a summative rating. What teachers sometimes forget is that they have voted for such a system and have had a hand in designing it. Unless a teacher receives a superior rating, the tendency is to resent the supervisor who gave the lower rating. The resentment may be diminished if the system is perceived as being as fair and evenhanded as possible.[2]

PROBLEMS WITH SUMMATIVE EVALUATIONS OF TEACHERS

Supervisors need to be aware that there are several unsupportable assumptions about summative evaluation of teachers. Precipitous action based on these assumptions can lead to legitimate grievances against supervisors. Consider the following examples.

Assumption 1. There is a clear set of criteria or standards understood and accepted by all with which a teacher's performance can be evaluated.

Rebuttal. There is no conclusive and incontrovertible research that any specific teacher behavior or any set of teacher behaviors causes learning to take place in any specific student. What evidence there is points to relatively weak correlations between some sets of teacher behaviors and some increase in aggregate scores on tests of basic competency. In these cases there is evidence that teachers teach directly to the test and ignore what is not on the test.[3] This leads to clear distortions in student learnings, as other legitimate learning outcomes are neglected.

Assumption 2. Sporadic, unannounced classroom visits, with no prior conversations and no subsequent discussion, are a legitimate and acceptable way to assess teacher performance.

Rebuttal. The visitor has no understanding of why the teacher is doing what he or she is doing. Until the final judgment, the teacher has no way of knowing what the visitor thinks about what is going on, and has no way of changing his or her own behavior, assuming there is agreement that it is inappropriate. There is also the assumption that what the visitor sees is a fair sample of what the teacher tends to do in most classrooms, an assumption not supported by the research.[4]

Assumption 3. Student achievement of course objectives is the only way to evaluate teacher performance.

Rebuttal. What is meant by "student achievement"? If it refers to mean aggregate scores on standardized tests, then what really is being measured and who determines what is measured? Even if these tests were accepted as legitimate measures of teachers' and school goals for student learning, a pretest of students' readiness levels would be necessary. Are baseline data available that

[2] Milbrey Wallin McLaughlin and R. Scott Pfeifer, *Teacher Evaluation: Improvement, Accountability, and Effective Learning,* New York: Teachers College Press, 1988.

[3] See Michael Kirst, "Interview on Assessment Issues with Lorrie Shepard," *Educational Researcher,* vol. 20, no. 2, pp. 21–23, 27, March 1991; Lorrie A. Shepard, "Why We Need Better Assessments," *Educational Leadership,* vol. 46, no. 7, pp. 4–9, April 1989.

[4] Susan Stoldowsky, "Teacher Evaluation: The Limits of Looking," *Educational Researcher,* vol. 13, no. 9, pp. 11–19, 1984.

allows for computation of gains or losses in mean test scores? Even when pre-
and postintervention data are available, educators must deal with the mean
scores of a group of students. What if the teacher is successful in teaching
slower students and not as successful with brighter students, or vice versa?
Does that count for nothing? What if the teacher is good at teaching creativity,
collaboration, research skills, and artistic criticism, but the tests do not measure student achievement in those areas?

Suppose, on the other hand, that student achievement is evaluated in terms
of grades. Suppose the grades range from A to F. Is a teacher rated on his or
her ability to increase the number of A students in the class? What if F students improve from a very low F to a very high F? In other words, how much
improvement in each student's performance counts for how much in the scale
of teacher ratings? Teachers must work with the hands they are dealt; why
should one teacher receive a low rating for less than spectacular student
achievement when her students are two or three grade levels behind to start
with? What if student average daily attendance is abysmal, so that there are
rarely the same twelve (out of twenty-seven) students in class on any given
day, and hence it is impossible to assume any continuity of classroom experience for most of the students? Clearly, evaluations must take many additional,
contextual factors into account besides the student achievement of course objectives.

Assumption 4. Evaluation of teacher performance should deal only with observable classroom behaviors.

Rebuttal. This assumption is derived partially from clinical supervision, in
which supervisors attempt to avoid subjective judgments by concentrating on
observable behaviors, pointing out patterns in both teacher and student behaviors. One of the problems is that this observational posture assumes a sepa-
rateness from content considerations; for example, it fails to consider whether
the teacher was teaching his or her subject matter accurately. Counting the
number of times the teacher gives positive or negative feedback, the number
of times the teacher calls on the same student, the number of seconds of wait
time after a question, the number of times the teacher uses visual displays
does not indicate whether the teacher did a good job teaching quadratic equa-
tions or the causes of the First World War. Furthermore, the connection between observable teacher behaviors and student achievement on a variety of
measures appears tenuous, according to some research evidence.[5]

These four assumptions do not stand up under rigorous cross-examination. If
a supervisor, acting on these assumptions, were to render a recommendation
or a decision not to rehire a teacher or not to grant tenure, the supervisor
would encounter legal and professional difficulty. Courts have established
very clearly that teachers, even beginning teachers, must be given due process.

---

[5] Michael Scriven, "Can Research-Based Teacher Evaluation Be Saved?" *Journal of Personnel
Evaluation in Education,* vol. 4, pp. 19–32, 1990.

The essence of due process is that teachers know beforehand the criteria or standards as well as the procedures by which they will be evaluated, and that these procedures and standards have in fact been followed. Beyond due process concerns, the very criteria and standards that a school or school system establishes for such evaluation can be challenged.

DUTIES-BASED TEACHER EVALUATION

Michael Scriven has proposed a different set of criteria for summative evaluations of teachers.[6] Claiming that the present criteria for summative evaluation of teachers are not ethically, scientifically, or legally supportable—due to lack of incontrovertible evidence of causality, observer bias, infrequent observations of classroom practice, and lack of other kinds of evidence besides classroom practice—Scriven offers "duties-based evaluation" as the answer.[7] By "duties" he means a list of teacher job specifications that answer the question: "What is a teacher hired to do?" He distinguishes between primary duties (teaching students worthwhile knowledge to the extent of the students' abilities) and secondary duties (talking to parents, supervising corridors or playground, referring students to counselors, etc.). While secondary duties are ancillary to primary duties, they are nonetheless essential. Using duties as the basis for evaluating teachers enables those charged with the administration of the schools to report that teachers are performing the required duties. Figure 14-2 shows Scriven's extensive, detailed list of the teacher's professional duties.

Scriven proposes that multiple sources of evidence be gathered on each of these duties, using more than one evaluator (and more than two if there are discrepancies in the evidence). Over the course of over 5 years, many educators from the United States and Australia developed several drafts of the list, so there is a reasonable claim for the validity of the list, at least for those two countries. To date, however, this list of teacher duties for the purposes of summative evaluation has not been used frequently enough to measure its effectiveness. Nevertheless, the duties-based approach appears to have sufficient merit for school systems to attempt it as an alternative to the present evaluation systems, which Scriven rightly criticizes. A sample of his criticism may indicate its persuasiveness. The first relates to the listing of multiple indicators of effective or competent teaching (as many as 29 in one state evaluation system, as many as 52 in another) as though they made up some organically integrated set.

One cannot fail to be concerned, also, about the problem of combining multiple indicators. Very few of the (research) studies will support general claims about the ex-

---

[6] See Michael Scriven, "Evaluating Teachers as Professionals: The Duties-Based Approach," in James Popham (ed.), *Teacher Evaluation: Six Prescriptions for Success,* Alexandria, Va.: Association for Supervision and Curriculum Development, 1988, pp. 110–142.

[7] See Michael Scriven, "Can Research-Based Teacher Evaluation Be Saved?" *Journal of Personnel Evaluation in Education,* vol. 4, no. 1, pp. 19–32, 1990.

1. Knowledge of duties
   The teacher is responsible for knowing all the duties for
   which he or she may be held accountable.

2. Knowledge of school and community
   The teacher should understand the special characteristics
   of the school, its students, and the surrounding
   environment, in order to shape learning activities that
   respond to those characteristics.

3. Knowledge of subject matter
   The teacher should have adequate and up-to-date knowledge
   of subjects he or she is hired to teach in order to
   represent the matter clearly and accurately to the
   students, as well as in accross-the-curriculum subjects such as
   English, study skills, computer skills, etc.

4. Instruction design
   The teacher should be able to develop a detailed course
   plan; select or create appropriate learning materials and
   aids; evaluate the impact of the curriculum on students;
   and respond to special groups of students such as the
   sensory-impaired, nonnative speakers, etc.

5. Gathering information about student learning
   The teacher should be able to construct, administer, and grade
   a wide variety of student performance appraisals and
   tests. This includes understanding the relative merits of
   various testing protocols, and the correct use of various
   grading procedures.

6. Providing information about student learning
   a) to the student
   b) to the administration
   c) to parents, guardians, and other appropriate authorities

7. Classroom skills
   a) Communication skills
      Teachers should be able to present material clearly and
      efficiently and maintain student attention.
   b) Management skills
      Teachers should know how to control and direct conditions.

8. Personal characteristics
   a) Professional attitude
      The teacher should conduct himself or herself according
      to accepted standards of the teaching profession.
   b) Professional development
      The teacher should engage in self-evaluation and seek
      to improve in various areas that relate to increased
      student learning.

9. Service to the profession
   The teacher should be knowledgeable about the profession,
   its history, its present problems, its standards of
   ethics, and work in service to the profession in one or
   more of a variety of activities.

tent or absence of interactions between the indicators studied, and in the absence of solid evidence on this point, it is not clear that scores on the indicators can be combined to give an additive indication of merit, in the way that is quite common, nor that one can recommend the adoption of one of these aspects of (teaching) style regardless of interactions with other aspects already in place.[8]

Another criticism concerns the use of indicators that have no justification in a teacher's list of duties.

> One of the popular entries is the use of advance organizers, provided to the class verbally or in writing. . . . Research has allegedly shown that this activity "characterizes effective teaching." As many of us know from interviews or direct observation, many teachers rated as outstanding by peers, pupils, and principals do not normally use advance organizers, except possibly when visitor/evaluators are present. It's not their style, and they see it as wasting time. They know what they're after, and they jump straight in, letting what they do—and have the class do—speak for itself. Should they be penalized if the evaluator observes or discovers that they do not use this approach? For the duties-based approach, of course, the answer is no, because there is no duty to provide advance organizers, nor does doing so flow from any duty. . . . Does a good teacher become a better teacher by adding this to their teaching approach and give up the time it takes and the rigidity many teachers say it tends to encourage? Nobody knows, because correlational research doesn't address that question.[9]

EVALUATION FOR ACCOUNTABILITY AND SCHOOL IMPROVEMENT

Efforts to develop summative evaluation systems in several states seem to falter on some of the same unstable grounds that Scriven points out.[10] Pressured by state legislatures and state departments of education for greater accountability in their use of tax dollars, school systems have attempted to show that they are being accountable, and are working toward improving student learning, by devising teacher assessment systems. As one reads accounts of comments by administrators who use these systems of accountability, it is not difficult to perceive the subtext under the word "accountability," which is "Get rid of incompetent teachers." That message was heard, and many of these new

---

[8] Ibid., p. 20.

[9] Ibid., p. 30.

[10] See the case studies reported and analyzed in Milbrey Wallin McLaughlin and R. Scott Pfeifer, *Teacher Evaluation: Improvement, Accountability, and Effective Learning,* New York: Teachers College Press, 1988; see also the theme issue, "Progress in Evaluating Teaching," *Educational Leadership,* vol. 44, no. 7, April 1987; Penelope L. Peterson and Michelle A. Comeaux, "Evaluating the System: Teachers' Perspectives on Teacher Evaluation," *Educational Evaluation and Policy Analysis,* vol. 12, no. 1, pp. 3–24, Spring 1990.

◄———————————————————————————

FIGURE 14-2   The teacher's professional duties (*Source: Summarized from Michael Scriven, "Evaluating Teachers as Professionals: The Duties-Based Approach," in James Popham (ed.),* Teacher Evaluation: Six Prescriptions for Success, *Alexandria, Va.: Association for Supervision and Curriculum Development, 1988, pp. 129–134.*)

evaluation systems initially focused on establishing defensible standards for doing just that. In many instances, one of the items highlighted in reports to the state was how many incompetent teachers had been identified and induced to resign under the new system.

Influenced by research on effective classrooms, these school systems enlisted the assistance of university-based consultants to help them generate evaluation items directly tied to this research. In the interests of fairness, many of these school systems also instituted ambitious staff-development programs for training in the very skills listed in the evaluation instrument. Teachers who wanted to avoid negative evaluations or whose evaluations pointed out deficiencies could avail themselves of these staff-development opportunities. Through these workshops both teachers and administrators learned a common vocabulary and absorbed a unified view of what constituted acceptable or effective teaching. Teachers felt protected, because they were learning how to get good evaluations. Administrators felt fulfilled because teachers were showing increased attention to "effective" teacher protocols. Because such evaluation schemes and staff-development schemes have been listed in the school renewal literature as comprising "school improvement," administrators could point to their systemwide effort at school improvement effort. Everyone agreed that teachers were the key to improved student learning, and improved student learning was what school improvement was all about. Accountability, effective learning, and school improvement were linked in a neat, logical formula.[11]

A DEEPER LOOK AT STUDENT LEARNING

While there is no doubt that all teachers can improve their effectiveness with students, and no doubt that students can and should be learning more and at a deeper level of personal appropriation, are these newly devised teacher assessment instruments the primary factor in increased student learnings and improved teacher instructional effectiveness? Or, are there other factors, perhaps equally as influential on student learnings within the school? As was indicated in Chapter 7, family background factors have been shown to account for the greatest variability in student school performance.[12] Looking within the school, may one say that the teachers' classroom behavior is the single most important in-school influence on student learning? The research is by no means conclusive on this question. As studies of mastery learning indicate, students' time on task seems to be clearly related to student learning as well as students' academic self-concept or students' sense of self-efficacy. Other studies show that students' sense of their future, their sense of controlling their own fate or destiny, also influences student learning.

[11] McLaughlin and Pfeifer, op. cit., chap. 4.
[12] See James S. Coleman et al., *Equality of Educational Opportunity*, Washington D.C.: U.S. Office of Education, National Center for Educational Statistics, 1966; Christopher Jencks et al., *Inequality: A Reassessment of the Effects of Family and Schooling in America*, New York: Basic Books, 1972.

Rather than focus on a one-to-one correspondence between teacher behaviors and student learning, educators must look at a critical *intervening* variable—the students' state of mind as they approach the learning task. How motivated are students to learn the material? Even at the level of an extrinsic motivation of wanting to get a good grade (regardless of whether the learning holds any personal significance to the student), is getting a good grade valued by this student? Do students have a sense that getting a good grade, getting promoted, and getting the school diploma are meaningful? Is schooling connected to getting a job? What kind of job is seen as possible in students' minds? Do students have a sense that they control their own destiny, that by working hard, obeying the rules, they can get ahead in life? Or do they feel that their chances are in the hands of others, or, worse, are a matter of luck and street smarts, not at all related to the "stuff" that schools deal with? In other words, if students approach the learning task with a sense that learning this material really doesn't matter, then whether the teacher employs 29 or 52 effectiveness protocols, the chances of improved student performance are slim at best.

Besides the teachers' classroom efforts to motivate students to learn, to improve their academic sense of self-efficacy, to engender a sense that they have a bright future if they apply themselves, the school as an *institutional environment* must contribute to student motivation and academic self-concept.[13] Is the school as a totality "user-friendly"? Is it a place where children are respected and cared for, a place made bright and colorful by the adult community, a place where student performances are on display, where pride and self-esteem are carefully nurtured? Does the whole school environment express a concern that the curriculum be related to students' experiences; that it be seen to have practical applications not only to the world of work but also to the world of family and neighborhood; that learning be seen as involving self-expression, building teamwork, engendering pride in the achievement of student projects; that the curriculum offer quality learning experiences that students will cherish?

Or is the school not user-friendly? Do students get the feeling that their interests and desires do not count in the school environment, that the adults see them as untrustworthy, as the adversary to be controlled, coerced, intimidated, and badgered into learning? Do students perceive the school as a place that demands uniformity, passive conformity, automatic obedience, suppression of spontaneity; as a place of constant correction and punishments or threats of punishment such as grades, demerits, detention, teachers' sarcastic and humiliating remarks in front of their friends; a place where hall monitors scowl at them, security guards check them into and out of school; a place

---

[13] See A. S. Bryk and M. E. Driscoll, *An Empirical Investigation of the School as Community,* Chicago: University of Chicago, Department of Education, 1988; Thomas B. Gregory and Gerald R. Smith, *High Schools as Communities: The Small School Reconsidered,* Bloomington, Ind.: Phi Delta Kappa Educational Foundation, 1987.

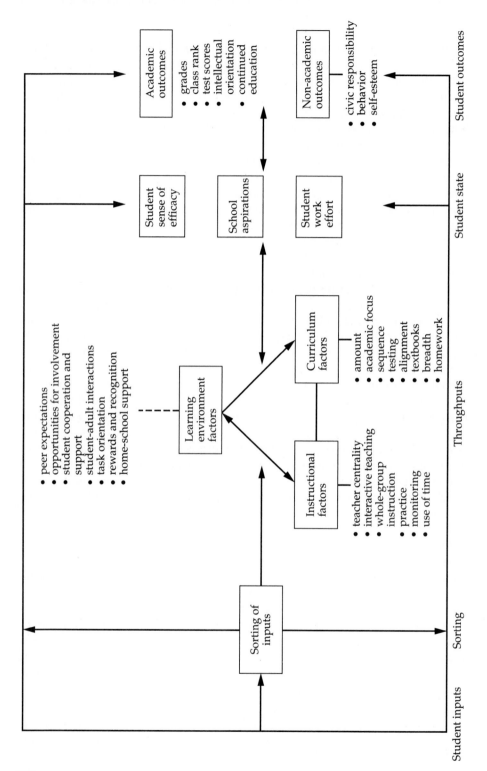

where the school bell is the enemy, demanding them to get to class, wolf down their food, interrupt an interesting or funny conversation?

Figure 14-3 presents a larger picture of other variables in the school, besides instructional factors, that affect student learning. As shown, the learning environment is an important factor that affects student learning. Teachers do not have complete, or even the major, influence over the learning environment. The general student-adult interaction throughout the school building and grounds communicates a positive or a negative feeling to students. Peer expectations and peer subculture affect the learning environment. School learning may not only not be valued within the peer culture, it may be seen as a kind of "selling out" to the authorities, an act of disloyalty to the group's cohesive resistance to the school authorities. When questions of accountability are raised, they should include the question, "What is the school administration doing to create a positive learning environment throughout the school?" Without a positive institutional learning environment, an individual teacher cannot be held exclusively accountable for the lack of progress of his or her students.

The same may be said for the influence of the curriculum. There are obvious technical questions about how well the curriculum is put together, its scope and sequence, the authentic relationship of tests and grades to the learning implied in the curriculum. Beyond the technical concerns, there are questions of perceived connections to reality and perceived relevance to students. This does not mean that the curriculum should be watered down to simplistic elements of teen music or video game culture. Rather, learning Shakespeare must have some connection to understanding oneself and one's world. Learning how to read a map of one's state or one's country can be an exercise in memorizing nonsense or it can be a very exciting journey, enabling students to see connections between rivers and mountains and highways and population and industrial centers. Is the curriculum viewed as a list of things to be memorized, a collection of right answers, an approved anthology of what others have deemed to be important information? If so, then teachers who use effectiveness protocols may have little success in improving students' academic outcomes.

Any form of teacher assessment that is tied to the rhetoric of accountability is unbalanced, and indeed unfair, if it is not integrated with school assessment. If it is possible to say that the whole school, as a total institution, has done its best to create an environment conducive to student learning, then looking at how teachers capitalize on that or fail to capitalize on that makes eminent professional sense. By the same token, when the institutional framework of the school is inimical to student learning, blaming teachers for inadequate levels of student learning makes no sense.

FIGURE 14-3   A conceptual model of influences on student outcomes. (*Source: Joseph Murphy and Philip Hallinger, "Equity as Access to Learning: Curricular and Instructional Treatment Differences,"* Journal of Curriculum Studies, *vol. 21, no. 3, 1989, p. 132.*)

ASSESSMENT FOR AUTHENTIC STUDENT LEARNING

Mounting evidence indicates that teacher assessment based on lists of class-room effectiveness protocols, when tied to student outcomes on tests, leads teachers to teach to the test. However, although test scores on basic skills rise as a result of these teaching methods, scores *decline* in other academic outcome areas such as writing essays, analytical reading, solving mathematics prob-lems, reasoning in science.[14] This evidence leads to further questions about the wisdom of creating assessment instruments based on effectiveness protocols of teaching. Besides questions raised by Scriven about the research base from which these protocols are derived, and about the logic and validity of combin-ing various protocols as though they were organically related, there are other questions prompted by reflections on the nature of learning itself.

Despite their protestations to the contrary, proponents of teaching effective-ness and teacher assessments based thereon impart a fundamentally passive role to the learner. The learner is to absorb what the teacher is teaching. Through drill and seat exercises, the student acquires sufficient familiarity with the material and with the way the tests solicit information about the ma-terial to score well on tests about that material. Defining learning as this kind of ability to absorb instructional material and score well on tests that elicit that absorption is to reduce learning to a model of passive intake and repetition of intake on exams. Teaching then becomes reduced to generating these kinds of student outcomes on examinations.

When students really learn something, they take it inside themselves and relate it to a network of other learnings in a framework of meaning and per-sonal significance; they understand those connections; they are able subse-quently to retrieve that learning and use it to interpret new material, reconfig-ure new information, analyze and name new problems, and express a new series of relationships. This kind of learning is not a guaranteed outcome of what a teacher does. The *student* does the learning. Rather than simply re-spond passively to a stimulus, the student has to internalize the material, look at it, fiddle with it, go back and ask the teacher something about it, come back and fiddle some more. Gradually the student understands how the material works, how it applies, what it means, how it is connected to other things or sit-uations or people. The student does this work. Learning is active, it is con-structive, it involves the whole person of the learner—body, intellect, imagina-tion, feelings, memory, present view of the world.

What the teacher does is to try to bring the student to the activity of learn-ing. The teacher cajoles, persuades, entices, threatens, encourages, supports, stimulates, invites, teases, explains, tells interesting stories, describes, demon-

---

[14] See Linda Darling-Hammond and Arthur E. Wise, "Beyond Standardization: State Standards and School Improvement," *Elementary School Journal,* vol. 85, pp. 315–335, 1985; see also Brian Rowan, "Commitment and Control: Alternative Strategies for the Organizational Design of Schools," in Courtney B. Cazden (ed.), *Review of Research in Education,* vol. 16, Washington D.C.: American Educational Research Association, 1990, pp. 353–389.

strates, suggests, nudges. The most important questions to ask about a teacher's work with students are: "Does the teacher bring the student to the activity of learning? Does the teacher get the student to engage the material actively? Does the teacher have the degree of versatility, patience, creativity, persistence, and clarity in using a wide variety of strategies necessary to engender in the student a curiosity about and interest in the material under study?" In evaluating teaching, educators must look at student activity and ask: Are students engaged? Is the process of leading them to the material caring, respectful, accepting of their readiness? Is the teacher's activity also challenging, demanding, relentless, so that the students stay with the material? Is the teacher's facilitating activity intelligent, that is, does it encourage students to make connections with larger patterns of meaning? Does the teacher's activity lead student learning toward those larger learning goals of the school's mission statement?

Consistent with our claim that the institutional support of a positive learning environment is critical to student learning, the process of teacher assessment should also include questions such as the following: What kind of home environment are these youngsters coming from? What is their sense of self? What is their sense of efficacy? Are they willing to work, to dig into the material to learn something valuable? What do they aspire to? How do they connect this learning activity with what they consider to be real in their lives, in their futures? Is this classroom reflective of a larger institutional environment that encourages initiative, pride, self-esteem, community, caring about their world? Do youngsters arrive in this classroom with little or no sense that the work expected of them has any intrinsic meaning or value to them? The answers to these questions should provide the person performing the summative evaluation of a teacher with some perception of the chances for success in that teaching/learning endeavor. If youngsters begin that endeavor with no feeling of support from the institutional environment and with feelings of alienation and conflict toward that environment, then that should be noted at the beginning of the teacher's assessment. Administrators, in the process of reviewing such assessments, should take note of the grade the institution receives for promoting a learning environment.

If assessment is to be linked to student learning and to school improvement, then the teacher assessment must include an assessment of the students' state as they approach the learning activity, as noted in Figure 14-3. The evaluator should try to discover whether and in what direction that state is influenced primarily by the teacher or primarily by the institutional environment. When both the institutional environment and the teacher's activities simultaneously and conjointly communicate positive support for students' motivation, sense of efficacy, and connectedness to real life, the evaluator should note how the interface works to increase student learning. When the institutional environment and teacher efforts are at odds, teachers and evaluators should discuss what needs to be done.

SUMMARY

In this chapter we explored the controversial topic of teacher evaluation. From the start we situated teacher evaluation within the context of the school as a community of learners. Summative evaluation relates to decisions about membership in that community, and to ways the community can honor outstanding contributions. Summative evaluations can be used to make various personnel decisions. In cases of possible termination of teacher contracts, these evaluations lead to administrative processes. We also looked at examples of summative evaluations for periodic assessment of tenured teachers. These examples provided maps of the terrain of summative evaluation. We then considered what might legitimately constitute standards for summative teacher evaluations. Michael Scriven offers one approach, which seems to avoid the pitfalls of many systems in use in the schools. We suggested that student learnings are as much influenced by institutional supports for a positive learning environment as they are by teachers' activities. Assessment of teachers should not be carried on independently from institutional assessment. Furthermore, a deeper look at what is meant by student learning provided a different base for constructing a different set of questions to ask in a system of summative teacher evaluation.

Because summative evaluation relates to the members of a community deciding whom to admit, whom to retain, and whom to honor for enhancing that community, the process often is hindered by adversarial and legal considerations. Ideally, summative evaluation should be used to identify and celebrate extraordinary contributions to the learning community.

CHAPTER 15

SUPERVISION AS TEACHER DEVELOPMENT AND RENEWAL

IT is generally assumed that the overarching purpose of supervision is to help teachers improve. The focus of this improvement may be on what the teacher knows, the development of teaching skills, the teacher's ability to make more informed professional decisions, to problem-solve better, and to inquire into her or his own practice. Traditionally, improvement has been sought by providing formal and informal in-service programs and activities and by providing an array of staff-development opportunities for teachers. Supervisors are placed in the driver's seat, taking responsibility for the whats, hows, and whens of improvement as they plan and provide in-service and staff-development programs. Frances Bolin, Judith Falk, and their colleagues[1] suggest that though in-service programs and staff development may be legitimate and important in their own right, neither are expansive and penetrating enough to fully tap the potential for teachers to grow personally and professionally. For example, Bolin writes,

> What would happen if we set aside the question of how to *improve* the teacher and looked instead at what we can do to encourage the teacher. . . . Asking how to encourage the teacher places the work of improvement in the hands of the teacher. It presupposes that the teacher desires to grow, to be self defining, and to engage in teaching as a vital part of life, rather than as unrelated employment. This leads to looking at teaching as a commitment or calling, a vocation . . . that is not adequately contained in the term *profession* as it has come to be used.[2]

According to Bolin, when supervision shifts away from providing improvement experiences and opportunities to encouraging teachers, in-service and staff development give way to *renewal*. Supervision as renewal is more fully integrated into the everyday life of the school as teachers move from the back seat to the driver's seat by assuming fuller responsibility for their own growth.

In this chapter we examine in-service programming, staff development, and renewal as alternative frameworks for creating a growth-oriented supervision. All three have a role to play, but the full range of growth opportunities for teachers, we suggest, are available only when renewal is emphasized and supported by staff development as needed. In contrast, in-service programming

---

[1] See, for example, the articles that appear in Frances S. Bolin and Judith McConnel Falk (eds.), *Teacher Renewal Professional Issues, Personal Choices*, New York: Teachers College Press, 1987.

[2] Frances S. Bolin, "Reassessment and Renewal in Teaching," in Bolin and Falk, ibid., p. 11.

should play a very limited role. This ordering of the three is in direct contrast to that which now dominates current practice. In-service programming dominates, supported by staff development. Renewal, to the extent that it exists, remains at the periphery.

The three frames are contrasted in Figure 15-1. In-service, for example, is a highly directive and structured process. Responsibility for in-service is usually in the hands of someone other than the teacher, and the emphasis is on the development of job-related skills through the provision of training and practice experiences. The workshop featuring a tell, sell, and practice format is often the vehicle for delivering in-service. When in-service is the sole or primary vehicle for promoting growth, teaching comes to be viewed as a job with teachers as workers who, it is apparently assumed, possess limited capacity or will to figure out things for themselves. Though teacher in-service has a long history, teachers do not always regard the process with enthusiasm. It is often too formal and bureaucratic and characterized by a high degree of administrative planning and scheduling. Too often, in-service serves less to provide growth and more to meet legal requirements of one sort or another. Program activities often are selected and developed for uniform dissemination without giving serious consideration to the purposes of such activities or to the needs of individual teachers. Structure, uniformity, and tight control from above result in a training rather than education emphasis. We are not suggesting that in-service be abandoned, for it can be useful under proper circumstances. We are suggesting, however, that a commitment to teacher growth requires much more than in-service programming.

The concept of staff development, in contrast, seems more in tune with the view of teaching as a profession. The emphasis is on the development of professional expertise by involving teachers in problem-solving and action re-

FIGURE 15-1   Frameworks for growth.

In-Service	Staff Development	Renewal
○ Assumes teaching is a job	○ Assumes teaching is a profession	○ Assumes teaching is a vocation
○ Focuses on development of job-related skills	○ Focuses on development of professional expertise	○ Focuses on development of personal and professional self
○ Through training and practice	○ Through problem solving and inquiry	○ Through reflection and reevaluation

Institutional Responsibility — Other-directed .... Self-directed — Personal Responsibility

search. Teachers and supervisors share responsibility for the planning, development, and provision of staff-development activities, and the focus is much less on training than on puzzling, inquiring, and solving problems.

Renewal as still another growth frame focuses on the development of the personal and professional self through reflection and reevaluation. Renewal is not driven so much by professional problems as by one's commitment to teaching as a vocation. As Bolin suggests, renewal implies doing over again, revising, making new yet restoring, reestablishing, and revaluing.[3] In renewal the emphasis is on the individual teacher and his or her personal and professional development.

Neither staff development nor renewal are imposed by the school upon the teacher; the teacher engages in these processes for her- or himself. In-service, on the other hand, typically assumes a deficiency in the teacher and presupposes a set of appropriate ideas, skills, and methods that need to be developed. In-service works to reduce the teacher's range of alternatives—indeed, to bring about conformity. Staff development and renewal assume a need for teachers to grow and develop on the job. Rather than reducing the range of alternatives they seek to increase this range. Teacher growth is less a function of polishing existing skills or of keeping up with the latest developments and more a function of solving problems and of changing as individuals. Growth occurs when teachers see themselves, the school, the curriculum, and the students they teach in a new light.

We begin this examination of supervision as development and renewal by first considering various dimensions of teaching competence. A design for development and renewal composed of five critical components is then provided. Next, we focus attention on the issue of who should assume responsibility for the provision of growth opportunities, pointing out that responsibility is in part a function of the approach one uses. Three approaches—traditional, informal, and intermediate—are discussed. Characteristics of effective staff-development programs are then considered, and we conclude our discussion by revisiting the question of purpose. Throughout this chapter we build a design that not only addresses issues and synthesizes basic concepts but can serve as a framework for planning, developing, and providing teacher growth programs and opportunities.

TECHNICAL COMPETENCE IN TEACHING

Teaching as an expression of technical competence, the most basic of the four competency types that will be discussed in this section, is the driving force behind most models of supervision and evaluation in use today. It is as well the basis for most teacher improvement programs and efforts. An example of an emphasis on technical competence is a focus on a list of teaching behaviors found to be linked to certain dimensions of teaching effectiveness. When tech-

[3] Ibid.

nical competence is overemphasized, such teaching behaviors inevitably are found on evaluation checklists and become the basis for developing companion supervisory strategies designed to check for and encourage their use. Completing this picture are workshops and other in-service efforts that teach educators how to use the behaviors and to provide tips to supervisors as to how they might be assessed.

As a general rule, the type of teaching competence being addressed and its resulting view of teaching determine the kind of supervision and the frame for teacher growth that are used. Technical competency is indeed important to successful teaching and learning. But over the long run this type of competency should not be the major concern in teaching or the major focus of growth and development efforts. Once technical competence is assured, primary attention should be given to clinical, personal, and critical teaching competencies.

CLINICAL, PERSONAL, AND CRITICAL TEACHING COMPETENCIES

In a groundbreaking synthesis of a broad range of philosophical, theoretical, and research knowledge on successful teaching practices, Nancy Zimpher and Kenneth Howey describe four major types of teaching competence that they believe can be facilitated by appropriate supervisory and staff-development practices: technical, clinical, personal, and critical.[4] The four are depicted and discussed in Table 15-1. Zimpher and Howey maintain that all four competency types are essential to good teaching and that each should be considered in choosing appropriate supervisory practice, determining appropriate emphasis in teacher growth programs, and deciding on the right mix of in-service, staff-development, and renewal as frames for planning.

When the emphasis is on clinical competence the teacher functions as a problem solver and expert clinician who frames problems and issues and comes to grips with solutions. The images of teaching as problem solving and decision making are at the heart of clinical competence. Supervisory efforts that enhance inquiry, encourage reflection, build problem-solving skills, and help teachers make more informed decisions about their practice address the clinical competence. Building clinical competence is the major goal of the staff-development frame.

When the emphasis is on personal competence the teacher functions as one able to understand and interpret his or her teaching in a manner that provides for meaning and significance. Supervision addresses personal competence by helping increase teacher self-awareness, understanding of teaching practice, and interpretive capacities.

Critical competence deals with issues of value and importance in the hid-

[4] Nancy Z. Zimpher and Kenneth R. Howey, "Adapting Supervisory Practice to Different Orientations of Teaching Competence," *Journal of Curriculum and Supervision*, vol. 2, no. 1, pp. 101–127, 1987.

TABLE 15-1
ZIMPHER AND HOWEY: FRAMEWORK FOR EXAMINING FOUR TYPES OF TEACHING COMPETENCE

	Technical competence	Clinical competence	Personal competence	Critical competence
Conception of the teacher	Determines in advance what is to be learned, how it is to be learned, and criteria by which success is to be measured	Instructional problem solver; clinician frames and solves practical problems; takes reflective action; inquirer	Understanding of self; self-actualized person who uses self as effective and humane instrument	Rational, morally autonomous, socially conscious change agent
Focus of supervision	Mastery of methods of instruction: specific skills (how to ask good questions); how to apply teaching strategies; how to select and organize curriculum content; how to structure the classroom for learning what techniques to use to maintain control	Reflective decision making and action to solve practical problems (what should be done about disruptive behavior) as well as reconsideration of intents and practices to take action to solve practical problems	Increase self-awareness, identity formation, and interpretive capacities, e.g., self-confrontation; values clarification; interpersonal involvement; small-group processes; develop personal style in teaching roles	Reflective decision making and action to form more rational and just schools, critique of stereotypes/ideology, hidden curriculum, authoritarian/permissive relationships, equality of access, responsibilities, and forms of repressive social control
Conception of the supervisor	Technical expert/master provides for skill development and efficient/effective use of resources in classroom; translator of research theory into technical rules for application in classrooms	Fosters inquiry regarding the relationship of theory and practice; fosters reflection about the relationship of intents and practice and reconsideration/modification of intent/practice in light of evaluation of their conscience	Expert in interpersonal competence and theories of human development; nondirective participant: warm and supportive learning environment, responsiveness to teacher-defined needs and concerns, wisdom in guiding free exploration of teaching episodes, diagnosing theories-in-use	Collaborator in self-reflective communities of practitioner-theorists committed to examining critically their own/institutional practices and improving them in interests of nationality and social justice; provides challenges and support as do other participants in dialogue

TABLE 15-1 (CONTINUED)

Type of theoretical knowledge	Technical guidelines from explanatory theory; analytic craft knowledge about what constitutes "good" practice	Synthesis of normative, interpretive, and explanatory knowledge to form intellectually and morally defensible practical judgments about what to do in a particular situation	Analytic and interpretive theory to understand and make explicit reasons underlying symbolic interaction essentially those which occur in the class	Critical theory of education; unite philosophical analysis and criticism and causal and interpretive science
Mode of inquiry	Applied science, functional and task analysis, linear problem solving to determine how to accomplish given ends	Practical action research to articulate concerns, plan action, monitor action, and reflect on processes and consequences to improve our teaching practices; rationale building	Phenomenological, ethnographic, hermeneutic analysis and interpretation; analyze elements of teaching episodes	Collaborative action and reflection to transform the organization and practice of education; group inquiry regarding conditions of communicative interaction and social control
Level of reflectivity	Specific techniques needed to reach stated objectives involve instrumental reasoning; means-end (if, then) relative to efficiency/effectiveness	Practical reasoning and judgment relative to what should be done (best course of action under the circumstances)	Interpretation of intended meaning of verbal and nonverbal symbols and acts; introspection relative to self-awareness/identity	Critical self-reflection; reflexivity and social critique to uncover contradictions/inadequacies and different conceptions of educational practice as values with society
Range of complexity	From: Learning/using specific skills To: Learning/using complex curricular and instructional systems	From: Examining what one is doing in the classroom and making needed changes (inquiry and reflection about one's teaching) To: Action research and practical deliberation among colleagues in school/district to solve common educational concerns	From: Self-awareness and survival concerns To: Using knowledge of adult moral and cognitive development to inform teacher practice	From: Consciousness raising about school practices that are self-defeating in terms of learning and teaching, such as exposing hidden curriculum To: Collaboration of critical inquirers to reconstruct/transform schooling/society

Source: Nancy L. Zimpher and Kenneth R. Howey, "Adapting Supervisory Practices to Different Orientations of Teaching," Journal of Curriculum and Supervision, vol. 2, no. 2, 1987. This table combines tables 1 and 2 from their article. Zimpher and Howey acknowledged the major contribution of Sharon Strom, a doctoral candidate at the University of Minnesota, in the development of tables 1 and 2.

den meanings that underlie teaching practice. Within the critical competence, teaching is viewed as an ethical science concerned with worth and purpose. Technical competence, for example, emphasizes doing things right. In contrast, critical competence emphasizes what is worth doing and doing right things. Personal and critical competence are the major goals of the renewal frame.

Zimpher and Howey's description of each of the four types of competence can be used by supervisors to evaluate the balance of emphasis that characterizes present school practice. Using Table 15-1, readers might, for example, examine teacher-evaluation practices now in use in their schools, the dominant models of supervision that accompany these practices, and the content and structure of teacher growth and development programs that have been implemented over the past two years. Then using a total of 100 points, assign points to each of the four critical competencies to reflect the emphasis that characterizes current practice. The following grid might be helpful:

	Technical competence	Clinical competence	Personal competence	Critical competence	Total points
Evaluation practices					100
Supervision models					100
Teacher growth and development purposes, content, structure					100
Total					300

A best distribution among the four types of teaching competence cannot, of course, be determined separate from the characteristics of the situation at hand. A school with a large proportion of novice teachers might well need more attention to the technical competencies of teaching, and, in contrast, a school with a large proportion of highly accomplished and experienced teachers might need more attention to other types of teaching competence. Total the points in each of the competency columns; using 300 points as base, determine the percentage of emphasis across the four competency areas.

A DESIGN FOR TEACHER GROWTH AND DEVELOPMENT

In the sections that follow, a design for teacher growth and development is presented. This design is composed of five critical components: *intents, substance, performance expectations, approach,* and *responsibility*. The design requires supervisors and teachers to be concerned about program intents and substance and, in turn, to match these with appropriate approaches, competency levels, and responsibility designations. Consider each of the components separately.

Intents

Teacher growth and development programs and activities are typically designed around such themes as presenting information, helping teachers understand this information, helping teachers apply this understanding in their teaching, and helping teachers to accept, and be committed to, these new approaches. Presenting information is a *knowledge*-level intent. For example, a program might be designed to introduce a group of science teachers to the concept and language of inquiry teaching. Promoting understanding is a *comprehension*-level intent. The intent here might be to help teachers to understand how inquiry teaching might affect the way they presently plan and organize instruction. Using inquiry methods effectively in teaching a particular biology unit is an example of an *applications*-level intent. Though each of these levels is necessary, none is sufficient to gain sustained use of inquiry methods by teachers. Teachers may be able to demonstrate such methods on demand but are not likely to use them once out of the spotlight unless they believe in, and are committed to, such methods. Becoming committed to inquiry methods as a useful approach to science teaching is a *value*- and *attitude-integration*-level intent.

Often only knowledge and comprehension levels are considered in planning. But programs and activities specifically designed to meet intents at these levels are not likely to be sufficient for such higher levels as value and attitude integration. By the same token programs and activities designed for higher-level intents, when only knowledge-level intents are necessary, may well be too elaborate, wasteful, and exhausting for both supervisors and teachers.

Substance

Louis Rubin has identified four critical factors in good teaching, each of which he believes can be improved through appropriate teacher growth and development activities:

The teacher's sense of purpose
The teacher's perception of students

The teacher's knowledge of subject matter
The teacher's mastery of technique[5]

Sense of purpose and perception of students are part of a teacher's *educational platform* and as such represent values, beliefs, assumptions, and action theories a teacher holds about the nature of knowledge, how students learn, appropriate relationships between students and teachers, and other factors. One's educational platform becomes the basis for decisions one makes about classroom organization and teaching, and, indeed, once a platform is known, key decisions the teacher will make can be predicted with reliability.

A teacher who considers his or her purpose to impart information is likely to rely heavily on teacher talk and formal classroom arrangements. Likewise, a teacher who perceives youngsters as being basically trustworthy and responsible is likely to share responsibilities for decisions about learning with the class. If a supervisor were interested in reducing teacher talk and/or increasing student responsibility, he or she would have to contend with the critical factor of purpose and perception of teachers. His or her target is the restructuring of educational platforms of teachers.

In describing the importance of knowledge of subject matter, Rubin notes:

> There is a considerable difference between the kind of teaching that goes on when teachers have an intimate acquaintance with the content of the lesson and when the acquaintance is only peripheral. When teachers are genuinely knowledgeable, when they know their subject well enough to discriminate between the seminal ideas and the secondary matter, when they can go beyond what is in the textbook, the quality of the pedagogy becomes extraordinarily impressive. For it is only when a teacher has a consummate grasp of, say, arithmetic, physics, or history that their meaning can be turned outward and brought to bear upon the learner's personal experience. Relevancy lies less in the inherent nature of a subject than in its relationship to the child's frame of reference. In the hands of a skilled teacher, poetry can be taught with success and profit to ghetto children.[6]

Though content versus process arguments continue from time to time, both aspects of instruction are necessary for effective teaching. Our observation is that the less the teacher knows about a particular subject the more trivial the teaching and the more defensive the pedagogy. By defensive pedagogy we mean dominance by the teacher and strict adherence to curriculum materials. But one can have a great appreciation for a particular field of study and still not be able to communicate its wonder and excitement effectively. Mastery of technique, classroom organization and management, and other pedagogical skills make up the fourth critical dimension of effective teaching. Each of the

[5] Louis J. Rubin, "The Case for Staff Development," in Thomas J. Sergiovanni (ed.), *Professional Supervision for Professional Teachers*, Washington, D.C.: Association for Supervision and Curriculum Development, 1975.
[6] Ibid., p. 47.

critical factors in good teaching can be understood and developed as technical, clinical, personal, or critical teaching competence.

These dimensions are the basis for deciding the substance of staff-development programs. Comprehensive programs are concerned with all four—the teacher's conception of purpose, sensitivity to students, intimacy with subject matter, and basic repertory of teaching techniques. Purpose and sensitivity remain key, for they shape the teacher's reality and become the basis for making teaching decisions about subject matter and technique. This observation raises questions about viewing technical, clinical, personal, and critical competency types as being rigidly developmental. Developmental thinking leads supervisors to reason that they must first provide in-service to build basic technical skills, shifting only later to staff development and renewal frames for "higher" levels of competency. It turns out that personal and critical competency may be so fundamental in shaping the teacher's basic view of teaching that they influence as well the development of basic teaching skills. Following this reasoning, the competency levels might best be viewed as a pattern for defining teaching that can be addressed by the provision of in-service, staff development, or renewal opportunities as appropriate. Multiple frames leads us to conclude that providing options (to be discussed in the next chapter) and encouraging teachers to make informed choices among them should be at the crux of a school's overall teacher growth strategy.

Performance Expectations

What are the major performance expectations for which teachers should be accountable? It is reasonable to expect that teachers *know how* to do their jobs and keep up with major developments. But knowing and understanding are not enough. Teachers also are expected to put their knowledge to work—to demonstrate that they *can do* the job. Still, demonstrating knowledge is a fairly low-level competency. Most teachers are competent enough and clever enough to come up with the right teaching performance when the supervisor is around. The proof of the pudding is whether they *will do* the job of their own free will and on a sustained basis. Finally, as professionals, teachers are expected to engage in a lifelong commitment to self-improvement. Self-improvement is the *will-grow* performance expectation. Self-employed professionals (doctors, accountants, etc.) are forced by competition and by visible product evaluation to give major attention to the will-grow dimension. Teachers, as organizational professionals whose "products" are difficult to measure, have not felt this external pressure for continuing professional growth. Increasingly, however, school districts are making the will-grow dimension a contractual obligation, and indeed teachers who are perfectly satisfactory in the know-how, can-do, and will-do performance expectations face sanctions (including dismissal) for less than satisfactory commitment to continuing professional growth.

The relationships between performance expectations, intents, and substance

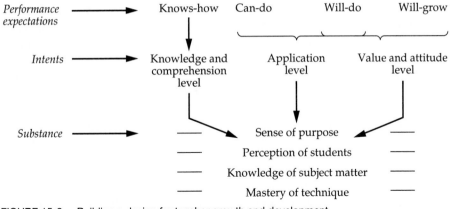

FIGURE 15-2   Building a design for teacher growth and development.

are summarized in Figure 15-2. For example, in the know-how area, teachers are expected to know and understand purposes, students, subject matter, and techniques. In the can-do area, teachers apply this knowledge of substance to their classrooms. Will-do, however, requires not only ability to apply this knowledge but a commitment to its application over time. Teacher growth programs aimed at the will-do dimension must have "value and attitude" as well as application intents. If performance and commitment are to be sustained over time, teachers must see value in what they do and believe it is important to commit themselves. Will-grow is equally dependent upon value and attitude intents. Thus supervisors working with teachers in the will-do and will-grow areas and who choose strategies suited only to knowledge and comprehension are not likely to be successful.

Approach and Responsibility

We have now discussed three of five design components for planning and providing teacher growth and development opportunities: intents, substance, and performance expectations. Two more remain: the *approach* used and the locus of major *responsibility*. Approaches can be grouped into three general categories: traditional, informal, and intermediate. Traditional approaches generally are more formal and structured and designed to meet specific and uniform objectives. They emerge from the in-service frame. Informal approaches, on the other hand, are loosely structured and rely on discovery and exploration techniques. Often objectives are not predetermined but are discovered or assessed after the fact. Intermediate approaches are moderately structured with a predetermined agenda that permits a great deal of flexibility. Both are aligned with the staff-development and renewal frames.

In-service

Traditional Approaches and Supervisory Responsibility   Traditional approaches to staff development are well known to supervisors and administrators and need little elaboration. They seem best suited when a problem can be defined as a deficit in knowledge of some kind. Traditional approaches typically are accompanied by clear objectives and rely on conventional, though well-executed, instruction. Teachers generally assume passive roles and are exposed to logically structured programs or activities. Techniques most often used are lecture, illustrated lecture, demonstration, and observation, often followed by guided discussion activities.

Traditional approaches seem well suited to routine information updating of the latest books, techniques, principles, and ideas relating to one's work. It is not assumed that a particular group is considering adopting something new, but that the group is only learning more about it. As intents change from learning to understanding, to applying, to integrating new things into one's repertoire of behavior, approaches will need to change if efforts are to be effective. The widespread use of traditional approaches to the virtual exclusion of other approaches would lead one to conclude that educators have an insatiable appetite for knowledge but are not interested in doing very much with this knowledge.

The locus of responsibility for traditional approaches to teacher growth and development is with the administration as it executes its personnel administration functions. Though traditional approaches have a place and should remain administrative responsibilities, alone they represent a minimum commitment to teacher growth and development.

Renewal
Informal Approaches and Teacher Responsibility   Perhaps the most innovative and provocative approaches to teacher growth and development are those that rely on exploration and discovery by teachers. It is assumed that by providing teachers with a rich environment loaded with teaching materials, media, books, and devices, and that with generous encouragement and support from principals and supervisors, teachers will interact with this environment and with each other through exploration and discovery. Exploration and discovery can help many teachers to find themselves, to unleash their creativity, to learn more about their own capabilities as people and teachers, and at the same time to pick up new teaching ideas, activities, and methods.

Thelen notes that in the most useful teacher growth and development programs "one finds intensity of personal involvement, immediate consequences for classroom practice, stimulation and ego support by meaningful associates in the situation and initiating by teacher rather than outside."[7] Informal approaches seem best able to meet these criteria, and because of their enormous potential, such approaches should play an important role in school district planning. Major responsibility for informal approaches rests with teachers. They can take a variety of forms: two teachers sharing ideas; a team or family

---

[7] Herbert Thelen, "A Cultural Approach to In-Service Education," in Louis Rubin (ed.), *Improving In-Service Education*, Boston: Allyn and Bacon, 1971, pp. 72–73.

of teachers working and planning together; teacher involvement in an in-building resource center; and participation in district or area teacher centers. Informal approaches should be encouraged and supported.

Teacher centers deserve special attention. They represent fledgling, but promising, attempts to elevate and legitimize the role of teacher in accepting some of the responsibility for their own growth and development. In describing such centers Kathleen Devaney notes:

> There is a notion of *teachers centers* which is essentially an image of a place—small, welcoming, hand-built—where teachers come voluntarily to make things for class-rooms, to exchange ideas, and to learn in a format of one-shot or short-series work-shops rather than semester-long courses based on lectures and texts. Because this place is non-institutional neutral ground, teachers can let down their hair, drop competitiveness and defensiveness, and thus find starting points for self-improve-ment and professional growth.[8]

Some centers indeed fit the "noninstitutional neutral ground" pattern, but no hard and fast rules regarding location exist. A teacher center can be developed and operated in a surplus classroom or perhaps in an overlooked or un-derutilized basement location of a particular school. The center could be limited to only teachers of that school or perhaps expanded to serve district or area teachers. The closing of schools in many districts is conducive to the establishment of a district or area teacher center in abandoned school buildings. Some centers can be located in storefronts and warehouses. Regardless of scale or location, some common aspects exist, the most notable being that the locus of responsibility for planning and operation is with teachers. Further common-alities are suggested by Devaney:

> The common purpose which stands out as a bond linking widely dissimilar teachers centers is the aim to help teachers enliven, individualize, personalize, enrich, elabo-rate, reorganize, or re-conceptualize the curriculum within their own classrooms. Study of scores of teachers center program offerings and calendars demonstrates center leaders' belief that help to teachers in the area of curriculum is the most teacher-responsive service they can offer. These centers teach teachers how to use manipulative, real-world, exploratory, frequently individualized curriculum materi-als and how to gradually reorganize classroom space and time to accommodate greater student activity and interaction. They engage teachers in adapting packaged curriculum materials, making their own materials, or building classroom apparatus, and often they involve teachers in some new study—often math or science—or craft so as to reacquaint them with the experience of being active, problem-solving learn-ers themselves.[9]

Changes of lasting quality in schools depend heavily on grass-roots pro-cesses. Further, it seems clear that teachers look to other teachers as important

---

[8] Kathleen Devaney, "What's a Teacher Center For?" *Educational Leadership*, vol. 33, no. 6, p. 413, 1976. This issue of *Educational Leadership* was guest-edited by Vincent Rogers, and its theme is teacher centers.

[9] Ibid., p. 414.

models for change. In two separate studies with similar themes both Emil Haller and Charles Keenan[10] asked teachers to identify to whom they go for help when they run into curriculum problems and to whom they could go for ideas and insights about teaching and learning. The Canadian and American teachers who responded to these questions also were asked which sources of new ideas were most creditable. Choosing from such categories as principal, supervisor, central office staff, professor, research journals, and so on, the overwhelming choice in response to each question was *other teachers.* Teachers go to other teachers for help and for sources of new ideas, and they believe in each other—potent reasons for supervisors to provide support for informal teacher growth and staff-development approaches.

Teacher Growth and Development
Intermediate Approaches and Supervisory Responsibility   The cornerstone of a comprehensive teacher growth and development program for any school or district is a *supervisory* system of staff development with shared responsibility. Informal approaches are low-keyed, classroom-focused, teacher-oriented, and particularistic. Traditional approaches, on the other hand, are high-keyed, more formal, system- or school-oriented, and universal. A supervisory system of teacher growth and development, in contrast, assumes an intermediate position whereby the supervisor enters into a relationship with teachers on an equal footing and assumes an active role along with teachers. The teachers' capacities, needs, and interests are paramount, but sufficient planning and structure is introduced to bridge the gap between these interests and school program and instruction needs.

Intermediate staff-development approaches usually have the following characteristics:

1 The teacher is actively involved in contributing data, information, or feelings, solving a problem, or conducting an analysis.
2 The supervisor shares in the contributing, solving, and conducting activities above as a colleague of the teacher.
3 In colleagueship the supervisor and teachers work together as professional associates bound together by a common purpose. The common purpose is improvement of teaching and learning through the professional development of both teacher and supervisor.[11] Neither the teacher's autonomy as a professional nor the supervisor's responsibilities

---

[10] Emil J. Haller, *Strategies for Change,* Toronto: Ontario Institute for Studies in Education, Department of Educational Administration, 1968; and Charles Keenan, "Channels for Change: A Survey of Teachers in Chicago Elementary Schools," doctoral dissertation, Urbana: University of Illinois, Department of Educational Administration, 1974.

[11] Our definition of colleagueship follows Morris Cogan, *Clinical Supervision,* Boston: Houghton Mifflin, 1973, chap. 5. In contrast, the relationship between supervisor and teacher in traditional approaches is more clearly superordinate-subordinate, and in informal approaches the supervisor is more of a helper, facilitator, or passive supporter. In the intermediate approach the supervisor is neither dominating nor passive but is involved, side by side, with the teacher as a colleague.

as a professional are compromised in the process, since the relationship is based not on authority but on a commitment to professional improvement.

4 Staff-development activities generally require study of an actual situation or a real problem and use live data, either from self-analysis or from observations of others.

5 Feedback is provided, by the supervisor, by other teachers, or as a result of joint analysis, which permits teachers to compare observations with intents and beliefs, and personal reactions with those of others.

6 The emphasis is on direct improvement of teaching and learning in the classroom.

CHARACTERISTICS OF EFFECTIVE STAFF-DEVELOPMENT PROGRAMS

By way of summary, excerpts from a study of staff-development programs conducted under the auspices of the Florida State Department of Education are provided. The study suggests a number of clear patterns of effectiveness consistent with the recommendations provided above:

School-based programs in which *teachers participate as helpers to each other and planners of in-service activities* tend to have greater success . . . than do programs . . . conducted by college or other outside personnel without the assistance of teachers.

In-service education programs that have *differentiated training experiences for different teachers* (that is, "individualized") are more likely to accomplish their objectives than are programs that have common activities for all participants.

In-service education programs that *place the teacher in an active role (constructing and generating materials, ideas, and behavior)* are more likely to accomplish their objectives than are programs that place the teacher in a receptive role. . . .

In-service education programs in which *teachers share and provide mutual assistance* to each other are more likely to accomplish their objectives than are programs in which each teacher does separate work.

Teachers are more likely to benefit from in-service programs in which they can *choose goals and activities for themselves,* as contrasted with programs in which the goals and activities are preplanned. [Italics added][12]

In their extensive review of the literature on staff development, experts Dennis Sparks and Susan Loucks-Horsley list the following as "well-known" effective practices:

Programs conducted in school settings and linked to school-wide efforts
Teachers participating as helpers to each other and as planners, with administrators, of inservice activities
Emphasis on self instruction with differentiated training opportunities

---

[12] Roy A. Edelfelt and Margo Johnson, *Rethinking In-Service Education,* Washington, D.C.: National Education Association, 1975, pp. 18–19, as quoted in Devaney, op. cit., p. 416. The original report is Gordon Lawrence, *Patterns of Effective In-Service Education,* Tallahassee, Fla.: State Department of Education, 1974.

Teachers in active roles, choosing goals and activities for themselves

Emphasis on demonstration, supervised trials and feedback; training that is concrete and ongoing over time

Ongoing assistance and support available on request[13]

Notice the importance given to teacher involvement in planning, differentiated experiences for different teachers, active roles, using ideas, materials, and behavior found in the actual teaching situation, teachers working with and helping other teachers, and teacher goals.

MAPPING TEACHER GROWTH AND DEVELOPMENT STRATEGIES

In this section the five critical components of teacher growth and development are arranged into a conceptual design to help in planning and decision making. This design for staff development is illustrated in Figure 15-3.

Before we begin to discuss this design, refer back to Figure 15-2 and note the relationship between three of the five design components. Here we suggested that intents at the knowledge and comprehension levels were suited to increasing teachers' knowledge; intents at the applications level, their can-do and to a lesser extent their will-do competence areas; and intents at the value and integration level, their will-grow competence area. The content, substance, or "subject matter" of intents could be concerned with one or a combination of four aspects of effectiveness in teaching: purposes, perceptions of students, knowledge of subject matter, and technique. In Figure 15-3 two additional critical components, approach and responsibility, are included, and all five are illustrated in a fashion to help monitor existing teacher growth and development programs or make decisions about new programs.

Consider the box in Figure 15-3 first. Notice that the box consists of four layers, each corresponding to aspects of teacher effectiveness. For illustrative purposes, refer only to the bottom layer, mastery of technique, and specifically to the technique of inquiry teaching. Intents are shown across the top of the box and teacher competency areas across the bottom of the box. If one is interested only in knowing about inquiry teaching, then one is concerned with knowledge-level intents and the know-how competency area. If one is interested in committed adoption and use of inquiry teaching, then one is concerned with value- and attitude-integration intents and will-do–will-grow competency areas.

The programs developed for the latter intents should be different from those for the former. To the left of the box appear the approach and responsibility components. Traditional (in-service), intermediate (staff-development), and informal (renewal) approaches correspond to supervisor, shared, and teacher responsibilities, respectively. The box area directly to the right of each approach-responsibility designation suggests which intents and performance

---

[13] Dennis Sparks and Susan Loucks-Horsley, "Five Models of Staff Development for Teachers," *Journal of Staff Development*, vol. 10, no. 4, p. 40, Fall 1989.

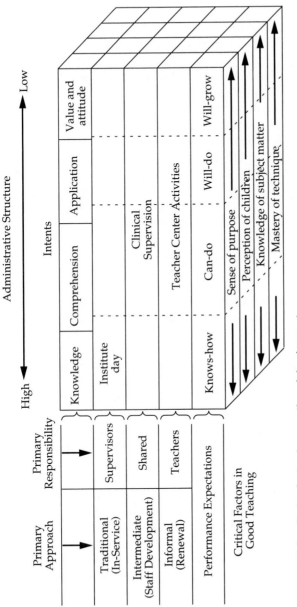

FIGURE 15-3   Design for teacher growth and development.

expectations are best served by that approach. Traditional approaches seem best suited to knowledge-comprehension intents. Intermediate approaches seem best suited to comprehension, application, and value- and attitude-integration intents. Similarly, informal approaches point toward applications intents, though these seem most potent for value- and attitude-integration intents.

What approaches to staff development should be used for our inquiry-method example? Who should assume major responsibility for this approach? The answer depends on the kind of purposes or intents sought. If one were interested only in knowledge and comprehension, then a supervisor directed-institute day might be best. Clinical supervision might be a strategy if inquiry teaching were seen as important to the school and the intent were committed implementation of this technique by teachers. Though informal approaches are typically more potent than others, agendas in this approach belong to teachers, and they may not choose to pursue inquiry teaching. If they did, then the approach might well be the most effective for achieving committed implementation of this technique by teachers.

INFORMING REFLECTIVE PRACTICE

In most schools and school districts technical teaching competence commands the major share of teacher growth and development attention and resources. The emphasis is on learning the facts, rules, and procedures and applying them to a presumably nonproblematic, relatively uniform, and stable teaching situation. Often these technical teaching skills are considered to be generic and thus universally applied to all situations, and sometimes this is indeed the case. At one level of abstraction, for example, it is true that positive reinforcement is positive reinforcement, wait time is wait time, on task is on task, and monitoring is monitoring regardless of the teaching and learning context. Supervision that responds to this focus seeks to train teachers in the appropriate techniques and to provide coaching directed to detecting and correcting errors as the techniques are applied.

In addition to professional knowledge construed as technical facts, rules, and techniques, Donald Schön proposes two other understandings: professional knowledge in the form of "thinking like a teacher" and professional knowledge as "reflection-in-action."[14] In thinking like a teacher one not only masters the appropriate facts and techniques but learns form of inquiry "by which competent practitioners reason their way, in problematic instances, to clear connections between general knowledge and particular cases."[15] In knowledge of this sort it is presumed that a right way exists to match every situation, and the emphasis is on how one analyzes situations and decides what is the appropriate, right way to apply. There is a link between this way of

[14] Donald A. Schön, *Educating the Reflective Practitioner,* San Francisco: Jossey-Bass, 1987.
[15] Ibid., p. 39.

knowing and professional knowledge construed in a technical sense. But the emphasis in thinking like a teacher is on learning how to decide when to use what. Supervision that emphasizes thinking like a teacher relies less on training and more on coaching, apprenticing, and other forms of mentoring.

In earlier chapters we pointed out that one problem with overemphasizing technical aspects of supervision that may be suitable for specific problems, stable environments, and deterministic teaching is that the real world is for the most part ambiguous, complex, and fluid. Teachers, for example, are often unsure of what their goals and objectives are, sometimes discover goals and objectives while they are teaching, and invariably pursue multiple goals and objectives that from time to time even conflict with each other. In the real world of teaching, plans rarely unfold as planned. Circumstances are typically not quite like those anticipated. Student reactions are difficult to predict. Subject matter, content, and concepts connect themselves in ways not expected, and so on. Teaching, then, is somewhat like surfing, and teachers ride the pattern of the wave of teaching as it uncurls. Teachers, therefore, need to learn to make new sense of uncertain unique and conflicting situations that they face in their practice. To do this, Schön suggests that professional knowledge be construed as "reflection in action." From this stance one does not assume that existing professional knowledge fits every case or that every problem has a right answer. Instead teachers will need to "learn a kind of reflection-in-action that goes beyond stable rules—not only by devising new methods of reasoning . . . but also by constructing and testing new categories of understanding, strategies of action, and new ways of framing problems."[16]

When professional knowledge is understood as reflection in action, staff development and supervision are drawn together. The context for reflection in action is the teacher's practice, and this practice takes place in the classroom, not in the school auditorium, during institute day, the cafeteria as setting for an after-school workshop. Staff development designed to inform reflective practice, therefore, needs to be largely classroom-based. In this sense, staff development, supervision, mentoring, and coaching should not be viewed as separate and distinct roles but as dimensions of the role of supervisor as he or she works to enhance the technical, clinical, personal, and critical competencies of teaching and to promote professional knowledge in its technical sense in the form of thinking like a teacher and in the form of reflective practice.

RENEWAL AS A STRATEGY FOR THE FUTURE

We began this chapter discussing three different frames for thinking about teacher growth and development: in-service, staff development, and renewal. We noted in Figure 15-1, for example, that within the in-service frame teaching is viewed as a job. With job as the metaphor, the development of job-related skills through training and practice becomes an important process of supervi-

---

[16] Ibid.

sion. In a sense, teaching is a job and such skills are important. But teaching is also a profession.

The staff-development frame views teaching as a profession within which the development of professional expertise through problem solving and inquiry are considered to be the main focus of supervision. Teachers assume much more responsibility for what happens in staff development as they work closely with their colleague teachers and their colleague supervisors.

Teaching, however, is not only more than a job but more than a profession, at least as defined in its technical sense. For example, much of teaching is a personal extension of the teacher. The act of teaching itself is moral, thus values and beliefs loom large in deciding what to do and in determining what happened and in assigning worth. The caring ethic as represented by deep commitment to service is yet another unique characteristic of teaching. Together, these characteristics define teaching as a vocation. Though one may join a profession, one is called to a vocation. In referring to the work of Dwayne Huebner, Bolin points out that "if we look at teaching as a vocation rather than as a profession we must attend to the meaning and valuemaking of the teacher. Activity of this kind involves . . . re-evaluation."[17] She continues, "renewal is full of meaning that suggests ways to think about teacher renewal. . . . There is a spiritual dimension to the term, especially in its first two levels of meaning: to do over again, revise; make new, or as new again."[18] Renewal and vocation go hand in hand. The idea of vocation is consistent with an emphasis on professional authority and moral authority as motivators for teachers and supervisors, a theme discussed in Chapter 2. When professional authority and moral authority become the focus, the in-service frame for teacher growth and development plays a minor role and the staff-development frame moves to a position of support for teacher renewal.

[17] Bolin, "Reassessment and Renewal in Teaching," op. cit., p. 12.
[18] Ibid., p. 13.

CHAPTER 16

PROVIDING OPTIONS FOR SUPERVISION

Principals and other supervisors struggle to sort out those aspects of schooling that need to be kept more or less uniform and those aspects that call for diversity. What is the right balance between uniform school rules and the different rules that teachers and teams work out with their students? What parts of the school schedule must be considered fixed and what parts can teachers create in use as they plan and teach? What content should be considered as curriculum imperatives and what content should emerge from teacher and student preferences, needs, and interests?

Resolving the tugs between the needs for uniformity and diversity requires a great deal of time and skill. The task is made a little easier if supervisors are able to develop a framework for making decisions. We believe that schools should be understood as learning communities. This understanding leads us to conclude that when considering how classrooms should be organized, which teaching styles to use, working arrangements for teachers, scheduling options, and methods of supervision the bias should definitely be in favor of diversity for both moral and practical reasons. From a moral perspective, democratic values include respect for individual differences and the rights of teachers to be involved in matters that affect them, including how they will work together, what they will do, and how they will be evaluated. From a practical perspective, when individual differences in preferences, style, and temperament are honored teachers respond with greater commitment, better performance, and increased satisfaction. Further, diversity in teaching styles, patterns of classroom organization, and interpretations of curriculum increases the range of possibilities and encourages learning among teachers.

In this chapter we are concerned about differences that teachers bring to their work. Accommodating these differences, we reason, requires abandoning commitment to a one best supervisory and evaluation system. In its place we propose a range of options and suggest that teacher preferences and needs should be primary in deciding which options make the most sense.

EXAMPLES OF OPTIONS

We propose that in every school a plan for supervision should be developed that includes at least five options: clinical supervision, collegial supervision, self-directed supervision, informal supervision, and inquiry-based supervision.[1] Further, we propose that teachers play key roles in deciding which of the options make most sense to them given their needs at the time. And finally, we propose that in implementing the options, supervision should be viewed as a process that is equally accessible to teachers and administrators. Equal access does not mean that principals and supervisors should be excluded from the process of supervision. They have important roles to play. But we do not believe that it is either right or sensible for supervisors to monopolize the process by excluding teachers from roles as supervisors or by relegating them to token roles.

Excluding teachers denies the reality that though formal supervisors bring expertise to the process, teachers as a group command the largest share of expertise in subject matter, knowledge about the particular students being taught, and the pedagogical knowledge needed to teach those students effectively. One problem with traditional conceptions of supervision is that they equate hierarchy with expertise by assuming that supervisors as a group know more about teaching than do teachers as a group.

In Chapter 2 we proposed that professional authority be taken seriously as a basis for what is done in schools. The viability of professional authority depends on whether the virtuous side of professionalism can be adequately defined and accepted as legitimate. The dimensions of virtue proposed included commitment to the following: exemplary practice, practice toward valued social ends, a concern for the practice of teaching itself rather than one's own practice solely, and the caring ethic. All four commitments provide compelling reasons for teachers to be involved in the process of supervision as equal partners. Together the four redefine teaching from a singular practice to a collective one. In a collective practice the supervisory process becomes a natural and informal part of the everyday lives of teachers at work.

From a practical perspective, disconnecting the process of supervision from hierarchic roles reflects what goes on in schools anyway. The research by both Emil Haller and Charles Keenan, for example, reveals that both the Canadian and American teachers they studied were very much inclined to depend upon each other when seeking help in solving problems, when searching for sources of new ideas about teaching, and when seeking other kinds of assistance.[2] Formal supervisors counted, but not nearly as much as other teachers. Further, teachers held the advice of other teachers in higher regard than advice from other sources. Though not officially acknowledged, there appears to be an in-

---

[1] The discussion of options for supervision presented in this chapter follows the views of Allan A. Glatthorn, *Differentiated Supervision*, Alexandria, Va.: Association for Supervision and Curriculum Development, 1984; and the discussion of options for supervision that appears in T. J. Sergiovanni, *The Principalship: A Reflective Practice Perspective*, 2nd edition, Boston: Allyn and Bacon, 1991, pp. 297–317.

[2] Emil J. Haller, *Strategies for Change*, Toronto: Ontario Institute for Studies in Education, Dept. of Educational Administration, 1968; and Charles Keenan, "Channels for Change: A Survey of Teachers in Chicago Elementary Schools," Ph.D. dissertation, Urbana: University of Illinois, Dept. of Educational Administration, 1974.

formal system of supervision in place in schools; the evidence suggests that this informal system is more important and useful to teachers than is the formal system. By disconnecting supervision from hierarchic roles and viewing it instead as a process accessible to both teachers and supervisors, educators can legitimize this informal system of supervision.

In the sections below an overview of the proposed options for supervision is provided. Attention is then given to the topic of individual differences among teachers, and ideas are presented that can help supervisors navigate through these differences in seeking to match options to teacher inclinations and need.

CLINICAL SUPERVISION AS AN OPTION

In Chapter 12 we proposed that clinical supervision be viewed as a partnership in inquiry shared by teacher and supervisor that is intended to help teachers modify existing patterns of teaching in ways that make sense to them. Clinical supervision is not for everyone, nor is it a strategy that can sustain itself over a long period of time. The process is demanding in the time it requires from both teacher and supervisor. There is a danger that continuous use of this approach can result in a certain ritualism as each of the steps are followed. Clinical supervision may be too much supervision for some teachers. That is, not all teachers will need such an intensive look at their teaching. And finally, teachers' needs and dispositions as well as learning styles vary. Clinical supervision may be suitable for some teachers but not for others when these differences are taken into consideration.

COLLEGIAL SUPERVISION

Allan Glatthorn uses the phrase *cooperative professional development* to describe a collegial process in which teachers agree to work together for their own professional development.[3] He defines this approach as a "moderately formalized process by which two or more teachers agree to work together for their own professional growth, usually by observing each other's classroom, giving each other feedback about the observations, and discussing shared professional concerns."[4]

Collegial supervision can take many different forms. In some schools teachers might organize themselves into teams of two or three. It might be a good idea in some cases for at least one member of the team to be selected by the principal or supervisor, but there are no rigid rules for composing collegial supervision teams. Once formed, the teams may choose to work together in a number of ways ranging from clinical supervision to less intensive and more informal processes.

[3] Glatthorn, op. cit.
[4] Ibid., p. 39.

Team members may, for example, simply agree to observe each other's classes and provide help according to the desires of the teacher being observed. The teachers might then confer, giving one another informal feedback and discussing issues of teaching that they consider important. An approach that relies on Madeline Hunter's teaching steps and elements of lesson design or on cooperative learning might be used.[5] In this case the emphasis on teaching might be narrowly focused on specific issues inherent in the model that the teacher deems important. On still another occasion the emphasis might be quite unfocused in order to provide a general feel or rendition of teaching. All that is needed is for team members to meet beforehand to decide "the rules and issues" for the observation and for any subsequent conversations or conferences.

Glatthorn describes five different forms collegial supervision might take:

Professional dialogue among teachers featuring guided discussion and focusing on teaching as a process of thinking. The purpose of professional dialogue is to enhance reflective practice.

Curriculum development featuring teachers working together on such themes as how to operationalize the existing curriculum, adapt the curriculum to the wide variety of students and situations faced in the classroom, and enriching the existing curriculum by inventing and developing new curriculum units and materials.

Peer supervision featuring observations of each other's teaching followed by analysis and discussion.

Peer coaching featuring collaborative development and practice of new teaching methods and skills in both "workshop" settings and under actual teaching conditions.

Action research featuring the study of problems being faced and the development of feasible solutions that result in changes in one's teaching practice.[6]

Traditionally supervision has come to mean some form of classroom observation. But collegial supervision extends well beyond classroom observation. It provides a setting in which teachers can informally discuss problems they face, share ideas, help one another in preparing lessons, exchange tips, and provide other support to one another. Some suggestions for implementing collegial supervision are provided in Table 16-1.

At issue in considering collegial supervision as an option is the nature of collegiality that emerges. For example, collegiality might be contrived if it is only an artifact of administrative arrangements. Andrew Hargreaves and R. Dawe describe contrived collegiality as bureaucratic procedures and admin-

---

[5] See, for example, Madeline Hunter, "Knowing, Teaching and Supervision," in Philip Hosford (ed.), *Using What We Know about Teaching*, Alexandria, Va.: Association for Supervision and Curriculum Development, 1984; and Robert E. Salvin, "Cooperative Learning." *Review of Educational Research*, vol. 50, no. 2, pp. 315–342, 1988.

[6] Allan A. Glatthorn, "Cooperative Professional Development: Peer-Centered Options for Teacher Growth," *Educational Leadership*, vol. 45, no. 3, p. 32, 1987. Action research and peer supervision in the form of clinical supervision are treated in this discussion as separate options. Both might involve collaboration with other teachers, a closer, more private relationship between formal supervisor and teacher, or, as in the case of action research, an individual initiative.

TABLE 16-1
GUIDELINES FOR IMPLEMENTING COOPERATIVE PROFESSIONAL DEVELOPMENT

1. Teachers should have a voice in deciding with whom they work.

2. Principals should retain final responsibility for putting together Collegial Supervision teams.

3. The structure for supervision should be formal enough for the teams to keep records of how and in what ways time has been used and to provide a general *nonevaluative* description of activities. This record should be submitted annually to the principal.

4. The principal should provide the necessary resources and administrative support enabling teams to function during the normal range of the school day. The principal might, for example, volunteer to cover classes as needed, or to arrange for substitutes as needed, or to provide for innovative schedule adjustments enabling team members to work together readily.

5. If information generated within the team about teaching and learning might be considered even mildly evaluative, it should stay with the team and not be shared with the principal.

6. Under no circumstances should the principal seek evaluation data from one teacher about another.

7. Each teacher should be expected to keep a professional growth log which demonstrates that she or he is reflecting on practice and growing professionally as a result of activities.

8. The principal should meet with the team at least once a year for purposes of general assessment and for sharing of impressions and information about the process.

9. The principal should meet individually at least once a year with each team member to discuss her or his professional growth log and to provide any encouragement and assistance that may be required.

10. Generally, new teams should be formed every second or third year.

Source: Thomas J. Sergiovanni, *The Principalship: A Reflective Practice Perspective,* 2d ed., Boston: Allyn and Bacon, 1991, p. 304.

istrative arrangements that are designed to encourage teachers to engage in joint teacher planning and consultation. Examples include peer coaching, mentor teaching, and training programs for those in consultative roles. To Hargreaves such initiatives are administrative contrivances designed to create collegiality in schools.[7] The receiving school culture is key in determining whether administratively induced collegiality becomes contrived or real. Grafted onto the existing school culture, collegiality is very likely to remain contrived. Collegiality becomes real when it emerges as a result of felt interdependence among teachers, and when teachers view it as an integral part of their professional responsibility to help others and to seek help from others when needed.

[7] See, for example, "Contrived Collegiality and the Culture of Teaching," Annual Meeting of the Canadian Society for the Study of Education, Quebec City, 1989; and Andrew Hargreaves and R. Dawe, "Paths of Professional Development: Contrived Collegiality, Collaborative Culture, and the Case of Peer Coaching," *Teaching and Teacher Education,* vol. 4, no. 3, 1990. See also Peter P. Grimmet, Olaf P. Rostad, and Blake Ford, "The Transformation of Supervision," in Clark Glickman (ed.), *Supervision in Transition: The 1992 ASCD Yearbook,* Alexandria, VA: Association for Supervision and Curriculum Development, 1992, pp. 185–202.

Mentoring as a Special Case

Mentoring is a form of collegial supervision. A mentor is a person entrusted with the tutoring, education, and guidance of another person who is typically new to teaching or new to a given school. The mentoring relationship is special because of its entrusting nature. Those being mentored are dependent upon their mentors to help them, protect them, show them the way, and develop more fully their skills and insights. The mentor is presumed to know more not only about matters of teaching but also about the school's culture so that the novice can navigate through this culture successfully. The unequal nature of the relationship makes it a moral one.

In some respects the tutorial, educational, and advisory aspects of the mentoring relationship are developmental. Initially most novices seek assistance. They want to know what they are supposed to do, where things are, how to make requests, and what are accepted practices. They want concrete help in setting up their classrooms, establishing routines, and getting started. They want, in other words, to be tutored by an individual they trust without worrying too much about having to make an impression.

Because of its dependent nature, the tutorial relationship often represents a source of great satisfaction for the mentor. In many respects the mentor becomes the center of the novice's life. But the purpose of mentoring is to help a novice become independent. For this to happen the mentoring relationship needs to evolve quickly from one of tutelage to one of mutual edification. This happens when novices ask less and mentors tell less and when both settle down to solving problems together. "How might I best do this?" is answered with, "What ideas do you have? That one sounds promising. Let's try it out." and eventually, "How do you think it's going?"

The mentoring relationship matures when it becomes reciprocal. The novice seeks advice from the mentor and the mentor seeks to transform the relationship from mentoring to colleagueship by soliciting advice in return, by sharing problems, and by valuing the perspectives of the newcomer. Given what is known about the importance of the school's inside culture, the informal norm system that exists among teachers, and the potential that exists for teachers to share talents, mentoring makes sense as a natural way to orient new teachers, give them a successful start, and invite them to become full colleagues.

SELF-DIRECTED SUPERVISION

In self-directed supervision teachers work alone by assuming responsibility for their own professional development. They might, for example, develop a yearly plan that includes targets or goals derived from an assessment of their own needs. This plan then might be shared with supervisors or other designated individuals. As the process unfolds teachers should be allowed a great deal of leeway in developing the plan, but supervisors should be responsible for ensuring that the plan and selected improvement targets are both realistic and attainable. At the end of a specific period, normally a year, supervisor and teacher meet to discuss the teacher's progress in meeting professional development targets. Teachers would be expected to provide some sort of documentation, perhaps in the form of time logs, reflective practice diaries, schedules, photo essays, tapes, samples of students' work, and other artifacts that illustrate progress toward goals. The yearly conference would then lead to the setting of new targets for future self-directed supervisory cycles.

There are a number of problems with approaches to supervision that rely heavily on target setting. For example, supervisors might be inclined to adhere rigidly to prespecified targets and to sometimes unnecessarily impose their own targets on teachers. Rigidly applying a target-setting format to supervision unduly focuses on the process. Teachers tend to direct their attention to prestated targets, and as a result other areas of importance not targeted can be overlooked or neglected. Target setting is meant to help and facilitate, not to hinder the self-improvement process.

Self-directed approaches to supervision are ideal for teachers who prefer to work alone or who, because of scheduling or other difficulties, are unable to work cooperatively with other teachers. This option is efficient in use of time, less costly, and less demanding in its reliance on others than is the case with other options. Further, this option is particularly suited to competent teachers who are able to manage their time well. Some guidelines for implementing self-directed supervision are provided in Table 16-2.

INFORMAL SUPERVISION

Included in any array of options should be a provision for informal supervision. Informal supervision is comprised of the casual encounters that occur between supervisors and teachers and is characterized by frequent informal visits to teachers' classrooms, conversations with teachers about their work, and other informal activities. Typically no appointments are made and classroom visits are not announced.

Successful informal supervision requires that certain expectations be accepted by teachers. Otherwise it will likely be viewed as a system of informal surveillance. Principals and other supervisors need to be viewed as principal teachers who have a responsibility to be a part of all the teaching that takes place in the school. They need to be viewed as instructional partners to every teacher in every classroom for every teaching and learning situation. When informal supervision is in place, principals and supervisors become common fixtures in classrooms, coming and going as part of the natural flow of the school's daily work. But this kind of relationship is not likely to flourish unless it is reciprocal. If teachers are to invite supervisors into their classrooms as equal partners in teaching and learning, teachers must in turn be invited into the process of supervision as equal partners.

Though we list informal supervision as an option, it should perhaps be understood as one kind of supervision that is included in any range of options

TABLE 16-2
GUIDELINES FOR IMPLEMENTING SELF-DIRECTED SUPERVISION

---

1. *Target setting.* Based on last year's observations, conferences, summary reports, clinical supervision episodes, or other means of personal assessment, teachers develop targets or goals that they would like to reach in improving their teaching. Targets should be few, rarely exceeding five or six and preferably limited to two or three. Estimated time frames should be provided for each target, which are then shared with the supervisor, along with an informal plan providing suggested activities for teacher engagement.

2. *Target-setting review.* After reviewing each target and estimated time frame, the principal provides the teacher with a written reaction. Further, a conference is scheduled to discuss targets and plans.

3. *Target-setting conference.* Meeting to discuss targets, time frames, and reactions, the teacher and principal revise targets if appropriate. It may be a good idea for the principal to provide a written summary of the conference to the teacher. Teacher and principal might well prepare this written summary together.

4. *Appraisal process.* Appraisal begins at the conclusion of the target-setting conference and continues in accordance with the agreed-upon time frame. The specific nature of the appraisal process depends on each of the targets and could include formal and informal classroom observations, an analysis of classroom artifacts, videotaping, student evaluation, interaction analysis, and other information. The teacher is responsible for collecting appraisal information and arranges this material in a portfolio for subsequent discussion with, and review by, the principal.

5. *Summary appraisal.* The principal visits with the teacher to review the appraisal portfolio. As part of this process, the principal comments on each target, and together the teacher and principal plan for the next cycle of self-directed supervision.

Source: Thomas J. Sergiovanni, *The Principalship: A Reflective Practice Perspective,* 2d ed., Boston: Allyn and Bacon, 1991, p. 305.

that a school might provide.[8] In addition to informal supervision, teachers should be involved in at least one other approach such as clinical, collegial, self-directed, or inquiry-based supervision. In selecting additional options, supervisors should accommodate teacher preferences and honor them in nearly every case. Nonetheless, final responsibility for deciding the appropriateness of a selected option should probably be reserved for the supervisor.

INQUIRY-BASED SUPERVISION

Inquiry-based supervision in the form of action research is an option that can represent an individual initiative or a collaborative effort as pairs or teams of teachers work together to solve problems. In action research the emphasis is on the problem-solving nature of the supervisory experience. Mixing the word "research" with such words as "action" or "supervision" may cause some initial confusion. Research, after all, is generally thought to be something mysterious, remote, statistical, and theoretical. And further, teachers and researchers

[8] Glatthorn, *Differentiated Supervision,* op. cit., p. 59.

have been thought to occupy two separate ends of a continuum. What is a teacher-researcher anyway? Glenda Bissex responds as follows:

> To dispel some traditional associations with the word *research*, I'll begin by saying what a teacher-researcher *isn't*.
>
> A teacher-researcher doesn't have to study hundreds of students, establish control groups, and perform complex statistical analyses.
>
> A teacher-research may start out not with a hypothesis to test but with a "wondering" to pursue: "I wonder how much my students think about their writing outside of class. Vicky mentioned today that she mentally revises compositions on the bus coming to school. What about the others now that they're writing on their own topics?"
>
> A teacher-researcher does not have to be antiseptically detached. He knows that knowledge comes through closeness as well as through distance, through intuition as well as through logic.
>
> When a teacher-researcher writes about what she's discovered, she need not try to make her writing sound like a psychology textbook. Her audience is herself, other teachers, her students, their parents, her principal, maybe even the school board—none of whom is likely to be upset by plain English and a personal style.
>
> A teacher-researcher is not a split personality with a poem in one hand and a microscope in the other.
>
> So what is a teacher-researcher?
>
> A teacher-researcher is an observer
> > a questioner
> > > a learner
> > > > and a more complete teacher.[9]

When action research is undertaken as an individual initiative, a teacher works closely with the supervisor in sorting out a problem and developing a strategy for its resolution and in sharing findings and conclusions. Implications for practice are then identified, and strategies for implementing these changes are then developed. When action research involves collaboration with other teachers, problems are "co-researched," findings are shared, and together teachers ferret out implications for changing in their teaching practice. Among all the options, action research requires the highest level of reflection and promises a great deal with respect to discovering new insights and practices.

Basic to action research is the belief that individual teachers and groups of teachers can undertake research to improve their own practice. Though increasing understanding and building one's store of conceptual knowledge is an important outcome of action research, its prime purpose is to alter the teaching practices of the researchers themselves. Florence Stratemeyer and her colleagues describe action research as "a process aimed at discovering new ideas or practices as well as testing old ones, exploring or establishing relation-

---

[9] Glenda L. Bissex, "What Is a Teacher-Researcher?" in Glenda L. Bissex and Richard H. Bullock (eds.), *Seeing for Ourselves,* Portsmouth, N.H.: Heinemann, 1987, pp. 3–4.

ships between causes and effects, or of systematically gaining evidence about the nature of a particular problem."[10]

Though usually articulated as steps, action research proceeds as a process that more accurately involves phases that are less clearly defined. Stratemeyer and her colleagues explain,

> For convenience, the phases of this process are frequently described in terms of steps although in reality they are neither neat nor discrete. Instead, there is usually a flow from one to another, sometimes back and forth, without clear demarcations. These phases are quite similar to the sequence of the problem solving process: the problem is identified and refined; hypotheses are formulated or hunches are advanced about its solution; the hypotheses are tested and evidence is collected, organized, and analyzed; and generalizations are drawn from the data and are retested for further validation of conclusions. In a controlled laboratory situation, the research process may closely parallel these so called problem solving steps. In the classroom situation, the process flow is usually quite different.[11]

Millie Almy and Celia Genishi propose the following as the basic steps for action research:

Step 1 Identify the problem
Step 2 Develop hunches about its cause and how it can be solved
Step 3 Test one or more of the hunches.
  (a) Collect data, evidence about the situation.
      Some hunches held initially or tentatively may have to be rejected when more of the facts of the situation are known. Hunches that seem reasonable after careful consideration become the hypotheses of scientific investigations.
  (b) Try out the hunches in action (the tryout may be in a test tube or in a classroom).
  (c) See what happens (collect more data or evidence).
  (d) Evaluate or generalize on the basis of evidence.[12]

For many teachers, action research works best when they engage in the process cooperatively. Problems that emerge might be of concern schoolwide or might be of concern to only two teachers whose classrooms are located across from each other. Action research as a collegial process often can result from other forms of supervision. For example, a cycle of clinical supervision might reveal pressing problems that are beyond the scope of understanding at the time. Adopting an action research stance, under this circumstance, may well be an attractive option. Examples of action research conceived as an individual activity and as a collegial undertaking are presented in Appendixes 16–1 and 16–2.

---

[10] Florence B. Stratemeyer, Handen L. Forkner, Margaret G. McKim, and A. Harry Passow, *Developing a Curriculum for Modern Living,* 2d edition, New York: Teachers College, 1957, p. 708.
  [11] Ibid.
  [12] Millie Almy and Celia Genishi, *Ways of Studying Children: An Observation Manual for Early Childhood Teachers,* revised edition. New York: Teachers College Press, 1979, pp. 3–4.

RENEWING INTEREST IN THE ADVISORY

During the sixties and seventies a great deal of interest was expressed in the concept of an *advisory system* as an alternative to traditional supervision. Writing in 1975, Theodore Manolakes noted,

> Possibly no other vehicle for improving instruction and the practice of teachers in the past decade has received more attention and effort than what has come to be known as the advisory system. The efforts to humanize and open up the schools that began in the late 60s have resulted in the appearance of a large number of professionals who do not view themselves as supervisors in the usual sense, but who are committed to aiding teachers to develop more effective educational programs for children. Some of these advisors are employees of school districts who have been relieved of teaching duties to carry on advisory functions, while others work in schools but are employed by private agencies or universities.[13]

Borrowed from the wave of professionalism that swept both Great Britain and the United States during the period, the advisory was a nonevaluative system of support and help made available directly to teachers.

According to Maja Apelman, an advisor:

1 provides assistance only upon request of the teacher
2 has no evaluative [traditional] or supervisory function
3 has no predetermined agenda and does not impose or implement mandated programs
4 provides assistance in terms of teachers' needs, goals and objectives
5 acts as a support and resource person for the professional growth of teachers and helps them develop more effective educational programs for children
6 respects teachers' autonomy and works towards strengthening teachers' independence
7 develops long-term collegial relationships based on mutual trust and respect.[14]

Adding the advisory as another option for supervision makes sense. Because of its confidential nature, the advisory option might be attractive to teachers who are experiencing classroom problems and want to deal with them systematically but privately. Similarly, many teachers might be ready for important significant changes in their teaching practice and would feel more comfortable working with someone on a more "off the record" basis.

---

[13] Theodore Manolakes, "The Advisory System and Supervision," in Thomas J. Sergiovanni (ed.), *Professional Supervision for Professional Teachers,* Washington, D.C.: Association for Supervision and Curriculum Development, 1975, pp. 51–64.

[14] Maja Apelman, "Working with Teachers: The Advisory Approach," in Karen K. Zumwalt (ed.), *Improving Teaching,* 1969 ASCD Yearbook, Alexandria, Va.: Association for Supervision and Curriculum Development, 1986, p. 116.

A CONTINGENCY PERSPECTIVE

A contingency view of supervision is based on the premise that teachers are different and that matching supervisory options to these differences is important. In recent years developmental theorists such as Carl Glickman[15] and Art Costa[16] have made considerable progress in suggesting how this matching might be done. These experts examine such dimensions as levels of professional maturity and cognitive complexity and suggest that as levels vary among teachers so should supervisory approaches and styles. Another group of theorists, such as R. S. Dunn and K. J. Dunn,[17] and David Kolb, Irwin Rubin, and James McIntyre,[18] have been interested in the concept of learning styles and how, as these styles vary, opportunities for learning, problem solving, and personal growth should also vary. Accounting for motives of teachers provides still a third dimension to the matching of individual teachers with supervisory options. Social motives theories such as those of David McClelland and his colleagues find that as important work motives such as the need for achievement, power, and affiliation vary among workers, the work conditions and settings they find motivating vary as well.[19]

Matching supervisory options to individual needs, therefore, has great potential for increasing the motivation and commitment of teachers at work. The section that follows *explores* these important individual dimensions and *suggests* compatible supervisory options.[20] Readers should not be under the illusion that tight and concise matching of supervisory options to individual needs and preferences is possible. It isn't. But more informed matching decisions can be made by considering the possibilities discussed.

PSYCHOLOGICAL TYPES AS METAPHOR FOR DIFFERENCE

Given the complexity of human nature, no discussion of individual differences can be exhaustive. Thus any set of ideas that seeks to chart and simplify individual differences can be viewed only as a metaphor. Carl Jung's theory of psychological types represents a preeminent metaphor for the range of individual differences in temperament that are likely to be found in any faculty and among any group of supervisors.[21] Further, the types can provide supervisors with helpful constructs and frames for understanding their own charac-

---

[15] Carl D. Glickman, *Supervision and Instruction: A Developmental Approach*, Boston: Allyn and Bacon, 1985.

[16] Art L. Costa, *Supervision for Intelligent Teaching: A Course Syllabus*, Orangevale, Calif.: Search Models Unlimited, 1982.

[17] R. S. Dunn and K. J. Dunn, "Learning Styles Teaching Styles: Should They . . . Can They . . . Be Matched?" *Educational Leadership*, vol. 36, no. 4, 1979.

[18] David A. Kolb, Irwin M. Rubin, and James M. McIntyre, *Organization Psychology: An Effective Approach to Organizational Behavior*, 4th edition, Englewood Cliffs, N.J.: Prentice-Hall, 1984.

[19] See, for example, David C. McClelland, J. W. Atkinson, R. A. Clark, and E. L. Lowell, *The Achievement Motive*, New York: Appleton-Century-Crofts, 1953; David C. McClelland and D. Burnham, "Power Is the Great Motivator," *Harvard Business Review*, vol. 54, no. 2, pp. 110–111, 1976.

[20] This section follows closely Sergiovanni, op. cit., pp. 306–315, 1991.

[21] C. S. Jung, *Psychological Types*, New York: Harcourt Brace & World, 1923.

ter and temperament and for sorting and understanding the differences among teacher-colleagues. Jung's theory is complicated, however, and thus this discussion will not be exhaustive. We are interested in only the essential elements of the theory and their application to the issue of providing options in supervision. For interpretations of Jung's theory we rely on the work of Isabel Myers,[22] David Keirsey and Marilyn Bates,[23] and Robert Benfari.[24]

According to the theory, psychological types are comprised of different combinations of preferences and temperaments that define each individual as a distinct personality. Four pairs of preferences are important: extroversion (E) versus introversion (I), intuition (N) versus sensation (S), thinking (T) versus feeling (F), and judging (J) versus perceiving (P). From the four pairs 16 different psychological types are thought to exist.[25]

According to Keirsey and Bates[26] the key words that differentiate each of the four preference sets are as follows:

- Extroversion from introversion; sociability over territoriality, breadth over depth, external over internal, and interaction over concentrating
- Sensation from intuition; experience over hunches, realistic over speculative, past over future, actual over possible, fact over fiction, practicality over ingenuity
- Thinking from feeling; objective over subjective, principles over values, laws over circumstances, impersonal over personal, criteria over intimacy
- Judging from perceiving; settled over pending, decided over gathering more data; fixed over flexible, plan ahead over adapt as you go, decided over tentative

Different combinations of preferences lead to very different realities for teachers and supervisors. Keirsey and Bates conclude that both introverted and extroverted teachers who also prefer sensation over intuition and judging over perceiving (known as "SJs," in the language of theory) are likely to be more structured in their teaching, favoring recitation, drill, composition, tests, quizzes, and demonstrations. They are likely as well to prefer well-established classroom routines, have well laid out and sequential plans, and to be "firm and fair disciplinarians who expect students to obey the rules of the classroom and institution."[27] Since these preferences are presumed to emerge from deep-rooted psychological temperaments, they are not too easily changed. A supervisor with a different bent will be hard pressed in trying to change the behavior

---

[22] Isabel Myers, *Manual: The Myers-Briggs Type Indicator,* Palo Alto, Calif.: Consulting Psychologists Press, 1962.

[23] David Keirsey and Marilyn Bates, *Please Understand Me: Character and Temperament Types,* Del Mar, Calif.: Prometheus Nemesis Book Company, 1978.

[24] Robert Benfari, *Understanding Your Management Style Beyond the Meyers-Briggs Type Indicators.* Lexington, Mass.: Heath, 1991.

[25] The 16 types are labeled according to the letters of preferences in each of the four pairs: ENTJ, INFJ, ESFP, ISTJ, etc.

[26] Keirsey and Bates, op. cit., p. 25.

[27] Ibid., p. 159.

and outlook of SJ teachers. Keirsey and Bates report that about 56 percent of teachers can be characterized as SJ.[28]

In contrast, introverted and extroverted teachers who prefer intuition over sensation and feeling over thinking (called "NFs") represent 32 percent of teachers according to Keirsey and Bates.[29] As a group, these teachers prefer teaching styles characterized by group projects, lessons that feature lots of interaction and discussion, exhibitions, simulations, and games. NFs are also likely to be more concerned with teaching the "whole child," to be in touch with the climate and temper of their classrooms, changing teaching topics and strategies accordingly, creating their own curriculum materials, giving more attention to values, allowing students more input, and teaching in more personalized ways.

IMPLICATIONS FOR SUPERVISION

From a psychological types perspective, preferences for particular styles of teaching, classroom climate, and curriculum arrangements may be as much a function of temperament as of reason or philosophy; this stance raises important and interesting questions. Just how far, for example, should supervisors go in trying to change the way teachers teach? How fruitful is deciding on a particular approach to teaching (i.e., the lesson cycle, direct instruction, or cooperative learning) and then insisting that all teachers use this approach? Does it make sense to require all teachers to work together in teams? Should all teachers be required to use a structured and sequential curriculum or, inversely, to create their own materials in use as needs and circumstances dictate? Or does it make more sense to encourage diversity in these matters and to invite teachers to work in ways that make sense to them? Depending on how one answers these questions, one has two alternatives: continue the present practice of developing singular and standardized supervisory systems, putting them into place, and evaluating everyone on the same terms or providing options for supervision and inviting teachers to play key roles in deciding which options make sense and in sharing responsibility for implementing the options.

Cynthia Norris believes that respecting differences and encouraging diversity are key in providing a supervision that enhances both leader development and student learning. In her words, "What can supervisors do to promote teacher development and enhance student learning? One answer lies with a renewed respect for those they supervise. Central to that respect must be an appreciation of each teacher's uniqueness and an understanding of how diversity enhances rather than limits the educational process. Supervisors must also become acquainted with their own unique style and understand how their behavior impacts those they supervise."[30]

[28] Ibid., p. 166.
[29] Ibid.
[30] Cynthia Norris, "Supervising with Style," *Theory into Practice*, vol. 30, no. 2, p. 128, 1991.

Building on Jung's theories[31] and the work of N. Herrmann,[32] Norris identifies four different temperament styles that shape not only how teachers teach but how supervisors supervise as well. Two of the styles—facts and form—stem from a decided preference for rationality, and two—futures and feelings—a decided preference for intuition. According to Norris's framework:

Teachers with Fact styles rely heavily on data, focus on the realities of the present, generalize from specific situations, conceptually view lessons as being comprised of segmented components, emphasize precision and efficiency, and value fairness and consistency. As teachers they are likely to be subject matter oriented and to rely on sequential thinking.

Teachers with Form styles adhere closely to policies and guidelines, value control and predictability, stick to the tried and true, are methodical and detailed, focus on the immediate situation, and concentrate on verifiable facts. Their classrooms are likely to be highly organized and structured and they feel most comfortable when they know exactly what is expected of them and have a fairly structured model of teaching to follow.

Teachers with Futures styles place much less emphasis on policies and procedures, look beyond what is to possibilities, avoid details, view situations holistically, and seek many sources of information. In teaching they give prime emphasis to student abilities, interests and needs and seek to develop open learning climates that provide support and encourage creativity. They are particularly good at self concept development.

Teachers with Feeling styles place concern for others above all other concerns, encourage student centered activities, focus on feelings and emotional tone in developing classroom climates, and try to understand why students feel and behave the way they do. In teaching they encourage originality and problem solving, push students beyond factual knowledge, emphasize discovery and pose "why" questions.[33]

Norris believes that "If supervisors seek to change a teacher's basic style and impose their own view of teaching, they fail to foster the development of that teacher's potential. Although growth should be expected of all teachers, that growth should not be measured against someone else's style (even the supervisor's). It is the supervisor's task to help develop the teacher's uniqueness."[34] Once again we are forced to conclude that accommodating diversity in styles and needs requires the abandoning of single-minded supervisory systems that treat everyone the same in favor of options.

THE QUESTION OF SUPERVISORY STYLE

Does honoring the differences among teachers and working with them to identify supervisory options that have appeal mean that diversity in supervisory styles should also be respected and encouraged? Following Norris's conceptual framework, supervisors too can be grouped into fact, form, futures,

[31] Jung, op. cit.
[32] N. Herrmann, *The Creative Brain*, Lake Lure, N.C.: Brain Books, 1988.
[33] Norris, op. cit., pp. 128–133.
[34] Ibid., p. 132.

and feelings categories. And each category spells a different supervision and a different way of working with teachers. Are they all equal? We suggest that they are not.

Facts supervisors, for example, are characterized by logical, detailed, and sequential thought. They are likely to be directive in approach, feeling compelled to structure the supervisory relationship, break down lessons into components, analyze lessons for the teacher, and point out shortcomings. They then are likely to place emphasis on developing verbal or written school improvement plans that include problems to be resolved, improvement objectives, and a schedule for implementation. Facts supervisors tend to use such phrases as:

- Your lesson concepts were not clearly defined.
- You should have included these key points.
- Many details, such as dates, were inaccurately presented.
- You will strengthen your lesson by elaborating on specific relationships, such as. . . .
- Let me outline some approaches you should use.
- If you plan to finish the course content, you cannot afford to waste time with a few students having difficulty.
- I'd like to list specific goals and targets for your improvement plan.[35]

Form supervisors are likely to emphasize the "correct methods" of teaching and to expect teachers to use these methods with precision and exactness. They are attracted to packaged teaching models and packaged evaluation systems that spell out lesson cycles, specific steps to follow, and lists of teaching behaviors to emulate. Their approach is likely to be conservative, detached, and impersonal as they take a judicial stance. They define good teaching by the accepted model, and their job is to note whether the model is being implemented or not and to follow up by giving suggestions to teachers that better align what they do with what they are supposed to do. Form supervisors tend to use such phrases as:

- You should better organize your teaching materials. Much time was wasted during the lesson.
- Students need established rules and procedures for classroom behavior.
- I observed inconsistency in your classroom discipline.
- Many students were off-task during the lesson.
- I suggest that you arrange the group according to a planned seating arrangement.
- Your lesson plan did not work for you.
- Follow the basic components of the lesson cycle.
- Your improvement plan should include the following objectives.[36]

---

[35] Ibid., p. 130.
[36] Ibid., p. 130.

Feeling supervisors are likely to rely more on their own intuition in deciding what to do and how. They expect teachers to be child-centered and believe that not much progress will be made academically unless the focus teaching is broad enough to include student developmental needs, the home situation, basic health concerns, and other characteristics that comprise "the whole child." They believe that in practice, cognitive and affective domains must be brought together. Thus they are likely to encourage teachers to individualize teaching and to encourage self-esteem building. Feeling supervisors seek to involve the teaching process in lesson analysis and in deciding other supervisory issues. They tend to use the following phrases:

- I get a special feeling when I walk into your classroom. The climate is conducive to learning.
- Discussion groups were a major feature of your lesson.
- What has made these groups effective?
- You seem to recognize that Billy was having difficulty in showing support. Explain some strategies you have used with him.
- The group project encouraged creative expression among the students.
- Do you have ideas for enlarging today's lesson through this method?
- Let's plan together some ideas for your continued development; what is especially important to you?[37]

Futures supervisors are likely to expect teachers to go beyond the factual by placing emphasis on higher-order thinking and by searching for questions as well as answers. They have little patience with unimaginative rote learning and recitation. They welcome input from teachers and try hard not to assume roles as experts with all the answers. As Norris explains, futures supervisors work to "build partnerships. Teachers are encouraged to search for their own solutions and to investigate a wide variety of possibilities. Emphasis is on 'why' rather than 'how.' "[38]

Futures supervisors tend to use the following phrases:

- Let's restructure today's lesson.
- I like your ideas on components you feel especially good about.
- If there are areas of discomfort, please address those, too.
- Together we'll explore some techniques that might work for you.
- Do you perceive some possibilities for further exploration in the comment made by Jim?
- How might you add to this concept?
- Have you considered focus areas for increased development?
- How may I assist you with your plan?[39]

The merit in Norris's framework is less in the particulars and more in the issues she frames and the general orientation to differences she provides. Few

[37] Ibid., pp. 130–131.
[38] Ibid., p. 131.
[39] Ibid., p. 131.

supervisors, for example, are likely to fit neatly into one or another category, and none of the categories captures completely the complexities involved. With this caveat in mind it is our position that some supervisory styles are more likely to be effective than others. For example, supervisors who bring to their practice features of the feeling and futures styles are likely to be more effective than those who emphasize the facts and form style. Norris points out that as a group, teachers prefer supervisors to be collaborative and nondirective, flexible in problem solving, and warm and accepting.[40]

Further, despite the reality that feeling and futures supervisors have distinct views about what is good teaching, their basically cooperative and problem-oriented style of supervision allows them to function successfully not only with the feeling- and futures-oriented teachers but also with the facts and form teachers. In contrast, the rigid and directive style of feeling and form supervisors seems not to be inclusive enough to accommodate feeling and futures teachers very well. Facts and form supervisors expect teachers to measure up to some preconceived standard and to adjust their teaching to fit the form of this standard.

SUPERVISORY STYLES AND COGNITIVE COMPLEXITY

Carl Glickman,[41] Art Costa,[42] and other developmental theorists believe that cognitive complexity levels of teachers should be an important consideration in matching supervisory options to teacher needs.

Cognitive complexity is concerned with both the content and the structure of teachers' thoughts, with particular emphasis on the structure.[43] For example, two teachers may share the same beliefs about the value of cooperative learning but may differ markedly in the complexity with which they view these beliefs. The content of the beliefs is similar but the structure is different. The first teacher views cooperative learning as being universally applicable rather than as one of many available strategies. The second teacher views cooperative learning as a strategy more appropriate in some instances but less appropriate in others. Though both teachers share common beliefs about cooperative learning, they differ as to the structure of those beliefs. The second teacher's thinking is characterized by higher levels of cognitive complexity than is the first. Teachers with higher levels of cognitive complexity are able to give attention to a number of different concepts relating to a particular issue and to see interconnections among these concepts. They are able to be more re-

---

[40] Norris cites authorities such as Arthur Blumberg and W. A. Weber, "Teacher Morale as a Function of Perceived Behavioral Style," *The Journal of Educational Research,* vol. 62, no. 3, pp. 109–113, 1968; and N. L. Whistler and N. E. Wallace, "How Teachers View Their Supervision," *Catalyst for Change,* vol. 14, no. 1, pp. 26–29, 1984.

[41] Glickman, op. cit.

[42] Costa, op. cit.

[43] O. J. Harvey, "System Structure, Flexibility and Creativity," in O. J. Harvey (ed.), *Experience, Structure, and Adaptability,* New York: Springer, 1966.

flective in their practice, to understand better the subtleties of teaching, and to make more complex decisions about teaching.

Lower levels of cognitive complexity are characterized by simple and concrete thinking and practice. Higher levels of cognitive complexity are characterized by more complex abstract thinking and practice. One important finding from the research on teaching is that teachers with higher levels of cognitive complexity provide a greater range of teaching environments to students. Their practice is characterized by a wider variety of teaching strategies and methods.[44] Further, it appears that students of teachers with higher levels of cognitive complexity tend to achieve more than do students of teachers with lower levels.[45]

N. A. Sprinthall and L. Theis-Sprinthall believe that cognitive complexity increases as teachers are exposed to more stimulating teaching environments.[46] For example, teachers who have more opportunities to interact with their supervisors and with other teachers about their teaching, who have greater opportunities for obtaining feedback about their teaching, and who have greater opportunities for experimenting in a supportive environment can all be expected to develop higher levels of cognitive complexity. One benefit of providing options for supervision is that opportunities for teachers to experience more stimulating teacher environments are increased.

MATCHING SUPERVISORY STYLES TO SITUATIONS

As suggested earlier, how supervisors decide to work with teachers can be referred to as their supervisory *style*. Styles are different from supervisory options. Within any particular option, supervisors might choose to behave differently. For example, when working with different teachers within the self-directed supervisory option it might make sense to be directive with one teacher, collaborative with another teacher, and nondirective with a third. The directive supervisory style emphasizes structure and more frequent interaction with the teacher; the collaborative emphasizes shared responsibility, joint decision making, and collegiality; and the nondirective emphasizes facilitating the teacher's plans and efforts in providing necessary support.[47] In Figure 16-1 Costa describes each of the three styles and gives examples of how they might look in practice.

The matching of supervisory styles to situations sounds deceptively simple in theory but is complex in practice. Basic to this discussion is the principle that any number of variables might be considered in defining the specifics of a situation. To this point we have discussed psychological types and cognitive

---

[44] David E. Hunt and Bruce R. Joyce, "Teacher Trainee Personality and Initial Teaching Style," *American Educational Research Journal*, vol. 4, no. 3, pp. 253–255, 1967.

[45] Harvey, op. cit.

[46] N. A. Sprinthall and L. Theis-Sprinthall, "Career Development of Teachers: A Cognitive Perspective." *Encyclopedia of Educational Research*, 5th edition, NY: Free Press, 1982.

[47] Glickman, op. cit.

	More directive style	**More collaborative style**
Direction	High *Directive Control*	*Directive Informational*
Behavior	The supervisor recalls and analyzes the data, proposes alternative strategies, and chooses one to implement.	The supervisor presents the data, invites the teacher to consider alternatives, suggests alternatives. Together they choose alternatives. The initiating supervisor presents the data, invites the teacher to analyze the data, proposes alternatives, and selects those to implement.
Example	Supervisor: "One reason why the class was shouting out answers is that you did not lay out the ground rules as to how they should respond. Also, your classroom was arranged so that they could interact more with you than with each other. You should arrange your class in a circle so they could see each other. Also, you must start the lesson by stating that you want them to take turns and listen to each other's ideas. In the future, I'd like to begin each lesson by setting some ground rules for how they should interact. Then you should plan to spend a few minutes at the end of the lesson evaluating how well they followed those rules. When we meet next Tuesday, I'd like you to share with me just how you intend to structure the lesson and the classroom that day."	Supervisor: "I noted today that several students were not taking turns as you hoped they would. Why is that, do you think?" Teacher: "I don't know. It's always a few kids who interrupt. They just don't seem to know how to listen to each other and wait. I scold them when they do it but they just keep right on." Supervisor: "Would it help, do you think, to lay down some ground rules at the beginning of the lesson?" Teacher: "It might. What do you suggest?" Supervisor: "I think you might tell them what you expect them to do. Take turns, listen to each other, raise their hands." Teacher: "You'd think they'd know that by now. You mean I should be more specific about my expectancies." Supervisor: "Yes. Perhaps, when the lesson is finished, you might take some time to evaluate how well they followed those rules." Teacher: "I can do that. That way the students will evauate their own behavior rather than making me do it." Supervisor: "Do you think the way you have the classroom arranged is conducive to total group listening and sharing?"

FIGURE 16-1   Levels and examples of directiveness in supervisory style. (*Source: Art Costa,* Supervision for Intelligent Teaching, *Orangevale, Calif., Search Models Unlimited, 1982, p. 114.*)

More nondirective style

Low

Collaborative

Nondirective

The supervisor invites the teacher to share the data, to analyze the data, to propose alternatives for himself or herself.

The teacher initiates by recalling data, analyzing, and prescribing. The teacher invites the supervisor to perform a role.

Supervisor: "How do you feel the lesson went today?"
Teacher: "Pretty well. However, I'm disappointed that so many students are still not taking turns. Did I make my directions clear, do you think?"
Supervisor: "I understand them."
Teacher: "I wonder if I changed the arrangement of the classroom, would that help, do you think?"
Supervisor: "When students sit in a circle, that is the position in which most students can see most other students. They can read each other's body language and facial expressions."
Teacher: "Mmm. That's what I'm trying to get them to do; to listen to one another. Next time, I'll try that. Is there anything else I could do to get them to take charge of their own behavior?"
Supervisor: "Having students evaluate themselves, you mean?"
Teacher: "Yes. When the discussion is over, I could take some time to have them discuss how well they listened to each other and took turns."

Teacher: "Today I noticed that there are still some students who are not taking turns and listening to each other. I've got to do something to help them take charge of their own behavior and to be courteous to each other."
Supervisor: "Like what?"
Teacher: "Well, I've gotten them into a circle where they can face each other, I've tried to model these behaviors in my own interaction, and I've talked privately with those students who have the problem. I guess I'm just going to have to lay down some ground rules for good discussion."
Supervisor: "Have you talked this over with the class?"
Teacher: "No, I haven't. Maybe if we'd have a whole class discussion to develop some criteria for good discussions, they could follow their own rules better than mine."
Supervisor: "That's possible."
Teacher: "Could you come into my classroom Tuesday morning during our class meeting? I'd like you to observe the students and me to see if they are setting their own ground rules and whether I'm helping them become more self-directed. Look for those students who are not taking turns and tell me if I could do anything more to help them learn to listen to each other."
Supervisor: "OK."

FIGURE 16-1   (Continued)

complexity as two variables that are worth considering. In the discussion that follows we add to this list of variables levels of maturity of teachers, their stages of concern, and their propensity for accepting responsibility. Depending upon which combination of these descriptors apply, educators can speculate (at least in a very general sense) about which supervisory style might make the most sense and which supervisory option might be most appropriate. The relationships are described in Figure 16-2.

Different concerns of teachers, propensity for responsibility, and levels of maturity are indicative of different levels of cognitive complexity. For example, teachers who are primarily concerned with the problems, needs, and learning characteristics of students; who are able to accept responsibility; and who are growing in levels of maturity are likely to display moderate levels of cognitive complexity. In contrast, immature, dependent, and self-concerned teachers are likely to display low levels of cognitive complexity. Cognitive complexity, therefore, is an important construct in determining both supervisory style and appropriate supervisory option. The intersection line brings together dimensions of teacher development with levels of cognitive complexity and suggests the recommended supervisory style and supervisory option.

Teachers located at or near point 1 on the intersection line would probably benefit most from directive supervision regardless of the supervisory option

FIGURE 16-2   Matching teacher concerns, levels of responsibility, maturity and complexity, supervisory options, and supervisory styles. (*Source: Adapted from Thomas J. Sergiovanni, The Principalship: A Reflective Practice Perspective, 2d edition, Boston: Allyn and Bacon, 1991, p. 309.*)

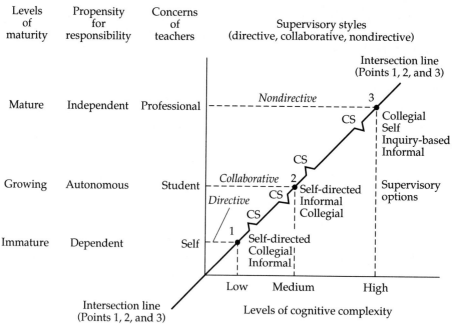

being used. Informal supervision, characterized by frequent and direct contact with the supervisor, might make sense as the most suitable option. Collegial and self-directed professional development would be appropriate as supplements. Should collegial supervision be chosen (for example, teaming the teacher with another teacher who might be located at point 3 on the intersection line), the supervisor may need to be involved to be sure that the point 1 teacher is receiving the needed direction and help.

The collaborative supervisory style might make sense for teachers at intersection point 2. In this case, both teacher and supervisor tackle problems together, plan activities and events, and make decisions cooperatively. Self-directed supervision is highly recommended as an option.

Mature teachers with more professional concerns who reflect higher levels of cognitive complexity in their practice will be found at or near point 3 on the intersection line. These mature professionals are more willing and able to assume responsibility for self-evaluation and improvement. When this is the case, supervision is more appropriately nondirective. Collegial supervision seems ideally suited to teachers at point 3. Here, groups of teachers work together as mature colleagues. Self-directed supervision may be selected by some teachers who might prefer to work alone. Point 3 is also the ideal setting for inquiry-based supervision. Informal supervision remains an important part of a comprehensive approach to supervision. For highly motivated and competent teachers the purpose of informal supervision is to provide needed recognition and support.

Peaks and dips appear periodically on the intersection line of Figure 16-2. Peaks represent occasions when teachers might desire more intense and prolonged help in the classroom, perhaps because they face a special problem or challenge. Dips represent trouble spots that might be identified by either the teacher or the supervisor. On these occasions clinical supervision can be an effective and appropriate option.

ACCOUNTING FOR MOTIVES OF TEACHERS

Many experts believe that the motives teachers and other workers bring to their jobs are important determinants of their outlook, and this outlook can influence preferences for supervision.[48] Three such motives that have been found to be particularly important are a person's need for achievement, power, and affiliation. David C. McClelland found that the three motives are present in all people but not to the same degree.[49] Some teachers are influenced greatly by the need for affiliation, only moderately by the need for power influence, and only modestly by the need for achievement. Other teachers might be very high on the need for achievement and comparatively low on the needs for affiliation and power and influence. The first group of teachers

---

[48] Benfari, op. cit.; Kolb, Rubin, and McIntyre, op. cit.

[49] David C. McClelland, *The Achieving Society*, Princeton, N.J.: Van Nostrand, 1961.

are likely to think more about social interaction, friendships, and human relationships at work and in controlling others at work than in job objectives and how well they can accomplish various teaching tasks. In contrast, the second group would probably be much more concerned with work issues and progress in achieving objectives than in interacting with and controlling others.

The achievement motive is associated with teachers wanting to take personal responsibility for their own success or failure; liking working situations where goals are clear and reasonably obtainable though challenging; preferring frequent and concrete feedback allowing them to gauge their success and failure rates in a continuous fashion. Teachers who are highly motivated by achievement are task-oriented, prefer short-range specific targets to more ambiguous and long-range targets, like to be on top of things, and seek personal responsibility for their actions. They find it difficult to delegate responsibility and to share authority with others. It is often difficult for them to emphasize human relationships and social interaction behaviors for their own sake. Teachers who have a high need to achieve are likely to be committed to building achievement-oriented classrooms with visible and detailed standards. They seek and accept responsibility for their own work behaviors and growth and gladly accept moderate risks in an effort to achieve personal success.

Supervisory options that encourage individual initiative, target setting, and charting of accomplishments are favored by high-achievement-oriented teachers. Individual professional development, for example, is ideally suited to them but they are likely to respond less favorably to cooperative professional development. They respond well to informal supervision if the feedback they desire is provided.

The affiliation motive is associated with people who have a high concern for warm and friendly relationships and for social interaction. Teachers for whom this need is important enjoy working with other teachers in group settings, find teaching and other assignments that require them to work alone, learn alone, or problem-solve alone to be less satisfactory. They depend heavily on other teachers for much of their work satisfaction and enjoy interacting with others about work. Affiliation-oriented teachers suffer more from isolation and experience more loneliness than do their achievement and power-influence counterparts. They need and seek opportunities to interact with other adults. Should they find this opportunity within the supervisory situation they respond with motivated behavior.

Self-directed supervision and other supervisory options that leave them to their own devices are not likely to be viewed favorably by high-affiliation teachers. On the other hand, collegial supervision elicits a very positive response. Affiliation teachers can feel uncomfortable when involved in informal supervision unless the supervisor makes a point of providing *supportive* feedback after every classroom visit.

Teachers who have a high need for power and influence are interested in influencing other people. They like group contacts and social interaction supervisory settings but view these less as opportunities for satisfying social interaction needs and more as opportunities that will enable them to exercise leadership. When provided with supervisory situations of this type the power-influence motive valve is opened and motivative behavior results.

High-power-influence teachers like to assume supervisory roles and will respond very positively to collegial supervision. Since they like to be in charge and enjoy assuming leadership roles they often resent competition in these areas from other teachers and from supervisors. An important strategy is to harness the motivational potential of high-power-influence teachers by delegating responsibility to them and in other ways sharing leadership roles and functions.

During the early stages of social motives research it was thought that the achievement motive was associated with increased performance at work and successful accomplishment of goals and that the other two motives actually interfered with the accomplishment of work. More recent research, however, suggests that none of the three emerges as being superior. Teachers with high needs for affiliation and teachers with high needs for power and influence can be every bit as productive and effective as teachers with high needs for achievement. Key to motivation is not the most pressing motive of a particular teacher but whether a person's work circumstances allow for expression of the motive.

PRESCRIPTIONS OR FRAMES?

Striking the right balance between uniformity and diversity may in the end be easier than dealing with the diversity side of this balance once it is acknowledged. For example, providing supervisory options will not in itself be an effective strategy unless teachers become involved in options that make sense. Matching A with B has a certain logic that can be misleading. As we've pointed out throughout the chapter, our speculations and recommendations are not prescriptions to be applied literally. They represent frames that might help both supervisors and teachers make better decisions about options. In the end, we believe that once options are provided, teachers should be allowed to choose to participate in those that make sense to them. When they do choose an option, however, they must demonstrate that it is indeed an effective one for them. If after implementing an option for a period of time they cannot compellingly argue for continuing in that direction, then supervisors may need to be more aggressive in advising, coaching, and, if need be, steering teachers into more promising options.

APPENDIX 16-1: An Example of Individual Action Research*

A fifth-grade classroom teacher, although concerned over a period of time about individual differences in reading ability among the members in his group, observed that variations among his students this year seemed to be even greater than usual. Aside from the teaching of reading, he noted other problems in planning for and with the youngsters because of these differences in reading achievement, interests, and motivations. He became sufficiently dissatisfied with the situation to search for some way of providing more adequately for these individual differences in reading as a first step toward improving the other aspects of the teaching–learning situation. He began by trying to discover what these differences were and how they manifested themselves. He assembled all the information available in the cumulative records, including results of standardized tests and measures of past achievement. He then studied some of the literature concerning reading and its effects upon other aspects of learning. From his examination of the literature, he decided that the picture of the students was incomplete and that he needed additional data in order to be able to define the problem more specifically.

As a next step, the teacher gave a diagnostic reading test to pinpoint some of the difficulties his students were encountering. He asked for reports on the kinds of materials the students read and had them keep a log of their reading over a two-week period. He obtained information from the parents as to the reading materials available in the home and the nature of the children's reading out of school. From these data the teacher identified a specific problem within the broad area of concern so that it could be studied. In addition to securing data about the reading skills and habits of the students, the teacher continued to study the literature about individualizing reading instruction. The evidence he collected about the students and the new insights he developed about individualizing reading instruction provided him with some hunches or hypotheses that he could test in his classroom.

This teacher believed that if he set aside more time for working with students in groups of two or three on reading skills, and discontinued the larger reading groups he had been using, then three benefits could result: the students' reading skills would increase, their interests in literature would expand, and their ability to work with similar materials in other class units would grow. He decided to test his hypothesis by providing direct reading instruction to students in very small groups for a two-month period. He continued to collect evidence about their reading skills and interests, and noted their behavior in using printed materials in a study of the community in which they were engaged. Then he tried his direct reading instruction plan and, at the end of the test period, gathered data about growth in the areas with which he was concerned.

In analyzing the evidence, he found that the work in small groups did help attain certain desired goals but that it made little difference in other areas of concern. Analysis of the data suggested some leads for other possible means of individualizing instruction. He believed, for example, that the additional use of multi-level reading materials seemed a good way to meet the needs of different individuals. The teacher then planned to test his hypothesis about the value of multi-level materials in reading instruction.

---

*From Florence B. Stratemeyer, Hamden L. Forkner, Margaret G. McKim, and A. Harry Passow, *Developing a Curriculum for Modern Living*, New York: Teachers College, 1957, pp. 709–710.

APPENDIX 16-2: An Example of Cooperative Action Research†

Some of the faculty members of a small rural high school, in examining the performance of their top students on a state-wide scholarship test, found that, although the pupils did reasonably well on certain parts of the examination, they were far below youth from other schools in understanding and appreciation of the arts, in handling concepts and abstractions, and in their breadth of reading. These were areas in which the teachers saw important educational goals.

The discussion of the findings resulted in several possible explanations. Two teachers raised the question as to whether this was a general condition or something which only occurred with these particular students. Some faculty members volunteered to gather comparable data for students who had taken this examination over the previous four or five years. Their report was submitted at the next meeting of the group and indicated that the condition had been essentially the same for previous students. Many guesses were made as to why the students in this school should do so much more poorly in these parts of the test than students from other schools, especially since the scores were comparable in sections requiring factual knowledge, and low only in appreciations, attitudes, and generalizing skills. Another meeting followed in which members reported additional findings about the experiences of learners in the areas of art, music, literature, and the assimilation of ideas. Other staff members summarized articles and reports about the achievements of youth in other small rural high schools.

After several sessions, the problem began to be clearer and to take on manageable proportions. The teachers decided that the reason their students did less well in certain parts of the examination probably was that they lacked meaningful experiences in these areas. The group hypothesized that if the students were to participate in a seminar, which offered cultural experiences that now seemed to be missing, their attainments in these areas would rise to a point where their understandings would show up favorably in the annual state-wide scholarship examination in comparison with youth from larger urban schools.

The teachers then set up the machinery for testing their hypothesis. Students whose records would cause one to predict that they would achieve the highest results on the examination were invited to participate in a special three-hour session one afternoon each week. Three teachers with differing interests and specializations volunteered to serve as seminar leaders and shifts were made in their teaching schedules to free them for this assignment. These leaders met for weekly preplanning sessions and reported regularly on their activities and problems to a faculty discussion group. A theme was selected and resources were made available. The students helped plan experiences which consisted of listening to symphonic music; reading more mature literature, poems, and plays; viewing television productions; visiting the nearest art museum which was forty-five miles distant; and listening to special resource persons discuss their areas of expertness. In general they explored cultural areas beyond those normally provided in their regular programs. The teachers compiled anecdotal and behavioral data about growth of individual students during the course of the year.

Eventually, these students took the state-wide examination and their scores, particularly in the areas which had concerned the faculty group earlier, were higher than those

† From Florence B. Stratemeyer, Hamden L. Forkner, Margaret G. McKim, and A. Harry Passow, *Developing a Curriculum for Modern Living*, New York: Teachers College, 1957, pp. 710–712.

received by former students during previous years. The faculty group then examined the validity of this test of their original hypothesis and came up with generalizations for further testing. For example, was the provision of the kind of teaching–learning situation which extended the students' cultural orientation and discussion of ideas and concepts the important thing? Assuming it might be, the faculty group began to explore possible modifications in the curriculum design and adaptations in teaching methods which they might try out the following year to see if the values of the seminar could be extended to other students.

PART FOUR

A LOOK TO THE FUTURE

CHAPTER 17

SUPERVISION AND THE RENEWAL OF SCHOOLS

Supervisors would not, in the minds of teachers, superintendents, policy-makers, and critics, be the ones expected to start a revolution in schools. They are traditionally seen as those who oversee the appropriate implementation of new policies or the following of standard operating procedures. In all the discussions over restructuring schools, the focus has been on the state legislature and state department of education to legislate major changes, or on the teachers at the school site who will participate in site-based change efforts. In either case, supervisors are not considered as major sources for change. In the state-initiated teacher assessment programs, supervisors have been called in as players in implementing those initiatives, but they have had little to say in forming the policies.

If supervisors are to play a significant part in the renewal of schools, they will have to move beyond their traditional roles of working within the given environment to exercising leadership in the transformation of that environment. In other words, the process of supervision, whether exercised by a department chair, an assistant principal, a principal, or a district supervisor, has to be seen as requiring more than seeing that the job is done according to standard criteria. The supervisory process has to be seen as an intellectual process of "re-imagining" the learning situation, of re-imagining the learning environment of the classroom and of the school. The re-imagining, of course, will be done with teachers and administrators as they work together on problems of practice. The supervisor needs to come to that task with a moral commitment to move the activity of teachers, students, and administrators beyond a technical rendition and acceptance of services to the activity of a community that is bound together by common values and meanings.

Those who engage in supervision have a unique perspective to bring to the job of school renewal. Supervising brings the supervisor into contact with many teachers, with many classrooms, with many different groups of students whose varied approaches to the demands of learning may be strikingly different. The supervisor's view is larger than the individual teacher's view. It is larger because the supervisor sees many teachers, all of whom exhibit different talents and who express their approaches to the design of learning activities differently. It is larger because the supervisor moves back and forth between different institutional levels of administration and policy and therefore has a better sense of the whole school than any individual teacher.

Moreover, the supervisor is closer to the realities of the classroom and of student engagement with or resistances to the learning tasks than are school administrators who do not exercise supervisory responsibilities. The supervisor can speak as an advocate for students and for teachers in discussions with administrators about making the school environment more "user-friendly." The supervisor, in short, is the one person whose work is involved with all levels of the school, or at least with most of them.

Because of these contacts with a variety of people in the school, the supervisor is in a unique position to articulate a new vision of teaching and learning, to bring a super-vision to the discussions with various school personnel. One might say that the supervisor is potentially the primary reflective practitioner in the school; besides reflecting with individual teachers, and with groups of teachers (in departmental level or grade level meetings), the supervisor reflects with administrators and district personnel about staff-development programs, curriculum redesign, and resource allocation in administrative staff meetings. The supervisor is in an ideal position to be a carrier of ideas, a conduit of new thinking, a map maker who can help teachers and administrators reconceptualize the terrain of their work.

People who supervise usually have two or three (or more!) additional responsibilities. Sometimes supervision is considered the least important task in the supervisor's job description. Yet, were the supervisor to reconceptualize supervisory work as a central activity for school renewal, and make supervision the centerpiece of his or her work, it might enable a better integration of the other tasks. More specifically, how might that role be worked out in practice?

INTELLECTUAL AND MORAL DIMENSIONS OF SUPERVISORY LEADERSHIP

First, supervisors would need to see the leadership possibilities in the supervisory process, see it as involved in the *educational* mission of the school, rather than as a bureaucratic activity fulfilling bureaucratic demands for control and record-keeping. Supervisors would need to appreciate the intellectual dimension of their work. As professionals who have studied the complexities of teaching and learning and human motivation and curriculum design, they should be conversing with other educational professionals about how to make the schools work better for youngsters. Besides being diagnosticians of instructional performances, they should be diagnosticians of curriculum units, of student readiness for learning, of the learning environment within the school, and, perhaps most important, they must be diagnosticians of the community, sensing when it is sick and what might restore its health. That is intellectual work. Supervisors are perhaps better positioned than most to re-imagine how the parts might work together more effectively.

Supervisors also need to appreciate the moral foundation of their authority as supervisors. That authority derives from the shared values held by the community. When the school is not a community but simply a legally constituted organization that provides services to clients—much the way a hospital does to patients or an automotive shop does to car owners—then the authority of the supervisor remains predominantly at the legal and technical level. When a school is a community, youngsters are happy to go there in the morning; such cannot be said for hospital patients or car owners on their way to their respective institutions.

In the school as a learning community, supervisors' moral authority is based on the trust that youngsters and teachers place in them to care for them, to respect and honor the integrity of each of them, as they engage in the demanding pursuit of the mission of the school. As a community their common mission is to explore and understand their past and their present, understand their natural and human environment so they can preserve and enhance it through their intelligent labor, understand themselves and their mutual responsibilities to each other, and understand the difficult but fulfilling challenge of communal self-governance. Within that mission, teachers are committed to nurture the intellectual, social, and personal growth of every youngster. Within that mission supervisors are committed to support and enhance the teachers' work with the youngsters, and to facilitate and enhance those institutional supports for the community's task of learning. There is a moral expectation, then, for supervisors to maintain a super-vision of what the school is supposed to be; a moral expectation that they will remind teachers and students and administrators, gently, diplomatically, but firmly, of that vision; a moral expectation that they will work with members of the community to enhance the community's commitment to its mission. This implies an intrinsically moral leadership in school renewal.

A TRANSITION FROM BUREAUCRATIC TO ORGANIC MANAGEMENT

This view of supervisory leadership, however, typically assumes that it will be exercised within the present hierarchic, bureaucratic management of school systems. A more decentralized management of schools is already being tried in various cities and states in what has come to be known as restructuring, or site-based management and participatory decision-making. Centralized bureaucratic management still provides the larger umbrella of authority, but where decisions involve the actual teaching-learning process, teachers have a greater say.

As it becomes more apparent that teaching is a complex technology exercised in rather fluid classroom contexts, it likewise becomes apparent that teachers should have the autonomy and authority to decide what is best to do in any given circumstance, rather than having to respond to bureaucratic policies and rules that assign a decontextualized uniformity and simplicity to teaching and learning. In other words, schools are moving toward more organic processes of management in order to enable those with the expertise to make those practical decisions needed to respond to the fluctuating and unpredictable situations in schooling. Organic management is beginning to replace some of the bureaucratic, hierarchic management. Instead of pervasive, centralized bureaucratic authority that controls the teaching-learning process through standardized operational procedures and uniform measures of input and output, small clusters of professional authority are emerging in schools where groups of professionals are deciding how best to promote learning.

Central office administration of school systems will continue, but probably with a reduced central office staff of supervisors and program directors. As more and more authority is transferred to local schools, more discretion over the allocation of resources will flow to the individual school. Various central office functions may remain, especially those that provide economies of scale. State departments of education, on the other hand, may remain rather sizable, and perhaps increase, as state legislatures increase their effort to improve education throughout each state.

Granting that most school systems have a long way to go in organic management at the school site, suppose for the moment that this way of managing schools were to became a major force in most school systems. In such redesigned schools, would there be any place for supervisors? The answer is that we really do not know. We can speculate, though, that supervision in these redesigned schools, if present at all, would be quite different from what it is today. Supervisors would probably function much more in a resource capacity, as facilitators of networking, as troubleshooters, as the ones who, after brain storming and discussing among teachers, may be designated by the teachers to come up with a tentative redesign of a curriculum or a learning space or a series of comprehensive student performance assessments.

There is some evidence that even teachers who have had good experiences with site-based management find the time spent at planning and coordination meetings a heavy burden, one that distracts them from their teaching responsibilities. While they find the sharing of information about their work rewarding, they are less enthusiastic about having to spend so much time on administrative procedures. Supervisors may have some role in relieving teachers of these burdens.

Various staffing differentiations among teachers have been promoted, such as lead teacher or head teacher or mentor. Much of the work of these positions involves coaching and mentoring beginning teachers, running staff-development programs, working with probationary teachers. In other words, some teachers have been largely removed from classroom responsibilities to deal with instructional matters and professional growth matters. These teachers appear to be the ones who will do much of what supervisors used to do, except that they are not viewed as part of the administration—at least not yet.

Between the present, more traditional organization of schools and school systems and the future, redesigned school and school systems, there is much that those who exercise supervisory leadership can do. Precisely as schools struggle to make the transition, supervisory personnel can arbitrate the disagreements and misunderstandings that arise between administrators and teachers. As both groups grope toward redefining their respective authority within the school, supervisors can serve as brokers and mediators, bringing to the attention of both the overriding mission they are supposed to be pursuing, namely the education of youngsters. Supervisors could be the primary spokespersons for the community as it experiences the strains of realignment of roles and responsibilities.

There is also another crucial task for supervisors in these efforts at school reform, and it involves a greater attention to a significant segment of the community that has been overlooked during the national flurry over school reform, namely, the students. Most of the discussion about granting teachers greater autonomy over instructional matters seems to imply that that autonomy will be exercised in classrooms and schools as they are currently structured, without questioning whether such structures are obstacles to student learning.

Few people are asking whether the learning environments in schools as they are presently structured are stimulating, flexible, and supportive, or whether students learn what they do *in spite of* spaces and time schedules and curriculum units that *inhibit* their learning potential. Moreover, few are analyzing the passive position most students must assume in relationship to adults in schools. They are told what to do, when to do, how to do, and what they definitely should *not* do. They rarely encounter teachers who are interested in what they think, what they dream about, what they fear. Students encounter a massive effort of most adults in the school to get them to pay attention to their agenda, with little concern whether that agenda has even the remotest connection to the youngsters' experience of life.

Traditionally supervisors have the responsibility to work with teachers to improve their instruction, with the assumed goal, of course, of enhancing student learning. Both supervisors and teachers, in this traditional conception of supervision, rarely discuss the students' state of mind as they approach the learning task. It is as though by focusing on the clearer presentation of the subject matter, or the use of various media representations, or the dividing of the class into work groups, there will be some automatic increase in learning in students who have been generalized into a group mind. If teachers can just get the instruction right, the group mind, sitting there awaiting enlightenment, will absorb the new knowledge.

More detailed studies of learning, however, show it to be a much more complex and individualized process affected as much by the youngsters' emotional state—their self-image, their sense of efficacy and control over the future, their life history and the residue of affect attached to words and images—as it is by what appears to be a more absolute trait of intelligence. In other words, learning is a highly contextualized matter. The state of mind youngsters bring into the classroom or to learning activities assigned outside the classroom very much determines the quality of the learning. Hence, both teachers and supervisors need to give much more attention to the frame of mind youngsters are in when they face a learning task, and attempt to deal with features of that frame of mind that inhibit readiness for engaging in the learning activity. Obviously, in settings of group instruction and group learning activities, complete awareness of each student's frame of mind in each hour of the school day is impossible. Insofar as they have some control over the learning environment, however, educators can remove from the environment those features that have a negative impact on the feelings and self-image of the student.

It is here that the supervisor may have a major role to play. If the supervisor sees the school as needing to be a *community* for it to maximize student growth and to maximize the potential of teachers to stimulate that growth, then the supervisor can make the promotion of community a centerpiece of his or her super-vision. In a school environment that promotes community, youngsters are more likely to feel cared for and respected. In a learning community environment they are more likely to be invited to explore the subject matter *with* the teacher, rather than experience academic work as something indifferently pressed upon them with warnings about the dire consequences of failing to do the assignment. In a learning community, students' questions are more likely to be given a sensitive hearing and an honest answer. In a learning community, knowledge will more likely be seen as a precious heritage of the community, rather than as property to be accumulated by individuals in a competition for scarce rewards. In other words, the environment of a learning community will affect the state of mind students bring to the learning tasks. Within the context of a learning community, supervisors can indeed work with teachers in exploring better ways to engage the students in this or that unit of learning, but the focus on the teaching protocol will also include attentiveness to the students' frame of mind.

The first wave of school reform focused on mechanisms of control: bureaucratic mandates for more courses, longer school days and years, more rigorous tests, and enforcement of nonpromotion policies. The second wave of school reform emphasized increasing the commitment of teachers to improving their instruction: By stressing their professional expertise, teachers were to be given greater autonomy and authority over decisions affecting the teaching-learning process. But few have talked about the need to increase *students'* commitment to the learning task. To be sure, there are stories in the literature about principals who constantly exhort students to improve their grades, to stay focused on their academic tasks. But these exhortations are simply part of the external control apparatus, linked with grades, class ranks, promotion, and graduation criteria. Nothing there about the intrinsic worth of learning something well; nothing about the connections between what they are learning and understanding themselves and their world; nothing about the awesome collective responsibility they have to understand their world, since they will be running it in the future; nothing there about the excitement of exploring the world with others, of coming into contact with the soaring of the human spirit in the humanities and the sciences; in short, no super-vision of learning, no super-vision of a learning community.

The various attempts at school renewal will fall short of their goal unless there is greater attention to nurturing a positive frame of mind among learners. Supervisors and teachers working together can begin to transform the learning environment into a more user-friendly environment, into an environment that communicates caring and respect for each student, into an environment supportive of a community of learners. That remains a primary intellectual and moral challenge of supervisory leadership. That is what all these chapters have centered around: attention to climate and culture, motivation and platform, curriculum and assessment, clinical supervision, reflective practice, staff development.

These concerns all affect how the learning community manages its affairs in the pursuit of its super-vision of schooling. If supervision is not to be left on the sidelines passively watching the spectacle of school reform, but, rather, to play a significant part in school renewal, then it must take up the intellectual and moral challenge of promoting this super-vision of what the school can become—an authentic community of learners.

INDEX